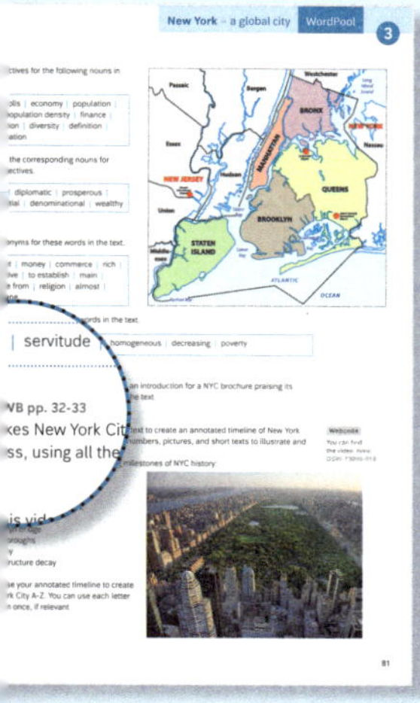

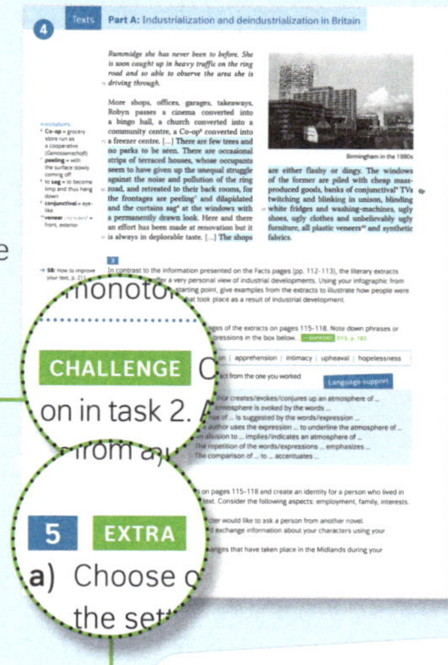

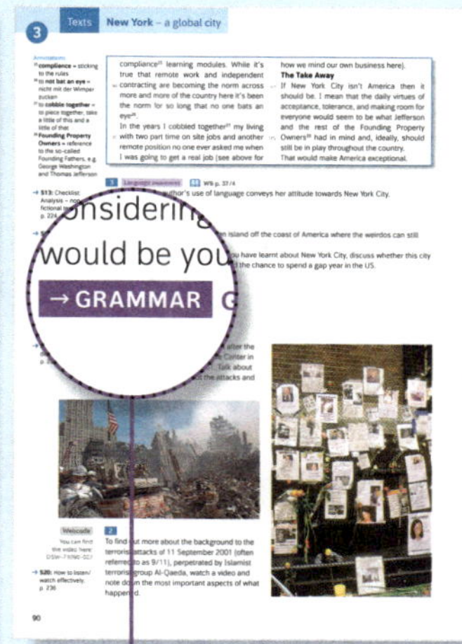

Die **Texts**-Seiten enthalten unterschiedliche Materialien und abwechslungsreiche Aufgaben aus allen Kompetenzbereichen.

Grammar-Verweise verweisen auf Einheiten im **Grammatik**-Anhang.

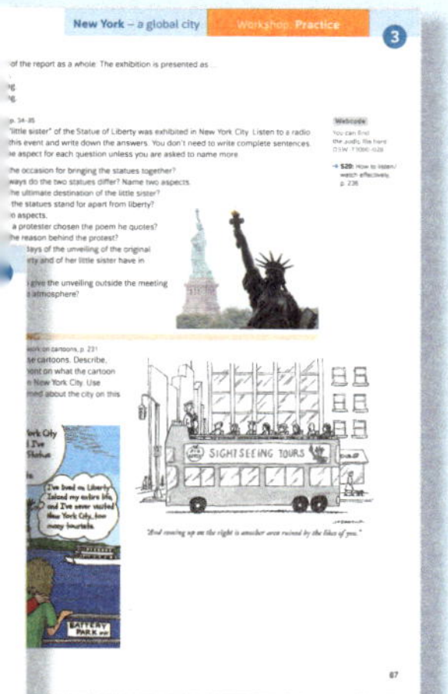

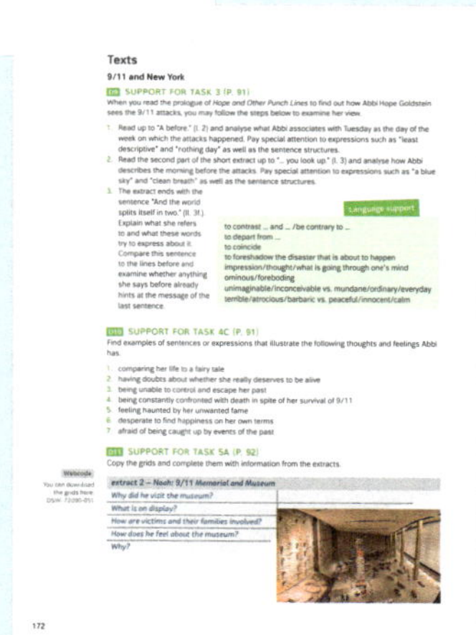

Grüne Unterlegung dich auf Differenzierungsangebote hin. So gekennzeichnet sind etwas anspruchsvollere **CHALLENGE**-Aufgaben, zusätzliche **EXTRA**-Aufgaben und **CHOOSE**-Aufgaben, bei denen du aus mehreren Optionen auswählen kannst. Außerdem macht dich der Hinweis **→ SUPPORT** auf Unterstützungsangebote in der **Diff section** aufmerksam.

Deine interkulturelle Kompetenz trainierst du mit dem Sonderelement **Across cultures**. Die vielfältigen Aufgaben zur Sprachbewusstheit sind als **Language awareness** gekennzeichnet.

Am Ende des Buches erwarten dich Übungs- und Nachschlageanhänge zu wichtigen **skills** und zur **Grammatik** sowie ein **Glossar**.

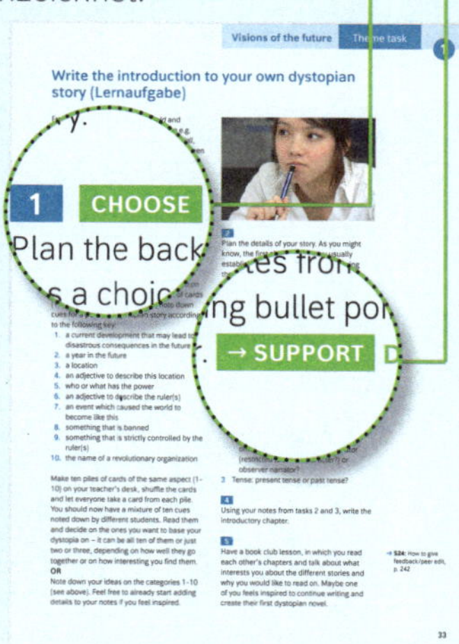

Am Ende jedes Kapitels wird als **Theme task** eine Lernaufgabe angeboten, die verschiedene Kompetenzen verknüpft und als kreativer Kapitelabschluss dient.

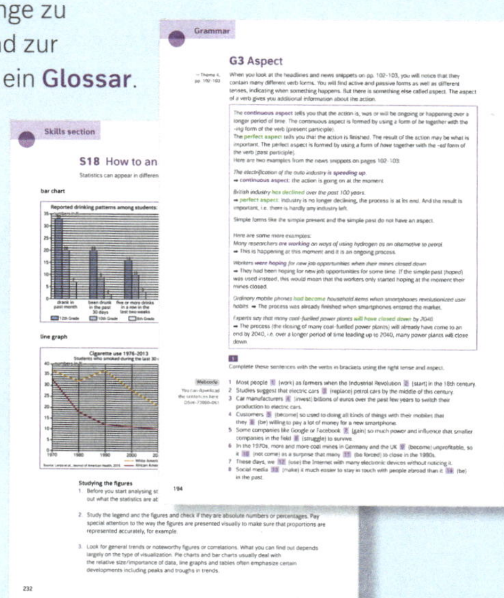

Tilman

westermann

CAMDEN TOWN Oberstufe

Einführungsphase

Erarbeitet von

Juliane Brunner
Pamela Hanus
Luzie Kage
Christoph Reuter
Mirja Schnoor
Sylvia Wauer

Fachliche Beratung

Friedrich Frenzel
Alexander Heim
Claudia Reiserer
Tom Schrock
Christian Schulze

Symbole und Abkürzungen:

AE	American English
BE	British English
e.g.	exempli gratia (Latin) = for example
i.e.	id est (Latin) = that is
infml.	informal
pl.	plural
sb	somebody
sth	something
vs.	versus

Material für Schülerinnen und Schüler:

- Arbeitsheft (978-3-425-73091-2)
- Vokabeltrainer-App iOS (978-3-425-73086-8)
- Vokabeltrainer-App Android (978-3-425-73087-5)

Materialien für Lehrkräfte:

- Materialien für Lehrkräfte (978-3-425-73092-9)
- Klausurvorschläge (978-3-425-73093-6)

BiBox

Vorbereiten. Organisieren. Durchführen.
BiBox ist das umfassende Digitalpaket zu diesem Lehrwerk mit zahlreichen Materialien und dem digitalen Schulbuch. Für Lehrkräfte und für Schülerinnen und Schüler sind verschiedene Lizenzen verfügbar.
Nähere Informationen unter **www.bibox.schule**

Webcodes
Auf manchen Seiten findest du Webcodes, die dich zu zusätzlichen Materialien führen.
Gib dazu einfach den Code auf **www.westermann.de/webcode** ins Suchfeld ein.
Eine Übersicht zu allen Webcodes findest du alternativ auch unter diesem QR-Code:

© 2023 Westermann Bildungsmedien Verlag GmbH, Georg-Westermann-Allee 66, 38104 Braunschweig
www.westermann.de

Das Werk und seine Teile sind urheberrechtlich geschützt. Jede Nutzung in anderen als den gesetzlich zugelassenen bzw. vertraglich zugestandenen Fällen bedarf der vorherigen schriftlichen Einwilligung des Verlages.

Die enthaltenen Links verweisen auf digitale Inhalte, die der Verlag bei verlagsseitigen Angeboten in eigener Verantwortung zur Verfügung stellt. Links auf Angebote Dritter wurden nach den gleichen Qualitätskriterien wie die verlagsseitigen Angebote ausgewählt und bei Erstellung des Lernmittels sorgfältig geprüft. Für spätere Änderungen der verknüpften Inhalte kann keine Verantwortung übernommen werden.

Druck A[1] / Jahr 2023
Alle Drucke der Serie A sind inhaltlich unverändert.

Redaktion: Thorsten Schimming, Dr. Philippa Söldenwagner-Koch, München (www.lektoratbilingual.de), Dr. Martin Walter
Umschlaggestaltung: LIO Design GmbH, Braunschweig
Layout: Visuelle Lebensfreude, Hannover
Druck und Bindung: Westermann Druck GmbH, Georg-Westermann-Allee 66, 38104 Braunschweig

ISBN 978-3-425-**73090**-5

Contents

Contents

1 Visions of the future

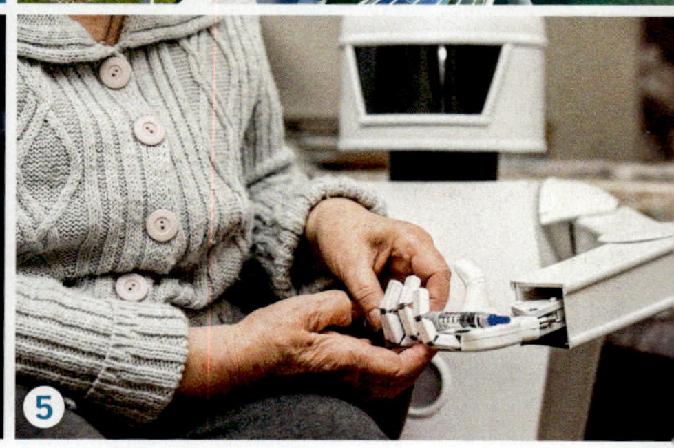

Webcode

You can download a word list for the Theme here: DSW-73090-001

1

Pair work Look at the pictures on this page. One partner describes the positive associations that come to mind, the other partner describes the negative associations.

2

Pair work Think about what life will be like in the future. Note down both positive and negative aspects. Consider areas such as politics, the media, the job market, education and social life.

3 Think-Pair-Share

a) Think about the daily routine of a teenager living in 2050. Note down your ideas.
b) **Pair work** Exchange your ideas with your partner's.
c) Share your ideas in class.

4

Pair work Not only have visions of the future been a popular theme in literature, they have also been the subject of numerous films and TV series. Take a look at the film stills on the next page and match them to the titles on the right and to the descriptions of the films/TV series.

The Rain
Divergent
The Hunger Games
The Handmaid's[1] Tale

Annotations
[1] **handmaid** = female servant
[2] **concubine** /ˈkɒŋkjʊbaɪn/ = in the past, a woman who had a sexual relationship to an important man without being married to him

Descriptions

1. This popular TV series is based on a novel and first aired in 2017. Both the novel and the series display a world in which only some women are still fertile. The USA has been replaced by a fundamentalist theocratic dictatorship, which forces these women to live as concubines[2].
2. This series deals with a brutal virus carried by the rain that wipes out most of the population and leaves behind two young siblings who embark on a dangerous journey.

6

7

8

9

3. In a futuristic Chicago, society is divided into five factions based on virtues. However, the protagonist does not fit into any of the factions. When the government plots to eliminate all those who are factionless and she uncovers this conspiracy, she teams up with the mysterious Four to overthrow the government and save the world.
4. Set in a future North America known as Panem, the Capitol annually selects one boy and one girl from each of the twelve districts to compete in a televised fight to the death. The protagonist Katniss Everdeen volunteers to save her sister. She is then rushed to the Capitol to undergo intense training. Luckily, she already has the skill to use a certain weapon.

Preview

In this Theme, you will learn about different visions of the future in literature.
In the **Workshop** you will work on extracts from two novels, focusing on
- ✓ narrative perspective and techniques
- ✓ characters

5 Group work

a) Each group member watches one of the following official trailers from popular TV series or films online:
The Giver • *Black Mirror – Arkangel* • *The Road* • *Never Let Me Go*
While watching, take notes on the society presented in the trailer.

→ **S20:** How to listen/watch effectively, p. 234

b) Watch the trailer again to find out which overall topics regarding the future the film/TV series seems to deal with (e.g. technology).
c) Read the following definition and explain whether the trailers present dystopian fiction.
d) Present your results to the other group members.
e) Choose one of the films/TV series you would like to watch. Explain your choice to the other group members.
f) EXTRA In your group, talk about other books, films or TV series you know that display a futuristic world. Discuss whether these visions of the future are more positive or negative.

> Dystopian fiction displays visions of the future that challenge readers or viewers to reflect on current issues in society. In this respect, these works of fiction often show what could happen by projecting current trends into the future. They deal with topics such as environmental ruin, surveillance and control through technology and governmental oppression.

UTOPIA VS. DYSTOPIA

There are (and always have been) countless visions of what the future might bring. Simply put, if these predictions are positive, they are called utopias; if they envision a dark, threatening future, they are called dystopias. The term "utopia" was coined by Thomas More in his 16th century work of the same name, in which he depicts an ideal society. The term derives from the Greek words for "not" and "place", thus describing a place that cannot (yet) be found in reality. Since then, many fictional and non-fictional works have dealt with the question of what the future may hold.

DYSTOPIAN FICTION

While utopian fiction does not really exist anymore, dystopian fiction has been a popular genre for decades and has even increased its popularity in recent years through young adult novels like Suzanne Collins' *The Hunger Games* or Lois Lowry's *The Giver* as well as motion picture films and series. The most important aspect when it comes to dystopian fiction is that it usually criticizes current issues – such as surveillance technology, social media or cloning – and projects them into the future in a "what if" scenario. For instance, a dystopian vision of the future might describe a society in which these technologies are used in extreme ways, thus illustrating possible negative consequences of current trends. However, initially these visions may seem ideal – even utopian –, since the societies in these works often seem to have been able to harness these technologies in a way which furthers the common good. But it soon becomes apparent that it is a "utopia gone wrong" and thus a dystopian world which is described in these works.

DYSTOPIAN ELEMENTS – FORMS OF CONTROL

Another typical element of dystopian fiction is a catastrophic background story, which is supposed to justify the society that has been created. For example, a war or revolution has led to a restructuring of society – as in *The Hunger Games* – or natural disasters or other climatic events have resulted in dramatic changes in the way people live, e.g. in *The Giver*.

Many dystopias are characterized by a totalitarian form of government and a small ruling elite, which oppresses its citizens and controls them with measures such as surveillance, medication, censorship and numerous rules and prohibitions. Even all-time classics from the first half of the 20th century such as Aldous Huxley's *Brave New World* (1932) and George Orwell's *1984* (1949) already use these motifs. While the latter is particularly known for its Big Brother who is always watching, the former already includes forms of genetic engineering and conditioning of embryos as well as the drugging of the citizens as a controlling measure.

LOSS OF INDIVIDUALITY

These forms of control typically cause a loss of individuality and lack of autonomy and independence, which is accepted by most citizens because they are either afraid to stand up for themselves or because they are not aware of the fact that they are being brainwashed. This is the case in Ray Bradbury's *Fahrenheit 451* (1953), in which all books are burned and people watch television all day, not being able to think independently anymore.

However, there is usually one character – sometimes a group of characters – who comes to realize that their society is far from ideal. This is the protagonist, who has always questioned or starts questioning the society he or she lives in throughout the course of the novel or film. It becomes their goal to destroy the system or, if that is not possible, at least to escape from it.

TECHNOLOGY

Another element that can often be found in dystopian fiction is advanced technology, often conceptualized by projecting current technological trends into the future. Apart from surveillance technology, robots are another classic example. Robots are machines that operate autonomously from human supervision. They can be built for any purpose and are meant to replace humans. Today robots are mainly used in manufacturing, by the military and by scientists. They can take on any form, though in fictional works, they often resemble humans. These kinds of robots are called "androids". In fiction, they often become too independent and rise up against their human creators.

1
Complete the grid. Use a dictionary to check your results.

noun	verb	adjective
...	*to envision*	...
...	*to depict*	
...	*to criticize*	...
...	*to project*	
...	...	*ideal*
restructuring	...	
...	*to oppress*	...
censorship	...	
prohibition	...	...
individuality	...	...
autonomy		...
independence		...
supervision	...	
creator	...	...

Webcode
You can download the grid here:
DSW-73090-002

2
a) Match these definitions with words from the text.
1. to force sb to accept your ideas or beliefs, e.g. by preventing the person from thinking independently
2. government control of what can be written in a book or newspaper or shown in a film etc.
3. to explain or defend one's actions
4. a description of how things might happen in the future
5. a small group of people who are often very powerful or influential
6. the act of carefully watching a person

b) **Pair work** Use other words from the text or from task 1 to create a partner taboo. One of you explains the word without using it, the other one has to guess the word.

3
a) Language awareness Look at the words highlighted in the text on the left. The words below describe the same or a very similar concept. Match them to the highlighted words and fill them into a grid with three columns. The first one has been done for you. In some cases, there may be three words which belong together.

to educate | reform | to rule | editing | drug | surveillance | to enlighten | to leave | subject | extensive | revolution | uncontrolled

positive	neutral	negative
	extensive	*extreme*

b) Discuss your results in class.

4 WB pp. 4-7
Use the terms "utopia" and "dystopia" as well as at least ten other words from tasks 1 to 3 to explain the quotation below. Make sure your explanation contains some examples.

If we don't change direction soon,
we'll end up where we're going.
Irwin Corey

Step by step Working on novel extracts

Preview

In this Workshop, you will work on novel extracts, focusing on
- analysing narrative perspective and
- analysing characters.

PRE-READING

1

George Orwell (1903-1950)

In 1948, the English author George Orwell completed what would become his most famous work, the dystopian novel *Nineteen Eighty-Four*. One of the most important examples of the genre to this day, it is set in a dystopian future. Orwell wrote the novel as a warning because of what he saw as very worrying developments in European politics at the time.
In the fictional world of the novel, much of the world is in a state of constant war. What we know today as Great Britain has become a province in a superstate called Oceania. Oceania is ruled by the Party.

a) The following slogans are the motto of the ruling Party and their state.
WAR IS PEACE.
FREEDOM IS SLAVERY.
IGNORANCE IS STRENGTH.
Speculate on the type of society Orwell describes in *Nineteen Eighty-Four*.

→ **S20:** How to listen/watch effectively, p. 234

b) Watch the trailer for the 1984 film version of the novel and check whether you were right. Note down what else you learn about Orwell's vision of the future.

COMPREHENSION

2

a) Read the first extract from George Orwell's novel and list elements that give you clues about the kind of society the protagonist, Winston Smith, lives in.
b) **Pair work** Exchange your ideas with a partner's.
c) Outline Winston's actions and their consequences.

→ **S9:** How to structure a text, p. 212

Nineteen Eighty-Four
by George Orwell

Extract 1

Winston turned round abruptly. He had set his features into the expression of quiet optimism which it was advisable to wear when facing the telescreen[1]. [...] He [...] sat down at a small table that stood to the left of the telescreen. From the table drawer he took out a penholder[2], a bottle of ink, and a thick, quarto-sized blank book with a red back and a marbled[3] cover.
For some reason the telescreen in the living room was in an unusual position. Instead of being placed, as was normal, in the end wall, where it could command the whole room, it was in the longer wall, opposite the window. To one side of it there was a shallow alcove[4] in which Winston was now sitting and which, when the flats were built, had probably been intended to hold bookshelves. By sitting in the alcove, and keeping well back, Winston was able to remain outside the range of the telescreen, so far as sight went. He could be heard, of course, but so long he stayed in his present position he could not be seen.
It was partly the unusual geography of the room that had suggested to him the thing that he was now about to do. But it had also been suggested by the book that he had just taken out of the drawer. It was a peculiarly beautiful book. Its smooth creamy paper, a little yellowed by age, was of a kind that had not been manufactured for at least forty years past. He could guess, however, that

Annotations
[1] **telescreen** = TV screen that also functions as a means of surveillance
[2] **penholder** = *Federhalter*
[3] **marbled** = looking like marble
[4] **alcove** = *Nische*

the book was much older than that. [...] Even with nothing written in it, it was a compromising possession. The thing that he was about to do was to open a diary. This was not illegal (nothing was illegal, since there were no longer any laws), but if detected it was reasonably certain that it would be punished by death, or at least by twenty-five years in a forced-labour camp. Winston fitted a nib[5] into the penholder and sucked it to get the grease off. The pen was an archaic instrument, seldom used even for signatures, and he had procured[6] one, furtively and with some difficulty, simply because of a feeling that the beautiful creamy paper deserved to be written on with a real nib instead of being scratched with an ink pencil. Actually he was not used to writing by hand. Apart from very short notes, it was usual to dictate everything into speakwrite[7], which was of course impossible for his present purpose. He dipped the pen into the ink and then faltered[8] for just a second. A tremor[9] had gone through his bowels[10]. To mark the paper was the decisive act. In small clumsy letters he wrote:

April 4th, 1984.

He sat back. A sense of complete helplessness had descended upon him. To begin with, he did not know with any certainty that this was 1984. It must be round about that date, since he was fairly sure that his age was thirty-nine, and he believed that he had been born in 1944 or 1945; but it was never possible nowadays to pin down any date within a year or two.

For whom, it suddenly occurred to him to wonder, was he writing this diary? For the future, for the unborn. His mind hovered for a moment round the doubtful date on the page, and then fetched up[11] with a bump against the Newspeak word doublethink. For the first time the magnitude of what he had undertaken came home to him. How could you communicate with the future? It was of its nature impossible. Either the future would resemble the present, in which case it would not listen to him, or it would be different from it, and his predicament[12] would be meaningless.

For some time he sat gazing stupidly at the paper. The telescreen had changed over to strident[13] military music. It was curious that he seemed not merely to have lost the power of expressing himself, but even to have forgotten what it was that he had originally intended to say. For weeks past he had been making ready for this moment, and it had never crossed his mind that anything would be needed except courage. The actual writing would be easy. All he had to do was to transfer to paper the interminable[14] restless monologue that had been running inside his head, literally for years. At this moment, however, even the monologue had dried up. [...]

Suddenly he began writing in sheer panic, only imperfectly aware of what he was setting down. [...]

His eyes refocused on the page. He discovered that while he sat helplessly musing he had also been writing, as though by automatic action. And it was no longer the same cramped[15] awkward handwriting as before. His pen had slid voluptuously[16] over the smooth paper, printing in large neat capitals –

DOWN WITH BIG BROTHER

DOWN WITH BIG BROTHER

DOWN WITH BIG BROTHER

DOWN WITH BIG BROTHER

DOWN WITH BIG BROTHER

over and over again, filling half a page. He could not help feeling a twinge[17] of panic. It was absurd, since the writing of those particular words was not more dangerous than the initial act of opening the diary; but for a moment he was tempted to tear out the spoiled pages and abandon the enterprise altogether.

But he did not do so, however, because he knew that it was useless. Whether he wrote DOWN WITH BIG BROTHER, or whether he refrained from writing it, made no difference. Whether he went on with the diary, or whether he did not go on with it, made no difference. The Thought Police would get him just the same. He had committed – would still have committed, even if he had never set pen to paper – the essential crime that contained all others

Annotations

5 **nib** = *Schreibfeder*
6 to **procure** = to buy
7 **speakwrite** = technology converting the spoken word into writing
8 to **falter** = to hesitate
9 **tremor** = shudder, quick shaking
10 **bowels** (*pl*) = *Gedärme, Eingeweide*
11 to **fetch up** = to land suddenly
12 **predicament** = dilemma, difficult situation
13 **strident** = loud and hurtful to the ear
14 **interminable** = without end
15 **cramped** = *verkrampft*
16 **voluptuous** = pleasant and opulent
17 **twinge** = small, quick pain

in itself. Thoughtcrime, they called it. Thoughtcrime was not a thing that could be concealed forever. You might dodge[18] successfully for a while, even for years, but sooner or later they were bound to get you. It was always at night – the arrests invariably happened at night. The sudden jerk[19] out of sleep, the rough hand shaking your shoulder, the lights glaring[20] in your eyes, the ring of hard faces round the bed. In the vast majority of cases there was no trial, no report of the arrest. People simply disappeared, always during the night. Your name was removed from the registers, every record of everything you had ever done was wiped out, your one-time existence was denied and then forgotten. You were abolished, annihilated: vaporized was the usual word. For a moment he was seized by a kind of hysteria. He began writing in a hurried untidy scrawl[21]:

theyll shoot me i dont care theyll shoot me in the back of the neck i dont care down with big brother they always shoot you in the back of the neck i dont care down with big brother –

Annotations
[18] to **dodge** = to avoid, keep out of the way
[19] **jerk** = sudden, violent movement
[20] to **glare** = to shine unpleasantly brightly
[21] **scrawl** = quick writing that is difficult to read

ANALYSIS: NARRATIVE PERSPECTIVE

3

→ **S12:** Checklist: Analysis – prose, p. 220

→ **S23:** How to quote, p. 239

a) Read the info box and identify the narrative perspective in the extract from *Nineteen Eighty-Four*. Pay special attention to the part highlighted in orange. Explain the effect the use of this particular narrative perspective has on the reader in a short paragraph. Include quotations to support your findings. → SUPPORT D1, p. 156

Language support

- The author **chooses/employs** ... to present ... in a ... way
  ... is written from ...'s perspective **because/so that** ...
- The ... narration offers a fairly **neutral/extremely detailed/rather one-sided/reliable/not very reliable** ...
- The .... narration directly **reveals** ...'s thoughts/feelings ...
  ... allows the reader to **gain insight into** ... and to understand ...
  ... allows the reader **access** to ...'s mind/thoughts/reasoning/feelings ...
- Using ... creates a feeling of **closeness/understanding/distance/openness/intimacy** ...
- The ... narrator comments on the story, thus **influencing/prejudicing** the reader ...

Info

Narrative techniques: perspective, point of view, mode of presentation, pace

There are different ways to tell a story. The author has a choice of different narrative perspectives: depending on the point of view from which the story is told, the effect on the reader may vary considerably.
Here are the most common **narrative perspectives** and **points of view**:

- **first-person narration**
  A first-person narration uses *I* and *me* and the narrator is often the novel's central character. The reader can easily identify with the first-person narrator, but since the narrator provides a very personal, subjective view of events, including their own feelings, the information may not always be reliable.
- **third-person narration**
  In a third-person narration, the characters in the story are referred to as *he, she, they*. Depending on the point of view, the narrator can be closer to or more distant from the characters and the action in a story.
  Within third-person narration, there are these points of view:
  a) omniscient point of view
  The omniscient narrator knows everything about the characters. The narrator can look inside their minds and knows their thoughts and feelings. They may comment on events and/or the behaviour of the characters or choose to merely report without an explicit comment. They also

know how the plot will develop and can switch between places and times. Thus they can refer to past events in a flashback or foreshadow future developments.

b) limited point of view
The limited narrator's insight into thoughts and feelings is restricted to one of the characters. They see and judge the development of the story through the eyes of that particular character only.

c) neutral point of view
An observer narrator merely reports the events without having access to the characters' minds, so the reader does not find out anything about the characters' thoughts and feelings.

- **multiperspectivity**
  There are multiple narrators telling the story alternatingly, often in opposition to each other or to illuminate different elements of a plot. Thus the reader is presented with different views of an event and the reasons behind it, as each narrator contributes new aspects and viewpoints.

Modes of presentation: interior monologue and stream of consciousness
Sometimes used interchangeably, **interior monologue** and **stream of consciousness** describes two ways of narrating a character's thoughts in a particularly direct way.

- **interior monologue**
  An interior monologue always presents a character's thoughts "directly", without the apparent intervention of a summarizing and selecting narrator.
- **stream of consciousness**
  This method attempts to give the written equivalent of the character's thought process. Stream-of-consciousness writing is usually regarded as a special form of interior monologue. It is characterized by associative leaps in thought and lack of some or all punctuation. Furthermore, it presents the reader with all of a character's impressions and perceptions in an unstructured, seemingly spontaneous way.

Pacing/narrative pace
This refers to the speed at which a story is told, which is not necessarily identical to the speed at which the story takes place. The pace is determined by the length of the scenes, how fast the action moves, and how quickly the reader is provided with information. The author can use certain devices to increase or decrease the pace of a story. Examples include:

- **increase:** dialogue, short sentences, frequent paragraphing, omissions
- **decrease:** description of details, introspection, flashbacks, foreshadowing

Flashbacks and foreshadowing can be used to break up the flow of the action and to explain it in more detail, develop a character, or add structure to the narrative.

b) Now focus on the passage highlighted in green. The narrator presents this passage as a kind of automatic writing, but it can also be regarded as a stream of consciousness. Write a short paragraph to explain the effect this passage has on the reader.

→ **S9:** How to structure a text, p. 212

Language support

The automatic writing can be regarded as an expression of Winston's ...
Winston's writing in the notebook offers the reader an insight into his mind/consciousness, showing his .../showing him to be ...
The stream of consciousness creates a closeness between ... and ...
... gives us insights into ...
... presents the character as very ...
... underlines his feelings/emotions/state of mind ...
Winston is portrayed as anxious/petrified/terrified/intimidated ...
The reader learns about his innermost feeling, his dread/distress/alarm/trepidation, expressed by ...
Winston's state of mind is exposed, showing his .../showing him to be ...

→ S23: How to quote, p. 239
→ S9: How to structure a text, p. 212

c) CHALLENGE Language awareness Focus on the narrative pace in the extract. Explain why the author chooses this pace and what effect it has on the reader. Include quotations to support your findings.

Language support

The short, straightforward sentences/The parataxis create/creates a fast pace/accelerate/accelerates the pace of ... This affects the mood of the scene, making it more ...
The long, complex sentences/The hypotaxis create/creates a slow pace/slow/slows down the pace of ... This gives the reader time to pause and think about .../This puts the focus on the development of ... rather than the action ...

COMPREHENSION

4

→ S1: Checklist: Summary, p. 198

a) Read the second extract from the novel and summarize Winston's encounter with Syme at their workplace cafeteria.
b) Using your own words, explain what "Newspeak" is and what purpose it seems to serve.

Extract 2

He turned round. It was his friend Syme, who worked in the Research Department. Perhaps 'friend' was not exactly the right word. You did not have friends nowadays, you had comrades: but there were some comrades whose society was pleasanter than that of others. Syme was a philologist, a specialist in Newspeak. Indeed, he was one of the enormous team of experts now engaged in compiling the Eleventh Edition of the Newspeak Dictionary. He was a tiny creature, smaller than Winston, with dark hair and large, protuberant[1] eyes, at once mournful and derisive, which seemed to search your face closely while he was speaking to you. [...]
'Did you go and see the prisoners hanged yesterday?' said Syme.
'I was working,' said Winston indifferently. 'I shall see it on the flicks[2], I suppose.'
'A very inadequate substitute,' said Syme. His mocking eyes roved over[3] Winston's face. 'I know you,' the eyes seemed to say, 'I see through you. I know very well why you didn't go to see those prisoners hanged.' [...]
'It was a good hanging,' said Syme reminiscently. 'I think it spoils it when they tie their feet together. I like to see them kicking. And above all, at the end, the tongue sticking right out, and blue – a quite bright blue. That's the detail that appeals to me.'
'Nex', please!' yelled the white-aproned prole[4] with the ladle[5].
Winston and Syme pushed their trays beneath the grille[6]. On to each was dumped swiftly the regulation lunch – a metal pannikin[7] of pinkish-grey stew, a hunk[8] of bread, a cube[9] of cheese, a mug of milkless Victory Coffee[10], and one saccharine[11] tablet.
'There's a table over there, under that telescreen,' said Syme. [...] Neither of them spoke again till they had emptied their pannikins. From the table at Winston's left, a little behind his back, someone was talking rapidly and continuously, a harsh gabble[12] almost like the quacking of a duck, which pierced[13] the general uproar of the room.
'How is the Dictionary getting on?' said Winston, raising his voice to overcome the noise.
'Slowly,' said Syme. 'I'm on the adjectives. It's fascinating.'
He had brightened up immediately at the mention of Newspeak. He pushed his pannikin aside, took up his hunk of bread in one delicate hand and his cheese in the other, and leaned across the table so as to be able to speak without shouting.

Annotations
1 **protuberant** = *hervortretend*
2 **the flicks** *(BE)* = cinema
3 to **rove over** = to wander across
4 **prole** = sb from the lower ranks of society, not a Party member
5 **ladle** = large deep spoon used to serve soup
6 **grille** = *Gitter*
7 **pannikin** = small pan
8 **hunk** = large piece
9 **cube** = square piece
10 **Victory Coffee** = poor-quality coffee made by the Party
11 **saccharine** = a kind of sweetener
12 **gabble** = *Gebrabbel, Geplapper*
13 to **pierce** = to make a small hole

'The Eleventh Edition is the definitive edition,' he said. 'We're getting the language into its final shape – the shape it's going to have when nobody speaks anything else. When we've finished with it, people like you will have to learn it all over again. You think, I dare say, that our chief job is inventing new words. But not a bit of it! We're destroying words – scores of them, hundreds of them, every day. We're cutting the language down to the bone. [...]'
He bit hungrily into his bread and swallowed a couple of mouthfuls, then continued speaking, with a sort of pedant's passion. His thin dark face had become animated, his eyes had lost their mocking expression and grown almost dreamy.
'It's a beautiful thing, the destruction of words. Of course the great wastage is in the verbs and adjectives, but there are hundreds of nouns that can be got rid of as well. It isn't only the synonyms; there are also the antonyms. After all, what justification is there for a word which is simply the opposite of some other word? A word contains its opposite in itself. Take "good", for instance. If you have a word like "good", what need is there for a word like "bad"? "Ungood" will do just as well – better, because it's an exact opposite, which the other is not. Or again, if you want a stronger version of "good", what sense is there in having a whole string of vague useless words like "excellent" and "splendid" and all the rest of them? "Plusgood" covers the meaning, or "doubleplusgood" if you want something stronger still. [...] In the end the whole notion of goodness and badness will be covered by only six words – in reality, only one word. Don't you see the beauty of that, Winston? It was B.B.'s idea originally, of course,' he added as an afterthought.
A sort of vapid[14] eagerness flitted[15] across Winston's face at the mention of Big Brother. Nevertheless Syme immediately detected a certain lack of enthusiasm.
'You haven't a real appreciation of Newspeak, Winston,' he said almost sadly. 'Even when you write it you're still thinking in Oldspeak. [...] You don't grasp the beauty of the destruction of words. Do you know that Newspeak is the only language in the world whose vocabulary gets smaller every year?'
Winston did know that, of course. He smiled, sympathetically he hoped, not trusting himself to speak. Syme bit off another fragment of the dark-coloured bread, chewed it briefly, and went on:
'Don't you see that the whole aim of Newspeak is to narrow the range of thought? In the end we shall make thoughtcrime literally impossible, because there will be no words in which to express it. Every concept that can ever be needed, will be expressed by exactly one word, with its meaning rigidly defined and all its subsidiary meanings rubbed out and forgotten. Already, in the Eleventh Edition, we're not far from that point. But the process will still be continuing long after you and I are dead. Every year fewer and fewer words, and the range of consciousness always a little smaller. Even now, of course, there's no reason or excuse for committing thoughtcrime. It's merely a question of self-discipline, reality-control. But in the end there won't be any need even for that. The Revolution will be complete when the language is perfect. [...]'

Annotations
[14] **vapid** = weak
[15] **to flit** = to move quickly

ANALYSIS: CHARACTERS

5

To understand the characters and their roles in a novel better, you have to take a closer look at how the author presents them in his or her text and how the different aspects of their personalities are revealed.
Read the info box on the next page to find out how characters can be presented in a direct or indirect way. Then look at the two examples below it and decide which is an example of direct and which an example of indirect characterization of Syme.

1. "Syme was a philologist, a specialist in Newspeak." (ll. 7-8)
2. "'Did you go and see the prisoners hanged yesterday?' said Syme.
   'I was working,' said Winston indifferently. 'I shall see it on the flicks, I suppose.'
   'A very inadequate substitute,' said Syme." (ll. 17-21)

Info

Types of characterization

Telling technique: direct characterization	Showing technique: indirect (dramatic) characterization
The reader is told directly and explicitly about the character's looks, traits and attitudes. This can be done by the narrator, the character himself/herself or other characters.	The reader can learn a lot about a character by studying what he/she says and does, how he/she behaves in certain situations and interacts with others. The reader is thus invited to infer traits from the character's actions, clothing, body language and the language he or she uses.

→ S12: Checklist: Analysis – prose, p. 220

6

Work with a grid in order to take a closer look at Syme as presented in the extract. All aspects in the grid below are connected and, analysed together, can give you insights into Syme as a literary character. For instance, his character traits might be reflected in the way he talks, his background influences his behaviour and so on. All of these aspects contribute to the personality of a literary figure as constructed by the author. Nevertheless, it is helpful to organize the different aspects before writing the characterization. → SUPPORT D2, pp. 156-157

Webcode
You can download the grid for task 6 here: DSW-73090-003

a) Copy the grid on pages 20-21. Use a complete A4 page for your grid.
b) Read the quotations that have been highlighted in the second extract and copy them into the

aspect	quotation	direct/ indirect?	interpretation
1. Outward appearance physical features/clothes/body language	Syme has "large, protuberant eyes, at once mournful and derisive" (ll. 13-14).	direct and indirect	The way Syme's eyes are described directly, makes him seem physically rather unattractive. At the same time, they are also described as being reflective of his character: his eyes are both "mournful" (l. 14), showing sadness and perhaps regret, as well as "derisive" (l. 14). This second adjective suggests that Syme is full of contempt and scorn for others. It contradicts Winston's first introduction of Syme as his "friend" and we learn that Winston might not feel very positively towards Syme after all.
2. Character traits e.g. modesty, courage, uncertainty			

aspect	quotation	direct/ indirect?	interpretation
3. Behaviour How a character acts (or does not act) gives an impression of their motives, abilities or moral standing.			
4. Mood the emotional state of a character			
5. Language e.g. correct or incorrect use of grammar, simple or academic vocabulary, colloquial language; reflects a character's social background, education, attitudes, etc.			
6. Family/social background			
7. Relationships with others how a character interacts with others and is perceived by them			

appropriate sections of the grid.

c) To find out more about Syme as a character, find further relevant passages in the text and add them to your grid.

d) Decide whether the quotations are examples of direct or indirect characterization.

e) Explain what the quotations reveal about Syme (fourth column).

7

As you have already found out, everything in this extract is presented from a limited perspective as if seen through Winston's eyes. This is also true for the way the reader gets to see Syme. Therefore, it is necessary to have another look at the narrative perspective.
Read the info box and assess the reliability of the information the reader is given about Syme. You can use this quotation to support your assessment:
"His mocking eyes roved over Winston's face. 'I know you,' the eyes seemed to say, 'I see through you. I know very well why you didn't go to see those prisoners hanged.'" (ll. 22-25).

Info

Reliability

When trying to find out how reliable the presentation of a character is, look for clues that show you whether the information presented is true objectively or whether you can detect that it has been influenced strongly by a character or the narrator, in particular

- the way they want to present the character in question,
- their emotions,
- their personal agenda, motives etc.

→ S12: Checklist: Analysis – prose, p. 2220

→ S23: How to quote, p. 239

8

Analyse Syme and the way he is presented in the extract, emphasizing what seems to be special about him as a character. Use your results from tasks 6 and 7 to write a detailed characterization of Syme. Remember to provide evidence for your findings by referring to and quoting from the text.
→ SUPPORT D3, p. 157, D4, p. 158

Checklist

Follow these steps to plan and write your characterization:

Introduction

✓ State who you are writing about and what the focus of your analysis will be (central claim).

Main part

✓ Use the categories of characterization to organize the main part in topical order. This is preferable to a chronological order, as working through the text chronologically often produces unnecessary repetitions.
✓ Use direct and indirect characterization for your analysis.
✓ Include information on the reliability of the information where helpful.

Conclusion

✓ Summarize your results in a concise and general manner.
✓ Refer back to your central claim.

Language support

characterization

Introduction	Main part	Conclusion
... is the protagonist/antagonist/a major/minor character in the novel. ... appears to be an ambivalent character. ... describes ...'s behaviour and ...	The character is presented/described as .../in a ... way. His body language reveals/suggests ... When he claims that/comments on/protests that ..., it becomes obvious that ... The fact that he reveals/highlights/underlines that ...	As a result of the analysis, ... can be described as ... The detailed characterization proves that ..., but at the same time ... The essential outcome of the analysis is that ... is actually ...

9

CHALLENGE In recent years, sales of Orwell's *Nineteen Eighty-Four* have risen again. Many people feel nervous about current political developments and liken the world we live in today to Orwell's "post-truth" dystopia. Developments such as fake news, especially in the context of social media, the emergence of extreme right-wing political movements around the world, the questioning and undermining of formerly generally accepted truths and scientific research fuelled by their leaders and/or religious fanatics, and the use of media outlets for propaganda worry many people tremendously.

→ S8: How to improve your text, p. 209

Drawing on the extracts you have worked on and your knowledge of current events, try to explain what might make Orwell's more than 70-year-old novel appealing and even instructive for a modern audience.

Practice Working on novel extracts

PRE-READING

1

a) Watch the video and name the effects climate change has had on the Ghanaian village Ada Foah.

b) **Pair work** As you have already learned, dystopian literature usually depicts societies with which something is inherently wrong, often by criticizing current developments and projecting them into the future. Taking the situation in Ada Foah as a basis, work with a partner and note down a few ideas for a dystopian novel of your own. Explain
- what the people living in the village and other areas similarly affected by sea level rise might do, and
- what consequences this could have for other countries.

Webcode
You can find the video here: **DSW-73090-004**

→ **S20:** How to listen/ watch effectively, p. 234

COMPREHENSION

2 WB pp. 8-9

In the 2019 novel *The Wall*, the negative consequences of climate change indicated in the video clip in task 1 have led to a world in which the southern hemisphere cannot be populated anymore. In a reaction to the sheer endless number of displaced people trying to find a new home in other countries, Great Britain has built a wall around the island, keeping the so-called Others out. Young people have to do service on the Wall to protect the coastline. → SUPPORT D5, p. 158

a) Read the first four extracts from the *The Wall* on pages 23-24 and note down general information on the fictional world of the novel. Focus on
- the world before and after the Change
- roles, rules and tasks on (and around) the Wall
- additional important information

b) **Pair work** Compare your results with a partner's.

c) In class, identify typical aspects of a dystopian world.

The Wall
by John Lanchester

Extract 1

Sometimes we would be told about a flotilla[1] of Others who had been spotted and attacked from the air, just in case some of them had survived and might still be coming in our direction. Occasionally there would be some big-picture news about crops failing or countries breaking down or coordination between rich countries, or some other emerging detail of the new world we were occupying since the Change. Sometimes there would be news of an attack in which Others had used new or unexpected tactics, or attacked in surprising strength. If Others ever got through, we were told about it. The room would go very quiet.

Annotations
[1] **flotilla** = small number of boats

Extract 2

None of us can talk to our parents. By 'us' I mean my generation, people born after the Change. [...] It's guilt: mass guilt, generational guilt. The olds feel they irretrievably fucked up the world, then allowed us to be born into it. You know what? It's true. That's exactly what they did. They know it, we know it. Everybody knows it.

To make things worse, the olds didn't do time on the Wall, because there was no Wall, because there had been no Change so the Wall wasn't needed. This means that the single most important and formative[2] experience in the lives of my generation – the big thing we all have in common – is something about which they have exactly no clue.

Annotations
[2] **formative** /ˈfɔː(r)mətɪv/ = important in forming sth, e.g. sb's character

Extract 3

Ten thousand kilometres of Wall. [...] it's more than three hundred thousand people involved in defending the Wall. That's why everybody goes to the Wall, no exceptions. That's the rule.
Except for Breeders. It's a paradox. Because the Wall needs so many people, we need people to Breed, so that there are enough people to man the Wall. It's on a fine edge as things currently stand, and there's talk of the tours having to be made longer, two and a half or three years, to make up a shortfall. But people don't want to Breed, because the world is such a horrible place. So as an incentive to get people to leave the Wall, if you reproduce, you can leave. [...] Some people say that this isn't fair to the children, who are born into a world where they have to do time on the Wall in their turn.

Extract 4

Most Defenders stand on the Wall because that's where the manpower is needed, but the Wall isn't the only form of border and coastal protection. The Flight scans the seas for Others, locates them, sometimes 'takes them out' then and there. [...] The Defenders are there for the rest of the Others: the ones who get through, which is a significant number [...]. They come in rowing boats and rubber[3] dinghies[4], on inflatable[5] tubes[6], in groups and in swarms and in couples, in threes, in singles; the smaller the number, often, the harder to detect. They are clever, they are desperate, they are ruthless, they are fighting for their lives, so all of those things had to be true for us as well. We had to be clever and desperate and ruthless and fight for our lives, only more so, or we would switch places. [...] One in, one out: for every Other who got over the Wall, one Defender would be put to sea[7].

Annotations
[3] **rubber** = flexible material car tyres are made of
[4] **dinghy** /ˈdɪŋgi/ = small rubber boat
[5] **inflatable** = *aufblasbar*
[6] **tube** = *Rohr, Röhre*
[7] to **put** sb **to sea** = to leave sb out on the sea

3 Outline what is important to the company's cook, Mary, as presented in extract 5.

Extract 5

The Defenders are on a short holiday trip during their two weeks off. They are joined by Mary, the company's cook.

Mary was the next one up. She came out of the girls' tent yawning and stretching, her curly hair seeming to stretch too, up and out. She came over and helped herself to coffee – she was one of those temperamentally cheerful people who are hilariously moody in the morning until they've had some caffeine. [...] cooking was Mary's hobby and chief interest as well as her job: it was just her favourite thing to do. No need to ask her what her plans were for life after the Wall. It was her favourite topic of conversation, a running reverie[1] about what she'd do once she had the money to open her own place. (That part, the bit where she put together the money, was a little vague. But she had faith.) When she could cook whatever she wanted, as long as it was in season. She loved to talk about it.

Annotations
[1] **reverie** = daydream

→ **S9:** How to structure a text, p. 212

4 Describe Joseph and Mary's duties during their respective shifts on the Wall as depicted in extract 6.

Extract 6

Joseph, the protagonist of the novel, is in the middle of two weeks of night shifts on the Wall when – as usual – Mary, the company's cook, does her round among the Defenders, serving them hot drinks.

Right from my first day I had liked Mary's visits – there was nothing original about that, everyone loved Mary. It's hard not to like the person who comes bringing chat and laughter and company and a warm drink in the middle of a long lonely watch[1], but even so, her personality was perfectly adapted to the job. She was the kind of person who leaves most people smiling, most of the time. Even the look of her could make you smile, her round pretty pink face and curly near-ginger[2] hair which always seemed to be trying to escape from whatever she was wearing to control and contain

Annotations
[1] **watch** = period of time in which sb has to keep watch
[2] **ginger** = red/orange hair colour

it [...] Those long stretches of time made people cranky, and it was easy to have sharp swings in mood, passages of time when you felt sure you weren't going to get through it. Mary never had that: her job was a relatively privileged one, by comparison, and she knew it, and made it part of her job to make everyone else feel better.

The tenth night of that shift, Mary did her second set of rounds with dawn minutes away. I watched her on her usual routine, her bike stopping in each Defender's pool of light as she came along the ramparts[3], cup of warm drink and a few words for everyone. That night a gale[4] was blowing. The waves and the wind were so loud that it was hard to hear even the communicator earpiece[5]. [...]

Mary [...] came over to me. I took a scan of the Wall and the water and prepared to give her my full attention for the next couple of minutes.

'Oof,' she said when she arrived, 'hello darling, I swear I'm getting more unfit the longer I do this, that doesn't make sense, does it, should be the other way round. Coffee and a biscuit, not in that order. Here, hold this.' She reached into her shoulder bag and was holding out a packet of biscuits. I remember thinking: chocolate and orange jam, my favourite. I took them and put my rifle[6] down on the bench, still within arm's reach as per the rules, and unhooked[7] my metal cup from the outside of my rucksack while she fiddled with[8] the thermos flask. I was glad it was coffee rather than tea [...] As she reached forwards to pour it I saw she had spilt it over herself, though spilt it in a strange place, along her throat and the front top of her waterproof[9], and I thought, that's weird, I know she can be clumsy, but how did Mary manage to pour the coffee upwards, somehow to chuck[10] it up over herself? She made a small noise, a bit like the 'oof' when she stopped her bike, but quieter, more involuntary[11]; she sounded surprised. She dropped the thermos and looked down at herself and then all at once several things happened, simultaneously, but also slowly: The liquid was a strange colour. A strange texture too. Mary was backlit[12], a lamp behind her, so I couldn't see properly, and I realised, yes, it was the texture that was wrong, not the colour: the way the wetness was thick but also moving too fast for a mere spill; it can't be coffee, can she have spilt food on herself? but no it's a liquid, but no it's wrong for water, and it's not spilling it's pumping, it's not been poured over her it's coming out of her. There's only one thing it can be, it's blood. But how can it be blood? It's not a nosebleed, she hasn't thrown blood up[13] on herself, my that would be a very serious illness, one that had you throwing blood up on yourself, anyway it's not coming out of her mouth it's coming from further down, it's pumping out of her, it's I swear I can remember this whole train of thought, a line of argument running through my mind as if I was, I don't know, defending a PhD thesis[14] or something. It can only have taken a tiny fraction of a second, and then I understood: Mary had been hit by a bullet or a knife or something similar, it was a very bad wound that she probably wouldn't survive. We were under attack. The Others had come.

Annotations

[3] **rampart** = protective wall
[4] **gale** = storm
[5] **communicator earpiece** = earphone used for communicating with sb
[6] **rifle** = long gun one fires holding it to one's shoulder
[7] to **unhook** = *aushaken*
[8] to **fiddle with** = *fummeln*
[9] **waterproof** = jacket that protects against water
[10] to **chuck** = to throw
[11] **involuntary** = without wanting to
[12] to **be backlit** = to be lit from behind
[13] to **throw up** = *sich übergeben*
[14] **PhD thesis** = academic piece of writing to earn a doctorate

ANALYSIS

5 WB p. 10/3 → **S12:** Checklist: Analysis – prose, p. 220

Analyse Joseph's perception of Mary's death in extract 6. Focus on the use of narrative perspective and pacing and the effect these narrative techniques have on the way the reader learns about the situation.

6 WB p. 10/4, p. 11/5 → **S9:** How to structure a text, p. 212

Write a characterization of Mary based on what you learn about her in both extracts 5 and 6. Assess how important she is for Joseph, the narrator.

COMMENT

7 Language awareness WB p. 11/6

Comment on the fact that Britons like Joseph refer to the environmental developments that have led to their situation as "the Change". Consider how appropriate this choice of words is and how the Others might describe these developments.

→ **S6:** How to write an argumentative text, p. 206

Mediation: Parents as Big Brother?

1 WB pp. 12-13 → S19: How to improve your mediation skills, p. 232

In recent years, the app *Life360*, which allows parents to track their children's every move, has become very popular and controversial in the US. Your email friend John has told you about how his parents want to keep tracking him even with him moving out to attend college this summer. You have done some research and found out that this trend exists in German-speaking countries, too.

Write a sympathetic email to John and tell him about what you have found out about parents using tracking devices in Switzerland, the reasons they have for tracking their children and whether experts recommend using this kind of surveillance on children. Write about 200 words.

„Überwachungs-Apps werden missbraucht"

Von Andrea Fischer Schulthess, Tagesanzeiger: Mamablog, 23. Oktober 2018

Heimwehkinder, Uber-Eltern, Drohnen-Eltern – das Thema der übertriebenen elterlichen Fürsorge beschäftigt die Gemüter und die Medien. Und das ist gut so. Denn es beeinträchtigt auch viele Jugendliche. Vor allem, wenn ihre Eltern per Handyortung ständig überprüfen, wo sie sich gerade aufhalten. Was macht das mit den Kids? Was mit der Beziehung zu ihren Eltern? Und: Ist das überhaut noch legal? Ein Gespräch mit Sharmila Egger, Psychologin, Medienpädagogin und Lerncoach.

Frau Egger, Sie haben vor diesem Interview speziell noch eine kleine Umfrage in Schulkassen gemacht. Was ist dabei herausgekommen?
Das Bild hat sich bestätigt, dass mehr Mädchen als Jungen von ihren Eltern kontrolliert werden. Und dass es den Jugendlichen peinlich ist, so überwacht zu werden. Sie reden nicht gern darüber.

Ich selbst habe schon mehrfach von Jugendlichen gehört, dass sie sich einfach mit diesem sogenannten Tracking abfinden müssen. Nur dann erlauben ihnen ihre Eltern, auszugehen und Freunde zu treffen. Ist das überhaupt erlaubt?
Es fehlt bislang eine eindeutige gesetzliche Grundlage, welche die Installation von Überwachungs-Apps von Eltern bei ihren Kindern regeln würde. Es gibt auch noch kein Gerichtsurteil zu dem Thema. So bleibt es ein Abwägen zwischen dem Persönlichkeitsrecht des Kindes und der Fürsorgepflicht der Eltern. Es ist wohl davon auszugehen, dass bei Kindern bis zum 14. Lebensjahr in der Regel die Schutzpflicht der Eltern überwiegt. Später wird das Persönlichkeitsrecht des Kindes eine Rolle spielen und ab 18 ist es dann klar nicht mehr erlaubt.

Gibt es Fälle, in denen eine solche Überwachung per Handy-App sinnvoll ist?
Selten. Ich empfehle es Eltern nicht. Auch zeige ich ihnen keine entsprechenden Apps, denn in der Regel wird dieses Mittel meiner Meinung nach missbraucht. Aber klar, es gibt wie bei allem immer Ausnahmen. Ich hatte in der Beratung auch schon ein Kind mit Diabetes. Da waren sich alle Beteiligten einig, dass es sinnvoll ist, eine App zur Kontrolle zu haben für den Fall, dass das Kind krankheitsbedingt irgendwo in einer Notsituation liegen bleibt.

Weshalb sind Sie derart gegen Überwachungs-Apps?
Eine solche Kontrolle richtet mehr Schaden an, als sie nützt. Sie stört das Vertrauensverhältnis zwischen Jugendlichen und ihren Eltern. In diesem Alter geht es darum, Freiheiten zu bekommen und damit umgehen zu lernen. Zu streng überwachte Jugendliche werden aktiv in die Unselbstständigkeit gestoßen. Sie sind nicht richtig fit fürs Leben. Das kann doch nicht der Wunsch der Eltern sein. Und im Extremfall bewirkt ein Überwachen mit einer App, was Eltern eigentlich verhindern wollten: Wenn Kids etwa ihr Handy bei Kollegen deponieren, damit ihre Eltern den wahren Aufenthaltsort nicht kennen. Unter Umständen sind sie dann nachts ohne Handy unterwegs und könnten nicht mal Hilfe anfordern, wenn sie den letzten Bus verpasst haben.

Was empfehlen Sie besorgten Eltern als Alternative?
Sie sollen mit ihren Kindern reden. Ihre Ängste äußern und erklären, was sie brauchen, um Sicherheit zu gewinnen. Und sich zurückerinnern. Wir wollten als Teenies doch auch nicht, dass unsere Eltern ständig wussten, wo wir sind. [...]

Haben Eltern heute viel mehr Angst als früher?
Nein, das glaube ich nicht. Doch es gibt mehr Mittel zur Kontrolle. Hinzu kommt, dass das Internet für viele Eltern eine Art Blackbox ist. Man hat keine Ahnung, was in dieser unübersichtlichen Welt mit den Kindern geschieht, was sie sehen, erleben und wen sie treffen. Man liest so viel über Cybermobbing, Cybergrooming und Co. Das macht den Eltern natürlich Angst. Deshalb sollten sie an diesen Themen dran bleiben. Nur wer versucht, offen zuzuhören, gewinnt das Vertrauen der Jugendlichen und kann auf Risiken hinweisen, ohne dass die Kids gleich auf Durchzug schalten. (581 Wörter)

The Circle: A contemporary dystopian novel

1
Pair work In the novel *The Circle* by Dave Eggers, the protagonist, a young woman called Mae, starts working at an influential company and is very excited about it. Imagine what your ideal workplace would look like. Describe it to a partner or draw a sketch of it and then talk about it.

2
Not only the novel is called *The Circle*, but also the company the protagonist works for. This company uses several slogans, one of them is SHARING IS CARING. With a partner, speculate on the meaning of the slogan and on what it might be like to work for such a company.

3
Now read the beginning of the novel, when Mae first arrives at her new workplace.
a) Explain briefly why Mae describes her new workplace as "heaven".
b) Language awareness Analyse the atmosphere created at the beginning of the novel. Pay special attention to the choice of words.
c) Explain to what extent this beginning fulfils your expectations of dystopian fiction.

→ **S12:** Checklist: Analysis – prose, p. 220

The Circle
by Dave Eggers

Extract 1

My God, Mae thought. It's heaven.
The campus was vast and rambling[1], wild with Pacific color, and yet the smallest detail had been carefully considered, shaped by the most eloquent[2] hands. On land that had once been a shipyard[3], then a drive-in movie theater, then a flea market, then blight[4], there were now soft green hills and a Calatrava[5] fountain. And a picnic area, with tables arranged in concentric circles. And tennis courts, clay[6] and grass. And a volleyball court, where tiny children from the company's day-care center were running, squealing[7], weaving[8] like water. Amid all this was a workplace, too, four hundred acres of brushed steel[9] and glass on the headquarters of the most influential company in the world. The sky above was spotless[10] and blue.
Mae was making her way through all of this, walking from the parking lot to the main hall, trying to look as if she belonged. The walkway wound around lemon and orange trees and its quiet red cobblestones[11] were replaced, occasionally, by tiles[12] with imploring messages of inspiration. "Dream," one said, the word laser-cut into the red stone. "Participate," said another. There were dozens: "Find Community." "Innovate." "Imagine." She just missed stepping on the hand of a young man in a grey jumpsuit[13]; he was installing a new stone that said "Breathe."

Annotations
1 to **ramble** = to move around aimlessly
2 **eloquent** = *here:* skilful, tasteful
3 **shipyard** = place where ships are built
4 **blight** = *here:* wasteland, empty land
5 **Santiago Calatrava** (*1951) = Spanish-Swiss architect and artist
6 **clay** = *Sand (Tennisplatz)*
7 to **squeal** = *kreischen*
8 to **weave** = *here:* to move effortlessly through a crowd without touching anyone
9 **brushed steel** = polished steel which is not shiny but dull
10 **spotless** = perfect, without a mark
11 **cobblestone** = *Kopfsteinpflaster*
12 **tile** = *Fliese, Kachel, Platte*
13 **jumpsuit** = overall

4 Think-pair-share

Before you read the next extract from *The Circle* about the use of social media within the company, reflect on your own use of social media.

a) Think about which kinds of social media you use. Rank them from most used to least used.
b) **Pair work** Compare your ranking with a partner's. Talk about when, how often and why you use these specific social media platforms and not others.
c) Share your results in class. Discuss what would happen if you did not use social media.

5 WB pp. 14-16

→ S9: How to structure a text, p. 212
→ S12: Checklist: Analysis – prose, p. 220

After a few weeks at *The Circle*, Mae gets called into her boss's office to talk to him and two employees from Human Resources.

a) Outline the reasons why the company criticizes Mae's behaviour and her reaction.
b) Analyse Mae's behaviour towards the employees from Human Resources.
c) Assess to what extent you can relate to the perspectives of both Mae and the employees from Human Resources.

Extract 2

"Let's start with this past weekend. We know you left campus at 5:42 p.m. on Friday, and you got back here 8:46 a.m. on Monday."

"Was there work on the weekend?" Mae searched her memory. "Did I miss something?"

"No, no, no. There wasn't, you know, mandatory work here on the weekend. That's not to say that there weren't thousands of people here Saturday and Sunday, enjoying the campus, participating in a hundred different activities."

"I know, I know. But I was home. My dad was sick, and I went back to help out."

"I'm sorry to hear that," Josiah said. "Was this related to his MS[1]?"

"It was."

Josiah made a sympathetic face, and Denise leaned forward. "But see, here's where it gets especially confusing. We don't know anything about this episode. Did you reach out to any Circlers during this crisis? You know that there are four groups on campus for staffers[2] dealing with MS? Two of them are for children of MS sufferers. Have you sought out one of these groups?"

"No, not yet. I've meant to."

"Okay," Denise said. "Let's table[3] that thought for a second, because that's instructive, the fact that you were aware of the groups, but didn't seek them out. Surely you acknowledge the benefit of sharing information about this disease?"

"I do."

"And that sharing with other young people whose parents suffer from the disease – do you see the benefit in this?"

"Absolutely."

"For example, when you heard your dad had a seizure[4], you drove, what, a hundred miles or so, and never once during that drive did you try to glean[5] any information from the InnerCirclers, or from the larger OuterCircle. Do you see that as an opportunity wasted?"

"Now I do, absolutely. I was just upset, and worried, and I was driving like a maniac. I wasn't very present."

Denise raised a finger. "Ah, *present*. That is a wonderful word. I'm glad you used it. Do you consider yourself usually present?"

"I try to be."

Josiah smiled and tapped a flurry[6] into his tablet.

"But the opposite of present would be what?" Denise asked.

"Absent?"

"Yes. Absent. Let's put a pin[7] in that thought, too. Let's go back to your dad, and this weekend. Did he recover okay?" [...]

"He did. It was a false alarm, really."

"Good. I'm so glad to hear about that. But it's curious that you didn't share this with anyone else. Did you post anything anywhere about this episode? A zing[8], a comment anywhere?"

"No, I didn't," Mae said.

"Hm. Okay," Denise said, taking a breath. "Do you think someone else might have benefited from your experience? That is, maybe the next person who might drive two or three hours home might benefit from knowing what you found out about the episode, that it was just a minor pseudo-seizure?"

"Absolutely. I could see that being helpful."

Annotations
1 **MS** = multiple sclerosis, a serious, incurable illness
2 **staffer** = employee
3 **to table** = to leave aside
4 **seizure** = sudden worsening of an illness
5 **to glean** = to collect
6 **flurry** = sudden movement across a touchscreen
7 **pin** = *Reißzwecke, Reißnagel, Stecknadel*
8 **zing** = in the novel a status update one can send to all of one's followers

"Good. So what *do* you think the action plan should be?"

"I think I'll join the MS club," Mae said, "and I should post something about what happened. I know it'll be beneficial."

Denise smiled. "Fantastic. Now let's talk about the rest of the weekend. On Friday, you find out that your dad's okay. But the rest of the weekend, you basically go blank. It's like you disappeared!" Her eyes grew wide. "This is when someone like you, with a low Participation Rank, might be able to improve that, if she wanted to. But yours actually dropped – two thousand points. Not to get all number-geeky, but you were on 8,625 on Friday and by late Sunday you were at 10,288." [...]

Denise put her palms on the desk, as if she might get up. "Mae, you know this is a technology company, correct?"

"Of course."

"And that we consider ourselves on the forefront of social media."

"Yes."

"And you know the term Transparency, correct?"

"I do. Absolutely."

Josiah looked at Denise, hoping to calm her. She put her hands in her lap[9]. Josiah took over. He smiled and swiped his tablet, turning a new page.

"Okay. Let's go to Sunday. Tell us about Sunday."

"I just drove back."

"That's it?"

"I kayaked?"

Josiah and Denise registered[10] dual looks of surprise.

"You kayaked?" Josiah said. "Where?"

"Just in the bay."

"With who?"

"No one. Just alone."

Denise and Josiah looked hurt.

"*I* kayak," Josiah said, and then typed something in his tablet, pressing very hard.

"How often do you kayak?" Denise asked Mae.

"Maybe once every few weeks?"

Josiah was looking intently[11] at his tablet. "Mae, I'm looking at your profile, I'm finding nothing about you and kayaking. No smiles, no ratings, no posts, nothing. And now you're telling me you kayak once *every few weeks*?" [...]

Josiah softened. "But documentation aside, I'm just fascinated why you wouldn't mention anything about kayaking anywhere. I mean, it's a part of you. An integral part."

Mae let out an involuntary scoff[12]. "I don't think it's all that integral. Or interesting, really."

Josiah looked up, his eyes fiery. "But it is!"

"Lots of people kayak," Mae said.

"That's exactly it!" Josiah said, quickly turning red. "Wouldn't you like to meet other people who kayak?" Josiah tapped at his screen. "There are 2,331 people near you who also like to kayak. Including *me*."

Mae smiled. "That's a lot."

"More or less than you expected?" Denise asked.

"More, I guess," Mae said.

Josiah and Denise smiled.

"So should we sign you up to hear more about the people near you who like to kayak? There are so many tools ..." Josiah seemed to be opening a page where he could sign her up.

"Oh, I don't know," Mae said.

Their faces plummeted[13].

Josiah seemed angry again. "Why not? Do you think your passions are unimportant?"

"That's not quite it. I just ..."

Josiah leaned forward. "How do you think other Circlers feel, knowing that you're so close to them physically, that you're ostensibly part of a community here, but you don't want them to know your hobbies and interests. How do you think they feel?"

"I don't know. I don't think they'd feel anything."

"But they do!" Josiah said. "The point is that you're not engaged with the people around you!"

"It's just kayaking!" Mae said, laughing again, trying to bring the discussion back to a place of levity[14].

Josiah was at work on his tablet. "*Just* kayaking? Do you realize that kayaking is a three-billion-dollar industry? And you say it's 'just kayaking'! Mae, don't you see that it's all connected? You play your part. You have to *part*-icipate." [...]

After the interview, at her desk, Mae scolded herself. What kind of person was she? More than anything, she was ashamed.

Annotations

[9] **lap** = *Schoß*

[10] to **register** = to show, to display

[11] **intent** = determined, resolute

[12] **scoff** = sound of disapproval

[13] to **plummet** = to fall

[14] **levity** = light atmosphere

6

→ **S2:** Checklist: Creative writing, p. 199

After the meeting, both Mae and one of the employees from HR write a diary entry in which they reflect on the conversation. Write either Mae's or the HR employee's diary entry.

7

In addition to the slogan SHARING IS CARING, which you already know, the company uses two other slogans: SECRETS ARE LIES and PRIVACY IS THEFT.

→ **S12:** Checklist: Analysis – prose, p. 220

a) Analyse to what extent the employees in extract 2 stand for these slogans. Give evidence.
b) Choose one of the three slogans and explain its utopian and dystopian implications.

8

→ **S6:** How to write an argumentative text, p. 206

Discuss to what extent *The Circle* can be considered dystopian fiction. Also refer to other works of dystopian fictions you have come across in this Theme.

9

→ **S6:** How to write an argumentative text, p. 206

EXTRA Mae's ex-boyfriend tries to warn her about the dangers of the company:
"[...] you guys create [...] unnaturally extreme social needs. No one needs the level of contact you're purveying. It improves nothing. It's not nourishing."
Comment on this statement, also referring to your own use of social media.

10

→ **S1:** Checklist: Summary, p. 198

Read the extract from an online article about Dave Eggers' *The Circle* and sum up its message.

Dave Eggers' 'The Circle' uncomfortably close to Internet reality

by Silke Wünsch, 14 August 2014

[...] "The Circle" makes for an exciting read. And even though it is just fiction, the reality created in the novel will resonate with readers. It brings to mind the very real fear of the power of Google & Co. – of what is perhaps already possible, but what we can only cautiously hint at, because we know very well that we ourselves are the ones helping big Internet players acquire such power.
"Of course you can fight these developments," said computer scientist Stefan Ullrich. "In the end, technology doesn't just happen. It is actually used and manufactured by people. The question is whether people want to fight back." [...]

"The Circle" is often mentioned in the same sentence as the two most famous horror scenarios depicted in 20th-century literature – Aldous Huxley's "Brave New World," about people who are bred, cloned and conditioned, and George Orwell's classic "1984." Published at the end of the 1940s, the dystopian novel is also about total surveillance. In Orwell's world, there's the authoritarian government called "Big Brother." In Eggers' novel, it's a company that has the power. The difference is that the people couldn't fight against the oppressors in "1984." But there is something people can do to curb the all-pervading power of data-collecting Internet groups and intelligence agencies: stop feeding them.

Apple's headquarters in Cupertino, California

11

The article suggests that "technology doesn't just happen. It is actually used and manufactured by people." Explain this statement and give examples from your own life.

12 → **S6:** How to write an argumentative text, p. 206

According to the author, unlike in *1984*, the characters in *The Circle* can stop being oppressed by no longer feeding the company with their data. Discuss whether no longer sharing data online would be an option for you as well.

Brave New World: A classic dystopian novel

PRE-READING

1 Think-pair-share

a) Note down what freedom means to you.
b) **Pair work** Exchange your ideas with a partner's and discuss similarities and differences.
c) Write your ideas on the board and try to categorize them in class.

COMPREHENSION

2

In Aldous Huxley's 1932 dystopian novel *Brave New World*, people are not born by mothers but created in a laboratory. They are genetically modified and conditioned into five groups or castes (called Alphas, Betas, Gammas, Deltas and Epsilons) to fulfil certain roles and jobs within society and be happy with this, never doubting or questioning their roles.
Bernard and Lenina – members of the two highest and most intelligent castes (Alphas and Betas) – have spent a date in Amsterdam, attending the semi-demi-finals of the women's heavyweight wrestling championships (Lenina's choice), and are now on their way home. Read the extract from the novel and outline the topic of the conversation Bernard chooses and Lenina's reaction to it.

Brave New World

by Aldous Huxley

On their way back across the Channel, Bernard insisted on stopping his propeller and hovering on his helicopter screws within a hundred feet of the waves. The weather had taken a change for the worse; a south-westerly wind had sprung up, the sky was cloudy.
"Look," he commanded.
"But it's horrible," said Lenina, shrinking back from the window. She was appalled by the rushing emptiness of the night, by the black foam-flecked[1] water heaving beneath them, by the pale face of the moon, so haggard[2] and distracted among the hastening clouds. "Let's turn on the radio. Quick!" She reached for the dialling knob[3] on the dashboard[4] and turned it at random.
"... skies are blue inside of you," sang sixteen tremoloing[5] falsettos[6], "the weather's always ...".
Then a hiccough[7] and silence. Bernard had switched off the current. "I want to look at the sea in peace," he said. [...] "It makes me feel as though ..." he hesitated, searching for words with which to express himself, "as though I were more *me*, if you see what I mean. [...] Not just a cell in the social body. Doesn't it make you feel like that, Lenina?"
But Lenina was crying. "It's horrible, it's horrible," she kept repeating. "And how can you talk like that about not wanting to be a part of the social body? After all, everyone works for everyone else. We can't do without any one. Even Epsilons[8] ..."
"Yes, I know," said Bernard derisively. "'Even Epsilons are useful'! So am I. And I damned well wish I weren't!"
Lenina was shocked by his blasphemy. "Bernard!" she protested in a voice of amazed distress. "How can you?"
In a different key[9], "How can I?" he repeated meditatively. "No, the real problem is: How is it that I can't, or rather – because, after all, I know quite well why I can't – what would it be like if I could, if I were free – not enslaved by my conditioning."
"But, Bernard, you're saying the most awful things."
"Don't you wish you were free, Lenina?"
"I don't know what you mean. I am free. Free to have the most wonderful time. Everybody's happy nowadays."
He laughed, "Yes, but wouldn't you like to be free to be happy in some other way, Lenina? In your own way, for example; not in everybody else's way." [...]
"I don't understand anything," she said with decision, determined to preserve her incomprehension intact. "Nothing. Least of all," she continued in another tone, "why

Annotations
[1] **foam-flecked** = *mit Schaum gesprenkelt*
[2] **haggard** = tired-looking and thin
[3] **dialling knob** = *Drehknopf*
[4] **dashboard** = board containing the controls of a car, plane, etc.
[5] to **tremolo** = to make a slightly shaking effect when singing, playing a violin, etc.
[6] **falsetto** /fɔːlˈsetəʊ/ = a male voice singing unnaturally high
[7] **hiccough** = *Schluckauf*
[8] **Epsilons** = in the novel, the lowest caste in society and conditioned to do the most meaningless tasks
[9] **key** = *here:* tone

you don't take *soma*[10] when you have these dreadful ideas of yours. Instead of feeling miserable, you'd be jolly[11]. *So* jolly," she repeated and smiled, for all the puzzled anxiety in her eyes, with what was meant to be an inviting and voluptuous[12] cajolery[13]. He looked at her in silence, his face unresponsive and very grave – looked at her intently. After a few seconds Lenina's eyes flinched away [...].

When Bernard spoke at last, it was in a small tired voice.

"All right, then," he said, "we'll go back."

Annotations
[10] **soma** = a drug the people in the novel take to stay happy
[11] **jolly** = happy
[12] **voluptuous** = sexually exciting
[13] **cajolery** = act of persuading sb with praise or pleasant talk

ANALYSIS

3 → GRAMMAR G1, p. 189

a) Explain both Bernard and Lenina's attitudes towards the society they live in, especially with regard to their definitions of freedom.

b) Language awareness Analyse how Lenina and Bernard's different attitudes towards their set roles in the society of *Brave New World* are conveyed to the reader. Consider narrative techniques as well as language.

→ **S9:** How to structure a text, p. 212

→ **S12:** Checklist: Analysis – prose, p. 220

4

Compare the two characters' ideas of freedom with your own ideas from task 1.

→ **S8:** How to improve your text, p. 209

COMMENT

5

Brave New World is either a perfect-world utopia or its nasty opposite, a dystopia, depending on your point of view [...]

Margaret Atwood, Canadian author of e.g. The Handmaid's Tale

a) Evaluate Atwood's statement on the basis of what you have found out about the world in Huxley's novel and the characters Bernard and Lenina.

b) If you have not done so in a), comment on the widespread use of a drug like soma in a world in which everyone is originally created and conditioned to be happy all the time.

→ **S6:** How to write an argumentative text, p. 206

CREATIVE WRITING

6 CHOOSE WB p. 16/1, pp. 18-19

Back home Lenina sits down to write about her day in her diary. Write her diary entry. Consider her conversation with Bernard and the reactions and emotions it might have prompted in her as a well-conditioned Beta female. Use emphatic *do*, inversion and cleft sentences to add emphasis to what you write.

OR

Write an interior monologue from Bernard's point of view, starting at the end of the extract you have read, in which he reflects on his attempt to have a critical conversation with Lenina. Use emphatic *do*, inversion and cleft sentences to add emphasis to what you write.

→ **S2:** Checklist: Creative writing, p. 198

Write the introduction to your own dystopian story (Lernaufgabe)

From classics like *Brave New World* and *1984* to more contemporary works like e.g. *The Hunger Games*, *Divergent* and *The Wall*, dystopian novels (and films) have always been very popular. Reading dystopian stories from different eras can give you an insight into the topics and developments the authors at the time worried about and wanted to criticize. Work on these tasks to write a first, introductory chapter to your own dystopian story.

1 CHOOSE → SUPPORT D6, p. 158

Plan the background of your story. Your class has a choice here.

In your class, hand out cards in different colours or labelled with the numbers 1-10 on the back. Every student gets one deck of cards (1-10). On the front of the cards, note down cues for a potential dystopian story according to the following key:

1. a current development that may lead to disastrous consequences in the future
2. a year in the future
3. a location
4. an adjective to describe this location
5. who or what has the power
6. an adjective to describe the ruler(s)
7. an event which caused the world to become like this
8. something that is banned
9. something that is strictly controlled by the ruler(s)
10. the name of a revolutionary organization

Make ten piles of cards of the same aspect (1-10) on your teacher's desk, shuffle the cards and let everyone take a card from each pile. You should now have a mixture of ten cues noted down by different students. Read them and decide on the ones you want to base your dystopia on – it can be all ten of them or just two or three, depending on how well they go together or on how interesting you find them.

OR

Note down your ideas on the categories 1-10 (see above). Feel free to already start adding details to your notes if you feel inspired.

2

Plan the details of your story. As you might know, the first chapter of a story usually establishes an atmosphere by introducing the setting and some of the characters. It is supposed to create suspense and motivate the reader to find out more about the dystopian world, the protagonist(s), etc. Have another look at your notes from task 1 and create an outline, using bullet points, for your introductory chapter. → SUPPORT D7, p. 158

3

Decide on narrative techniques. Choose from the following options:

1 Narrative perspective: first-person narration or third-person narration?

2
- If you chose first-person narration: do you want to use interior monologue or stream of consciousness?
- If you chose third-person narration: omniscient narrator, limited narrator (restricted to which character?) or observer narrator?

3 Tense: present tense or past tense?

4

Using your notes from tasks 2 and 3, write the introductory chapter (350 words).

5

Have a book club lesson, in which you read each other's chapters and talk about what interests you about the different stories and why you would like to read on. Maybe one of you feels inspired to continue writing and create their first dystopian novel.

→ **S24:** How to give feedback/peer edit, p. 240

2 Postcolonial experiences

1888 1

2

Webcode

You can download a word list for the Intro, WordPool and Facts pages here: **DSW-73090-005**

1

Look at the map above and read the quotations.

a) Use the map to explain the quotations.

b) Note down any questions you would like answered.

> We hold dominion over palm and pine[1]
>
> from a poem by British author Rudyard Kipling (1865-1936)

> ... this vast empire on which the sun never sets[2], and whose bounds nature has not yet ascertained.
>
> George Macartney (1737-1806), British statesman and diplomat.

> Powerful, prosperous, peace-loving, with the seas all round us and the Royal Navy on the seas ...
>
> Violet Bonham Carter (1887-1969), British politician and author

> Rule Britannia!
> Britannia, rule the waves!
> Britons never never never shall be slaves.
>
> lyrics of a patriotic song written by James Thompson (1700-1748) and Davis Mallet (1703-1765)

Annotations

[1] **pine** = tree that has needles instead of leaves

[2] to **set** (sun) = to go down

2

a) Read the text "The development of the British Empire" on page 38 and try to find answers to any questions you had in 1b.

b) Put the following sentences in a chronological order.

1. In the 19th century, the British Empire continued to grow in Asia and Africa.
2. In the 17th century, some colonies were set up along the coast of North America and in the Caribbean.
3. The British monarchs Henry VII and Elizabeth I sent ships to explore the coast of North America.
4. By 1922 the British Empire was at its height and ruled over 25% of the world's population.
5. At the end of the First World War, the Treaty of Versailles (1918) awarded further territories to Britain.
6. Having defeated the French and the Dutch in a number of wars, Britain became the most important colonial power in 18th century Europe.
7. During the American War of Independence, thirteen North American colonies declared their independence from Britain.

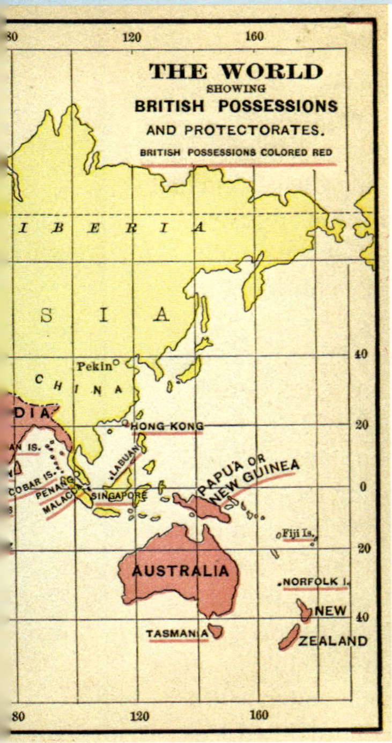

3 1902

3 Think-pair-share

Choose one of the two cartoons 1 and 3 above and analyse it. → **S17:** How to work on cartoons, p. 229

- Note down your own ideas.
- Compare your ideas with those of a partner and reach an agreement on the following points:
  - description of the cartoon
  - message
- Now talk to two students who have chosen the other cartoon and present your results to each other.
- In your groups, discuss the views of colonialism expressed in the cartoons.

4

a) Read the following definition of postcolonialism and explain it in your own words. → SUPPORT D1, p. 159

The term postcolonialism refers to the effects of colonization on cultures and societies. On the one hand, the term has a chronological meaning and is used by historians to signal the end of colonialism and the beginning of a new historical period. On the other hand, the scientific field of post-colonial studies explores what is often termed the postcolonial present, i.e. the lasting legacy of colonialism both in the former colonies and the mother countries in contemporary times.

b) From what you know about Great Britain, think of possible legacies of colonialism in Great Britain and in the former colonies today.
→ SUPPORT D2, p. 159

Preview

India

The first part of the Theme is about the history and current situation of India. In the **Workshop**, you will analyse articles.

Canada

The second part of the Theme gives you a brief introduction to Canada.

South Africa

In this part, you will find out about the past and present of South Africa.

Nigeria

In the fourth part of the Theme, you are going to find out about life in Nigeria.

Europe and the colonial past

This part is about how Europe deals with its colonial past.

THE RISE OF THE BRITISH EMPIRE

At its prime around 1900, the British Empire was the largest empire in history. With the unmatched power of its Royal Navy, Britain was able to exercise control over territories all across the globe and came to be known as 'the empire on which the sun never sets'.

During the 17th and 18th centuries, England and later Britain was only one colonial power among many and the emancipation of thirteen North American colonies from British rule in the late 18th century was a massive blow to British dominance. However, after the French defeat in the Napoleonic Wars, Britain was able to rise to almost unrivalled world domination during the 19th century and especially in the age of imperialism in the decades leading up to the First World War.

CANADA

When 13 North American colonies formed the USA in the late 18th century, the colonies in what is now Canada remained British. Whereas the 17th and 18th centuries had been dominated by Anglo-French rivalry in that region and a series of wars between the two powers, the French defeat in the French and Indian War (1754-1763) had spelt the end of French rule in Canada. In 1867, the British Canadian colonies became largely independent as they formed the new Dominion of Canada.

INDIA

India was Britain's most important colony. At the start of the colonization process stood the British East India Company. This private enterprise established a number of trading posts in India and over time took control of more and more of the country, enforcing its control by military means. Popular resistance led to a massive rebellion in 1857, which was crushed after a year. As a consequence, the British government took over control of the country.

In 1947, India became independent from Britain. However, continuing tensions between Hindus and Muslims led to the partition of the country into two independent countries, India and Pakistan. Today's India is a land of contradictions. The country is marked by extreme disparities: between backward rural areas and fast-growing cities, extreme poverty and massive wealth, staggering progress in many areas and the persistence of conservative social norms. One example is the caste system, which sustains the oppression of the Dalit, who are still marginalized. Moreover, women are yet to gain an equal role in society, with female employment levels still very low.

COLONIALISM IN AFRICA

By the 15th century, European powers had already started establishing trading posts along the West African coast. During the second half of the 19th century, the Europeans massively expanded their spheres of influence, finally holding sway over most of the continent towards the end of the century.

The first Europeans to have a lasting impact on South Africa were the Dutch, who established a trading post there in 1652. In the following centuries, many European settlers moved to the region, displacing local Bantu and Khoisan peoples. Conflicts between Dutch settlers and their descendants and British colonists led to a series of wars at the end of which stood the Union of South Africa, a British dominion established in 1910. However, the descendants of the original Dutch settlers remained politically dominant and the Black South Africans oppressed. This state of affairs only ended with the first free elections in 1994.

In the 1860s, the British tightened their grip over the territory which is now Nigeria so that more and more of the different peoples populating the region had to submit to British dominion. Apart from economic and military endeavours, missionary activities were another crucial factor in the colonization process.

THE LEGACY OF COLONIALISM

After the Second World War, especially in the 1960s, many colonies gained their independence. In independent Nigeria, the legacy of colonialism can still be felt in many areas: the ethno-religious tensions between the predominantly Muslim north and the Christian south, as well as the dominance of British and multinational oil companies in the Niger delta region where many people feel exploited and oppressed, are at least in part a consequence of British imperial rule. However, the aftermath of colonialism can also still be felt in Britain. For example, many people have immigrated from the former colonies since the mid-20th century.

1 WB p. 20

Read the definitions and find the corresponding words highlighted in the text. More words are highlighted than you need.

1 a group within the social hierarchy, e.g. of India
2 a vast territory of different countries which are governed by the same ruler
3 situation or consequence that exists due to events that happened in the past
4 gaining political or legal rights that people did not have before
5 political freedom from the control of another country's government
6 official power to govern a country and its people
7 term referring to the political system of colonialism, often used with a negative connotation
8 inequalities in age, rank, wealth or living conditions
9 period of time after a catastrophic event such as a natural disaster, accident or war, when people still have to deal with the consequences

2

a) Learning a new word can open up a whole range of new words when you consider the word family. Use the given words to extend your vocabulary by filling in the grid. Work with a dictionary if necessary. Sometimes more than one word is possible, especially when prefixes are added.

b) Use six of the new words in meaningful sentences about colonialism or the postcolonial era.

noun	*verb*	*adjective*
colony *colonialism* *colonization*	*to colonize* *to decolonize*	*colonial* *postcolonial*
dominance *dominion* *domination*	...	...
...	*to progress*	...
...	*to oppress*	...
employment	...	...
resistance	...	...
...	*to exploit*	...
...	*to populate*	...
...	*to submit*	...
...	*to marginalize*	...

Webcode

You can download the grid for task 2 here: **DSW-73090-006**

3

Many words are often used in a particular combination. These are called collocations. Find the collocations by combining 1-10 with A-J. In some cases, you will need to insert *of* or *to*.

1 rural		A influence
2 colonial		B system
3 to exercise		C rule
4 sphere		D norms
5 to hold		E domination
6 social	of/to	F area
7 caste		G independence
8 to gain		H colonialism
9 aftermath		I sway
10 to submit		J control

4

Read the following text and fill in the missing words from the box in the correct form. There are more words than you need.

During the time of the British Empire, colonies were of great economic relevance: not only did the people have to 1 to British rule, the colonists also 2 the natural resources of the countries. This explains why after gaining 3, many former colonies found it hard to establish a productive industrial sector. As a 4 of colonialism, social injustice often prevailed. Today a new ruling class often profits from globalization, while a great part of the population in many former colonies is 5, especially in 6 areas. As the gap between rich and poor widens, regional 7 provide further obstacles to nation-wide progress and development. In countries that are 8 by many different ethnic and religious groups, a particular attempt to connect to their own cultural heritage is a crucial part of 9.

emancipation
to marginalize
disparities
tension
to submit
to exploit
empire
independence
legacy
to populate
rural

From Empire to Commonwealth

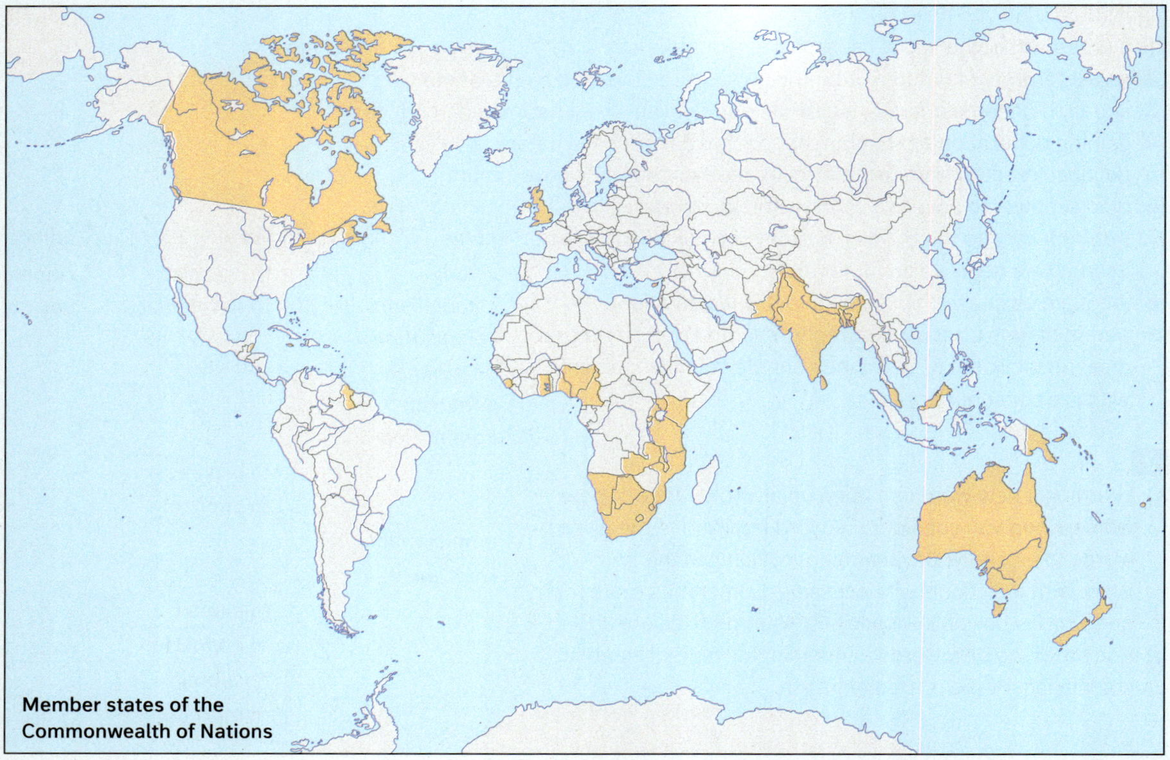

The development of the British Empire

England became an important seafaring nation during the reign of Elizabeth I (1558-1603) and ships were sent to explore the coast of America and the Caribbean. During the 17th century, the first colonies were established in this region. Britain lost its 13 American colonies in 1783 after the American War of Independence but retained its colonies in Canada, which had been acquired after defeating France in the Seven Years War in 1763. In the 19th century, Britain continued to expand its Empire around the world, reaching its peak at the beginning of the 20th century when nearly a quarter of the world's population lived under British rule.

Many historians regard the loss of the 13 North American colonies as a watershed moment for the British Empire. This is why the history of the Empire is often subdivided into two phases: the First Empire before 1783 and the Second Empire after 1783.

Britain's main interest as a colonial power lay in promoting her own trade and thus increasing her wealth. India, called "the jewel in the crown of the Empire", was an important source of raw cotton, tea and spices. Raw cotton was needed for the expanding British textile industry and finished cloth "made in Britain" was then exported to the Empire and other countries around the world, in many cases destroying domestic production as a result.

Other colonies, such as Australia, New Zealand and the Cape Colony in South Africa, were primarily used for the settlement of British people and as markets for British goods. As a result, the English language and also British traditions and institutions were spread around the globe. Cricket, for example, is a national sport in Australia, India, Pakistan, South Africa and New Zealand and competitions between these countries are of huge national interest.

Some colonies were also of great strategic importance. Control of Egypt meant control of the Suez Canal. Similarly, control of Gibraltar, Cyprus and Malta was deemed vital to ensure a safe passageway for British trading ships on their way to colonies in Asia. Before the Second World War, Britain maintained a huge fleet of ships in the Mediterranean.

From Empire to Commonwealth

In the late 19th and early 20th centuries, some of the colonies within the British Empire began to demand and to acquire greater autonomy. Thus began the Empire's process of decolonization. However, keeping close ties to the former colonies was regarded as important both economically and politically. So in 1931, the British Commonwealth of Nations was founded with six initial members: Canada, New Zealand, Australia, South Africa, the Irish Free State (later to become the Republic of Ireland) and Newfoundland, which is now part of Canada.
The Second World War changed the nature of the British Commonwealth. After the independence of India and Pakistan in 1947, the Commonwealth began to acquire its modern shape. It dropped the word *British* from its name, the allegiance to the crown from its statute, and became an association of decolonized nations.
From 1960 onwards, the Commonwealth expanded rapidly with new members from the Caribbean, the Mediterranean and the Pacific. Nations which enter the Commonwealth do so voluntarily. Today it is a group of 54 member states, all of which (except two) were formally part of the British Empire. They are republics (33) such as India, constitutional monarchies such as Canada – recognizing the British monarch as their head of state (16) – or monarchies in their own right. All of the member states recognize the monarch as the head of the Commonwealth.

Organization and aims of the Commonwealth

Unlike the United Nations, Commonwealth members have no binding obligations, but members commit themselves to the statements of beliefs set out by their heads of government. The Commonwealth has no constitution or charter, however, the heads of government of its member states hold Commonwealth Heads of Government Meetings (CHOGM) every two years to discuss issues of common interest. Since 1965, the heads of government have elected a Secretary-General every four years to lead the executive arm of the Commonwealth with its headquarters in London.
The Commonwealth draws its main strength from its moral authority. Committed to human rights and democratic principles, the Commonwealth suspends members who do not uphold these values. Pakistan, Nigeria and Zimbabwe are three of the countries which were suspended for political reasons. The suspensions were lifted as soon as democracy was restored. South Africa chose to leave the Commonwealth in 1961 when it became clear that its apartheid policy would not be tolerated.
Although the Commonwealth has been criticized for being more symbolic than useful, membership brings some practical benefits through the Commonwealth Fund for Technical Cooperation (CFTC). This is the main way in which the Commonwealth promotes economic and social development and the alleviation of poverty.
For many people, the Commonwealth Games is what brings the organisation to life. This multi-sport event has taken place every four years since 1930 (only the Games in 1942 and 1946 were cancelled because of the Second World War). The Games are the third largest multi-sport event in the world after the Olympic Games and the Asian Games.
The monarch attends the Commonwealth summits and the Commonwealth Games. Also, on every Commonwealth Day, which is the second Monday in March, he or she broadcasts a message to all member countries.

1

a) Read the text and outline the main developments from Empire to Commonwealth.
b) **CHALLENGE** Examine the future of the Commonwealth in the light of Britain's decision to leave the European Union.

→ **S8:** How to improve your text, p. 209

India – a country of contrasts

Webcode

You can download a word list for Part A here: **DSW-73090-007**

1 WB p. 21/1

India promotes the idea of "unity in diversity" to celebrate its diverse landscapes, cultures, religions and languages.

a) Start a mind map on the diversity of India and note down what you already know about the subcontinent.

b) **Pair work** Compare your mind map with a partner's.

	India	Germany
Area (km²)	2,973,190	357,022
Population	1,366,418,000	83,175,000
Population density (per km²)	455	230
Per capita GDP (USD)	2,098	45,733
Agriculture / manufacturing / services percentage of GDP	16.0%/24.9%/49.9%	0.8%/29.7%/69.5%
Agriculture / manufacturing / services percentage of labour force	42.4%/25.6%/32.0%	1.2%/27.2%/71.6%
Doctors per 1,000 inhabitants	0.8	4.3
Human development index	0.645 (rank 131)	0.947 (rank 6)

2

Have a look at this grid giving you some basic information on India as compared to Germany. Note down three sentences about what you consider the most important differences. Also explain what, if anything, surprises you.

3

India is often referred to as a country of contrasts.

a) Choose two photos from this page that can be seen as a contrast and describe them. → **S15:** How to describe pictures, pp. 228-229

b) **Pair work** Find a partner who has worked on other photos and talk about your choices and the impressions of India your photos convey.

c) **Pair work** Suppose you were planning to travel to India. Work with the photos to decide which aspects of the country you would be interested in.

4 EXTRA

Imagine you were travelling in India and wanted to send some photos home to your friends.

a) Choose three photos from the ones on this page and write short texts you would add to them. Refer to what can be seen in the photos as well as your expectations or emotions. → SUPPORT D3, pp. 159-160

b) **Group work** Read your texts to each other and discuss why you would or would not like to travel to India.

5

Use your results from tasks 2-4 to add to your mind map from task 1.

India – past and present

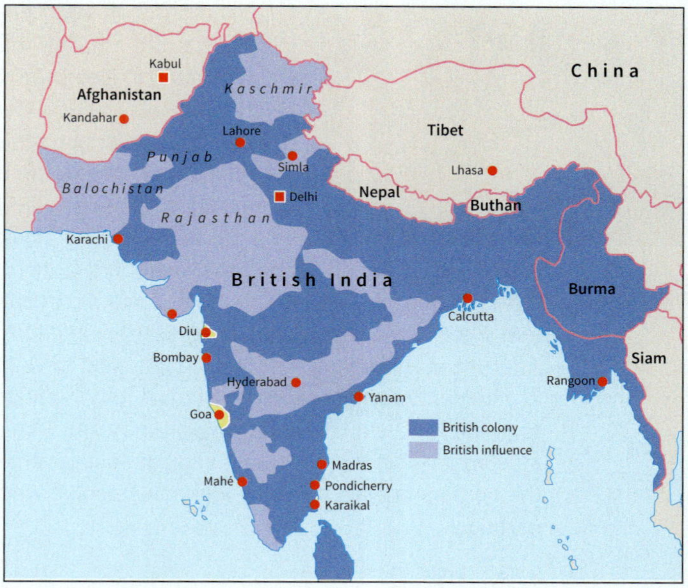

The British in India

When the British and other European powers came to India in the early 17th century, a large part of the country was ruled by the Muslim Moghul Empire. But there were also many different independent states.

The British came to India as traders. Starting with a few trading posts on the coast, a private trading company called the East India Company over the centuries took over more and more Indian territory. Having led several wars against Indian states in the process, the East India Company had established itself by the end of the 17th century as one of the dominant economic, political and military powers in India.

However, while British traders made their fortunes, many Indians starved. The heavy taxation and other policies left many impoverished. They were also upset by the cultural changes imposed on them by the British and worried that the two main traditional religions, Hinduism and Islam, would be replaced by Christianity. These factors led to the great Indian rebellion of 1857. It took the British a whole year to crush the uprising and as a consequence, the rule of the East India Company was abolished. Control of India passed to the British government and Queen Victoria became Empress of India in 1876.

British rule lasted until 1947, when India gained its independence. During British rule India was governed by the British Viceroy and his Executive Council. Their policies were enforced by the Indian Civil Service, which was run by British officials. The country was defended by the Indian Army, consisting of both British and Indian troops under the command of British officers. All were responsible to the British Parliament in London.

Rule over India brought wealth and prestige to Britain and poverty and sometimes famine to India. India was the "brightest jewel in the crown" of the Empire and a vital source of raw materials such as cotton, silk and tea as well as an important market for British exports. India also underwent an industrial revolution, leading to the construction of railways, canals and roads. But these changes were predominantly made to increase British wealth at the expense of local industry and agriculture.

The struggle for independence

By the beginning of the 20th century, resentment about British rule was growing fast. The history of India in the first half of the 20th century was dominated by the struggle for independence and the emergence of an outstanding personality in that struggle, Mahatma Gandhi.

Gandhi was a lawyer who had studied law in England and lived in South Africa for 20 years, acting on behalf of Indians living and working there. He returned to India in 1915 and dedicated his life to the cause of Indian self-rule. He identified himself with rural life and encouraged the masses to take up a programme of self-reform and passive resistance to British rule. Under his leadership, the farmers took up cotton spinning and weaving in their homes and wore homespun cloth, burning British-manufactured cloth in protest against British domination. He was the champion of the poor against the wealthy and powerful, whether Indian or British. He also urged Muslims and Hindus to end their traditional animosity and unite against the British.

During the First World War more than 1.3 million Indian soldiers served in the British Indian army. After the war, in 1919, Indians were given more representation in the governing of their country, but Gandhi continued to lead campaigns of civil disobedience and to press for complete Home

Gandhi on the 1930 salt march

Rule. Famously, in 1930 he led a 24-day march to the sea to make salt in defiance of the British monopoly on salt. In 1935 self-government was finally granted to eleven provinces and an All-India Federal Parliament was set up. Gandhi's National Congress Party took part in the first elections. Unfortunately, the outbreak of the Second World War resulted in the suspension of self-government under special emergency powers. When the Viceroy once again declared war on India's behalf without consulting Indian leaders, the Hindu-dominated National Congress Party opposed the war and in 1942 Gandhi and other members launched the "Quit India" movement, resulting in the imprisonment of Gandhi and other leaders. Great parts of the Indian population, especially Muslims and Sikhs, however, supported the British war effort.

After the war Britain announced its decision to withdraw from India. Sectarian violence flared up as independence approached. In June 1947 representatives of Hindus, Muslims and Sikhs agreed to divide India along religious lines, Hindu and Sikh areas remaining part of India, while the mainly Muslim areas in the northwest and the east became Pakistan. Millions of refugees flooded across the borders in each direction and many people were killed in the sectarian violence that followed partition.

Modern India

India is the largest democracy in the world with a population of around 1.4 billion people. However, there have been many challenges facing this new nation. The region of Kashmir, in particular, has been a constant source of conflict. Part of the region belongs to India and part to Pakistan. Conflicts over control of the region have resulted in two wars between India and Pakistan. Since both countries are nuclear powers, this conflict poses a considerable threat to world peace.

India's independence was an important turning point in its economic history. The country was extremely poor and the vast majority of the population were illiterate. Under India's first Prime Minister, Jawaharlal Nehru, the state was to play a leading role in economic progress by regulating and protecting indigenous industries. India set its hopes on a planned economy and introduced restrictive licensing regulations to discourage private enterprise, both Indian and foreign.

In the 1980's, Prime Minister Rajiv Gandhi recognized the need for economic reform. He began to liberalize the economy and provided subsidies to increase industrial production. Moreover, he increased government spending on education, science and technology. These changes have increased the country's economic standing, allowing it to compete with developed nations in sectors such as technological infrastructure and e-commerce. India is fast becoming a global player.

Despite the great progress made by India since independence, the country still faces severe problems. Many people in the country still suffer from extreme poverty, and the state needs to invest more in healthcare, education, and infrastructure. Moreover, its crime rates, particularly in areas such as rape, kidnapping and domestic violence, are worryingly high.

Webcode
You can download the timeline here:
DSW-73090-008

1

Copy and complete the timeline showing the development of India from a British colony to a global economic player. Note down the events that took place in the years given at the bottom.

2

→ **S9:** How to structure a text, p. 212

a) Outline Mahatma Gandhi's role in the Indian struggle for independence.

b) CHALLENGE Do some research on Gandhi and find out how his non-violent protest forms have influenced political leaders around the world.

Step by step Analysing an article

Preview

In this Workshop you are going to focus on analysing an article. In order to do so you will look at structure, language and rhetorical strategies.

COMPREHENSION

1

a) Read the info box on the Indian caste system and speculate on the meaning of the headline of the article on pp. 44-45, "India's 'untouchable' women face discrimination even in schemes meant to help them".

Info

The caste system

Despite laws that aim to create equality, the caste system still has a strong impact on Indian society. The system is believed to go back about 3000 years and splits up Hindus into four groups according to their work and birth: the Brahmins (the priestly class); the Kshatriyas (the ruling, administrative and warrior class); the Vaishyas (the class of artisans, traders, farmers and merchants); and the Shudras (manual workers). There are also people who fall outside the system, including tribal people and the Dalits, who used to be known as "untouchables".

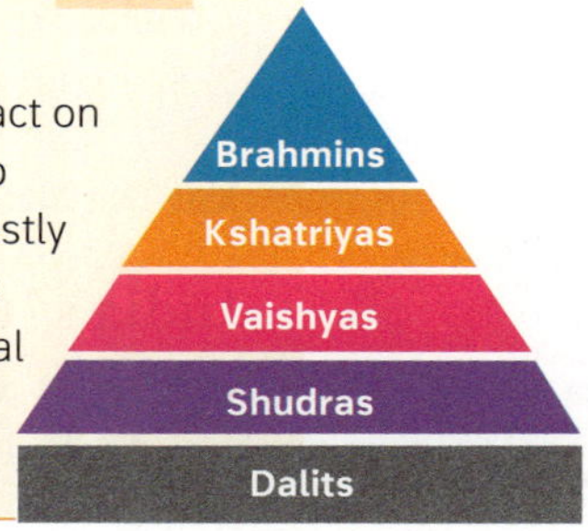

b) Language awareness Explain the wording of the headline and what it reveals about the author's attitude towards the topic.

→ **S13:** Checklist: Analysis – non-fictional texts, pp 222

2

There are different types of articles. Read the info box. Then scan the article on pp. 44-45 and explain which kind of article it is.

Info

Types of articles

News article: The main focus of a news article is on factual information and therefore it provides mainly answers to the who, what, where, when, why and how of an incident.

Feature article: It is an article that explores a news story in depth. Its main purpose is not to tell you what has happened, but to look at the wider context of a news story. The author's opinion may shine through, but it should always be based on the analysis of the situation, not a personal attitude or bias.

Opinion piece: In this type of article the author clearly expresses his or her view on a certain issue. The style of writing may be argumentative, entertaining, biased or evaluative. Opinion pieces can be subdivided into:

- **Editorial:** This article is always written by the paper's editor or senior editorial staff. It is clearly marked as an editorial and usually unsigned.
- **Column:** This article may be written by a regular or a guest columnist. Such pieces may be strongly opinionated, and the opinion expressed is that of the writer and not (necessarily) of the paper.

3

When you are working on an article, the first step is to summarize what it is about.

a) In the introductory sentence of your summary, you should include a reference to the author, the title of the article, the date of publication and the gist of the article. From the options 1-3 on p. 44, choose the one that best sums up the article. Explain your choice.

The article "India's 'untouchable' women face discrimination even in schemes meant to help them" was written by Kanika Meshram and published on theconversation.com in 2022. It deals with …

1 the situation of Dalits whose attempts to lead a better life are thwarted both by the people around them as well as by Indian institutions.

2 the discrepancy between the official end of caste-based discrimination, declared in 1950, and the actual treatment of Dalits in India's society today..

3 that Dalit women are frequently excluded from the financial support that help programs offer and consequently have little chance to cimb the social ladder.

b) When you are working on comprehension tasks, it is important to be precise and focus on what is essential. This depends on the exact wording of the task. Read the following two tasks carefully and identify the keywords that determine your selection of information from the text. Then take notes on what you would write. → SUPPORT D4, pp. 160-161

1. Outline the situation of Dalits in modern India as depicted in the article.
2. Point out what the author criticises about programs to support Dalit women in India.

KANIKA MESHRAM **The Conversation, 28 December 2022**

India's 'untouchable' women face discrimination even in schemes meant to help them

Seema and her husband did quite well when they first opened a samosa[1] stall in the local market of a town in Bihar state, northeastern India. But then other vendors found out who Seema was. They yelled at her customers for buying her samosas. They threatened her husband for "polluting" the market by selling food prepared by her. She put up with it for months before giving up.

What had Seema done wrong? She had been born a Dalit, a member of the "untouchables", the lowest group in India's ancient and now officially obsolete caste system. Seema didn't look, talk or behave any differently. But someone had found out her family name, which indicated she was descended from pig farmers, a job only done by Dalits. That was enough.

[…] India officially outlawed caste-based discrimination in 1950. But it continues to be a fact of life for the estimated 200 million of India's 1.4 billion population who are Dalits. They are even discriminated against when applying for programs established to help them.

I met Seema in the summer of 2019, through a non-government organisation that provides vocational training[2] to women. It was about two years since she'd given up her stall. Now she was completing a cooking course. From the course she would gain a certificate she hoped would improve her chances of getting a microloan from a government bank, backed by the Reserve Bank of India[3] […]. Seema's plan was to relocate to a bigger city and start a restaurant. She had already applied for a microloan 18 months before, with no success. When she enquired about her application's status, she said, staff at the bank brushed her off[4] with comments such as "we have to be extra careful with some applicants", "I can tell just by looking at your name here on the first page that doing business will be tricky for you" and "I don't think it's in your blood". My research suggests this is a common experience for Dalit women.

Since being pioneered by economist Muhammad Yunus and the Grameen Bank in Bangladesh in the 1970s, microloan programs have been embraced as a poverty-reduction policy in many developing nations, including India. […] But there are increasing concerns about the poor implementation of microfinance programs. My research involves the lack of outcomes for Dalit women entrepreneurs in India. In Bihar I interviewed almost 30 Dalit women completing vocational

Annotations

[1] **samosa** = a small fried pastry filled with meat or vegetables

[2] **vocational training** = programmes or courses that focus on the knowledge and skills needed for a particular job

[3] **Reserve Bank of India** = India's central bank

[4] to **brush** sb **off** = to refuse to talk to sb

courses to improve their prospects for a microloan. I asked them the same question: why had they not succeeded?

The typical response was an uncomfortable silence, then tears, and then a story of being humiliated when applying for a microloan – of help being refused when filling in a form, of being told not to sit on the same chairs as other bank customers, and of their application being rejected for no good reason. Research by myself and associates, analysing the microloan-lending decisions of 43 branches of a major bank with more than 2 million microloan customers, found 66% of rejected applications were from Dalit women. [...]

Dalit women face a catch-22[5]. To qualify for a program to assist Dalits, they had to prove they're a Dalit by supplying a government-issued caste certificate. But this certificate then became the means for them to be identified as Dalits and discriminated against. The women I interviewed told me how much attitudes changed when bank staff saw their caste certificates. They were called "freeloaders"[6] and "privileged".

Dalit women, being at the bottom end of the social and patriarchal hierarchy, will seldom request a reassessment. They have already been hit with a double whammy[7] of caste and gender discrimination, and the instruments put in place to help them have become bureaucratic weapons to perpetuate this exploitation and ostracism[8].

There are no simple solutions, but the first step is to understand the extent of the problem. A full audit[9] by the Reserve Bank of India of microfinance programs and their treatment of Dalit women is the obvious place to start. India's history has its fair share of nice ideas failing in practice. The work to end discrimination against Dalits will take decades. Seema may never live to see the day when revealing her family name doesn't risk disgust. But there's still a chance for Seema's two young children to live in such a world.

Annotations

[5] to **face a catch-22** = a dilemma from which there is no escape because of mutually conflicting or dependent conditions

[6] **freeloaders** = *Schmarotzer*

[7] **double whammy** (*coll.*) = *doppeltes Pech*

[8] **ostracism** /ˈɒstɹəsɪzəm/ = banishment or exclusion from privileges

[9] **audit** = an examination of an individual's financial situation

ANALYSIS

4

In an analysis, the structure of an article is an important aspect. Read the info box on structure and line of argument and subdivide the article. Use the language support below to explain the functions of the different parts. → SUPPORT D5, p. 160

→ **S9:** How to structure a text, p. 212

Info

Structure of an article

Introduction
In order to raise interest, the article can be introduced by a slice of life story, an anecdote, a quotation, a reference to history, literature or a scientific experiment, etc.

Main body
The main body may be organized in different ways:
- topical: dealing with different aspects of equal relevance, one after another
- antithetical: weighing the pros and cons
- chronological: organizing information according to time
- climactic: moving from the least important to the most important aspect

Conclusion
The conclusion expresses the main idea in a concise way and might end in a quotation, an appeal, or a plea.

Language support

Introduction	Main body	Conclusion
... introduces the topic of ... by referring to .../by comparing .../by illustrating ... with ...	... presents his/her view of .../formulates the thesis that .../states concern about .../ proves the necessity to ... ... claims/acknowleges/concedes that ... ... provides examples from ... ... argues in favour of/against ...	... concludes the article by referring back to .../by appealing to .../by demanding ... In his/her article, ... reinforces the need to .../the demand for ... by ...

Webcode
You can download the grid for task 5 here: DSW-73090-009

5 Read the info box below. To analyse the language and communicative strategies used by the author of the article, copy the grid and find more examples in the article to complete it.

Info

Language and rhetorical strategies

To convince the reader of their view, writers can employ several rhetorical strategies:

Language
- choice of words: words with negative/positive connotations; word fields such as sports, war, family relations, etc.
- stylistic devices: alliteration, repetition of key notions, contrast, metaphorical language, enumeration, rhetorical question, etc.

Rhetorical strategies
- quotations from
  - scientists, politicians, etc. as experts
  - ordinary people who are impacted by the issue as eye-witnesses
  - famous writers or philosophers
- examples to illustrate the situation/issue the author refers to
- facts and figures to prove the author's claims
- inclusive language (e.g. first-person plural)

device/strategy	*quote (evidence)*	*function/effect*
Choice of words/word fields		
words with negative connotations	*"yelled" (l. 6), "threatened" (l. 7)*	*to reveal how intimidating the behaviour of the people in the market must have felt*
word field exclusion/ social marginalisation	*"discriminated", "refused", "rejected", "ostracism", …*	*to underline the futility of Dalit women's attempts to improve their situation*
Rhetorical devices		
rhetorical question	*"What had Seema done wrong?" (l. 11)*	*to focus on possible reasons for her failure thus unmasking the strong impact of caste in Indian society*
imagery/metaphor	*"pioneered by economist Muhammad Yunus … in the 1970s" (ll. 51-53)* *"catch-22" (l. 79)*	*to present the concept of microloans as an important innovation in the fight against poverty* *to underline that the situation of Dalit women is a dead end with no way out*
enumeration	*"Seema didn't look, talk, or behave any differently" (ll. 15-16)*	*to prove she was exactly like others in all the different aspects*
Communicative strategies		
quotation	*"polluting" (l. 8)*	*to reveal the unfair accusation of people that the mere touch of food by Dalits would make it unedible/poisonous*
facts and figures	*"the estimated 200 million." (ll. 22-23)*	*to underline the huge number of people who still suffer caste discrimination*

→ **S23:** How to quote, p. 239

6 Use your results from the previous tasks to write an analysis of the article. Analyse how the author structures her article and how she uses rhetorical strategies to convince her readers of the need to overcome casteism. Remember to provide evidence for your findings by quoting from the text.

Practice Analysing an article

COMPREHENSION

1 WB p. 23/1, p. 24/2

Read the following article and outline the aims of the Gandhi Nagar initiative, the difficulties involved and the achievements.

→ **S9:** How to structure a text, p. 212

Full steam ahead: India's first women-run train station blazes a trail[1]

Annie Banerji, 10 October 2018, Reuters

As Chandra Kala heard the blaring horns of a train, she quickened her pace, zig-zagged and elbowed across a teeming[2] platform while hauling[3] a sack of wheat, a suitcase and a backpack.

She placed the luggage inside a carriage just as the train began to chug[4] out of Gandhi Nagar railway station, which in February became India's only major terminal where women run the show.

Kala is a rare female porter[5] in the conservative, desert state of Rajasthan in western India, and one of about 40 women holding positions traditionally held by men.

"Earlier, I used to feel very shy," said Kala, a widow with two children. "How should I speak to passengers, how can I lift luggage? It all felt very weird."

She had taken over her husband's porter job when he passed away[6] last year, and she now supports her children from her earnings of about 3,000 rupees ($40) a week.

"It does not feel weird any more," said Kala. "It feels really good."

From ticket sellers and conductors, to station managers and cleaners, these trailblazers are upending sexist views and providing hope in a country where women are slowly vanishing from the workplace.

India is one of the world's fastest growing major economies but the rate of female employment is startlingly low, in large part due to social prejudices and general disapproval of working women.

At least 20 million women – the combined population of New York, London and Paris – have left the workforce of Asia's third-largest economy since 2005, World Bank data shows, with only 27 percent now employed.

The Gandhi Nagar initiative is part of efforts by the state-run railway – India's biggest employer – to empower women in its workforce of 1.3 million people.

Indian Railways officials are planning to replicate the all-women staff model in other stations, according to Tarun Jain, a spokesman for the railways ministry.

The experiment has also created a financial windfall[7], according to Jain, who said Nagar station has experienced "record earnings" since women took over.

Each year, millions of tourists flock[8] to ancient fortresses and camel-back desert safaris in Rajasthan, which is also home to some of India's poorest villages where age-old customs like purdah[9], or veiling[10], often dictate a woman's life.

At Gandhi Nagar station in the state capital of Jaipur, 25 trains pass through every day with about 7,000 commuters – mostly from conservative rural and tribal areas – witnessing women carrying out jobs many have only seen men do before.

Bewildered, surprised and even upset, many gawked at[11] the women when they first took over the station and often undermined their authority, asking for a "male manager",

Annotations

1 to **blaze a trail** = to do sth that has never been done before; to set an example
2 **teeming** = crowded
3 to **haul** = to drag or carry sth heavy, often with difficulty
4 to **chug** = to make the sound of an engine
5 **porter** = sb who carries luggage
6 to **pass away** = to die
7 **windfall** = an amount of money that one gets without expecting it
8 to **flock** = to gather
9 **purdah** /ˈpɜː(r)də/= practice of hiding women from the public and requiring them to cover parts of their body
10 **veiling** = wearing a veil to cover one's face
11 to **gawk at** sb = to stare at sb in shock

according to Neelam Sharma, a reservation supervisor.

"Some people reacted quite angrily," said Sharma, adding that passengers would say things like, "We do not know how any work will get done here."

However, as the months rolled by, Sharma said commuters were pleased to see improvements at the station, including faster service, smaller queues, better information and cleanliness.

"Now those same people come to us and really appreciate us and say things like, 'Madam, we really like coming here, our work gets done quicker', and, 'The men did not explain things to us properly,'" Sharma said.

"Passengers are quite happy now." [...]

Members of the team credit this success to their motivation to prove themselves in what is commonly considered a male bastion.

"[We] are giving our 100 percent efforts," said station master Angel Stella, sitting behind a control panel with color-coded track lines and buttons that send signals to incoming trains in order to prevent accidents.

But it was not easy getting to this point, she said.

The women, who were mostly transferred from stations in smaller towns, had to overcome their own doubts and fears of running a station by themselves.

They had to get comfortable working night shifts and working in positions of responsibility traditionally held by men, said Stella.

"We were scared and we thought, 'How will we do this?'"

It was also a challenge for those who lived with their children or in-laws[12] to strike the balance between work and family, Stella added.

To ensure their comfort and safety, authorities equipped the station with CCTV cameras, deployed an all-women police force, installed sanitary pad vending machines, and created a temporary daycare.

Female employees said they hope to inspire young girls passing through the station, and trigger a change among people who think a woman's place is at home.

Annotations
[12] **in-law** = sb you are related to through marriage

ANALYSIS

2 Language awareness WB p. 24/3

Analyse how the author Annie Banerji structures her text and how she uses language to convince her readers of the magnitude of the success and of the obstacles that had to be overcome.

→ SUPPORT D6, p. 161

→ **S13:** Checklist: Analysis – non-fictional texts, p. 222

COMMENT

3 WB p. 24/4

Discuss the importance of projects like the Gandhi Nagar initiative for the improvement of the situation of women in India.

→ **S6:** How to write an argumentative text, p. 206

Working on a short story

1

You are going to read the short story "Death on Facebook" by Claude Forthomme. Consider the title and speculate on what might happen in the story.

2

a) Read the first part of the short story on pp. 49-50 and describe the conflict between Anamika and her brother. → SUPPORT D7, p. 162

b) Point out what the conflict reveals about the situation of many women in Indian society.

→ **S9:** How to structure a text, p. 212

→ **S8:** How to improve your text, p. 209

Death on Facebook

by Claude Forthomme

Extract 1

"Anamika, don't deny it! I saw you on Facebook." He pulled out the pictures he had downloaded and threw them on her desk.

"You were at that despicable party. No mistake, that's you!"

She didn't bother to look. She kept her head low and he glared at her shiny black hair pulled back in a modest bun at the nape of her delicate neck. All he could see of her face was an expanse of white forehead, as smooth as porcelain. At least, she had the decency to wear a sari[1]. It was the one their mother had given her when she had left home to study in Mumbai. He recognized the green silk, it came from the same material their mother used for her own dress.

"Who's this Vikram?" He growled. That was the name that was tagged on his face in the picture. "Vikram Chaudhry is his name, right? I'm waiting for an explanation!"

"There isn't any." Her voice was so low he could hardly hear.

"What do you mean? You're sitting on this man's knees. And here you're in his arms about to kiss him. Who's he?"

She shrugged. "He's a doctor at the Hospital."

"A doctor? You think that's a good excuse? I bet his real name isn't Chaudhry ..." He paused and glowered before adding with force: "He's trying to hide the fact he's a Dalit[2]. That's what they all do ... He's a Dalit, isn't he?"

No answer.

Her brother sighed. "With that face he's not a Brahmin[3], that's obvious! He looks so ... dark, how could you? Anamika, I can't believe you were in that filthy boy's arms, drinking wine!"

"It wasn't wine. I don't drink."

"That's not the point and you know it. Father and Mother are furious."

"Vikram is perfectly respectable. He does cancer research, he's brilliant. And he wants to marry me!"

"Marry you?" He stopped again and frowned. "Never. He cannot marry you. You're a Brahmin and don't forget it!" A pause. He stared at his big sister. He had been so proud of her when she had gone to study in Mumbai – the new generation reaching out to the world, and his sister was part of it. What a mistake ... "Our parents were too good with you, too lenient" he continued. "They should never have let you attend the Hospital College. This fixation of yours with medicine. Ridiculous. It's not the kind of work any woman belonging to our family should ever get into. I told them something bad would happen to you. I was sure of it."

"You told them?" She was amazed. Here was treason! He used to look up to her. Ever since childhood, she had been convinced they were on the same wave length. She didn't recognize her sweet Adinah, the math prodigy, the computer techie, the clever boy in the family. [...]

Their mother was always objecting to new ideas. Not surprisingly: she was the pillar of the home, the guardian of traditions. That was her role in the family.

When Anamika had decided to attend the famous college linked to the Tate Memorial Hospital, all hell had broken loose. As expected, their mother had made it sound like a desperately sinful place on the other side of the planet – as if it were in America.

Annotations

[1] **sari** = traditional Indian piece of clothing for women: a very wide, long piece of cloth worn wrapped around the waist and draped over the shoulder

[2] **Dalit** = a member of the "untouchable" caste in India, the lowest of the castes

[3] **Brahmin** = a member of the priest caste in India, the highest of the castes

Fortunately her father had come to the rescue. "With the Deccan Queen train it's only three and half hours away," he pointed out. "Anamika can come home every weekend!" Anamika knew there was an implicit order in that apparently innocent remark.

She had tried to keep up her end of the bargain and come to the family homestead in the old city of Pune as often as she could. But now that college was finished, she had been overwhelmed with work at the hospital. She welcomed the extra work: she knew it meant her real career had started at last – she was doing what she had always wanted to do. What she was meant to do in her life. It was exhilarating. In the last few weeks, she hadn't found the time to go back home. She hadn't even thought of it.

Then there was Vikram. The work at the hospital and a new life opening up with Vikram, everything came together.

Adinah stood up. "You have to come home with me," he said, his voice cold.

"I won't." He didn't understand, there was just too much to do at the hospital. It was too important, people were sick, people needed her.

"Oh, but you are coming home. That's why I'm here, you're coming with me. Now."

"I'm not."

He shrugged. "Pack your things. There's no time to lose. The train leaves in an hour. At 5:10 sharp."

He looked for her luggage and saw a couple of suitcases piled up in a corner. He threw the bigger one on the bed and opened it with a flourish.

For the first time since he'd come, she turned her face up to him but remained seated on the chair. Her little brother could scream as much as he liked, she wasn't going home with him.

"Get moving, pack!" He was so angry he choked on his words.

She still didn't move. He walked across the room and slapped her on the face, hard.

She stood up and walked away, applying the cool palm of her hand to her burning cheek. It helped. She looked out the window. [...]

She loved Mumbai, she was going to miss it.

"Adinah, what has gotten into you? We used to be friends!" she murmured. He repeated, his tone icy. "Get moving. Pack!"

There was no point in answering. Her brother didn't know, couldn't understand what it meant to be committed to work, to fall in love and know this man was the right one, the only one to share everything with. Adinah would say that kind of love was a degenerate Western idea. A Brahmin could never love someone from a lower caste. [...]

"What are you looking at?" he asked, his voice cracking with irritation.

"Nothing."

"Ok, if you're not going to pack, I'll do it for you!" he said, grabbing her clothes out of the wardrobe as if they were rags. He threw them in the suitcase and within seconds had made a mess of them. She stared at the rumpled clothes overflowing onto the bed and the floor.

"Let me do it," she said.

3 Language awareness

→ **S12:** Checklist: Analysis – prose, p. 220

Analyse how the author reveals Adinah's aggressive attitude towards his sister and the fact that he is gradually gaining control. Consider the choice of words used to describe his behaviour.

4

→ **S2:** Checklist: Creative writing, p. 198

After the quarrel with his sister, the scenes of their confrontation are still vivid in Adinah's mind. Write his interior monologue and include:

- references to his childhood days with Anamika,
- recollections of his feelings when first seeing her photo on Facebook,
- his emotions when confronting her,
- thoughts about his behaviour and his role.

Remember that an interior monologue reveals the thoughts going through a person's mind. It has similar elements to spoken language like questions, elliptical (unfinished) sentences and exclamations. → SUPPORT D8, p. 162

5

Pair work Anamika returns to her family. Talk to a partner about how you think they will react. Speculate how her life will go on for her.

6

Read extract 2 of the short story and outline how Anamika's life develops after her return.

Extract 2

The train ride was longer than Anamika remembered it. Her brother didn't speak and neither did she. When they reached home, night had fallen.

For the first time, it didn't feel like home to her.

The air, redolent[1] with the smell of spice and flowers, was warm and moist as usual at this time of year and it was the only thing she recognized.

[...] She didn't listen to her father's speech. She closed her eyes. She wished she could close her ears. All she heard was the conclusion. "You will stay in your bedroom until such time as you see the light," he said. "In the meantime, we shall look for a suitable man for you to marry!"

Her brother threw her luggage in her room and her mother locked her in.

She had never been locked in her own bedroom before. She had a fit of rage[2]. She grabbed the door knob and shook it with all her might. It wouldn't budge. Then she hammered the door until her fists hurt. She screamed and scratched her face. [...]

She went to the water basin, washed herself and looked into the mirror. The scratches on her cheeks stood out, wisps of wet hair clung to her face, she looked like a witch.

She couldn't stop her tears. They kept flowing out, in silence. Ah, the angel face Vikram had loved was no more. She would never see him again. What was the point of living?

She hardly ate, rarely moved out of bed.

The only person who looked after her was her mother – who always locked the door after tending to her. "Your father has found someone willing to marry you!" she said one day. "You must eat and look good for him!" But Anamika shook her head and wouldn't eat.

Her mother began to worry. The girl was too thin, she looked like a scarecrow. Who would ever accept to take her as a wife? Then she noticed something worse: after a month her daughter still showed no sign of menstruation. Might she be pregnant? What a scandal! No, this was inconceivable.

One morning, she found Anamika retching[3] helplessly over the water basin, her legs shaking.

"What's the matter?" she asked.

"I'm feeling nauseous[4] ..." whispered Anamika, her forehead glistening with perspiration.

"Are you pregnant?"

Anamika shrugged.

She took her daughter by the shoulders and swung her around, like a rag doll. "Are you pregnant?" she screamed. Anamika's silence drove her mad. "You made love with that swine, didn't you?"

[...] "We had found a husband for you and now you've made it impossible! No one will ever want you, you are as dirty as a Dalit!" She wailed[5], wringing her hands. "How could you, my one and only daughter, the light of my eyes!" and she ran out of the room, locking the door.

What was she to do now? This planned marriage was a good one, the father of the groom had already sent a lavish gift of sweets. How was she to tell her husband? There was no question Anamika's father had been too soft with her. [...] Anamika was weak, she was bound to trip[6] and fail. And now, there was no coming back to an earlier, happier time. There was no remedy.

Or perhaps there was one.

She repaired[7] to the largest room in the house, the one in the center where a sacred picture had been hung high, a six-foot picture of *Venkateshwara*[8], the Vishnu god. She looked up at him and he frowned down on her, fierce and ready to combat sin. She let the god's vibrations flow down to her.

For a long time she stood immobile, waiting for her resolve to gather strength. She could feel it coming. She said a prayer of thanks and grabbed the biggest silk pillow she could find. She climbed up to her daughter's bedroom, unlocked the door and found the young woman still lying on the bed, facing the wall.

That made it easier.

She pushed the pillow down on her head and smothered[9] her. "Your soul is saved", she murmured in her ear.

Annotations

1 **redolent** /ˈred(ə)lənt/ = *here:* filled with a particular smell
2 **fit of rage** = *Wutanfall*
3 to **retch** = *würgen*
4 **nauseous** /ˈnɔːziəs/ = feeling as if you will be sick
5 to **wail** = to make a long high-pitched sound
6 to **trip** = to fall because you caught your foot on sth
7 to **repair to** = to move to
8 **Venkateshwara** reincarnation of the God Vishnu (Venkata meaning "destroyer of sins")
9 to **smother** sb /ˈsmʌðə(r)/= to kill sb by covering their face so that they cannot breathe

7

Analyse how Anamika's mother is presented. → SUPPORT D9, p. 163

→ **S12:** Checklist: Analysis – prose, p. 220

Webcode

You can download a word list for Part B here: DSW-73090-010

Introduction to Canada

General information

Canada is the second-biggest country in the world with an area of almost 10,000 square kilometres. However, it is also one of the most sparsely populated countries with only about 38 million inhabitants. The capital and seat of government is Ottawa, its fourth-largest city after Toronto, Montreal and Vancouver. It is in these cities and in the area close to the US border that the majority of people live. Canada is officially bilingual in English and French, reflecting the British and French colonization of the country in the 18th and 19th centuries . French is primarily spoken in Quebec. The national symbols are the maple leaf, to be seen in their flag, and the beaver.
Canada is one of the most prosperous nations in the world. It is one of the world's major exporters of agricultural products, although its economy is dominated by the service industry, which employs about 75% of the population. Other important industries include transport, timber, minerals, natural gas, fish products and chemicals. Canada is a member of the G7 and the OECD.

Indigenous population

When the first explorers arrived in Canada, the country was populated by an estimated 500,000 indigenous First Nation and Inuit people. As a consequence of European colonization, their numbers declined rapidly. In the beginning, the relations between the settlers and the indigenous peoples were relatively peaceful. However, in the 19th and early 20th centuries, attempts were made to force indigenous peoples to adapt to a European way of life. These initiatives focussed on Christianisation and promoted education and agriculture. Some peoples even had to relocate to reserves, where it was easier for the government to control them. From 1847 to 1996, the Canadian government and the Catholic Church ran 130 residential schools for indigenous children, who were forcibly separated from their parents. The discovery of hundreds of unmarked children's graves at the sites of former residential schools in recent years has reignited the demand for justice by the indigenous population of Canada. The First Nations population have also been active in demonstrating for the protection of the environment against government measures to economically develop their ancestral lands.

Diversity

Canada is a very liberal country and proud of its diversity. It is also a nation of newcomers. During and after the two world wars, waves of immigration brought many new cultures and languages into the country. With this came the first laws to encourage diversity. In 1971, Canada became the first country to have an official policy of multiculturalism. Today immigrants represent 25% of the population and the figure is rising. However, not everyone is allowed to immigrate to Canada. The government employs a points system for immigration. It distinguishes between skilled workers and other kinds of immigrants and factors such as education, language proficiency, work experience, age, health and whether the applicant has an outstanding job offer play a decisive role in who is allowed to become a Canadian and whose application is rejected. People who are likely to be a burden on the health and welfare system will most likely be refused.

1 WB p. 24/1, p. 25/2-3

a) Read the text about Canada and match the illustrations to relevant parts of the text.

b) Write captions for the illustrations.

What it means to be Canadian

1

a) Watch an excerpt from a speech by Canada's Prime Minister, Justin Trudeau. Choose three adjectives from the box which you think best describe the picture he paints of Canada.

> progressive | diverse | multicultural | nationalist | inclusive | prosperous | unbiased | tolerant | liberal | open-minded

b) **Pair work** Compare your results with a partner's. Explain why you chose your three adjectives, giving evidence from the speech.

c) Say which pieces of information in the text on p. 52 contradict the picture painted by Trudeau.

Webcode
You can find a link to the video here: **DSW-73090-011**

→ **S20:** How to listen/watch effectively, p. 234

2 WB p. 26/1, p. 27/2

a) Now read the following article on what it means to be Canadian and note down what you find out about Canadian identity.

b) Analyse the means the author uses to develop her (line of argument in pursuit of a) definition of Canadian identity.

c) In class, discuss the advantages and disadvantages of living in a country where there is "no core identity, no mainstream" (ll. 48-49).

→ **S6:** How to write an argumentative text, p. 206

What does it mean to be Canadian?

Quincy De Vries, 22 December 2022, Varsity.co.uk

'There is no way to quickly sum up Canadian culture when someone asks you in passing': Quincy De Vries shares her experience of attempting to define her Canadian identity.

For Canadians [...] the assumption that we are American is, I'm certain, one that we have all become used to. This is not something I mind, but it has forced me to reflect. When I meet new people and am asked about the country's culture, I struggle to come up with a cohesive[1] answer that encompasses the Canadian experience. There are a few common things one tends to hear about Canadians: we are nice, we like poutine[2], we have free health care, and our country is very cold. These are not false, but surely there is more to Canada than that. But putting exactly what this is – what Canada really means to me – into words is much harder than I anticipated. Put simply, I have one question: what does it mean to be Canadian?

In my search for an answer to this question, I turned to some well-known Canadian citizens. Surely, they must have a unanimous explanation. But, to my frustration, they all had different answers. Donald Sutherland[3] spoke of Canada's legacy in the Netherlands after World War Two; David Suzuki[4] of Canada's reaction to the Cold War; and Margaret Atwood to the beacon of light Canada represents to our southern neighbours. Even when speaking to friends and family I got a variety of answers. A few people said Tim Hortons,

Annotations
[1] **cohesive** = to be naturally or logically connected
[2] **poutine** /puˈtiːn/ = a dish of chips with cheese curds and gravy sauce
[3] **Donald Sutherland** = Canadian actor who starred in *The Hunger Games* franchise
[4] **David Suzuki** = Canadian professor of genetics and environmental activist

Annotations
5 to **be stumped** = to be puzzled or clueless
6 to **venerate** = to have and show a lot of respect for sb or sth
7 As of September 2022, King Charles III. The $20 note still features a portrait of the Queen.
8 to **adorn** = to decorate sth
9 **ethos** = a set of moral ideas and attitudes connected to a person, group or society

Canada's coffee chain of choice. My friends mentioned that we love to say sorry to everyone no matter the situation. No one gave me the answer I was searching for. I was stumped[5]. Next, I turned to the leader of Canada, Prime Minister Justin Trudeau. I was sure he must have said something about the Canadian identity in the past. And I was correct – he had. But it was not at all what I was expecting. In his words, "there is no core identity, no mainstream in Canada." These are the words of our leader. Can you imagine the head of any other nation saying anything like that? I certainly can't. It is not that I disagree, but Canada is unique in embracing the fact that none of us seem to know what being Canadian means.

The history of the nation is another element that makes answering this question difficult. Canada has been both a French and English colony and now welcomes immigrants from all over the world. There are large Eastern European, Irish, and Chinese groups (among others) living in Canada who played and continue to play a central role in our history. Many of these minority groups have faced racism and prejudice at the hands of the ruling elite throughout our history and Canadians are still coming to terms with the horrible treatment of the indigenous peoples of Canada. Acknowledging the darker parts of our history is just as important as celebrating the good parts when reflecting on what it means to be Canadian.

The United States has a similar history in being a nation built by immigrants, but it doesn't seem to suffer from the same identity crisis. I believe this is because Canada does not have a venerated[6] national myth like America, and many other countries. We did not have a war for independence. The British Queen[7] is still our head of state and adorns[8] our money. There is an entire province, Quebec, that speaks a different language. Combined, these factors make it difficult to create a national ethos[9].

As I continued to ponder what it meant to be Canadian, I was struck by the simple fact that I was not going to find an answer. There is no way to quickly sum up Canadian culture when someone asks you in passing, but this is what makes the country special. We celebrate the fact that we are all different, that people come to Canada and can retain elements of their identity and become part of our community. Canada continues to highly encourage immigration: an average of 300,000 immigrants come to Canada each year and roughly 21.5% of our population are immigrants with permanent residency. Yes, we are polite and say sorry a lot, but this is not what defines us. We celebrate our differences and encourage new perspectives.

Canada is not perfect. We have a long way to go in many areas, especially when it comes to our treatment of indigenous peoples. But to be Canadian means to belong to a country that is united by our diversity. Next time someone asks me about being Canadian, I am not going to look for a simple answer. I have realised that I don't want one.

A short history of South Africa

Webcode
You can download a word list for Part C here: **DSW-73090-012**

1
Pair work Look at these terms and names that are closely associated with South African history. What do you know about them? The photographs on the next page will give you some clues. Talk to a partner and note down any questions you may have.

apartheid | ANC (African National Congress) | Nelson Mandela | Afrikaans

2
a) Watch the video and note down
- what event in South African History it deals with.
- what the speaker says about its significance and how it is highlighted.

b) Now describe the graph and relate the information to the event shown in the video.

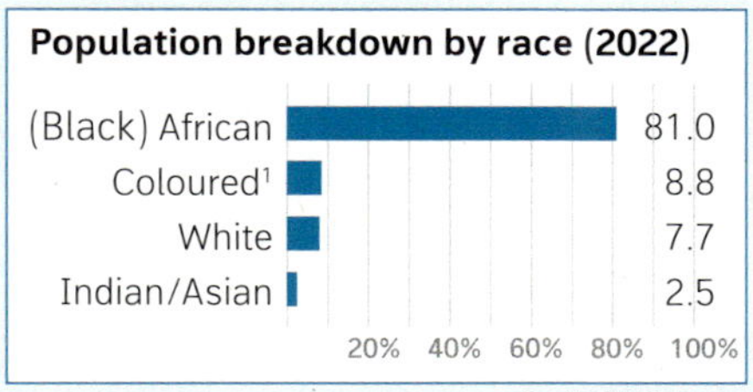

Quelle: Statista.com

Webcode
You can watch the video here: **DSW-73090-013**

→ **S18:** How to analyse statistics, p. 230

3 **Group work (3)** WB p. 28/1
a) Each of you works on one part of the text (A, B, and C) on South African history until 1994. Read your part and prepare to tell the other group members the most important information.
1. Note down the most important information. Try to find answers to the questions from task 1.
2. Note down important words and terms on slips of paper.
3. Prepare four questions to ask your group members.

b) Take turns to present your part of the text to the other group members.
1. Do it chronologically and use your notes.
2. In order to make sure that everyone has understood your presentation, ask your listeners the questions you have prepared.

c) Prepare a timeline of important events in the history of South Africa. Compare your timeline with one produced by another group and make any necessary changes.

d) In class, organize the words and terms you have collected alphabetically and compile a (digital) glossary.

Annotations
[1] In South Africa, the term 'coloured' refers to members of multiracial ethnic communities. It is not to be confused with the term 'colored (or coloured)', which was the dominant term for African Americans in the 19th and first half of the 20th century.

4 EXTRA
Do some research on one of the people or events mentioned in the text. Prepare a short digital presentation to show the class.

A

Early colonial history
From the end of the 16th century, European trading ships on their way to East Africa and India regularly sailed past the Cape of Good Hope, the most southern part of Africa. However, it was not until 1652 that the Dutch East India Company established a permanent base there. Gradually, more and more Dutch farmers, known as Boers, were encouraged to settle in the region and the first colony, the Cape Colony, was established. Slaves were brought in from other parts of Africa and Asia. The Boers fought the indigenous population, the Khoisan, who were also farmers, gradually taking over their land and expelling them from the region.

The Union of South Africa
At the end of the 18th century, the British captured the Cape Colony and many British settlers moved into the area. The Boers resented British rule. They wanted to speak their own language, Afrikaans, and control their own affairs, so they moved northwards and established two new republics – the Orange Free State and Transvaal. After the discovery of gold and diamonds there, the hostility between the Afrikaners (descendants of the Dutch settlers) and British settlers escalated, culminating in a series of wars. In the so-called Boer War (1899-1902), in the course of which thousands of Boer men, women and children were interned in concentration camps, the Boers were eventually defeated and the British annexed their land and destroyed their farms. In 1910, a united

South Africa, consisting of the British colonies (the Cape Colony and Natal) and the former Boer republics (the Orange Free State and Transvaal) was given a constitution and became known as the Union of South Africa. It was a British dominion, but the Boers were granted certain concessions.

B

Apartheid

Black, Coloured and Asian[2] people in South Africa were very much second-class citizens, although white people[3] made up only about 20% of the population. Non-whites were not allowed to vote and only allowed to own land in certain areas.

To appeal to white farm, mine and factory workers, who had lost their jobs during the 1930s Great Depression, Afrikaner leaders founded the National Party in 1934 and promoted the idea of white supremacy. They believed that "racial mixing" was a sin. The idea of apartheid was born. The National Party won the election of 1948. Their campaign, promising to free South Africa from British rule and to introduce apartheid, appealed particularly to the rural population and white industrial workers returning from the Second World War, who felt their existence again threatened by black workers.

The National Party's policy of apartheid was soon put into practice. The 1950s witnessed the passing of many acts of parliament designed to separate the various ethnic groups. Everyone was classified according to race. The black population was sent to so-called homelands. The Coloured and Asian populations were also forced to relocate. Mixed marriages and sex between different racial groups were prohibited. An inferior school curriculum ensured that non-whites would pose no threat to white workers in the future. However, as black workers were needed to do menial jobs in the towns, they could not all be sent to the homelands. So some black people lived in "townships" close to the towns, but still apart from the white population. They went to separate schools and had to use separate transport and other public facilities.

Annotations

[2] Black people were descended from the original native African population. The Coloured community had mixed ancestry. The Asian community was descended from Indian immigrants.

[3] The white population consisted of those of Dutch, German and French descent, who spoke Afrikaans and called themselves Afrikaner, and the English-speaking colonists of British descent, who were in the minority.

C

Opposition to apartheid and repression

As daily life for non-whites became a fight for survival, the African National Congress (ANC) and other political groups opposed to apartheid grew in strength. One common form of protest was the burning of the "passes", the identity papers that black people had to carry at all times. In 1960, such a demonstration in Sharpeville ended in a massacre, the police killing or wounding more than 200 people, some of them children. The government then banned the ANC and other anti-apartheid organizations. The events at Sharpeville led to a worldwide condemnation of apartheid, but many countries continued to trade with South Africa.

Peaceful opposition to Apartheid had made no impression on the government, so that some leading members of the ANC, including Nelson Mandela, decided to go underground and prepare for an armed struggle. In 1962, Mandela was caught by the police and sentenced to life-imprisonment after being convicted of planning to overthrow the government. Many of those detained by the Security Police died as a result of the brutal treatment they received during interrogation. Steve Biko, leader of the Black People's Convention, was one of the most prominent victims of police violence.

Opposition to the government's education policy was particularly strong. The South African Student Movement organized the protest against the government's decision to teach half the school curriculum in Afrikaans, a language which many teachers and students did not understand. In 1976, a peaceful demonstration in Soweto, a township outside Johannesburg, became violent after the shooting of a thirteen-year-old boy by the police. Rioting continued for weeks until the government finally gained control of the situation.

The wind of change

But the anger of the non-white population could not be resisted indefinitely. Resistance movements increased their pressure on the government and a campaign to release Mandela was widely supported both at home and abroad. The international community started an economic and cultural boycott of South Africa, which gradually weakened the economy. In 1989, the new Prime Minister, F.W. de Klerk, realized that there was no future for apartheid and instigated the first reforms. The ANC was legalized, political prisoners, including Nelson Mandela, were released and most of the apartheid legislation was abolished. On 27 April 1994, the first free elections were held and Nelson Mandela became the first president of a democratic South Africa.

Living under apartheid

1

The following extract is taken from South African comedian Trevor Noah's autobiography called *Born a Crime*. Look at the book cover and the title of the book and note down what they reveal about the author and his background. What crime might be associated with his birth?

2 WB p. 29/1 (Living under apartheid)

a) Skim the extract from the first chapter on pages 57-58 and explain the title of the book.

b) Read the extract closely and note down the effects of apartheid on the daily lives of non-white South Africans. → SUPPORT D10, p. 164

c) Examine the picture Trevor Noah paints of his mother in this extract. → SUPPORT D11, p. 164

→ **S12:** Checklist: Analysis – prose, p. 220

Born a Crime

by Trevor Noah

I grew up in South Africa during apartheid, which was awkward because I was raised in a mixed family, with me being the mixed one in the family. My mother, Patricia Nombuyiselo Noah, is black. My father, Robert, is white Swiss/German, to be precise, which Swiss/Germans invariably are. During apartheid, one of the worst crimes you could commit was having sexual relations with a person of another race. Needless to say, my parents committed that crime.

In any society built on institutionalized racism, race-mixing doesn't merely challenge the system as unjust, it reveals the system as unsustainable and incoherent. Race-mixing proves that races can mix – and in a lot of cases, *want* to mix. Because a mixed person embodies that rebuke[1] to the logic of the system, race-mixing becomes a crime worse than treason.

Humans being humans and sex being sex, that prohibition never stopped anyone. There were mixed kids in South Africa nine months after the first Dutch boats hit the beach in Table Bay[2]. Just like in America, the colonists had their way with[3] the native women, as colonists so often do. Unlike in America, where anyone with a drop of black blood automatically becomes black, in South Africa mixed people came to be classified as their own separate group, neither black nor white but what we call "colored". Colored people, black people, white people, and Indian people were forced to register their race with the government. Based on those classifications, millions of people were uprooted and relocated. Indian areas were segregated from colored areas, which were segregated from black areas – all of them segregated from white areas and separated from one another by buffer zones of empty land. Laws were passed prohibiting sex between Europeans and natives, laws that were later amended to prohibit sex between whites and all non-whites.

The government went to insane lengths to enforce these new laws. The penalty for breaking them was five years in prison. There were whole police squads whose only job it was to go round peeking[4] through windows – clearly an assignment for the finest law enforcement officers. [...]

Under apartheid, if you were a black man you worked on a farm or in a factory or in a mine. If you were a black woman, you worked in a factory or as a maid. Those were pretty much your only options. My mother didn't want to work in a factory. She was a horrible cook and never would have stood for some white lady telling her what to do all day. So, true to her nature, she found an option that was not among the ones presented to her. She took a secretarial course, a typing class. At the time, a black woman learning how to type was like a blind person learning to drive. It's an admirable effort, but you're unlikely to ever be called upon to execute[5] the task. By law, white-collar jobs and skilled-labor jobs were reserved for whites. Black people didn't work in offices. My mom, however was a rebel, and, fortunately for her, her rebellion came along at the right time.

Annotations

1 **rebuke** = criticism
2 **Table Bay** = bay on the South African coast, now part of Capetown
3 to **have** one's **way with** sb = to have sex with sb against their will
4 to **peek** = to look quickly
5 to **execute** = to do, carry out

In the early 1980s, the South African government began making minor reforms in an attempt to quell international protest over atrocities and human rights abuses of apartheid. Among those reforms was the token[6] hiring of black workers in low level white-collar jobs. Like typists. Through an employment agency she got a job at ICI, a multinational pharmaceutical company in Braamfontein, a suburb of Johannesburg.

When my Mom started working, she still lived with my grandmother in Soweto, the township where the government had relocated my family decades before. But my mother was unhappy at home, and when she was twenty-two she ran away to live in downtown Johannesburg. There was only one problem. It was illegal for black people to live there.

The ultimate goal of apartheid was to make South Africa a white country, with every black person stripped of[7] his or her citizenship and relocated to live in the homelands, the Bantustans[8], semi-sovereign black territories that were in reality puppet states[9] of the government in Pretoria. But this so-called white country could not function without black labor to produce its wealth, which meant black people had to be allowed to live near white areas in the townships, government-planned ghettos built to house black workers, like Soweto.

Soweto

The township was where you lived, but your status as a laborer was the only thing that permitted you to stay there. If your papers were revoked for any reason, you could be deported back to the homelands.

To leave the township for work in the city, or for any other reason, you had to carry a pass with your ID number; otherwise you could be arrested. There was also a curfew. After a certain hour, blacks had to be back home in the township or risk arrest. My mother didn't care. She was determined to never go home again. So she stayed in town, hiding and sleeping in public restrooms until she learned the rules of navigating the city from the other black women who contrived[10] to live there: prostitutes.

Many of the prostitutes in town were Xhosa[11]. They spoke my mother's language and showed her how to survive. They taught her how to dress up in a pair of maid's overalls[12] to move around the city without being questioned. They also introduced her to white men who were willing to rent out flats in town. A lot of these men were foreigners, Germans and Portuguese who didn't care about the law and were happy to sign a lease[13] giving a prostitute a place to work in exchange for a steady piece on the side[14]. My mom wasn't interested in any such arrangement, but thanks to her job she did have money to pay the rent.

Johannesburg

Annotations

[6] **token** = merely symbolic, without any substance or real consequence
[7] to **strip** sb **of** sth = to take sth away from sb
[8] **Bantustan** = derived from the Afrikaans name for black people, Bantus
[9] **puppet state** = state which is totally dependent on another one
[10] to **contrive** to do sth = to make a real effort in order to achieve sth
[11] **Xhosa** /ˈkɔːsə/ = one of the main ethnic groups of black South Africans
[12] **maid's overalls** = Domestic workers all wore a similar kind of uniform called overalls. They were allowed to be in the city.
[13] **lease** = contract allowing sb to rent a flat
[14] **piece on the side** = some extra money

Info

Patricia Nombuyiselo Noah

- born ca. 1959, grew up in Soweto
- left her mother's home aged nine to live with her aunt in Transkei
- attended a missionary school at the age of 21 and learned English
- secretly rented a flat from a Swiss-German, Noah's father

3 Language awareness

Despite the serious nature of Trevor Noah's subject, the implicit mood he creates is light-hearted and humorous. Find examples of his humour in the text and explain why they make the reader smile. → SUPPORT D12, p. 164

→ **S2:** Checklist: Creative writing, p. 199

4 EXTRA

Write Patricia's story from her point of view.

Truth and reconciliation

1
Read the excerpt from a speech given by Archbishop Desmond Tutu in Canada and summarize the developments in South Africa since the end of apartheid.

→ **S9:** How to structure a text, p. 212

2 WB p. 29/1 (Truth and reconciliation)
Explain the role played by the Truth and Reconciliation Commission in preventing a civil war in South Africa.

→ **S8:** How to improve your text, p. 209

Info

Truth and Reconciliation Commission
Nelson Mandela's new government was faced with a number of challenges. Mandela wanted a united South Africa and a peaceful transition to democracy. However, many people in the country saw a need to uncover injustices committed during the apartheid era. For this purpose the Truth and Reconciliation Commission (TRC) was created in 1995 under the chairmanship of Archbishop Desmond Tutu. The aim of the commission was to reveal the truth about atrocities committed by all sides during the apartheid era, to encourage forgiveness and thus to help the South African people to come to terms with their past. Between 1995 and 1998, the TRC gave both victims and perpetrators the opportunity to talk about their experiences. The commission had the power to grant amnesty to those who committed human rights violations if they disclosed them fully and if their actions were considered to have been politically motivated. The commission was also able to grant reparations to victims.

Speech by Archbishop Desmond Tutu given at the University of Toronto on 24 February 2000

I am very greatly honoured in being asked to give the keynote address for this major international symposium: "Justice, Memory, and Reconciliation".
[...] we [the South African people] are the beneficiaries of the commitment of many who demonstrated on our behalf, who staged rallies for us, who agitated for sanctions against the apartheid government. And here we are – today we are free, democratic, seeking to be non-racial and non-sexist. We have won a spectacular victory over the awfulness of apartheid's injustice and oppression. If you asked even the most sober students of South African affairs what they thought was going to happen to South Africa a few years ago, then, almost universally, they predicted the most ghastly catastrophe would befall us; that we would be devastated by a blood-bath. It did not happen. Instead the world watched with amazement, indeed awe, at the long lines of South Africans of all races, snaking their way to their polling booths on April 27, 1994. And they thrilled as they witnessed Nelson Mandela being inaugurated as the first democratically elected president of South Africa on May 10, 1994. And nearly everyone described what they were witnessing, a virtually bloodless, reasonably peaceful transition from injustice and oppression to freedom and democracy, as a miracle. [...]

When the disaster did not overtake us at the transition, there were those who said, "Wait until a black-led government takes over. Then these blacks, who have suffered so grievously in the past, will engage in the most fearful orgy of revenge and retribution against the whites." Well, that prediction, too, was not fulfilled. Instead, the world saw something quite unprecedented. They saw the process of the Truth and Reconciliation Commission, when perpetrators of some of the most gruesome atrocities were given amnesty in exchange for a full disclosure of the facts of the offence for which they had applied for amnesty. Instead of revenge and retribution, this new nation chose to tread the difficult path of confession, forgiveness and reconciliation. It has not been an easy path to walk, but it is now nearly six years since we embarked on this experiment in race relations, seeking to weld[1] former adversaries, alienated from one another by deliberate government policy, to weld them into a nation that would seek to celebrate its diversity and glory in being the rainbow nation of God. [...]

You have to say that we, South Africans, have not done too badly. We have already had a fairly uneventful second general election. Not only that, we have witnessed a transition from a highly revered and charismatic first democratically elected president, Nelson Mandela, to the more hands-on, pragmatic Thabo Mbeki. The turmoil and instability that many feared would accompany these crucial events have not occurred. Why? Well, first, you have prayed for us and, if miracles had to happen anywhere, South Africa was a prime site for a miracle of this sort.

We have been richly blessed to have had at such a critical time in our history a Nelson Mandela. He was imprisoned for 27 years. Most expected that when he emerged from prison, he would be riddled with[2] bitterness and a lust for revenge and retribution. Instead, the world has been amazed at this one who, instead of spewing[3] calls for revenge, has urged his own people to be ready to forgive and to work for reconciliation. He has preached this gospel[4] of forgiveness and reconciliation a great deal more by example than by precept[5]. He invited his former jailer to attend his presidential inauguration

Nelson and Winnie Mandela in the Johannesburg soccer stadium shortly after his release from prison in 1990

as a VIP guest. He has had lunch at the presidency with Percy Yutar, who was the prosecutor in the Rivonia trial, where Mandela and his colleagues were sentenced to life imprisonment. He invited to lunch the man who had argued for the death sentence to be passed in that trial.

Wonderfully, Nelson Mandela has not been the only person committed to forgiveness and reconciliation. [...] Many of the previously more anonymous, faceless victims of apartheid have shown that they are the real heroes and heroines of our struggle. [...]

We were exhilarated as we heard people who had suffered grievously, who by rights should have been baying for the blood of[6] their tormentors, utter words of forgiveness, reveal a willingness to work for reconciliation, demonstrating magnanimity and nobility of spirit. [...]

We have not been particularly virtuous. We are not particularly smart. God wants to point at us as this unlikely bunch[7] and say to the trouble spots of the world: "Look at them. They had a nightmare called apartheid. It has ended. Your nightmare, too, will end."

Annotations
1 to **weld** = *schweißen*
2 to **be riddled with** = to be full of
3 to **spew** = to spit
4 **gospel** = *Evangelium*
5 **precept** = principle
6 to **bay for the blood of** sb = to be determined to badly hurt or kill sb
7 **bunch** = a large group of people

3

Analyse the means Archbishop Tutu uses to convince his listeners of his message.

→ **S14:** How to analyse a speech, p. 223

4

Desmond Tutu describes how the Truth and Reconciliation Commission could grant "perpetrators of some of the most gruesome atrocities" amnesty. The Commission's work has been hailed by some as exemplary and criticized by others for preventing the punishment of perpetrators of some gruesome crimes.
Comment on this special South African way of coming to terms with the country's past.

→ **S6:** How to write an argumentative text, p. 206

South Africa today

1 → **S20:** How to listen/watch effectively, p. 234

a) Watch the short film *My Backyard* and say what impression it makes on you.

b) Watch it again and note down keywords to describe the problems prevalent in South Africa in the 21st century. → SUPPORT D13, p. 165

Webcode
You can watch the video here:
DSW-73090-014

2

Examine Zach's attitude towards South Africa. → SUPPORT D14, pp. 165-166

→ **S9:** How to structure a text, p. 212

3 CHALLENGE

Identify the message of the film and analyse how the cinematic devices are used to convey it. Consider camerawork, special effects and the use of flashbacks.

→ **S16:** Checklist: Analysis of a film scene, p. 227

4 EXTRA

Imagine you were told to look for important current problems in Germany "in your own backyard". Describe what you would see.

5 Group work (4)

a) Choose one set of statistics each and note down the issue(s) it deals with and the information it gives you.

b) Present your statistic to the rest of your group.

c) In your group, compare the issues you identified with your results from task 1 b). Consider to what extent the problems presented in the film can be supported by the statistical information.

→ **S18:** How to analyse statistics, p. 230

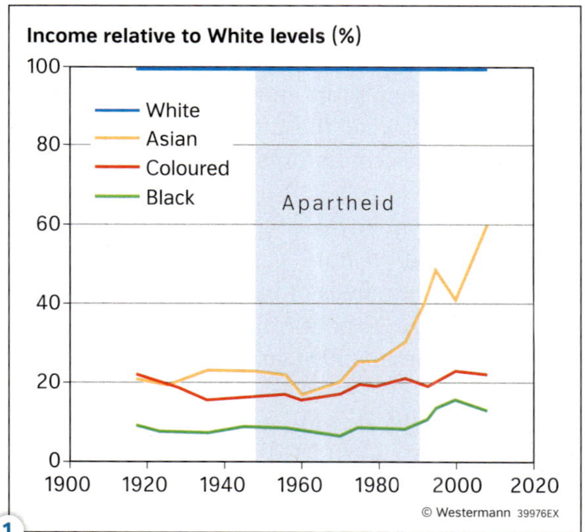

1

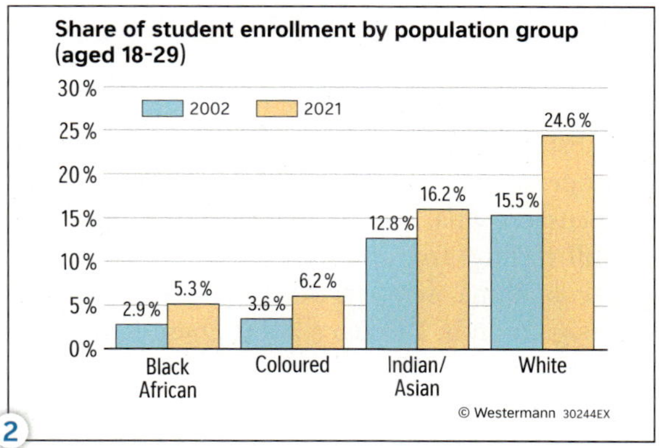

2

HIV in South Africa (2021)

7.5 million people living with HIV

18.3% adult HIV prevalence (ages 15-49)

210,000 new HIV infections

72,000 AIDS-related deaths

75% of adults on antiretroviral treatment (of those living with HIV)

48% of children on antiretroviral treatment (of those living with HIV)

Source: UNAIDS Data 2023

3

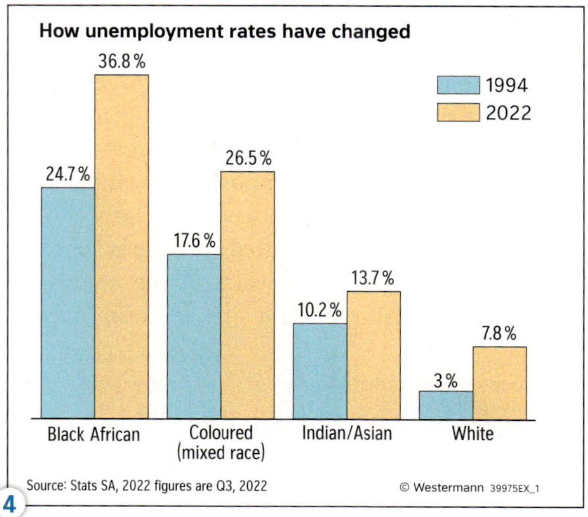

4

6 WB pp. 30/31, 1-3

Now work on the following newspaper article from the *Washington Post*.

a) Read the headline and the sub-headings. Keep in mind that the article was written in 2019, 25 years after South Africa became a republic. Speculate on the kind of picture the author will paint of South African democracy 25 years after the first free elections. Give reasons for your answer.

b) Read the article and state the author's view of South African democracy.

c) Read the article again and note down
- positive developments in South Africa since the first free elections
- problems facing South Africa today.

d) The author uses a number of useful collocations/adjective-noun combinations in his article. Scan it and find synonyms for the expressions in the box on the right.

considerable achievement | long-standing issues | unstable character | legendary triumph | proper houses | imminent ballot | improved/revived attempt

EVAN LIEBERMANN

The Washington Post, 27 April 2019

South Africa's apartheid regime ended 25 years ago

Democracy has taken root with substantial success.

It was 25 years ago today when South Africans of all races went to the polls to mark the end of apartheid government and over three centuries of institutionalized white supremacy. In 2019, with democracy under threat in various countries around the world, South Africa offers a surprising counterpoint[1]: Once mired[2] in bitter conflict, democracy has taken root with substantial success.

Understandably, many contemporary analysts focus on what's gone wrong. South Africa is still reeling[3] from the disastrous presidency of Jacob Zuma, who served from 2009 until his resignation in February 2018. There have been corruption scandals, power outages[4], problems with education – along with unemployment and low economic growth.

Where is South Africa today?

[...] After almost three decades of return visits and research, following an initial trip to South Africa in 1991, I remain impressed by a series of quite significant accomplishments, indicative of the value of democracy writ large[5]. The persistence of deep-seated problems should not surprise us in the wake of the country's troubling history. And in certain cases, perceptions of problems, such as crime, may be worse than the realities.

We must recall the perilous nature of South Africa's initial political transition. In February 1990, State President FW de Klerk announced the release of Nelson Mandela, signifying that the old regime was coming to an end. This political opening did not, however, provide clarity about what the future would bring, or if South Africa could forge[6] a stable democratic settlement.

In those days, virtually every office building required that visitors pass through a metal detector, as hundreds of people had been killed in more than 20 politically motivated attacks between February 1990 and June 1991. [...]

The April 1994 election was largely peaceful

South Africa's April 27, 1994 election – which led to Mandela's inauguration as the country's first black president – was a storied[7] success, largely calm and peaceful.

Since then, South Africans have held four additional national elections plus five local elections. Freedom House and other international organizations continue to give the country top scores for upholding high democratic standards. [...]

South Africa remains a violent country for citizens, and politics is still a perilously dangerous job. But there is no serious threat of (another) civil war.

Annotations

1 **counterpoint** = sth that is very different
2 **mired** = caught in a bad situation
3 to **reel** = to shake, move unsteadily
4 **outage** = when sth does not work anymore
5 **writ large** = in a bigger form
6 to **forge** = *schmieden*
7 **storied** = legendary

It was a different story 25 years ago

In 1991, when I visited squatter[8] camps outside Cape Town and townships around Johannesburg, I found nothing but squalor[9]: Most black South Africans lived in shacks[10] without basic services. Countrywide, less than half of all households had access to piped water[11], and less than 60 percent lived in "formal" dwellings[12] or had access to electricity. The poverty contrasted sharply with the wealth and comfort of white South Africa.

Inequality and poverty persist. But townships, such as Khayelitsha in Cape Town, are markedly changed, with roads, basic infrastructure and services that were virtually absent in the early 1990s. Moreover, about 78 percent of South Africans now live in formal structures, including millions of units built by the government since 1994. Additionally, 85 percent have access to electricity, and 90 percent have piped water.

South Africa has become a global leader in the protection of human rights, and the courts have served as an important political vehicle for citizens to challenge a government when it fails to meet its constitutional obligations. Through democratic pressures, the government switched course from one of the most delinquent[13] responses to AIDS, to one of the most ambitious treatment programs on the planet.

Yes, the racial divide remains wide

Just like in America, more than 50 years after the passage of the U.S. Civil Rights Act, race-based inequality, racism and racial resentment are still rife[14]. But the landscape has changed radically from just 30 years ago, when much of South Africa remained officially segregated. Before the 1994 election, millions of black South Africans were assigned to be citizens of sham[15] "homeland" governments, and none could vote for the leadership of the South African government.

Many white South Africans today complain of a "reverse discrimination" and of lack of security. But the country maintains a white population the size of Denmark that is largely prosperous and enjoys standards of living comparable to that in the world's wealthiest countries.

South Africans want better lives

Democratic politics offer hope for more equality and needed change, and the upcoming election highlights the valuable pressures of democratic competition.

Trying to stem a tide of political losses in the 2016 local elections, ANC leader Cyril Ramaphosa, in his February State of the Nation Address conceded many government failures, especially corruption. Unlike his counterparts in Tanzania and Uganda, he has not repressed the opposition or sought to muzzle[16] the media or social media.

Instead, Ramaphosa has tried to convince voters that the ANC can do better. He has proposed concrete solutions, including a renewed effort to attract foreign investment. The ANC's main challengers, the Democratic Alliance and the Economic Freedom Fighters, along with several other parties, are offering important alternatives on election day.

Annotations

8 **squatter** = illegal settler or resident
9 **squalor** = dirty, unpleasant living conditions
10 **shack** = hut, small simple building
11 **piped water** = tap water
12 **dwelling** = place where sb lives
13 **delinquent** = inadequate, failed
14 **rife** = widespread
15 **sham** = not real
16 **to muzzle** = to silence

7 Analyse the means the author employs to support his view of present-day South Africa. Refer to rhetorical devices and strategies.
→ SUPPORT D15, p. 166

Language support

The author makes a case for/against ... | The author employs/uses ... in order to underline/emphasize/support his view that ... | The author relies on different strategies to persuade/convince the reader of his arguments/opinion/point of view/assessment/judgement/impression.

8 CHALLENGE
With reference to the text and to the statistical information in task 5, assess the success of the ANC in transforming South Africa from a despotic apartheid state into a modern democracy.

→ S9: How to structure a text, p. 212

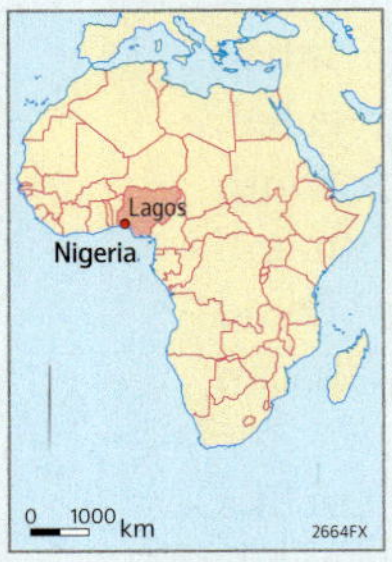

→ **S15:** How to describe pictures, p. 226

Webcode

You can download a word list for Part D here: **DSW-73090-015**

Nigeria: past and present

1

With over 211 million inhabitants, Nigeria has the biggest population in Africa and its economy, which is largely based on oil, is also the biggest economy on the continent. Yet in 2020, the human development index (HID), which is used by the United Nations to measure progress, ranked Nigeria at number 161 out of 189 countries worldwide. Almost half of the Nigerian population lives on less than 2$ a day, below the international poverty line.

a) Across cultures Describe the photos. Assess what impression they give of Nigeria.

b) **Pair work** Discuss to what extent the photos reflect the economic situation of Nigeria.

1

2

3

4

5

2 WB p. 32

a) Read the text on Nigeria's history and draw a timeline of the most important events.

b) Look at the map on p. 65 and describe the most important differences between the regions.

Pre-colonial and colonial times

For centuries, the territory of modern-day Nigeria has been populated by hundreds of different ethnic groups. The biggest among these are the Yoruba (in the west), the Fulani and Hausa (in the north) and the Igbo (in the south-east). Since the unification of Nigeria as a British colony in 1914, these different ethnic groups have been in constant rivalry with each other. They have had different religious beliefs and have generally had very little in common.

In the 19th century, the British began Christian missionary activity in Southern Nigeria, which led to the Christianisation of large parts of the Igbo and Yoruba populations. The missionaries built schools in the area and sent teachers to help with reading and writing. However, at the same time the missionaries imposed their language and culture on the indigenous population, which helped to destroy parts of the native social structure.

By the end of the 19th century, Britain controlled the whole of the territory which makes up modern-day Nigeria, but keeping the vast territory under control remained a major problem. Only by introducing "indirect rule", where local chiefs maintained considerable power, was it possible to appease the north. Meanwhile, in the south, the British government exercised control directly. As a result, the ethno-religious differences between the Muslim north and the Christian south became more obvious, with the northern Hausa and Fulani peoples able to keep many of their local social structures and the southern Igbo and Yoruba peoples having to submit to direct British rule.

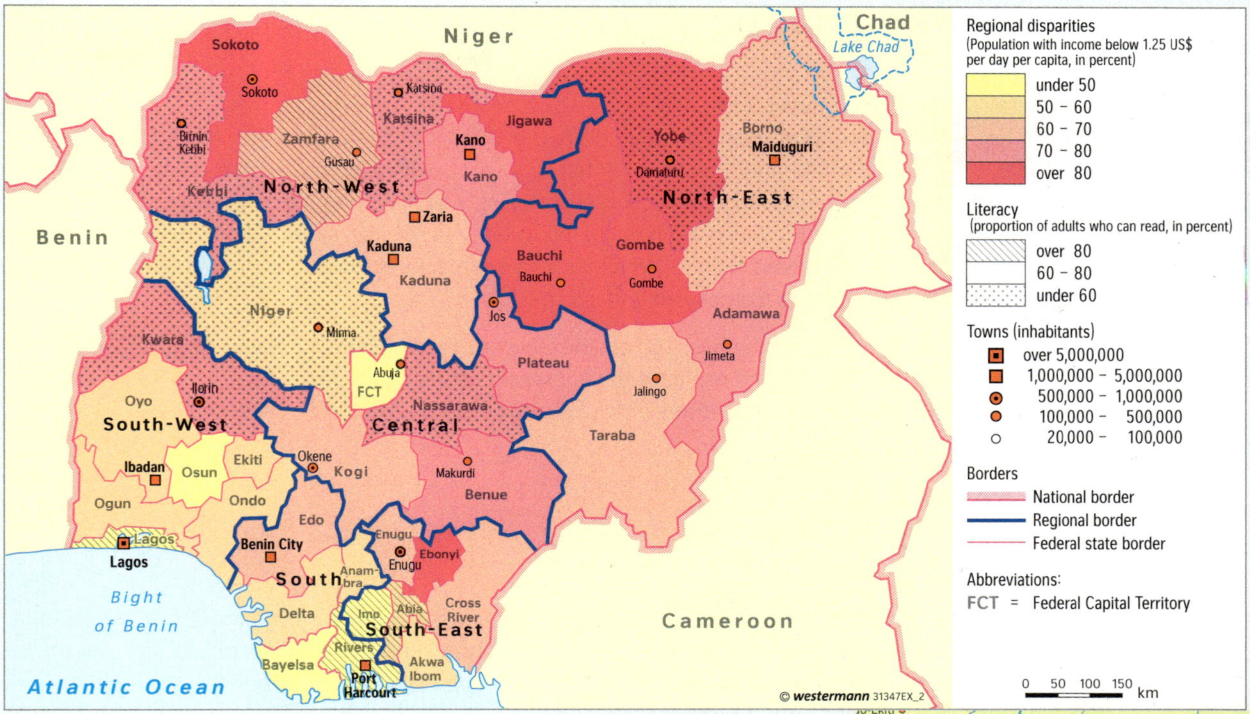

When oil was discovered in the south-east of the country in 1956, the colonial government granted Shell British Petroleum a monopoly to produce oil. Multinational and, above all, British companies continue to dominate the oil sector in Nigeria to this day.

Independence and ethno-religious conflicts

In October 1960, Nigeria gained full independence from Britain, but hostilities among the different Nigerian ethnic groups have been a feature of independent Nigeria from the start until the present day. Various civil and military governments were unable to ease the ethnic tensions between the north and the south, which led to the massacre of thousands of Igbo people in the north in 1966. This resulted in a mass migration of Igbo people back to their “homeland” in the southeast and eventually triggered the breakaway from Nigeria of the Igbo region calling itself the Republic of Biafra in 1967 (see the small map in the right column). After a bloody civil war, the Biafran forces had to surrender in 1970 and the region was reintegrated into Nigeria.

But the problems still remain. There have been frequent changes between military and civil governments, but no government has succeeded in overcoming the ethno-religious hostility between the different groups and assuring a lasting peace and national identity for all Nigerians.

One example of recent religious conflict has been the activities of the radical Islamic group Boko Haram, which has been involved in around 30,000 killings in the last decade. The group’s first known attack occurred in 2003 and they have been active ever since, being responsible for kidnappings, killings and political disturbances. The most high-profile act was the 2014 kidnapping of 276 teenage girls from a boarding school in northern Nigeria. This sparked global outrage and a social media campaign (#bringbackourgirls), headed by celebrities like Michelle Obama. UNICEF estimates that Boko Haram has kidnapped more than 1,000 children in north-eastern Nigeria since 2013.

Nigeria has the largest population in Africa and is the seventh most populous country in the world. It offers a bigger market than most African countries put together and is one of the ‘Next Eleven’ (N-11) countries which are expected to have the largest economies in the 21st century. However, at the present time, the economy cannot create jobs fast enough to keep up with the growth in population. So many highly-skilled Nigerians and students are leaving their country.

Working on novel extracts

1 WB p. 33/1

In her novel *Americanah*, published in 2013, Chimamanda Ngozi Adichie tells the story of Ifemelu and Obinze, who fall in love at university. But as the political situation in military-ruled Nigeria becomes increasingly difficult, Ifemelu emigrates to the US. Due to a stricter US immigration policy following 9/11, Obinze cannot join Ifemelu in the US and goes to Britain instead. When his visa expires, he is forced to return to Nigeria, where he eventually becomes rich and successful.

→ **S9:** How to structure a text, p. 212

a) Read extract 1 from the novel and outline Obinze's relationship to Ifemelu. → SUPPORT D16, p. 167

b) Describe the setting and explain what impression of Nigeria is created.

c) In class, discuss which features of Nigerian society are reflected in this description.

Americanah

by Chimamanda Ngozi Adichie

Extract 1

When Obinze first saw her e-mail, he was sitting in the back of his Range Rover in still Lagos traffic, his jacket slung over the front seat, a rusty-haired child beggar glued outside his window, a hawker pressing colourful CDs against the other window, the radio turned on low to the Pidgin English news on Wazobia FM, he skimmed the e-mail, instinctively wishing it were longer. *Ceiling*[1]*, kedu?*[2] *Hope all is well with work and family. Ranyinudo said she ran into you some time ago and that you now have a child! Proud Papa. Congratulations. I recently decided to move back to Nigeria. Should be in Lagos in a week. Would love to keep in touch. Take care, Ifemelu.*

He read it again slowly and felt the urge to smooth something, his trousers, his shaved-bald head. She had called him Ceiling. In the last e-mail from her, sent just before he got married, she had called him Obinze, apologized for her silence over the years, wished him happiness in sunny sentences and mentioned the black American she was living with. A gracious e-mail. He had hated it. He had hated it so much that he Googled the black American – and why should she give him the man's full name if not because she wanted him Googled? – a lecturer at Yale, and found it infuriating that she lived with a man who referred on his blog to friends as "cats", but it was the photo of the black American, oozing intellectual cool in distressed[3] jeans and black-rimmed glasses, that had tipped Obinze over, made him send her a cold reply. *Thank you for the good wishes, I have never been happier in my life*, he'd written. He hoped she would write something mocking back – it was so unlike her, not to have been even vaguely tart in that first e-mail – but she did not write at all and when he e-mailed her again, after his honeymoon in Morocco, to say he wanted to keep in touch and wanted to talk sometime, she did not reply.

The traffic was moving. A light rain was falling. The child beggar ran along, his doe-eyed expression more theatrical, his motions frantic: bringing his hand to his mouth, again and again, fingertips pursed together. Obinze rolled down the window and held out a hundred-naira note. From the rear-view mirror, his driver, Gabriel, watched with grave disapproval.

"God bless you, oga[4]!" the child beggar said.

"Don't be giving money to these beggars, sir," Gabriel said. "They are all rich. They are using begging to make big money. I heard about one that built a block of six flats in Ikeja!"

"So why are you working as a driver instead of a beggar, Gabriel?" Obinze asked, and laughed, a little too heartily. He wanted to tell Gabriel that his girlfriend from university had just e-mailed him [...] His phone rang and for a confused moment he thought it was Ifemelu calling from America.

Annotations

1 **Ceiling** = nickname Ifemelu had given him when they were a couple

2 **kedu?** (*Igbo*) = how are you?

3 **distressed** = made to look old and worn

4 **oga** = Nigerian word meaning boss or sir

2

Read extract 2 and sum up what you learn about Obinze's life.
→ SUPPORT D17, p. 167

Extract 2

On Lekki Expressway, the traffic moved swiftly in the waning rain and soon Gabriel was pressing the horn in front of the high black gates of his home. [...] Inside was the furniture imported from Italy, his wife, his two-year-old daughter, Buchi, the nanny Christiana, his wife's sister Chioma, who was on a forced holiday because university lecturers were on strike yet again, and the new housegirl, Marie, who had been brought from Benin Republic after his wife decided that Nigerian housegirls were unsuitable. The rooms would all be cool, air-conditioner vents swaying quietly, and the kitchen would be fragrant with curry and thyme, and CNN would be on downstairs, while the television upstairs would be turned to Cartoon Network, and pervading it all would be the undisturbed air of well-being. He climbed out of the car. His gait was stiff, his legs difficult to lift. He had begun, in the past months, to feel bloated from all he had acquired – the family, the houses, the cars, the bank accounts – and would, from time to time, be overcome by the urge to prick everything with a pin, to deflate it all, to be free. He was no longer sure, he had in fact never been sure, whether he liked his life because he really did or whether he liked it because he was supposed to.

"Darling," Kosi said, opening the door before he got to it. She was all made-up, her complexion glowing, and he thought, as he often did, what a beautiful woman she was [...]

She laughed. The same way she laughed, with an open, accepting enjoyment of her own looks, when people asked her "Is your mother white? Are you a half-caste[1]?" because she was so fair-skinned[2]. It had always discomfited him, the pleasure she took in being mistaken for mixed-race.

"Daddy-daddy!" Buchi said, running to him in the slightly off-balance manner of toddlers. She was fresh from her evening bath, wearing her flowered pyjamas and smelling sweetly of baby lotion.

"Buch-buch! Daddy's Buch!" He swung her up, kissed her, nuzzled her neck and, because it always made her laugh, pretended to throw her down on the floor.

"Will you bathe or just change?" Kosi asked, following him upstairs, where she had laid out a blue caftan[3] on his bed. He would have preferred a dress shirt or a simpler caftan instead of this, with its overly decorative embroidery, which Kosi had bought for an outrageous sum from one of those new pretentious fashion designers on The Island[4]. But he would wear it to please her.

"I'll just change," he said.

"How was work?" she asked, in the vague, pleasant way that she always asked. He told her he was thinking about the new block of flats he had just completed in Parkview. He hoped Shell would rent it because the oil companies were always the best renters, never complaining about abrupt hikes[5], paying easily in American dollars so that nobody had to deal with the fluctuating naira.

"Don't worry," she said, and touched his shoulder. "God will bring Shell. We will be okay, darling."

The flats were in fact already rented by an oil company but he sometimes told her senseless lies such as this, because a part of him hoped she would ask a question or challenge him, though he knew she would not, because all she wanted was to make sure the conditions of their life remained the same, and how he made that happen she left entirely to him.

Annotations

[1] **half-caste** = person of mixed race or ethnicity
[2] **fair-skinned** = having (relatively) light skin
[3] **caftan** = a long robe or tunic
[4] **The Island** = an area in Lagos separated from the mainland by a channel
[5] **hike** = increase in price

3

Analyse how the narrator presents Obinze's feelings about his life. Support your findings with evidence from the text. → SUPPORT D18, pp. 167-168

→ **S12:** Checklist: Analysis – prose, p. 220

Oil production in the Niger Delta

Info

Oil production in the Niger Delta

The extraction of oil in the Niger Delta region started towards the end of British colonial rule, when Shell was allowed to explore the region for oil. Other multinational companies have followed. Between 1976 and 1991 alone, nearly 3000 oil spills have led to massive environmental damage and robbed local farmers and fishers of their livelihoods.

In 1990, inhabitants of the region formed the Movement for the Survival of the Ogoni People (MOSOP) to fight the oil companies. When nine leaders of the movement were put on trial in 1995 and later executed, this radicalized many activists, who formed new, more militant groups. These groups try to drive the oil companies away using military force. In recent years, their activities have disrupted oil production on a large scale, which has had a massive impact on the Nigerian economy.

1

In his novel *Oil on water*, published in 2010, Nigerian author Helon Habila depicts the journey of two Nigerian journalists, Rufus and Zaq, who are trying to find the kidnapped wife of a white oil executive in the oil-polluted Niger Delta. The continued resistance against the oil companies and the pollution have produced a society marked by violence, corruption and the everyday struggle for survival.

a) Read extract 1 from the novel and outline the living conditions Rufus finds his family in.

b) Describe how their current life has changed both the mother and the father and explain why Rufus's father does not want him to stay.

c) Analyse how the author reveals the effect of social decline in the description of Rufus's mother.

Oil on water

by Helon Habila

Extract 1

Here I was with my certificate[1], going back home, leaving Port Harcourt[2] for good, I hoped. But when I at last located my family, it was not where I had left them, in the town where I was born and raised. I found out that after moving to a succession of smaller houses, they had finally moved to a town called Junction, whose economy rode on the back of[3] the two asphalt roads that neatly divided the town into four equal parts. My mother looked thinner, tired, and she didn't talk very much. She had appeared briefly excited at my return, hugging me and asking me questions about my time in Port Harcourt; then, as if that display of emotion had drained her of her little reserve of energy, she retreated to the kitchen, not to cook but to stare into the flames in the hearth. My father, on the other hand, was full of energy, almost fidgety[4] with it, unable to sit still.

– Come.

He took me to a large barn at the back of the house. Even before he opened the door I could smell the petrol, and when he turned on the light I saw more than ten drums, most of them empty. We sat on two wooden stools in a clear space between two drums.

– Now that you have your certificate, what are your plans?

He hadn't even touched the certificate. He had only glanced at it and nodded distractedly.

– I don't know. I'll look around and maybe open a photo shop –

– No, not in this town. There's nothing here.

He pointed at the empty oil drums.

- This is the only business booming in this town. I buy from little children. I buy cheap and I sell cheap to the cars that come here at night. Emmanuel, John's father, is my partner. You remember your friend John? Well, Emmanuel has proved himself to be a true friend. He's the only one of my former

Annotations

[1] **certificate** = Before he became a journalist, Rufus spent three years in Port Harcourt as an apprentice photographer. At the end of his apprenticeship, he was given a certificate.

[2] **Port Harcourt** = large city in the Niger Delta region in southern Nigeria

[3] **to ride on the back of** sth = to rely on sth completely

[4] **fidgety** = unable to stay still

colleagues whom I can still call a friend. He came up with this plan. We started the whole thing with his savings. It's not a bad business, really. We get by, we give the police a little something to look the other way, but sooner or later they'll get greedy. They'll arrest us, or take over the whole business themselves. I don't want you to be here when that happens. There's nothing for you here. Go back to Port Harcourt. You're smart. Talk to your master. You'll find something. And when you do, don't forget us. Don't forget your mother and especially your sister.

All I could ask, after he had finished speaking, was, Where do the children get the petrol you buy from them?

– They come to me with their little gallons and I don't ask them where they get it.

In the two days I spent at home before returning to Port Harcourt, I saw how much my father had changed. He had turned his back on religion, and now smoked and drank *ogogoro*[5] almost non-stop. He left home early in the morning in a pick-up truck to go to the bush, where he and his partner bought the petrol from the kids, and he returned home only after midnight, often drunk. The house stank of petrol and cigarettes. He said he smoked just to kill the petrol smell.

Annotations

[5] **ogogoro** = a west African alcoholic drink

2

Seven years later Rufus is employed by Mr Floode, one of the white executives of a foreign oil company in Nigeria, who wants him to find the people who have kidnapped his wife. When Rufus meets him in his villa to report on his findings, a news programme is shown on TV.

a) Read extract 2 and describe the content of the broadcast.

b) Outline Mr Floode's view of Nigeria and compare his view to that of Rufus.

Extract 2

Next, there was a shot of picketing[1] youths holding placards in front of an oil-company building in Port Harcourt. This segment[2] was accompanied by a long, rote-like[3] voiceover about poverty in Nigeria, and how corruption sustained that poverty, and how oil was the main source of revenue, and how because the country was so corrupt, only a few had access to that wealth.

Floode turned off the TV and turned to me.

– Such great potential. You people could easily become the Japan of Africa, the USA of Africa, but the corruption is incredible.

I said nothing, looking to the door to see if the maid[4] was coming in answer to Floode's ring. He warmed to this topic, scratching his chin vigorously as he spoke.

– Our pipelines are vandalized daily, losing us millions ... and millions for the country as well. The people don't understand what they do to themselves ...

– But they do understand.

– What?

– Have you ever heard of a town called Junction?

– No. I don't think so ...

– I'm from there. Almost five years ago I came home from Lagos after graduating from journalism school and found half the town burned down. The newspapers said the villagers brought it upon themselves by drilling[5] into the pipelines to steal oil ...

– Yes, I have heard of that, isn't that a place called Jesse?

– That is a different place. There are countless villages going up in smoke daily. Well, this place, Junction, went up in smoke because of an accident associated with this vandalism, as you call it. But I don't blame them for wanting to vandalize the pipelines that have brought nothing but suffering to their lives, leaking into the rivers and wells[6], killing the fish and poisoning the farmlands. And all they are told by the oil companies and the government is that the pipelines are there for their own good, that they hold great potential for their country, their future. These people endure the worst conditions of any oil-producing community on earth, the government knows it but doesn't have the will to stop it, the oil companies know it, but because the government doesn't care, they also don't care. And you think the people are corrupt? No. They are just hungry, and tired.

– Hmm, well. I've read about it before. A tragedy. But it does illustrate my point –

– No, actually, it illustrates my point.

Annotations

[1] to **picket** = to prevent other workers from entering your place of work during a strike

[2] **segment** (news) = a short piece of news

[3] **rote** = sth learnt word-for-word but not understood

[4] **maid** = a woman employed to do housework

[5] to **drill** = to make a hole in sth using an electric tool

[6] **well** = a hole in the ground from which you can get water

→ **S8:** How to improve your text, p. 208

3

The people in the Niger Delta have suffered from years of oil pollution. Read the two articles and explain

- why Nigerian communities from the Niger Delta have tried to take legal action against Shell
- what difficulties they were confronted with
- why the decision of the British Supreme Court is a major breakthrough for communities suffering from pollution caused by multinational corporations

Shell in Nigeria: Polluted communities 'can sue in English courts'

BBC, 12 February 2021

The UK Supreme Court has ruled that oil-polluted Nigerian communities can sue Shell in English courts.
The decision is a victory for the communities after a five-year battle, and overturns a Court of Appeal[1] ruling. The Niger Delta communities of more than 40,000 people say decades of pollution have severely affected their lives, health and local environment.
The oil giant had argued it was only a holding company for a firm that should be judged under Nigerian law. Shell described the legal ruling as disappointing.
What does the ruling say?
The Supreme Court, the UK's final appeal court for civil cases, ruled that the cases brought by the Bille community and the Ogale people of Ogoniland[2] against Royal Dutch Shell were arguable[3] and could proceed in the English courts.
Royal Dutch Shell did not dispute that pollution had been caused, but argued it could not be held legally responsible for its Nigerian subsidiary. Shell is responsible for about 50% of the delta's oil production.
Last year the Court of Appeal agreed with the company, but the Supreme Court said on Friday that that decision was flawed.

Annotations
[1] **Court of Appeal** = high court in the UK dealing with appeals from other courts
[2] **Ogoniland** = territory in the south of Nigeria on the coast of the Gulf of Guinea, east of Port Harcourt
[3] **arguable** = able to be dealt with in court

Fresh hope for justice

Ishaq Khalid, BBC News, Lagos, 12 February 2021

The Niger Delta pollution has continued despite years of promises by successive governments in Nigeria to clean it up. In 2016 President Muhammadu Buhari launched an ambitious clean-up operation in Ogoniland. The work is ongoing but residents say little progress has been made.
Continued oil spills from the activities of multinationals have also cast doubt on the impact of the clean-up exercise. "Things are getting worse by the day," Celestine Akpobari, an environmental activist from Ogoni, told the BBC.
The region provides most of Nigeria's government revenues but the communities say successive governments have neglected them. Mr Akpobari says people can no longer fish or farm because of the devastation. "People are dying, there are strange diseases and women are having miscarriages from the pollution", he says. But the communities and campaigners say the recent court victory gives them hope they will see justice.

How bad is the pollution?
In 2011 the UN concluded it would take 30 years to clear up the vast amounts of pollution in the Niger Delta.
The Ogale community of about 40,000 people are mostly fishermen or farmers who rely on Ogoniland's waterways. But pollution has all but destroyed fishing, turning their lush[1] home into a toxic wasteland.

Annotations
[1] **lush** = opulently green

There have been at least 40 oil spills from Shell's pipelines since 1989, lawyers say Shell's records reveal.

UN scientists have found an 8cm (3 inch) layer of refined oil floating on top of water that supplies the community's drinking wells – vastly higher than is legally permitted.

The water is now too dirty for people to drink. Despite promises to provide clean water, people must often either shell out[2] for bottled water or drink from contaminated sources.

Thick crusts of ash and tar[3] cover the land where oil spills have caused fires. Planting new vegetation to replace burnt crops or plants is almost impossible. Farmer Damiete Sanipe describes a wasteland where the trees and the mangrove have been destroyed.

"The habitat is gone, the river we used to swim in is gone. For a coastal community whose life revolved around the water, it's all gone.

"I don't think money can bring back what we have lost. Even if they want to revive the mangrove, it will take more than 30 years which is a long time."

On Friday Leigh Day[4] lawyer Daniel Leader said the ruling was a "watershed[5]" for "impoverished communities seeking to hold powerful corporate actors to account". The firm said the amount of compensation sought had yet to be determined. [...]

The decision on Friday is the latest case to test whether multinational companies can be held accountable for the acts of overseas subsidiaries.

Amnesty International welcomed the ruling. Mark Dummett, director of Amnesty International's Global Issues Programme, said the fight had not yet been won, but added: "This landmark ruling could spell the end of a long chapter of impunity[6] for Shell and for other multinationals who commit human rights abuses overseas."

Annotations

[2] **to shell out** = to pay money
[3] **tar** = *Teer*
[4] **Leigh Day** name of the British law firm that represents the communities
[5] **watershed** = *here:* breakthrough
[6] **impunity** = not being held legally accountable for sth

4 EXTRA → **S27:** Evaluating online sources, p. 245

Research other instances of pollution by multinational companies and its effects on local communities. Write a statement in which you present the case and explain why it is essential to hold multinational corporations accountable for the damage they cause.

Nollywood – Nigeria's dream factory

1

a) The Nigerian film industry, which produces more than 1,500 films per year, is called Nollywood. Explain the term.

b) A film can fulfill different functions, e.g. to entertain or to portray social problems. Watch the trailers of these three Nollywood films: *Half of a Yellow Sun* (2014), *The Arbitration* (2016) and *Nigerian Prince* (2018). Then discuss which functions each film fulfills. → SUPPORT D19, p. 168

→ **S9:** How to structure a text, p. 212

→ **S20:** How to listen/watch effectively, p. 234

2

In her book *Nollywood – the making of a film empire*, published in 2017, Emily Witt explores the development of the Nigerian film industry from the very beginning to the present. In the introduction to the book, Femi Oduagbemi, the founder of a documentary film festival in Lagos and producer of a popular soap opera, presents his view of the different phases and of their importance for Nigeria.

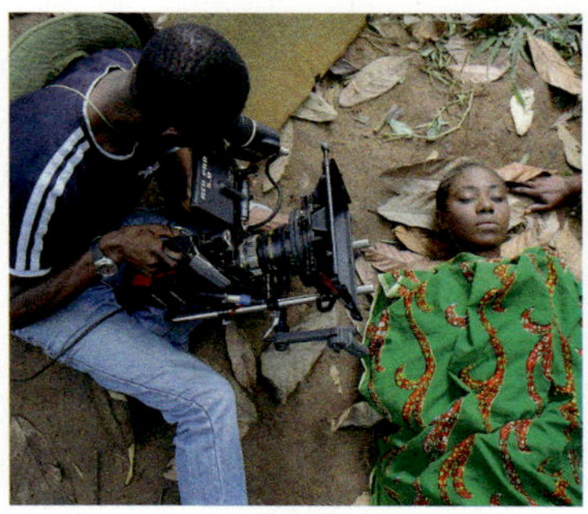

a) Read the text on p. 72 and explain how Oduagbemi sees the films of colonial times.

b) Describe how the Nigerian film industry started.

c) Explain to what extent Nigerian films have altered the perception of Nigeria in the world according to Oduagbemi.

d) Consider Oduagbemi's reference to Nollywood as "our voice", "our documentary", "our answer to colonial narratives". Discuss to what extent the development of Nollywood can be seen as an essential aspect of emancipation.

Up until the last twenty to thirty years the history and culture of African communities were the narratives[1] of the colonialists. Those narratives, quite frankly, beyond not being accurate, beyond not being authentic, were political.

Now: cinema is political. Every cinema is political. The only way cinema works for you is if you are in charge of it. Every colony used cinema – whether in the genre of documentary or the genre of drama – they used cinema to what? To alter behaviour. They used cinema to explain that it was civilised to use knives and forks to eat, as though the natives were not eating before they came. There was a replacement therapy and film was the tool. If you knew a god before they came, cinema was able to give you a greater god, and a better god, and explain to you why your god was rubbish. If you dressed a certain way before they came, they were able to use cinema to assure you that what the queen approved as gentlemanly was a suit. Film allowed you to be able to show, to tell, to wow, to entertain – while indoctrinating. Unless you were in control of that, your story was at risk. Your story was told by someone else.

When Nollywood started out in the 1980s, the executive producers were actually merchants who sold videotapes. Someone had the brilliant idea that the way to move[2] these videotapes was to put something on them. Now, at that time, locally produced soap operas were very popular on NTA, the Nigerian Television Authority. And a videotape salesman named Kenneth Nnebue thought to himself, if I could get one of these guys who made the soap opera at NTA to make me something like a soap opera, then we'll move the sales of the tapes. It turned out to be brilliant. But also at that time, like a perfect storm[3], security was an issue, the military regime was in place, and people wanted to stay at home. The tape players were new, and it was a sign of elitism to be able to watch a film in your own house. [...] So how did the tapes move? The merchants commissioned[4] the soap opera producers: Make me what was essentially an episode, write and direct it for me, and put it on tape. It moved the tapes. What they didn't sell, they wiped[5], and made another film.

The way to distribute it was simple: The tapes were simply placed in every electronics shop. It was at that time mostly urban, essentially sold in Lagos. And then, guess what? The house girls and house boys who came from the village and lived with their principals[6] in Lagos found it to be something to watch when madam and *oga* [Yoruba for "sir" or "boss"] were not at home. [...]

By bringing it on TV he gave it a value. In giving it value those people who were wiping could licence content. That's when Nollywood became international. [...]

From 2000 to 2010, a few things are beginning to come together. A star system is emerging: looking for storytelling in a formal sort of way is emerging; a class of writers and filmmakers and cameramen. There is a certain consciousness now that what we are doing actually has a meaning. It was at that same time that festivals began to be interested in what is this activity in this Nigeria, and curiosity. Remember, suddenly out of nowhere, a country is producing dramatic features[7] in the thousands.[...] Its originators were Nigerians, its performers were Nigerians, its audience were Nigerians. Why? They all shared a certain one common thing: the Nigerian experience.

[...]

They told urban tales people lived and swore by[8]. And the first thing to grow was not their storytelling capacity, it was their audience. That really was what made Nollywood unique across the world. The audience grew, before the birth, before those driving it. The audience embraced it even before the owners knew what it was. And you know what was even more interesting? The audience chose it before international foreign stuff. And that's enough for you to understand my constant conversation about Nollywood being documentary. It was the answer to colonial narratives. [...]

So whatever its imperfection, Nollywood, in 2000 to 2010, became our voice, and thus our documentary. We did not need you to create a space for us.

There were a lot of films in Nigeria through the years, but none spoke our voice. None recognized our existence as a distinct civilization, a distinct aspiration. We were just defined in one single ... you know what they call poverty porn? The little boy starving with big inflated[9] stomach defined our narrative. Well guess what? It was from Nollywood that people first realized that we build houses with huge big columns and we could afford it.

Annotations

[1] **narrative** = story
[2] to **move** = *here:* to sell
[3] **perfect storm** = an unusual or unlikely combination of events that bring a powerful or significant result
[4] to **commission** = to formally ask sb for a piece of their work
[5] to **wipe** = to delete
[6] **principal** = *here:* employer
[7] **feature** = *Spielfilm*
[8] to **swear by** sth = to believe in or depend on sth
[9] **inflated** = *aufgebläht*

Statues, monuments and other remnants of colonialism

Webcode
You can download a word list for Part E here: **DSW-73090-016**

1

In 2020 the violent death of George Floyd, who was killed by a US police officer, brought hundreds of thousands of people around the globe to the streets to protest against racial discrimination and white supremacy. Emerging in the US in 2013 after the young black man Trayvon Martin had been killed and a court ruling declared the white perpetrator not guilty, the Black Lives Matter movement brought attention to structural racism and has contributed to a growing awareness that the wrongs of European imperialism need to be confronted in order to understand the continued repression and injustice in our societies.

Info

Edward Colston was born in Bristol in 1636 and took over his father's business as a sea merchant mainly trading with Spain and Portugal. Gradually he became involved in the Atlantic slave trade, first as a member, later as deputy governor of the Royal African Company which held a monopoly on the English trade with slaves from Africa. Colston was considered a philanthropist since he used a great deal of his fortune to build schools, houses for the poor and hospitals in and around Bristol. More than 170 years after his death, his hometown, which he had also represented in parliament, honoured him with a statue.

a) Read the article on pp. 73-74 and describe the form the protest has taken in Bristol.
b) Outline the different views on the matter as presented in the article.

→ **S9:** How to structure a text, p. 212

Toppling of UK statue fuels debate on monuments to slave traders

Sonia Elks, Reuters, 8 June 2020

Anti-racism protesters who tore down a statue honouring a slave trader in a British port city have fuelled a hot global debate over how to deal with monuments to historic figures who profited from enslaving African people.

The toppling of the statue of Edward Colston, who made a fortune in the 17th century from trading in West African slaves, was condemned as petty vandalism by critics, while others hailed it as affirmative action against racist ideologies.

"It was an absolutely incredible feat that really shows the importance of us knowing our history," said Aliyah Hasinah, a curator and spokeswoman for protest group Black Lives Matter UK.

"Public art absolutely has an impact on our imagination and what we believe is at the core of our society because it's what we hail as important," she told the Thomson Reuters Foundation.

"That's why so many people politely petitioned to get the Colston statue removed ... They weren't listened to, so the city of Bristol made their voices heard in another way."

Colston's statue was pulled down by protesters joining a wave of worldwide demonstrations against racial inequality triggered by the death of unarmed black man George Floyd at the hands of U.S. police.

But the debate over buildings and monuments named after people involved in the trans-Atlantic slave trade has been brewing for some years fuelled by the world's recently adopted drive to end modern slavery.

Campaigners had previously called for the statue – still bearing a plaque describing Colston as "virtuous and wise" – to be removed, but had failed to persuade the authorities.

Debates over how to handle monuments and artifacts commemorating historic figures whose actions and beliefs are widely condemned today are also raging in other nations.

In the United States, Virginia Governor Ralph Northam announced plans last week to remove a statue of Confederate General Robert E. Lee in the state's capital city of Richmond.

In Belgium, an online petition calling for the removal of statues of colonial-era King Leopold II has garnered more than 30,000 signatures. His troops decimated Congo in the late 1800s.

Britain's interior minister Priti Patel condemned the toppling of the Colston statue as an "utterly disgraceful" act while prominent black British campaigner Nimco Ali said removing the statue was "not OK" and failed to tackle racism.

"Many of you who are super vocal about the Colston statue have been silent about the real & current inequities in Bristol. So this morning I am waiting for you to clean up and also campaign for real change," she wrote on Twitter.

But others hailed the removal as affirmative action against racial inequality and Britain's imperial legacies – although some added they would have preferred to see it done legally.

"It is important people see the reality of the growth of the British Empire and imperialism," said Richard Benjamin, head of the International Slavery Museum in Liverpool, northern England.

"The representation of Edward Colston was highly contentious and offensive to many, and in bringing him down, it is important to note we are not erasing history, but instead making history."

→ **S6:** How to write an argumentative text, p. 206

2 → SUPPORT D20, p. 168

Discuss whether historic monuments of people whose enterprises were based on human exploitation should be

- left untouched as part of our history
- demolished to wipe out the memory of them
- supplemented by information boards or plaques
- presented in museums.

Mediation: How Germany handles its colonial past

1 Across cultures → **S19:** How to improve your mediation skills, pp. 234/235

Your school is working on an intercultural learning project with a partner school in Britain. The current topic is how to deal with our colonial past. Like you, your British partner on the project would like to know what the situation is like in Germany. You have done some research online and found this article from 2020. Write an email of about 250 words to your partner in which you outline different approaches to changing the way the colonial past is remembered in Germany, the problems involved and different views on the matter.

Die Schatten des deutschen Kolonialismus

Von Christoph Hasselbach, Deutsche Welle, 18.06.2020

Der Streit um die Kolonialgeschichte hat Deutschland erreicht. Soll man dessen Symbole stehen lassen, besser einordnen – oder einfach entfernen? Die Statue des britischen Sklavenhändlers Edward Colston in Bristol wird in den Hafen geworfen; die Figur von Christoph Kolumbus in Boston wird geköpft; die Stadtväter von Antwerpen entfernen aus Sorge vor Zerstörung vorsorglich selbst ein Standbild von König Leopold II, der für schlimmste Gräueltaten in seiner „privaten" Kongo-Kolonie verantwortlich gemacht wird. Koloniale Symbole weltweit stehen derzeit als Ausdruck für weißen Rassismus unter Druck. Lange hat sich kaum jemand für sie interessiert. Das hat sich spätestens mit dem gewaltsamen Tod des Schwarzen George Floyd durch einen weißen Polizisten in den USA geändert.

Deutschland hatte eine nur kurze Kolonialgeschichte, von 1884 bis zum Ende des Ersten Weltkrieges, als es seine Kolonien in Afrika, Ozeanien und Ostasien wieder abgeben musste. Aber auf seinem Höhepunkt war das deutsche Kolonialreich immerhin das viertgrößte der Welt. Und Spuren davon gibt es bis heute.

Was tun mit der „Lüderitzstraße"?

Nach wie vor sind Straßen und Plätze in Deutschland nach Kolonisatoren wie Carl Peters, Adolf Lüderitz oder Gustav Nachtigal benannt. Der Befehlshaber der Schutztruppe in Deutsch-Ostafrika, Paul von Lettow-Vorbeck, war bis vor wenigen Jahren Namensgeber von Kasernen und Schulen. Es gibt nach wie vor eine Statue von Hermann von Wissmann, einem ehemaligen Gouverneur der Kolonie, in Bad Lauterberg im Harz und eine Büste von Nachtigal, der zeitweise Reichskommissar für Deutsch-Westafrika (heute Kamerun und Togo) war, in Stendal in Sachsen-Anhalt. [...]

Widerstand gegen Umbenennungen

Im so genannten „Afrikanischen Viertel" in Berlin gibt es bereits seit Jahren Streit um die Umbenennung von Straßen. Die Bezirksverordnetenversammlung hat bereits vor gut zwei Jahren beschlossen, sie nach Widerstandskämpfern gegen die deutsche Kolonialherrschaft umzubenennen.
Doch viele Bewohner und Geschäftsinhaber in den Straßen sind dagegen, oft nicht aus politischen Gründen, sondern, weil sie die Kosten von Adressenänderungen vermeiden wollen. Manche wollen auch einfach aus Gewohnheit an den alten Namen festhalten. Die Initiative Pro Afrikanisches Viertel hat einen kreativen Weg vorgeschlagen, wie die Namen bleiben könnten: Die Lüderitzstraße soll nach der namibischen Stadt gleichen Namens heißen, der Nachtigalplatz nach dem Theologen Johann Nachtigal. Und die Petersallee erinnert bereits seit 1986 offiziell nicht mehr an den Kolonialisten Carl Peters, der in Ostafrika brutal geherrscht hatte. Sie ist jetzt nach Hans Peters benannt, einem Widerstandskämpfer gegen den Nationalsozialismus. Manche meinen, damit weiche man dem Problem aus. Endgültig ist jedenfalls noch nichts, der Namensstreit hält an.

Kaum jemand möchte alles auslöschen

In Hamburg auf dem Gelände der ehemaligen Lettow-Vorbeck-Kaserne hat man Erklärtafeln zu den Büsten von Männern wie Paul von Lettow-Vorbeck und Lothar von Trotha gestellt, die an der Niederschlagung von Aufständen in den deutschen Kolonien maßgeblich beteiligt waren. Wie es mit dem Umgang damit weitergeht, ist noch nicht klar. Dem Senat geht es jedenfalls grundsätzlich darum, dass diese schwierige Geschichte auch künftigen Generationen im Bewusstsein bleibt: weder Glorifizierung noch Tilgung sollen das Konzept sein, sondern eher Mahnmale und Erinnerung.

„Gegendenkmäler" als Lösung?

Weiter geht der Verein Postkolonial. Er ist in rund 20 deutschen Städten aktiv. Postkolonial setzt sich etwa in Hamburg, so heißt es auf der Webseite, für eine „umfassende Dekolonisierung des Hamburger Stadtraums [...] und die Darstellung der Geschichte des antikolonialen Widerstandes sowie für ein ehrendes Gedenken an die Opfer von Kolonialismus und Rassismus" ein. Das schließt Straßenumbenennungen ein, aber es geht dem Verein nicht darum, alle Spuren des Kolonialismus einfach auszulöschen. Für Christian Kopp, Sprecher von Postkolonial in Berlin, kommen etwa auch Gegendenkmäler infrage. Nur eine kritische Informationstafel vor ein Denkmal zu stellen, ist ihm eindeutig zu wenig. [...]

Welche Maßstäbe kann man anlegen?

Aber kann man überhaupt historische Persönlichkeiten und Epochen mit heutigen Maßstäben messen? [Der Hamburger Historiker] Jürgen Zimmerer meint eindeutig ja, „sonst dürften wir uns ja auch von Hitler, Himmler und Co nicht distanzieren oder diese verurteilen". Es gehe aber in der gegenwärtigen Debatte vor allem darum, „ob die historischen Persönlichkeiten heute als zu ehrende Vorbilder geeignet sind, und damit sind unsere heutigen Maßstäbe maßgeblich. Wir verhandeln in Denkmälern auch unsere eigenen Werte und Vorstellungen".
Der deutsche Kolonialismus war bisher ein wenig beachteter Teil der Geschichte. Johann Hinrich Claussen, der Kulturbeauftragte der Evangelischen Kirche in Deutschland, gehört zu denen, die froh sind, dass sich die deutsche Gesellschaft durch die Proteste überhaupt damit befasst. Zwar könne man den Umgang in Deutschland und Ländern wie den USA oder Großbritannien mit Denkmälern nicht vergleichen. Doch inzwischen rücke der deutsche Kolonialismus endlich ins öffentliche Bewusstsein. Darin sieht Claussen eine große Bildungsaufgabe.

(738 Wörter)

Decolonizing the curriculum

1 WB p. 35/1

a) Read the headline of the following article and discuss what the term "decolonising schools" might imply.

b) Read the article and explain why according to the author changes in what is taught in schools would be a step towards racial equality.

→ **S9:** How to structure a text, p. 212

LOLA OKOLOSIE — **The Guardian, 10 June 2020**

'White guilt on its own won't fix racism': decolonising Britain's schools

The UK is finally facing up to the crimes of empire. Is it time to rewrite the curriculum?

The medley of jubilant black, brown and white faces cheering the destruction of Edward Colston's statue has had many rethinking. Discussing even. Britain, a nation not keen on making much of a fuss, is having to talk about slavery. For too long we would rather have dunked our digestives[1] into mugs of tea and not bothered with dredging up our past. But what if we had all learned at school that the history of our great British brew is inseparable from our history of empire? While Brits have been embracing lockdown baking, how many will know our national sweet tooth is the direct result of slave labour on Caribbean sugar cane fields?

At this moment, remaining ignorant about such history looks increasingly indefensible. Overnight, it has become a moral imperative to learn both the good and bad of British history. Meanwhile support for organisations that have long been working on "decolonising the curriculum" has skyrocketed since the killing of George Floyd.

Pran Patel, a consultant on decolonising the curriculum for schools in the UK and beyond, says that over the past two weeks the interest in his work from headteachers has been "crazy". For Patel, decolonising the curriculum means exposing kids to the richness of knowledge from what he calls the "global curriculum". Denying children a wider range of subjects and perspectives does them a disservice[2]. So too does a lack of consideration for how material is taught and who is teaching it. "Our curriculum leaves some of us feeling inferior and others, through no fault of their own, superior," says Patel. "Nobody wins in that scenario. When we teach literature, we should be teaching Dickens but we should also be talking about Tagore. When we teach poetry, we should absolutely be teaching Shakespeare and his sonnets but also Rumi[3]."

Signs declaring "White silence is violence" on our streets and social media feeds have forced thousands to act. According to Penny Rabiger, an ex-teacher and member of the Black and Minority Ethnic Educators Network, this "huge collective white guilt" has led to an enormous volume of traffic to the network's website. [...] Rabiger hits a cautious note, though, when she says: "White guilt is dangerous. It's a start but it's not going to 'fix' racism." White educators must, she says, continually ask themselves how racial inequality comes to exist and in what ways they perpetuate it.

Annotations

[1] **digestive** = (*BE*) biscuit
[2] to **do** sb **a disservice** = to do sth, often with good intentions, that is not good for sb
[3] **Rumi** = 13th-century Persian poet and Sufi mystic

Indian poet, playwright and philosopher Rabindranath Tagore (1861-1941), winner of the Nobel Prize for Literature in 1913

2

Analyse how the author introduces her topic in the first paragraph. → SUPPORT D21, p. 169

→ **S13:** Checklist: Analysis – non-fictional texts, p. 222

3 Across cultures WB p. 35/2-3

Consider your own lessons at school and assess to what extent they fulfil the requirements of a global curriculum according to Patel's concept and what could be changed.

Write a blog post on decolonization (Lernaufgabe)

Work on these tasks in order to write a blog post on an example of how the colonial past or the emancipation from colonialism is dealt with by a cultural institution (e.g. a museum, theatre or school) or a contemporary artist.

1

a) Read this text taken from the website of the Museum of British Colonialism and outline what the term decolonization originally meant and what it usually refers to today.

What is decolonization?

Initially, decolonization referred to the process that former colonies underwent to free themselves of the colonial supremacy and gain their independence. Today, the term has become much more than that: a [...] call that points to the fact that we are **still subject to the ideology of colonialism**.

There are so very many remnants of colonial times: from street names and statues that glorify people responsible for massacre and genocide, to objects in museums taken from their original owners, to the human remains of unidentified people held as collection artefacts. [...]

Decolonizing is about questioning our institutions: how and why are some forms of knowledge given priority and authority over others? [...] How do we contribute to a renewal of the canon with stories and reference frames that have been systematically erased from it? [...]

In short: how do we change the focus, how do we alter our perspective?

b) According to the text, the process of decolonization involves a change of perspective in the way colonialism is presented in society. What could be done to bring this about? Consider these areas:

- school/university curricula
- exhibitions, e.g. in museums
- the arts
- public spaces
- the media

2

Choose a topic. Here are some ideas:

A Visit some museum websites and find out how the museums approach the topic of decolonization. Here are some suggestions:

- the Canadian Museum of History
- the International Slavery Museum in Liverpool
- the British Empire and Commonwealth Collection in Bristol
- the Deutsche Historische Museum

B Examine historic representations of colonial times in paintings and statues or in the work of contemporary artists.

C Do some research on the role of film in the process of decolonization, e.g. by visiting the websites of film festivals dealing with postcolonialism.

3

Plan your blog post.

→ **S7:** Checklist: Writing a blog post, p. 208

Include the following aspects:

- Why did you choose to work on this particular topic?
- What did you find out? Present the project, exhibition, artist, etc. you have worked on.
- State your view on how successful the project is concerning a reassessment of colonialism.
- How has your work on the topic affected your own view of the matter?

4

Write your blog post. Present your information and your views in a way that will appeal to a young audience.

→ **S7:** Checklist: Writing a blog post, p. 208

- Think of a good title. Your title should capture your readers' interest and convey an idea of what your blog post will be about.
- Write a captivating introduction to grab your readers' attention right from the start.
- You can include pictures or links to film clips or interviews to support your text.
- Write a memorable ending to your blog post that will motivate your readers to engage with you via the comment section.

5

Edit your blog post.

- Reread your text to see if it flows well.
- Ask another student to read your text and to suggest improvements.
- Put your blog post on an online learning platform for your class.

→ **S24:** How to give feedback/peer edit, p. 240

3 New York – a global city

Webcode

You can download a word list for the Theme here: DSW-73090-017

1

a) Look at the photos of New York City and describe them briefly.
b) Match the photos to the topics below (1-14). Two topics do not have a corresponding photo.
c) Explain what image of New York the photos convey.

1 art: Guggenheim Museum | **2** Black culture: Black Lives Matter street art mural, Brooklyn | **3** civic center: City Hall | **4** contemporary architecture: The Vessel | **5** gentrification: Harlem brownstones | **6** international politics: United Nations headquarters | **7** money: Financial District | **8** multiculturalism: Steuben Parade | **9** perpetual rush hour: New York traffic and cabs | **10** religion: Hasidic Jews in New York | **11** remembering 9/11: Ground Zero | **12** sports and recreation: Pier 2 Brooklyn Bridge Park | **13** theatre scene: Broadway | **14** urban landscape design: High Line (urban public park)

2

Prepare a one-minute talk on a topic from task 1 or some other New York aspect of your choice. Convince your classmates that this is an important aspect of life in New York.

3

Choose one of the quotations about New York City (1-6) or research a different quotation that appeals to you. In class, explain what the quotation says about New York City and why you chose it.

1 New York has a thousand universes in it that don't always connect but we do all walk the same streets, hear the same sirens, ride the same subways, see the same headlines in the Post, read the same writings on the walls. That shared landscape gets inside of all of us and, in some small way, unites us, makes us think we know each other even when we don't.

Jay-Z, rapper, 2010

7

8

11

9

10

12

2 One good thing about New York is that most people function daily while in a low-grade depression. It's not like if you're in Los Angeles, where everyone's so actively working on cheerfulness and mental and physical health that if they sense you're down, they shun you. Also, all that sunshine is a cruel joke when you're depressed. In New York, even in your misery, you feel like you belong.

Mindy Kaling, actress and comedienne, 2011

Preview

This Theme covers several aspects of the global city New York.
In the **Workshop** you will work on different kinds of listening tasks.

3 New York is an ugly city, a dirty city. Its climate is a scandal, its politics are used to frighten children, its traffic is madness, its competition is murderous. But there is one thing about it: Once you have lived in New York and it has become your home, no place else is good enough.

John Steinbeck, writer, 1953

4 Being a New Yorker grounds you in every way. Before you walk out of the house, you can dress in the nicest clothes and be whoever you think you are, but when you're on those streets, you're just in the school of fish.

Awkwafina, rapper and actress, 2019

5 Each neighborhood of the city appeared to be made of a different substance, each seemed to have a different air pressure, a different psychic weight: the bright lights and shuttered shops, the housing projects and luxury hotels, the fire escapes and city parks.

Teju Cole, writer, 2012

6 New York is the meeting place of the peoples, the only city where you can hardly find a typical American.

Djuna Barnes, Writer, 1916

MEGACITIES

New York City is one of the world's current 33 megacities (as counted by the United Nations). Megacities are widely defined as metropolitan areas with more than 10 million inhabitants and a very high population density. But megacities are not only defined by size. Economic weight, political stability, and attractiveness for foreign capital are important categories, too. It is estimated that there will be a lot more megacities in the future, as the world population is still pulled towards the cities.

FACTS AND FIGURES

With a population of well over 20 million people in its metropolitan area, New York City is the most populous and the most densely populated major city in the United States. It has been awarded the title of the cultural, financial, and media capital of the world and has a huge influence on world trade, technology, research, politics, entertainment, education, art, fashion, and sports. New York City is also the most photographed city in the world. As the home of the headquarters of the United Nations, it is an important centre for international diplomacy and sometimes called the capital of the world.
The New York metropolitan area is one of the wealthiest regions worldwide – if it were a country, it would have the eighth-largest economy in the world. Moreover, the highest number of billionaires of any city in the world call New York City their home.

BOROUGHS

New York City is made up of five boroughs: Brooklyn, Queens, Manhattan, the Bronx, and Staten Island. If the boroughs were each independent cities, four of them (Brooklyn, Queens, Manhattan, and the Bronx) would be among the ten most populous cities in the United States. Within the boroughs, which each have their distinctive features, there are hundreds of neighbourhoods, many with a colourful history and individual character.

HISTORY

New York City was founded as a trading post on Native American land by Dutch colonists in 1624 and called Nieuw Amsterdam. It was renamed New York after the English had seized control of the island of Manhattan in 1664. From the late 19th century on, more and more immigrants started to come to New York City. Today, it still remains a symbol of prosperity, freedom and cultural diversity.

DIVERSITY

With the Statue of Liberty still a symbol of welcome to arriving immigrants, New York constitutes the premier point of entry for legal immigration to the United States. New York is home to more than 3.2 million residents born outside the United States, the largest foreign-born population of any city in the world. Among themselves, these residents speak over 800 languages, making New York City the most linguistically diverse city in the world.
In New York, no single country or region of origin dominates. The largest groups of foreign-born individuals in the city hail from the Caribbean, China, Mexico, Guyana, Ecuador, India and Russia. New York City is also home to the largest Jewish and Israeli communities outside Israel, with the Jewish population in the region numbering over 1.5 million. Residents of New York City possess a variety of denominations, among them Christianity, Judaism, Hinduism, Islam and Buddhism as the largest groups, as well as a growing number of atheists.
The gay and bisexual community in New York City is estimated at nearly 570,000 individuals, the largest in the United States and also one of the world's largest.
There is also a very wide range of wealth and income to be found, from the aforementioned billionaires to more than 80,000 homeless people, as many as 20,000 of them children.

9/11

There are many defining moments in New York City's history, but 9/11 is arguably the most important one in recent years. 9/11 describes a series of four coordinated terrorist attacks by the Islamic terrorist group Al-Qaeda against the United States on the morning of Tuesday, September 11, 2001. It was the deadliest terrorist attack in human history. New York City suffered the highest losses, as two of the four airliners hijacked that day were flown into the twin towers of the World Trade Center, destroying them and killing 2,192 civilians, 343 firefighters, and 71 police officers.

1

a) Find adjectives for the following nouns in the text.

metropolis | economy | population | (high) population density | finance | distinction | diversity | definition | coordination

b) Now find the corresponding nouns for these adjectives.

stable | diplomatic | prosperous | residential | denominational | wealthy

2

a) Find synonyms for these words in the text.

resident | money | commerce | rich | distinctive | to establish | main | to come from | religion | almost | aeroplane

b) Now find antonyms for these words in the text.

tiny | servitude | illegal | native | homogeneous | decreasing | poverty

3 WB pp. 36-37

What makes New York City so attractive? Write an introduction for a NYC brochure praising its uniqueness, using all the words highlighted in the text.

4

a) Use this video and the information from the text to create an annotated timeline of New York City from 1609 to the present. You can use numbers, pictures, and short texts to illustrate and annotate your timeline.
In your annotations, include the following milestones of NYC history:

1. Lenape People
2. Commissioners' Plan
3. New York & Harlem Railroad
4. construction of Central Park
5. elevated railroads
6. Brooklyn Bridge
7. Five Boroughs
8. subway
9. infrastructure decay

Webcode
You can find the video here: DSW-73090-018

b) **EXTRA** Use your annotated timeline to create a New York City A-Z. You can use each letter more than once, if relevant.

Step by step Listening

Preview

In this Workshop you are going to practise working on listening tasks. In an exam, you will encounter various test formats, sometimes in combination, for example:

- short answer questions: You are asked to answer questions, often in the form of notes.
- table completion: You are asked to complete a table by adding missing information.
- multiple choice: You have to choose one of usually three or four options.
- multiple matching: You listen to several shorter clips and have to match them to headings or statements that sum up the gist of these clips.

PRE-LISTENING

1

→ **S18:** How to analyse statistics, p. 230

a) Look at the graph and describe what it tells you about
- where New Yorkers have come from,
- how this has changed over time.

Language support

figures for ... increase/go up/rise slightly/sharply/suddenly/steeply/gradually/steadily
figures for ... decrease/go down/fall slightly/sharply/suddenly/steeply/gradually/steadily
figures for ... remain steady/do not change
figures for ... reach a peak/a bottom

Composition of New York City's foreign-born population by place of origin, 1800-2013

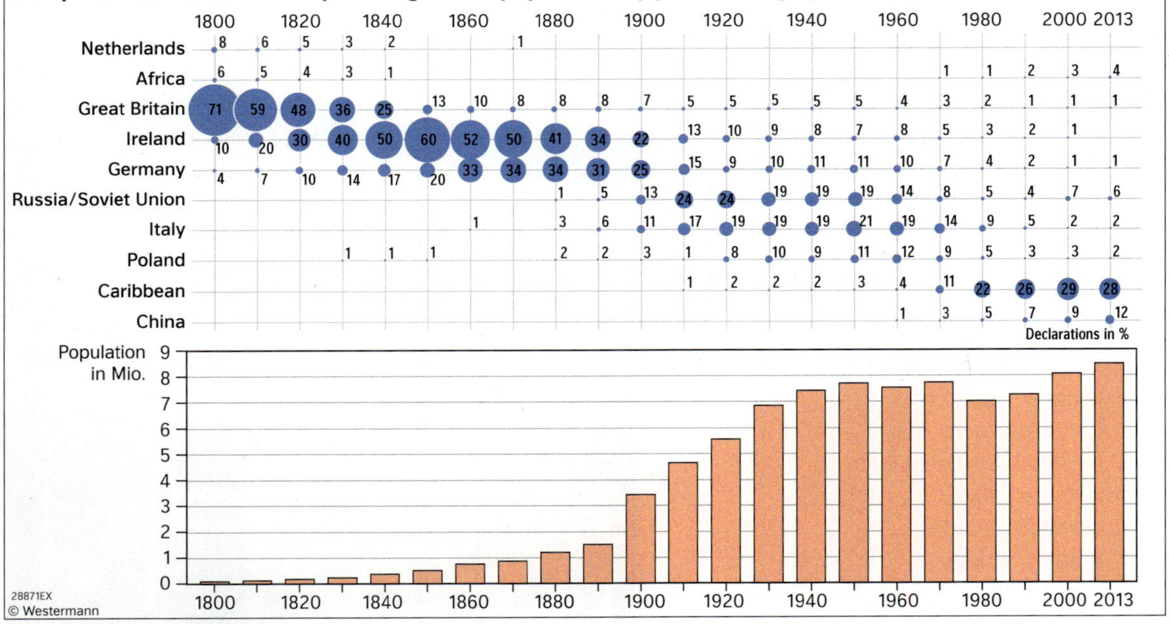

b) EXTRA Look up the following historical keywords and events. Using information from the graph, explain how they may have affected immigration to New York City.

New Amsterdam | the Irish potato famine | US Immigration Act of 1965 | World War I | World War II | German revolution of 1848/49 | Russian Revolution of 1917

c) Name possible consequences of these events and the different immigration waves on New York City.

LISTENING

Checklist

Before listening

Before you start listening to a recording, make sure that you are ready for what you are going to hear. Usually, you should have a fairly good idea of what kind of recording you can expect after following these steps:

✓ Read the instructions carefully. They often tell you what kind of listening text it is, e.g. a lecture, a call-in show, a podcast. This could give you a clue regarding
- the number of speakers you are likely to hear,
- the kind of language to expect (e.g. formal for a speech or informal for a call-in show),
- the variety of English (American/British/Australian/... English).

✓ In addition, the instructions as well as the overall context of the listening task hint at the topic of the listening text. You will probably have heard of the topic before or already worked on it in class. Therefore you may already know what the people are likely to talk about and may be familiar with a lot of the relevant vocabulary.

✓ Be careful: usually, only what is said in the listening text is relevant for the tasks, not what else you may know.

Example task

Listen to a speech by former US President Bill Clinton to students at Harvard University on the issue of racial inequality.

✓ kind of language: rather formal, use of stylistic devices
✓ variety of English: US English
✓ topic: different opportunities for people of different ethnic backgrounds

2

a) 1 Read the info box below.
2 Then listen to a short extract from an episode of the podcast "How to be American" commissioned by the Tenement Museum in New York. It deals with immigrants in New York City.
3 While listening, concentrate on the gist, i.e. the overall message of the extract.
4 Choose a, b, or c to complete this sentence. → SUPPORT D1, p. 169
The podcast host mainly focuses on
a the omnipresence of German culture in "Kleindeutschland".
b other immigrants' feelings about "Kleindeutschland".
c the size of the German community in "Kleindeutschland".

Webcode
You can find the audio file here:
DSW-73090-019

→ **S20:** How to listen/watch effectively, p. 23

Info

In a listening task, you may be asked to concentrate on different kinds of information:
- listening for gist: understanding the main idea
- listening for detail: finding out specific information
- inferring meaning: understanding what is said between the lines or how someone feels about something

b) Listen to the same extract again. This time focus on some of the details that are mentioned.
How could the presence of Germans be noticed in Kleindeutschland? Give two examples.
→ SUPPORT D2, p. 169

Webcode
You can find the audio file and questions here: DSW-73090-020

→ S20: How to listen/ watch effectively, p. 234

3

You will listen to another extract from the episode of the podcast "How to be American" on immigrant communities in New York City.
While listening, work on the tasks. → SUPPORT D3, pp. 169-170

1. In the middle of the 19th century, the inhabitants of Kleindeutschland
   a had a regional rather than a German identity.
   b had left their newly-founded nation state behind.
   c outnumbered those of any German city at the time.

2. The inhabitants of Kleindeutschland
   a had German ancestors.
   b shared their Christian faith.
   c constituted a large community.
3. John and Caroline Schneider's life together was special because
   a they were very young when they got married.
   b they started a saloon for the local German community.
   c it would have been an almost impossible match back in Europe.
4. Why were places like the Schneiders' saloon so important for the German community? Name two aspects.
5. Kleindeutschland disappeared when
   a it was officially renamed by the city.
   b fewer immigrants arrived from Germany.
   c its inhabitants left for other places in the US.
6. A wave of Caribbean immigrants
   a arrived about 100 years after the heyday of Kleindeutschland.
   b had advantages similar to those enjoyed by the German immigrants.
   c replaced Germans as the main group of immigrants to New York City.
7. What qualifies Christina Greer as an interview partner on Caribbean immigrants in New York City? Name two aspects.
8. One of Greer's key findings on various groups of immigrants is that they all
   a cultivated their original regional differences.
   b experienced divisions within their communities.
   c had the search for new business opportunities in common.
9. The main challenge for the community of Little Caribbean is that
   a it is more diverse than other black communities in the US.
   b there are tensions with Black Americans from the American South.
   c its special features are lost when seen as a part of Black America in general.

4

Webcode
You can find the audio file here: DSW-73090-021

→ S20: How to listen/ watch effectively, p. 234

a) Now listen to the beginning (0:00-0:50) of a radio feature about languages spoken in New York City to answer the question below using key words. You will have to listen for details.

   What is the reason for the enormous linguistic diversity of New York City?

b) Listen to the same extract again. This time you are asked to infer meaning, i.e. to listen "between the lines". Choose the correct answer. → SUPPORT D4, p. 170

   Why does Mark Turin, the reporter, refer to the expanse of New York City?
   a to raise doubts about the term "most linguistically diverse city"
   b to emphasize the exceptional nature of the language situation there
   c to express his surprise about the number of languages spoken there

5

Listen to a longer extract (1:25-4:52) from Mark Turin's report on New York City's languages and complete the grid. You need not write complete sentences. Name only one aspect each. → SUPPORT D5, p. 170

Annotations
Pidgin English = English mixed with words from other languages
Yiddish = a language based on German which was originally spoken by Jews in central and eastern Europe and has survived in some Jewish communities around the world

Webcode
You can find the audio file here: DSW-73090-022

→ **S20:** How to listen/watch effectively, p. 234

Webcode
You can download the grid here: DSW-73090-023

1	what is special about areas along subway line 7			
2	reason for choosing Queens as the starting point for the trip			
3	reason why Hoong Yee Lee Krakauer's family is in the US			
4	what confuses some shopowners when they meet Mrs Krakauer			
5	Complete the table with the languages Mrs Krakauer learnt as a small child and who she learnt them from.	**languages** **who she learnt them from**		
6	Asians' expectation connected with subway line 7			
7	what Mrs Krakauer associates with the different stops			
8	whom her organization contacted in 1991 about line 7			
9	Choose the correct answer. How does Mrs Krakauer see subway line 7? a as a symbol of immigrants' success b as an object of intensive academic study c as a metaphor for bringing ethnicities together			

POST-LISTENING

6

Read an article from gothamist.com, a news website run by New York Public Radio. Describe how experts try to save languages from extinction and why New York City is a good place to start.

→ **S9:** How to structure a text, p. 212

Dazzling Map Shows NYC's Incredible Linguistic Diversity

Christopher Robbins, 3 December 2019

Seke is a language spoken in just a handful of towns in Nepal – worldwide, there are fewer than 700 people who speak it. More than 100 of those people live in Brooklyn and Queens, according to the Endangered Language Alliance, a group that seeks to document and preserve smaller, minority, and Indigenous languages across New York City. Seke is one of 637 languages and dialects the ELA has mapped in roughly 1,000 locations across the five boroughs and New Jersey – more than three times the number represented in the census.

"Over 10 years ELA has built a network of linguists, community leaders, language activists, speakers, students, and just regular New Yorkers who either speak these languages or know people who do – so every point on the map was based on a conversation with someone knowledgeable about a community," said Ross Perlin, ELA's co-director.

The map [...] displays where there are languages spoken by large swaths of the neighborhood, and those that are spoken by just a few people. Around 40 percent of the languages represented are from Asia, 27 percent are from Africa, 18 percent from Europe, 14 percent from the Americas, and the remainder come from Oceania and the Pacific.

Perlin said that the map is a "first step" in helping to preserve endangered dialects and languages.

Practice Listening

PRE-LISTENING

1

a) New York City can be a rather expensive tourist destination. Collect ideas on how to save money on a trip.

b) Watch a video with advice on how to visit New York City on a budget.
  - Compare the advice to your ideas.
  - Choose the three tips that seem most promising to you.

c) In class, discuss which of the tips you would like to put to the test.

Webcode
You can find the video here: DSW-73090-024

LISTENING

Webcode
You can find the audio file and questions here: DSW-73090-025

2

Listen to a radio report about a multimedia exhibition at the Museum of the City of New York. Choose the correct answers. There is only one correct answer for each question.

1. According to the introduction, the main focus of the multimedia exhibition is on ...
   a the visual impression of New York sights.
   b the haptic impression of New York buildings.
   c the acoustic impression of places in New York.

2. Lidize Mora considers Grand Central Terminal to be ...
   a a place too busy with visitors.
   b a location fit for family celebrations.
   c a building she associates with a fairy tale.

3. Mora admires ...
   a the painted sky high above her.
   b the metal ornaments used for the handrails.
   c the special kind of stone the staircase is made of.

4. Professor Karen Van Lengen claims that by just using one's ears one ...
   a forgets about one's visual impressions.
   b perceives previously unnoticed sounds.
   c starts to move around the place in one's mind.

5. The sounds of Grand Central make Van Lengen ...
   a think of a stormy coast.
   b experience a sense of peace.
   c feel the building revolve around her.

6. Van Lengen's intention is to draw people's attention to ...
   a the power of one's senses.
   b the activities that define these sites.
   c the architectural beauty of buildings.

7. The New York Public Library is represented by sounds of people ...
   a moving objects for cleaning.
   b taking a seat when studying.
   c taking books from wooden shelves.

8. At the Rockefeller Center, Van Langen is reminded of ...
   a the sounds of the Industrial Revolution.
   b the history of the family the place is named after.
   c further places she would like to cover for her project.

9. Now think of the report as a whole: The exhibition is presented as ...
   a bizarre.
   b inspiring.
   c amusing.

3 WB pp. 38-39

In 2021, the "little sister" of the Statue of Liberty was exhibited in New York City. Listen to a radio report about this event and write down the answers. You don't need to write complete sentences. Name only one aspect for each question unless you are asked to name more.

Webcode
You can find the audio file here: DSW-73090-026

→ S20: How to listen/watch effectively, p. 234

1 What is the occasion for bringing the statues together?
2 In what ways do the two statues differ? Name two aspects.
3 What is the ultimate destination of the little sister?
4 What do the statues stand for apart from liberty? Name two aspects.
5 Why does a protester quote from a poem?
6 What is the reason behind the protest?
7 What do the days of the unveiling of the original Statue of Liberty and of her little sister have in common?
8 What helps to give the unveiling outside the meeting place a festive atmosphere?

POST-LISTENING

4 → S17: How to work on cartoons, p. 231

Choose one of these cartoons. Describe, analyse and comment on what the cartoon reveals about life in New York City. Use what you have learned about the city on this double page.

"And coming up on the right is another area ruined by the likes of you."

Webcode

You can listen to the song here: DSW-73090-064

Info

The full name of the song is "Empire State of Mind (Part II) Broken Down". It is a solo and "broken down", i.e. more basic, version of the original song "Empire State of Mind" by Alicia Keys and Jay-Z.

New York is not America

1 WB p. 40/1

a) One of New York-born singer Alicia Keys' songs is called "Empire State of Mind". Speculate why she might have chosen this title for a song about her hometown. → SUPPORT D6, p. 170

b) Listen to the song. Take notes on what impression of New York City and New Yorkers is conveyed by the song – both by the lyrics and the music.

Language support

Talking about music

Adjectives catchy | gloomy | happy | sad | upbeat | fast | slow | dreamy | dramatic | melodious | funky | old-fashioned | uplifting | groovy | monotonous | soothing | melancholy

Nouns tempo/pace | rhythm | beat | melody/tune | sound | words/lyrics

Verbs/phrases to make you feel ... | to evoke feelings/thoughts of ... | to be marked by a change in ... | to convey a sense of ... | to remind one of ... | to express what it means to ... | to combine ... with ...

c) Read the lyrics of the song and analyse how New York and New Yorkers are presented. → SUPPORT D7, p. 171

d) Briefly explain the "Empire State of mind" as presented in the song.

Grew up in a town
That is famous as a place of movie scenes
Noise is always loud, there are sirens all around
And the streets are mean

If I could make it here
I could make it anywhere, that's what they say
Seein' my face in lights
Or my name in marquees[1] found down on Broadway

Even if it ain't all it seems, I got a pocketful of dreams

Baby, I'm from New York
Concrete jungle where dreams are made of
There's nothing you can't do
Now you're in New York
These streets will make you feel brand new
Big lights will inspire you
Hear it for New York, New York, New York

On the avenue, there ain't never a curfew
Ladies work so hard
Such a meltin' pot, on the corner sellin' rock[2]
Preachers pray to God
Hail a gypsy cab[3] takes me down
From Harlem to the Brooklyn Bridge
Someone sleeps tonight with a hunger
For more than an empty fridge

I'm gonna make it by any means, I got a
pocketful of dreams

One hand in the air for the big city
Street lights, big dreams, all looking pretty
No place in the world that can compare
Put your lighters in the air
Everybody say yeah, yeah, yeah

Annotations

[1] **marquee** (*AE*) = display advertising a show, film etc. above the entrance to a theatre, cinema or other venue

[2] **rock** (*AE, infml*) = drugs

[3] **gypsy cab** (*AE, infml*) = illegal taxi

2 WB p. 40/2, p. 41/3

Read the article on pages 89-90, written by Remington Write, who grew up in a small town in Ohio. Outline what makes New Yorkers different from people elsewhere in the US according to her.

How New York City is not an American city

A few reasons why NYC isn't America

Remington Write, 18 March 2019

[...] It was my good luck that there is an island off the coast of America where the weirdos can still walk freely and be ignored. Here are some of the reasons I've found New York City not to be an American city:

We don't expect everyone to speak English

Remember the kerfuffle[1] that happened in Philadelphia when some smart guy put a sign on his cheese steak emporium[2] instructing customers to place their orders in English? Yeah. That's not going to happen here.

Some French tourists were having trouble understanding why they couldn't pay the bus fare with their dollar bills (crazy throwback[3] to the 60's I guess but the buses here only take coins or Metrocards[4]). I wasn't at all surprised when several passengers who spoke French went up to help.

51 percent of New Yorkers speak only English at home and it's estimated that up to 800 different languages are spoken in the five boroughs. And we all just roll with[5] that. And I'm not talking about only those of us poor boneheads[6] who only speak English; for the most part on a daily basis people manage to communicate with each other and get stuff done regardless of what language each brings to the table[7].

We mind our business

[...] We don't care if you're crying in public, fighting in public, making out in public, asking for money in public, practicing your scales[8] in public, or posing for your latest Instagram masterpiece in public. Just don't get in our way. We're in a hurry.

We move fast

We're not unfriendly and, if we have the time, we're happy to direct confused tourists to the right train. But speak up quick and be clear.

The energy here is intoxicating[9] and infectious[10]. Even when I'm not in a hurry here I'm in a hurry. Generally, however, I'm in a hurry. So are you and so is everyone else who, by God, is going to fit into this subway car. We get that and most of us remember to pass on the left and that the right lane is for the slower folks or those with walking casts[11] (it happens).

We don't expect anyone to do it the way we do it

Radical self-expression rules in New York City. Pimp that ride[12] just the way you like it and drive with pride, baby.

It does take a certain authority to pull it off, but people can and do wear whatever the hell they feel like wearing ... for the most part. Unfortunately homophobia, misogyny, and plain old stick-in-the-mud-ness[13] aren't exclusively American traits.

And this ability to transcend societal expectations in the matter of dress, while certainly pioneered by transgender people, is seen on every street in Manhattan at least daily. Cisgendered men in dresses, mini-skirts, and mink stoles[14] with a dashing lapel pin[15] holding it on the shoulder. Goth, total fashion plate[16], ethnic of every description, prints-with-plaid[17] (I don't understand either), tuxedos[18] in the afternoon, and a coat made out of shredded white garbage bags which float most becomingly[19].

We define what success means to each of us

It's true that I'm currently a paid up member[20] of the rat race[21] with a daily office awaiting me and great health care insurance. Before I get too comfy[22] here, though, let's remember that the position is being eliminated in six months (nice of them not to bother mentioning that in the job offer but that's how it goes in the 21st century). That's a drag[23] but here I know I can make a living in a hundred different ways that don't include a HR department[24] and corporate

Annotations

1 **kerfuffle** (*infml*) = a lot of talk or agitation about sth unimportant
2 **emporium** = place where sth is sold
3 **throwback** = sth that seems to belong to an earlier period of time
4 **Metrocard** = plastic card used as a means of payment on public transport in New York
5 to **roll with it/that** (*infml*) = to be OK with things that are changing
6 **bonehead** (*infml*) = idiot
7 to **bring** sth **to the table** = to contribute sth
8 **scale** = *Tonleiter*
9 **intoxicating** = very exciting
10 **infectious** = easily passed on, contagious
11 **cast** = *Gips*
12 to **pimp a ride** (*AE, infml*) = to restore a car, often in a lavish way
13 **stick-in-the-mud-ness** (*infml*) = resisting change
14 **mink stole** = the fur of a small animal worn around the shoulders
15 **lapel pin** = *here:* metal pin worn on a jacket as a decoration
16 **fashion plate** = sb who is very much into fashion
17 **plaid** = piece of cloth with a checked pattern of Scottish origin
18 **tuxedo** = formal suit
19 **becoming** = looking really good, suitable
20 **paid up member** = member who pays a regular fee
21 **rat race** = *Hamsterrad*
22 **comfy** = comfortable
23 **a drag** = *here:* annoying
24 **HR** (human resources) **department** = *Personalabteilung*

Annotations

[25] **compliance** = sticking to the rules

[26] to **not bat an eye** = *nicht mit der Wimper zucken*

[27] to **cobble together** = to piece together, take a little of this and a little of that

[28] **Founding Property Owners** = reference to the so-called Founding Fathers, e.g. George Washington and Thomas Jefferson

compliance[25] learning modules. While it's true that remote work and independent contracting are becoming the norm across more and more of the country here it's been the norm for so long that no one bats an eye[26].

In the years I cobbled together[27] my living with two part time on site jobs and another remote position no one ever asked me when I was going to get a real job (see above for how we mind our own business here).

The Take Away

If New York City isn't America then it should be. I mean that the daily virtues of acceptance, tolerance, and making room for everyone would seem to be what Jefferson and the rest of the Founding Property Owners[28] had in mind and, ideally, should still be in play throughout the country. That would make America exceptional.

3 Language awareness WB p. 41/4

→ **S13:** Checklist: Analysis – non-fictional texts, p. 222

Analyse how the author's use of language conveys her attitude towards New York City.

→ SUPPORT D8, p. 171

4 WB p. 41/5

→ **S6:** How to write an argumentative text, p. 206

"It was my good luck that there is an island off the coast of America where the weirdos can still walk freely and be ignored." (ll. 1-3)

Considering Write's article and what you have learnt about New York City, discuss whether this city would be your place of choice if you had the chance to spend a gap year in the US.

→ GRAMMAR G2, p. 191

9/11 and New York

1

→ **S15:** How to describe pictures, p. 226

Look at the photos. They were taken after the terrorist attacks on the World Trade Center in New York on 11 September 2001. Talk about what the photos reveal about the attacks and their consequences.

Webcode

You can find the video here: DSW-73090-027

→ **S20:** How to listen/watch effectively, p. 234

2

To find out more about the background to the terrorist attacks of 11 September 2001 (often referred to as 9/11), perpetrated by Islamist terrorist group Al-Qaeda, watch the video and note down the most important aspects of what happened.

3

Read the prologue of Julie Buxbaum's 2019 novel *Hope and Other Punch Lines* about Abbi Hope Goldstein, who survived the 9/11 terrorist attacks when she was a baby. Now a young woman, she tries to understand the impact 9/11 has had on her and other people's lives. Examine how she expresses that 9/11 was a life-changing event. → SUPPORT D9, p. 172

> Tuesday, the least descriptive day of the week. Neither beginning nor end, not even the sad, saggy middle. A nothing day. No. A before. Picture a blue sky. A beat, to breathe it in. All that blue. When you let out your last clean breath, you look up. And the world splits itself in two.

4

a) Read an extract from the first chapter of *Hope and Other Punch Lines*. State the reasons why Abbi has become famous.
b) Outline her plans for the summer holidays.
c) Analyse how Abbi feels about 9/11 and its effects on her life. → SUPPORT D10, p. 172

→ **S9:** How to structure a text, p. 212

→ **S12:** Checklist: Analysis – prose, p. 220

Hope and Other Punch Lines

by Julie Buxbaum

Extract 1

I've long outgrown fairy tales, but I still have trouble with the concept of time. Maybe it's because my own life has always been an exception to the rule: I lived once when I was supposed to die. And so this story, the one I'm telling you now, has two distinct beginnings. There's the one that starts with, and feel free to groan[1], a once upon a time. Or at least, it feels that way to me because I don't remember it happening, and yet, once upon a time, a click of the camera changed the entire trajectory[2] of my life. I know exactly the when: Tuesday, September 11, 2001, approximately 9:59 a.m. The morning of my first birthday. In the photograph, the one that turned me from Abbi Hope Goldstein into The Baby Hope, I'm being whisked away[3] to safety by Connie Kramer, one of the women who worked at the day-care center in the World Trade Center complex. I'm wearing a paper crown and holding a red balloon, and behind me the first tower is collapsing. An AP[4] photographer managed to capture the dust-filled moment, though I have no idea how. You've probably seen the picture. It's everywhere. You can find it hanging on living room walls and in dorms[5] and nursing homes and museums and even printed on T-shirts and tote bags[6]. I kid you not, I once saw baby me on a hat at Six Flags[7]. Like in an actual fairy tale, there are some sad parts to this story, which are an unfortunate narrative necessity. Let's get those out of the way as quickly as possible. Connie died seventy-five days ago. Her diagnosis was ovarian cancer[8]. Stage IV. Which for reasons I don't know—maybe because it's serious—is written with Roman numerals. She was only forty-six. XLVI.

Connie was thirty on September 11, 2001. In my house we all knew that Connie really died of 9/11 syndrome, the catchall[9] diagnosis for the group of health problems caused by the exposure to toxic chemicals in the air at Ground Zero. For some survivors, it starts with inflammation[10] of the lungs. For others, like Connie, it's mutations and tumors, the assault of that day being retold on the cellular level. On September 11, 2001, twenty-four thousand gallons[11] of jet fuel blew up. Those of us there breathed in a chemical bouquet that included crystalline silica[12] (which = bad), asbestos[13], carbon monoxide[14], hydrogen sulfide[15] (or "sewer gas"), and God only knows what else. No. We do know what else: human ash and human bone. Hair and teeth and nails and dreams. Before things get any more morbid, let me share an important bit of happily-ever-after. Not only did I survive on 9/11 (and get almost sixteen bonus years so far), but somehow, defying all statistical odds, so did my parents. My mom and dad both worked in One World Trade (the North

Annotations

1 to **groan** = to make a certain sound because you are unhappy or in pain
2 **trajectory** = the curving line in which an object moves through the air
3 to **whisk sb away** = to move sb away quickly
4 **AP** = Associated Press, a major news agency
5 **dorm** = dormitory, a room in which several people sleep
6 **tote bag** (*AE*) = small bag, e.g. for shopping
7 **Six Flags** = a theme or amusement park
8 **ovarian cancer** = *Eierstockkrebs*
9 **catchall** = vague and therefore covering several things
10 **inflammation** = *Entzündung*
11 **gallon** = 3.78 litres
12 **crystalline silica** = a chemical which can cause cancer
13 **asbestos** = *Asbest*
14 **carbon monoxide** = *Kohlenstoffmonoxid*
15 **hydrogen sulfide** = a highly toxic gas

Tower), on floors 101 and 105, respectively, when no one survived above the 91st floor. Ninety-five percent of the people in the company they worked for got wiped out. Had they been at their desks like they were supposed to be, I would be an orphan. Instead, when the planes hit, my parents were sipping Frappuccinos three blocks away at a ground-floor Starbucks, which is the best advertisement for dessert disguised as coffee I've ever heard. In 2001, my parents went to fifty-three funerals in one month. They bought condolence cards in bulk from Costco[16]. And then they went back for more. We live in Oakdale, New Jersey, which is the town outside New York City that had the highest number of 9/11 casualties, so the loss was everywhere: colleagues, neighbors, friends. Five kids from my class alone lost a parent on the same day, including my former best friend, Cat. Sixteen years later, Oakdale High is this weird hybrid of those who don't really care about September 11 and those whose whole lives were shaped by it. For the former, the event is just another chapter in our history books, like Pearl Harbor or the Vietnam War or landlines[17]. For the latter, it's forever part of our peripheral vision. We may not remember, but we can never forget. That's the first beginning, which I tell you only because otherwise the rest won't make any sense. To meet Abbi Hope Goldstein is to meet Baby Hope, and to understand that in my town, at least, I get pointed at – people know my name even though we've never met – and occasionally, someone will corner me in a supermarket line while my hands are full of deodorant and hummus and tell me where they were that morning, like it's something I want to know about them. The absolute worst is when I make strangers cry.

But as promised, there's a second beginning. Right here, right now, in a moment of rare triumph, the first days of summer vacation. Sunday night, nine p.m.: me, age sixteen, rocking out alone in my bedroom. I belt[18] a girl-power ballad into a makeshift microphone, aka a dry shampoo bottle, because I can't find my brush. Shimmy. Shimmy. Hair flip. Shimmy. Tomorrow I start as a counselor for four-year-olds at Knight's Day Camp, two towns away. When I visited for the interview, there were lush green lawns and an old-fashioned red barn and something they called the "plake," which is a hybrid pool/lake. We'll have pajama day and a bouncy castle water slide and a Color War. Also arts and crafts and potato-sack races and even a Dance Dance Revolution activity block. Knight's is a happy place, by far the happiest place I could find in the tri-state area[19], and believe me, I looked. Even went as far as to Google "happy places in New Jersey." Now I get to go there eight hours a day five days a week, and for two months, not a single person will look at me and see Baby Hope. Time is still confusing and slippery. Based on some unexpected medical developments, there's a good chance I'm running out of it. But for the next blissful eight weeks, I am going to be just Abbi Goldstein. I'll get to make little kids laugh and not a single stranger cry.

Annotations
[16] **Costco** = a big warehouse
[17] **landline** = non-mobile telephone
[18] **to belt** = to shout or sing loudly
[19] **tri-state area** = the New York metropolitan area, covering parts of the states New York, New Jersey and Connecticut

5

At summer camp, Abbi meets Noah, whose family's life has also been affected by 9/11. Abbi and Noah reflect on ways in which the memories of 9/11 are kept alive.

a) Concentrate either on Noah's (Extract 2) or Abbi's experiences (Extract 3). Take notes on what form of commemoration is presented in your extract and on how Abbi or Noah feels about it. → SUPPORT D11, p. 172

b) **Group work** Form mixed groups with experts on both Abbi and Noah.
- Present your extracts to each other with the help of your notes from a).
- Compare Abbi and Noah's attitudes.

c) EXTRA Analyse how Abbi's and Noah's attitudes towards remembering 9/11 are conveyed. Consider the choice of words and stylistic devices.

→ **S12:** Checklist: Analysis – prose, p. 220

Extract 2: Noah

Noah remembers a visit to the 9/11 Memorial and Museum with his friend Jack.

A few years ago, I dragged Jack on a research mission to the 9/11 Memorial and Museum, which turned out to be, at least for me, the weirdest weirdest freaking place on earth. It's free for family members of the victims. Not that anyone should have to pay. Obviously they shouldn't. But why would anyone want to go? Maybe one day when I'm older and possibly wiser, I'll find the museum cathartic[1] or beautiful or respectfully commemorative, and maybe I'll even be grateful for its existence. But at the moment, it pisses me off[2]. I can't understand why anyone would want to see the place where the most horrific thing you can imagine happening actually happened. Worse, why would you want that turned into a tourist attraction? Do some people think, While we're here, let's make sure to buy a commemorative hat from the gift shop. I've always wanted to turn a mass tragedy into a material possession! I'm pretty sure that's not what we mean by Never forget.

There's this whole special area reserved for VIPs, where you stand in the Reflection Room and view the remains repository. Those are literally the words they use, Reflection Room and remains repository, as if its patrons[3] are kindergarteners or Kardashians and take comfort in alliteration. This is an underground lookout point – a window onto a cavernous[4] room filled with mood-lit[5] drawers. A gold star to anyone who can guess what's in those nifty[6] cabinets. Yup, those lucky people who were so incinerated[7] there aren't even DNA traces left. That's what you're supposed to reflect on. In your free time. By choice. They provide complimentary tissues. Unidentified remains. Here's the strangest part of all: the museum has its own Twitter feed. A fucking Twitter feed. Of course it's about the most depressing shit imaginable. They don't even try to be funny.

Annotations
1 **cathartic** = healing in a psychological sense by confronting repressed emotions or memories
2 to **piss** sb **off** (*infml*) = to annoy sb extremely
3 **patron** = visitor
4 **cavernous** = like a cave
5 **mood-lit** = with low lighting
6 **nifty** (*infml*) = clever, elegant
7 to **incinerate** = to set on fire

Extract 3: Abbi

Abbi and her mother are on a walk through Oakdale, a New Jersey suburb. Cat is Abbi's friend.

We don't say anything until we pass the town's 9/11 memorial garden, which is a beautiful patch of green right next to the train station. Cat's father's name is engraved on the big slab of stone in the center of the courtyard, one of many, though when Cat talks about her dad now, she means Stewart, her stepfather.

Every year, on the anniversary of 9/11, my parents and I visit the monument and say the names of the lost out loud. We make two offerings to the Gods of Survivor's Guilt. One, a beautiful floral bouquet[1] so heavy that we have to drive the half mile from our house to deliver it. And two, I don't have – and have never had – a birthday party. Not when I was little and dreamed of having Spider-Man paint my face in our backyard, like Cat did. Not for the celebration of my bat mitzvah[2]. These are tiny sacrifices. Actually, they're not sacrifices at all. These are the minor material things we are lucky to be able to offer up in thanks for being alive.

Don't play even your tiniest violin for us. We don't deserve it. Because here is our shameful truth: The rest of the year? On almost-perfect nights like this? We stare straight ahead so we don't have to look at the monument. We do not take even a moment to stop and read the names in the quiet of our own minds. We go on like it never happened.

Annotations
1 **floral bouquet** = *Blumenstrauß*
2 **bat mitzvah** = Jewish ceremony celebrating a girl's entry into the religious community as a full member at the age of 12

6

Group work Abbi and Noah have been personally affected by 9/11 and express their views on how 9/11 is remembered. Discuss how a catastrophe, e.g. 9/11, an environmental disaster or the COVID-19 pandemic, as well as its victims, should be remembered.

→ **S6:** How to write an argumentative text, p. 206

New York – social disparities

1

Usually the headline and the subheading of an article already give the reader an idea of the author's attitude and the problem they are going to deal with. For the article below, point out which keywords are essential in this respect and explain what effect is created.

2

→ **S8:** How to improve your text, p. 209

a) Read the article and describe the socio-economic disparities the author presents.
b) Outline the process the author criticizes.

New York, New York, What a Less than Wonderful Town

Any city – any society – that lets the rich keep as much as they can grab is asking for big-time trouble.

Sam Pizzigati, 20 June 2018

The ultimate real-life test of "trickle down[1]" – the notion that we all prosper when the rich get richer – may well be New York. The Big Apple, after all, certainly abounds in[2] rich getting richer. No city in the world now hosts more of humanity's super rich.

Researchers at Wealth-X last month put the New York billionaire total at 103, ten more than Hong Kong. Top 1 percenters[3] in New York overall are now taking in over 40 percent of the city's income, about double the top 1 percent's income share nationally in the United States.

Numbers like these don't happen by accident. Local and state officials in New York have worked diligently for decades to make their city as attractive as possible to the ten-digit set[4].

"If we could get every billionaire around the world to move here," as then mayor of New York Michael Bloomberg, himself a billionaire, noted in 2013, "it would be a godsend."

At that mission, Bloomberg and his pals[5] would prove remarkably successful. The fantastically rich physically dominate New York as never before. Luxury residential towers over 75 stories tall now look down upon midtown Manhattan, casting shadows that darken ever wider swathes[6] of Central Park.

Fancy restaurants abound throughout Manhattan and beyond. Broadway is booming. Millions of tourists are trampling on streets free from grit[7] and grime[8]. New York, the city's most ardent cheerleaders proclaim, has never been a better place.

Never been a better place, counters long-time New York resident and writer Kevin Baker, only if you're talking about the rich.

[...] The poor, of course, have life the hardest in the new New York, and the city has many more of them. One in five New Yorkers – 19.6 percent – currently rate as officially poor. Back in 1970, that rate stood at 11.5 percent.

The ranks of the near-poor have swelled as well. Almost half the city lives a precarious existence, "just one paycheck away," writes Baker, "from disaster."

Most of the rest of New York's 8.6 million people strain to maintain a decent middle-class existence. The city is losing its "most treasured amenities," adds Baker's Harper's[9] analysis, those aspects of life most "essential to its middle-class character."

"Look at almost any public service or space in New York," he advises, "and you will see that it has been diminished, degraded[10], appropriated[11]."

[...] Some parks have simply disappeared. The new Yankee[12] Stadium sits on what had been, notes Baker, "two beloved public parks." Local, state, and federal officials graced[13] the owners of the Yankees with $1.2 billion in subsidies. The owners graced the city back with a ballpark that has 9,000

Annotations
1 to **trickle down** = for a liquid to flow down drop by drop
2 to **abound in** = to be rich in, to have a lot of
3 **top 1 percenters** = the richest one percent of the population or the one percent with the highest incomes
4 **ten-digit set** = people with an income or a wealth of at least one billion $ (ten digits)
5 **pal** = friend
6 **swathe** = large piece of land
7 **grit** = very small stones
8 **grime** = dirt
9 **Harper's Magazine** = a monthly publication
10 to **degrade** = to decrease the value of sth
11 to **appropriate** = to take into possession
12 **New York Yankees** = baseball team from the Bronx
13 to **grace** = to honour

fewer seats for the general public and 37 more luxury suites for the deep-pocket set[14]. For these deep pockets, New York has become a dazzling cornucopia of consumption options, with posh shops full of luxuries of every description. For those of more pedestrian means, the "warrens[15] of little shops and businesses" that used to sustain – and enliven – daily life are vanishing in one neighborhood after another. […]

Baker tells the story of a proprietor of one of New York's vanished small businesses. She had been paying $7,000 a month to rent the space for her laundromat[16]. The landlord upped that to $21,000.

Back in the mid-20th century days of Abbott and Costello[17], your landlord lived in your neighborhood. Today's New York landlord will more likely be a private equity empire, a lavishly financed international firm, […] "highly incentivized[18]" to replace low-rent tenants with more lucrative lessees[19]. The resulting high rents are driving away neighborhood-based commerce.

Driving people away, too. Between 2014 and 2017, rents for vacant apartments in New York rose 30 percent, about three times faster than the typical incomes of renting families. What happens when arithmetic like this happens? Homelessness happens. New York's Department of Homeless Services now on average shelters 60,000 people per night.

Annotations

14 **deep-pocket set** = people with deep pockets, meaning a lot of money
15 **warren** = *Gewirr*
16 **laundromat** = shop in which one can wash their clothes
17 **Abbott and Costello** popular duo of comedians in radio and TV shows of the 1940s and 1950s
18 to **incentivize** = to influence sb's actions by promising them sth if they act a certain way
19 **lessee** = sb who pays rent

3 Language awareness

Study how the author highlights his criticism.

a) Analyse his choice of words in ll. 1-37 and explain the effect on the reader. **→ SUPPORT D12, p. 173**

b) Examine the stylistic devices and rhetorical strategies the author uses to convince his readers. **→ SUPPORT D13, p. 174**

4

Decide which of these photos illustrates the topic of the article best. Explain your choice by referring to the image and to how it relates to the text. **→ SUPPORT D14, p. 174**

5 WB pp. 42-43

Write a text for the comment section of the online article like the one on the right.

a) First read the example and identify
- details that are based on information from the article
- phrases that are adopted from the article
- the presentation of a personal view

b) Now read the article again and collect phrases the author uses to refer to the rich and the poor. You can use them in your comment later.

c) Choose one of the roles from the box and imagine how this person would react to the information presented in the article. Write their comment. **→ SUPPORT D15, p. 175**

It is a relief that for once the "less than wonderful" side of New York City gets a mention. Many parts of the city are turning into the glitziest luxury places ever, but even if this NYC is highly attractive to the ten-digit set and to tourists from around the world, it is losing its spaces for the ordinary people. For me it's alarming to see that families find it hard to cope with rising rents, that more and more places once open to the public are privatized and that fees for pastime activities that used to be for free are forever increasing.

the owner of a little shop | the parent of two kids | a young adult about to finish school | a long-time Yankee fan | a real estate agent | a tourist board official | a young affluent owner of an apartment

The High Line

1

Urban renewal is important to adapt cities to the changing demands of the people who live and work there. But in densely built-up areas, space is a problem. An impressive example of how urban renewal can bring new life to a run-down and neglected neighbourhood can be found in Lower Manhattan: the High Line. Read about the history of the High Line and match the highlighted words to the definitions in the box.

in very poor condition due to disuse | to tear down | to gradually lose its quality | to use sth instead of sth else | goods that are transported by train or truck | to keep sth from being destroyed | with many different aspects | self-employed | people who walk the streets | high above street level

Joshua David and Robert Hammond together with actor Edward Norton (left)

The High Line looks back on a varied history. It was built in the meat-packing district on the lower westside of Manhattan to replace the original street level tracks of freight trains that had brought food into town since the 1850s. Those trains, running on street level, were especially dangerous for pedestrians. Until 1910 more than 540 people had been killed. In the 1920s, guards on horseback were hired to ride in front of trains to warn pedestrians, but accidents still occurred so that 10th Avenue was known as Death Avenue. So an elevated railroad was planned and in 1934 the first trains ran on the High Line.
However, the trains on the elevated tracks gradually lost their importance, as transport was increasingly taken over by trucks. In the 1960s parts of the High Line were demolished while the remaining part fell into decline. After the last train ran in 1980, the line was closed and the area became derelict.
In the 1990s, the remaining parts of the elevated railroad were meant to be demolished. But artist Robert Hammond and freelance writer Joshua David, who both lived in the area, decided they wanted to save the High Line from being torn down. So in 1999 they formed *Friends of the High Line*, a non-profit organization dedicated to preserving and developing the High Line. They were successful and in 2009 the first part of the High Line opened as a public park.

2

Ten years after the opening of the High Line it was time for an assessment.

→ **S9:** How to structure a text, p. 212

→ **S13:** Checklist: Analysis – non-fictional texts, p. 222

a) Read the article and describe the positive and negative aspects that are mentioned.
b) Language awareness Collect words and phrases the author uses to present the positive and negative sides of the new cityscape.
c) Language awareness Analyse the images used in the highlighted paragraph, explain their connotations and the criticism involved. → SUPPORT D16, p. 175
d) The High Line has become a masterplan for other cities. Explain what Kevin Dow, who is in charge of a similar project in Philadelphia, wants to achieve and which mistakes he wants to avoid.

New York's High Line park marks 10 years of transformation

New York's High Line has opened its final piece just days before the 10th anniversary of the opening of the first section on June 9, 2009.

Karen Matthews, Associated Press, 9 June 2019

When the High Line park opened in New York City, then-Mayor Michael Bloomberg predicted the transformation of the abandoned, elevated freight line into an artsy[1] public promenade would be "an extraordinary gift to our city's future."

A decade later, there's no question the High Line has been a resounding success as an engine for tourism and neighborhood revitalization.

An estimated 8 million annual visitors now visit the park, which threads 1.5 miles (2.4 kilometers) through a transformed part of Manhattan. Once a land of industrial buildings, parking lots and auto repair businesses, the neighborhood is now anchored[2] at one end by the dazzling new home of the Whitney Museum of American Art and at the other by Hudson Yards, a $25 billion development of skyscrapers, shops and a performing arts center.

But there's handwringing[3] about whether the High Line is a victim of its own success.

In the beginning, the park was remarkable for its ability to lift visitors above the streetscape[4] to a perch[5] with unique vistas[6] over mostly low-rise rooftops. It was a park in the sky. Now, it's nestled in[7] a canyon of tall, luxury condominium[8] buildings that have sprouted[9] along its sides. Still cool, but different, and often choked with out-of-town visitors.

And some critics blame the High Line for the neighborhood's hyper-gentrification.

"When I first used to go up there I was pretty wowed by[10] it," said Alex Reichl, a Queens College political science professor [...]. "But it started to feel to me more and more that it was such an exclusive space and so lacking in the diversity that New York is known for. To me, it's always been kind of a missed opportunity."

Robert Hammond, who co-founded the High Line with Joshua David and serves as the executive director of the nonprofit that

manages the park in partnership with the city, said it deserves neither all the credit nor all the blame for the ultra-luxury buildings now blocking some of its views.

"The High Line becomes a lightning rod[11] for love and hate," he said. "This neighborhood was going to change. It was a manufacturing neighborhood. It was going to be rezoned[12]." The net effect of the park, he said, has been incredibly positive. [...]

Julie Bauer, who bought an apartment a block east of the High Line shortly before it opened, said the area has changed dramatically.

"Tenth Avenue was always parking lots because everyone would come over from Jersey or wherever, come through the tunnel, park their car and then go do their business," she said. "And then the parking lots and garages all suddenly started getting converted to apartment buildings and galleries and things like that." [...]

The High Line's success has inspired dozens of efforts to turn abandoned pieces of infrastructure into parks, including about a dozen in the United States and Canada that are part of the High Line Network, set up by Hammond in part to help other projects navigate gentrification issues.

Kevin Dow, the executive director of Friends of the Rail Park in Philadelphia, said leaders of the Rail Park – whose first section opened last year – hope to create opportunities for development without alienating longtime residents or forcing them out.

"What we want to be able to do is engage deeply with our current community in a way that we retain that cultural fabric while adapting to the changing demographics that are coming in," Dow said.

Annotations

1 **artsy** (*infml*) = connected with the arts and culture
2 to **be anchored** = to be fixed in a place
3 **handwringing** = nervous or fearful squeezing of the hands
4 **streetscape** = street as seen from a distance
5 **perch** = small high place where sb can sit
6 **vista** = view
7 to **be nestled in** = to be tucked in, fitted in a small space in a comfortable manner
8 **condominium** = block of flats which are owned by the residents
9 to **sprout** = to grow, usually referring to a plant
10 to **be wowed by** sth = to be amazed by sth
11 **lightning rod** = Blitzableiter
12 to **rezone** = to develop in a completely new way

3 EXTRA
Visit the High Line website to find out more about the development and the current state of the project. Choose one aspect you find interesting and prepare a short presentation.

4
→ **S6:** How to write an argumentative text, p. 206

Discuss to what extent the High Line has been successful in improving life in New York. You can use the phrases you have collected in 2 b). → SUPPORT D17, p. 175

5 CHOOSE WB pp. 44-45
→ **S8:** How to improve your text, p. 209
→ **S27:** Evaluating online sources, p. 245
→ **S19:** How to improve your mediation skills, p. 232

Do some research on projects in your area in which disused industrial buildings or infrastructure have been revitalized. Describe the project and assess the benefit for the public.

OR

Mediation You are taking part in an international youth forum on the future of city life. Your topic is urban renewal, and you are asked to present examples of the creation of attractive public spaces on former industrial sites. You have found the website of a famous old colliery in the former mining district of the Ruhr.
Write an article of about 200 words for the website of the youth forum in which you describe the former use of the colliery, as well as the changes that have taken place. Also point out how the public profits from the development.

Zeche Zollverein

Vom Ort der Maloche zum UNESCO-Welterbe

Früher wurde hier malocht, heute bietet das Welterbe Zollverein Industriekultur vom Feinsten: Kunst, Konzerte, Festivals und Sportmöglichkeiten treffen auf eine imposante Kulisse.

Der Industriekomplex Zeche und Kokerei Zollverein, der 2001 als UNESCO-Welterbe ausgezeichnet wurde, gilt als eines der imposantesten Industriedenkmäler der Welt. Seit der letzten Schicht im Jahre 1986 hat sich Zollverein in eine Stätte für Kunst, Kultur und Kreativwirtschaft verwandelt, die jährlich rund 1,5 Millionen Besucher anzieht. Damit symbolisiert sie den Strukturwandel in der Metropole Ruhr wie kaum ein zweites Bauwerk.

Weltgrößte Steinkohlenzeche

In ihrer aktiven Industriezeit war die Essener Zeche die größte Steinkohlenzeche weltweit, die Kokerei so groß wie keine andere in Europa. Neben seiner außergewöhnlichen Größe ist aber auch die Architektur des Zollverein-Komplexes herausragend – nicht umsonst wird Zollverein auch als schönste Zeche der Welt bezeichnet. Der berühmte Doppelbock-Förderturm ist heute das bekannteste Wahrzeichen des Ruhrgebiets und Symbol für die Industriekultur einer ganzen Region.

Denkmalpfad und Museen

Einen besonders guten Einblick in die Zeit, in der die Anlagen noch aktiv waren, bieten die zahlreichen Führungen im Denkmalpfad Zollverein. Entlang riesiger stillstehender Maschinen folgen Besucher dem „Weg der Kohle" in den Übertageanlagen der Zeche und den Produktionsanlagen der Kokerei. Wer noch mehr über das Leben und den Alltag im Ruhrgebiet erfahren will, kann sich eine multimediale Ausstellungen und einen 360°-Film im Portal der Industriekultur in der ehemaligen Kohlenwäsche ansehen. [...]
Imposante orangefarbene Rolltreppen bringen die Besucher hoch ins Ruhr Museum, wo sie in der identitätsstiftenden Dauerausstellung oder den spektakulären Wechselausstellungen noch mehr über Geschichte und Gegenwart des Ruhrgebiets erfahren. Die unterschiedlichen Ausstellungsebenen, auf denen die Natur- und Kulturgeschichte der Region präsentiert wird, verbinden scheinbar rotglühende Treppen.
Design-Fans werden auch vom Red-Dot-Design-Museum im vom Stararchitekten Norman Foster umgebauten Kesselhaus begeistert sein, das sich ebenfalls auf dem Zollverein-Gelände befindet. In der anregenden Industriekulisse entdecken Besucher hier etwa 2000 Objekte, die sich durch eine hervorragende Gestaltung auszeichnen.

Festivals und Konzerte

Vor allem im Sommer bietet das Welterbe-Gelände zahlreichen Veranstaltungen wie Konzerten, Open-Air-

Kino oder auch einem Gourmet-Festival Platz. Zu den weiteren Highlights gehören die Kunstmesse contemporary art ruhr (C.A.R.) sowie Festivals wie die Extraschicht und die Ruhrtriennale.

Natur aus aller Welt

Zwischen den riesigen Hinguckern aus Stahl und Stein finden sich kleine Attraktionen, die oft erst bei genauerem Hinsehen auffallen: Auf den Brachflächen haben sich Pflanzen aus aller Welt angesiedelt. Sommerflieder und Japanischer Staudenknöterich aus Asien, Robinie, Nachtkerze und Goldrute aus Nordamerika, Schmalblättriges Greiskraut aus Südafrika sind durch Gütertransporte, mit dem Wind oder durch Mensch und Tier hierher gelangt.

Aber auch zahlreiche heimische, zum Teil seltene und geschützte Tier- und Pflanzenarten, leben im Schatten des Unesco-Weltkulturerbes. So hat sich an mancher Stelle ein dichter Gehölzbestand aus Roteiche, Schwarzerle, Traubenkirsche und Schwarzem Holunder entwickelt, andernorts bilden Birken, Weiden und Brombeergebüsche einen wilden „Industriewald". Rund um das Gelände des Zollverein-Parks führt eine 3,5 Kilometer lange Ringpromenade Radfahrer, Fußgänger, Jogger und Naturliebhaber durch die teils exotische, teils heimische Flora. In den Feuchtbiotopen der großen Brachfläche leben Frösche, Kröten und Molche, die es etwa auf einer Taschenlampenführung zu entdecken gilt.

Sport und Entdeckungen

Auf sportliche Gäste wartet im Winter eine Eisbahn, auf der Besucher inmitten der spektakulären Industriearchitektur ihre Runden drehen können. Zu einem ganz besonderen Erlebnis wird das Fahren nach Einbruch der Dunkelheit, wenn die Lichtinstallation der britischen Künstler Jonathan Speirs und Mark Major die Kokerei in blaues und rotes Licht taucht. Im Sommer ist Zollverein Anziehungspunkt für alle, die Abkühlung suchen, denn sie können während der NRW-Sommerferien im kostenlosen Werksschwimmbad abtauchen. Das Becken entstand 2001 im Rahmen eines Kunstprojekts aus zwei zusammengeschweißten Überseecontainern und war eigentlich nur für eine Badesaison gedacht. Wegen des großen Erfolgs öffnet es nun jedoch jeden Sommer.

(605 Wörter)

The arts and New York City

1

New York City has always been a centre for established artists and newcomers to the scene. It boasts more than 80 art museums, many of them world-famous like the Museum of Modern Art (MoMA) or the Guggenheim Museum, and 1,500 art galleries. The Public Art Fund, a non-profit organization, takes a different approach.

a) Look at these photos of art projects sponsored by the Public Art Fund and describe the impact the art has on the urban environment.

→ **S15:** How to describe pictures, p. 226

b) Read this mission statement from the Public Art Fund website and explain in your own words what the organization wants to achieve. What is special about their approach?
→ SUPPORT D18, p. 176

Tip
You can visit the website of the Public Art Fund to find out about artists and current exhibitions and projects.

As the leader in its field, Public Art Fund brings dynamic contemporary art to a broad audience in New York City and beyond by mounting ambitious free exhibitions of international scope and impact that offer the public powerful experiences with art and the urban environment. [...] Since its inception, Public Art Fund has presented more than five hundred artists' exhibitions and projects at sites throughout New York City's five boroughs, making it possible for artists to engage diverse audiences and, along the way, redefine public art in relation to the changing nature of contemporary art.

2

→ **S9:** How to structure a text, p. 212

a) Read the short descriptions of three different New York exhibitions and examine to what extent the approach of the Public Art Fund has been realized.
b) **Group work** Discuss what effect the different art projects might have on their New York audience.

In the exhibition **Back and Forth Disco**, photographs by Farah Al Qasimi are shown in an everyday urban surrounding: 100 bus shelters across all five boroughs serve as backdrop for the larger-than-life photographs, which reveal to commuters and pedestrians glimpses of city life that are colourful and enigmatic. Al Qasimi tries to reflect different styles and cultural traditions that are typical of this vibrant city. All photographs appear in 18 different neighbourhoods, so that the public has a chance to see all of her work without having to travel far.

Conquest was a performance initiated by Pope.L, who used the idea of his solo crawls for a group activity. For 40 years his crawls through different urban areas have drawn attention to the hardship of people living on the street. For "Conquest" he gathered more than 140 volunteers and chose a route through downtown Manhattan, including places of historical importance. People doing the crawl together were meant to experience the struggle of people less privileged than them and also gain an insight into the effect of collective action.

Tony Oursler can be considered one of the pioneers of working with light installations. For his project **Tear of the Cloud** he has chosen a real urban landscape in New York City, the buildings on the Hudson River and the water of the river itself, as the surface for his digital projections, which are accompanied by eerie music. In his installations, he utilizes images of different people like painters, musicians, inventors or other legendary figures related to New York. But he also includes references to recent developments like water pollution or the impact of the media. Anyone can visit the Riverside Park at night to experience this fascinating transformation of the New York scenery.

3 EXTRA

Present your hometown/city/surroundings in an unexpected way.
- Decide what you want to show, what the general topic could be.
- Take pictures from an unusual/unexpected angle, focus on certain details or take in a whole street scene.
- Write a text or captions to explain what you intend to show.
- Present your photos in class.

4 Across cultures

→ **S6:** How to write an argumentative text, p. 206

Art projects in public places – a way to make urban spaces more attractive or a waste of money? Discuss this question, referring to your area or hometown and/or to projects you have come across in this section.

Create your own New York podcast episode (Lernaufgabe)

The "city that never sleeps", the "capital of the world", the "Big Apple" – New York City has many nicknames that allude to its greatness. And there are many possible aspects that one could take a closer look at. Work in a small group and produce an episode of your podcast called "Empire State of Mind", which is aimed at young people interested in this special place.

1

First choose a topic you want your episode to deal with. Here are some ideas:

1 What if we could rebuild NYC?
New York is famous for its bold architecture and sprawling mass of skyscrapers – but what if we could start anew? Build a more livable, more sustainable, more climate-friendly NYC? Or would you do something else entirely? Research ideas on how to rebuild a megacity like NYC and explain your vision.

2 Disasters in NYC
The Coronavirus swept through NYC in 2020/21 and left many dead; on 9/11, an unprecedented terrorist attack claimed close to 3,000 lives in NYC alone. Further back in time, the PS General Slocum accident cost the lives of many German Americans in the worst maritime disaster in the city's history. Both natural and man-made disasters have left their mark on the city. Research one such event and focus on what happened, who was affected, and on how the disaster changed NYC.

3 Music from and about New York City
From Frank Sinatra to Jay Z, many (often local) artists have made songs about the greatest city on earth. Research famous NYC songs and compile your own top ten. Tell your listeners about New York in songs and explain why you chose these specific songs. Make sure to include some samples in your podcast.

4 Sports stars
Home to famous teams like the New York Knicks, New York Liberty, the Yankees, the Giants or the Mets, but also individual sports stars, NYC has great appeal for those interested in basketball, baseball, ice hockey, football and more. Choose your heroes, do some research and introduce your listeners to NYC's biggest and most successful athletes of all time.

5 New York City's "dark side" – homelessness, poverty and ways to help
Today, more New Yorkers are experiencing homelessness than ever before. In a city of more than 8 million people, about one in every 100 New Yorkers is homeless – that's nearly 80,000 men, women and children, who do not have a roof over their head, do not have food security, protection, access to facilities, information, education, ... Research organizations dedicated to the poor in NYC and lay out what they do, who they focus on, why their work is so important and how they hope to inspire others to help, too.

2 → **S27:** Evaluating online sources, p. 245

Research articles and websites regarding your topic. Collect facts, statistics, examples, and other ideas for your podcast.

3 → SUPPORT D19, pp. 176-177

Plan your episode. It should run for about 3 to 5 minutes. Come up with ideas for

- the title of your podcast episode. Remember: your podcast is called "Empire State of Mind" – play around with that as a starting point, if you want.
- the aim of your show – what do you want to achieve? What do you want your audience to learn, know, do?
- your target group – young people interested in NYC. How can you appeal to them?
- the separate parts of your show – intro and outro, parts spoken by the host(s), interview parts, music, sound effects, ...
- who in your group is going to do what.

4

When you have prepared everything, record your show. If possible, edit it afterwards, too. For that, consider

- (re)listening to your material.
- deleting noises or unwanted material.
- adding (more) music or sound effects.
- saving your finished podcast as an mp3 or other audio file.

4 Industrialization and globalization

Midlands Engine, 23 September 2020

Midlands region is ready to lead on UK's green economy recovery

Today, one-third of all jobs in the UK energy sector are based in the Midlands – reskilling and advancing the extensive skill set of our valued 'green collar' workforce is key. Sir John Peace […]: "[…] Our region was the birthplace of the industrial revolution and there is no question that today we have the industry expertise, skills and leadership needed to be at the heart of the next 'green' revolution." […] The pandemic has presented us with a 'once in a generation' opportunity to build back stronger, better and greener.

1

Express & Star, 3 June 2019

The die was cast[1] for Midland steel industry

Last week's news that British Steel, the last vestige of this once-great industry, has been placed into receivership[2] is a sad reflection of how British industry has declined over the past 100 years.

2

4 August 2020

New high-tech food manufacturing campus to create up to 4,500 jobs in Derby, UK

The UK government has agreed to provide £12 million in funding to help launch a revolutionary high-tech food manufacturing campus in Derby, which will create up to 4,500 jobs. It will also provide an additional £6.85m to establish a manufacturing research centre in the city.

3

Webcode

You can download a word list for the Intro and WordPool here: **DSW-73090-028**

Annotations

1 **The die is cast.** = *Die Würfel sind gefallen.*

2 **receivership** = external administration of a company that is bankrupt

1

Pair work Talk about

- the things you and your family possess, e.g. clothes, furniture, electrical goods, etc. Where have these things been designed and produced?
- the kinds of entertainment you prefer (TV series, films, music, games). Where does this entertainment come from?
- your interaction with other people. Are you in contact with people in or from other countries? How do you stay in touch with them?

2

Now read this definition and explain how your results from task 1 are linked to the process of globalization.

> Globalization is the word used to describe the growing interdependence of the world's economies, cultures, and populations, brought about by cross-border trade in goods and services, technology, and flows of investment, people, and information.

3

International trade is not a modern phenomenon, but it has developed significantly as a result of the process of industrialization, i.e. the widespread development of industrial manufacturing in a region or a country.

Webcode

You can find the video here: **DSW-73090-029**

→ **S20:** How to listen/watch effectively, p. 234

a) Watch a video on the process of industrialization and name the different stages.

b) Watch the video again and in a grid note down: → SUPPORT D1, p. 177
   - the dates of the different stages
   - key inventions and technologies
   - major changes and developments

c) **Pair work** Compare your notes with a partner's.

d) Name examples of places and companies that represent the first/second industrial revolutions on the one hand and the third/fourth industrial revolutions on the other.

14 May 2020

With Oil Industry in Slump, California Offers a Break on Some Well[3] Regulations

State regulators have signaled their willingness to postpone a deadline for oil and gas producers to pay fees and submit plans to manage thousands of unused oil wells after an industry group asked the Newsom[4] administration for help as it deals with the severe drop in petroleum
4 demand due to California's stay-at-home orders[5].

29 September 2020

Massive biotech hub planned for San Diego's waterfront

A life science development firm has unveiled plans to transform eight acres along San Diego's waterfront into a mixed-use hub that could attract numerous leading edge companies to the city.

16 February 2021

The electrification of the auto industry is speeding up – and shaking up the energy economy

The shift to decarbonize the planet is kicking into high gear. In few sectors are the risks or the ripple effects[6] greater than
5 in the auto industry.

6

4 → GRAMMAR G3, p. 192

The headlines, photos and news snippets above illustrate industrial developments in two different parts of the world.

a) Describe the photos and point out which sectors of industry they illustrate.

b) Skim the headlines and news snippets to check your results. Categorize these industries according to the sequence of industrial revolutions outlined in the video as far as possible.

c) Read the news snippets carefully and summarize
- what has happened/is happening to traditional industrial sectors, and
- what current trends are revealed.

5 EXTRA Language awareness → SUPPORT D2, p. 177

A good headline should catch the eye of the reader and make them want to read on.

a) Choose the headline that you think does this best and explain why.

b) Identify any rhetorical devices that are used.

c) Choose a headline that you think needs improvement and suggest how it could be changed using at least one rhetorical device.

Annotations

[3] **oil well** = oil extraction site
[4] **Gavin Newsom** = from 2019 governor of California
[5] **stay-at-home orders** = during the COVID-19 pandemic, many workers had to work from home
[6] **ripple effect** = the circles created by a stone dropped into water

Tip
You can find a list of rhetorical devices on pp. 248ff.

→ **S13:** Checklist: Analysis – non-fictional texts, p. 222

Preview

Industrialization and deindustrialization in Britain

The first part of the Theme is about industrialization and deindustrialization in Britain, with a focus on Wales and the Midlands. In the **Workshop**, you will work on extracts from a feature film.

Globalization

The second part of the Theme deals with the process of globalization, with a special focus on California and the US tech and entertainment industries.

Globalization is not a new phenomenon. There are different theories about when it started, but the Industrial Revolution is often considered to be one of the triggers of globalization.

THE INDUSTRIAL REVOLUTION

Britain became the first global economic superpower in the late 18th and 19th centuries because groundbreaking inventions such as the steam engine gave British manufacturing a technological edge and constituted the starting-point for factory-based production. Additionally, long-distance communication and transport was facilitated by the development of innovative technologies such as trains, steamships and the electric telegraph. The industrial weaving machine turned the textile industry into the first industry to be characterized by mass production. In 1771, Cromford Mill was the first water-powered cotton spinning mill, which marked the rise of the Midlands as the home of the British textile industry.

THE IMPORTANCE OF THE EMPIRE

With its vast empire, Britain exported manufactured goods to places all over the world. Consequently, Britain became not only the industrial powerhouse, but also the leading trading power worldwide. However, other countries such as France, Germany and the US followed suit over the course of the 19th and early 20th centuries and gradually increased the competition for markets worldwide.

THE 20TH CENTURY GLOBAL ECONOMY

In the periods after World War I (1914-18) and II (1939-45), it was the US that developed into the most powerful economy. As a champion of the free-market economy, the US encouraged developments such as the European Union, where tariffs between countries were abandoned. The end of the Cold War in 1989/90 allowed the previously separate spheres of influence – one dominated by the US, the other by the Soviet Union – to merge into, by and large, one global economy. Since then less economically developed countries (LEDCs) have competed with industrialized ones for jobs, especially those that do not require extensive training. Therefore many jobs in agriculture, mining and industrial production, but also some services such as call centres, have been outsourced to LEDCs in order to capitalize on cheap labour costs as well as lower environmental and social standards. Relocating facilities to far-away places, for example in Asia, has become an attractive option especially for large multinational companies, as transport and communication costs have fallen considerably over the past few decades. This has become possible due to progress in transportation, e.g. container ships and aircraft, and the advent of computer technology and the internet.

DEINDUSTRIALIZATION

Outsourcing of labour-intensive work has led to a decline of traditional manufacturing and therefore a process of deindustrialization in industrialized countries. A rise in unemployment in areas like the Midlands has made political attempts at rejuvenating former industrial centres and retraining the jobless for other lines of work necessary. Automation has put further pressure on the preservation of these jobs. Besides, in a growing number of jobs it has become irrelevant where someone lives and works as long distances can easily be bridged by access to the internet.

LIVING IN A GLOBAL AGE

All in all, globalization has led to a general rise in prosperity despite doubts about the sustainability of production and the hazards of insufficient health and safety regulations. However, the effects of globalization cannot only be felt on the production side. Consumers can increasingly choose between the same or similar products by multinational companies worldwide. Social media allows us to stay in touch with people all over the world. Modern transport allows us to explore the world.

RECENT CRITICISMS

In recent years, globalization has been criticized for its lack of sustainability, such as the overexploitation of natural resources, decreased biodiversity and its role in carbon dioxide emissions. Attempts at protecting national markets with the introduction of tariffs as well as discomfort in view of a growing dependence on global supply chains have called the existing economic model into question.

1 WB p. 46/1

Find expressions with the same/a similar meaning in the text.

1. the steps from the sourcing of raw materials to the manufacturing and sale of the product and finally to the customer
2. the manufacturing of goods on a large scale
3. advancement, improvement
4. an economic system in which the government does not interfere
5. charges that need to be paid when goods enter a country
6. a country with a rather basic economy
7. relocating jobs to another country, usually to save labour costs
8. businesses that are active internationally
9. a process that involves an increased use of machines, robots, etc.
10. wealth, economic well-being
11. laws/rules that keep people safe from injury and illness

1

2 WB p. 46/2

Find words or expressions in the text to match the pictures (1-6). Sometimes there is more than one solution.

2

3

3 WB p. 46/3

Find words or expressions that mean the opposite (antonyms) in the text.

1. to hinder, make difficult
2. to go down, fall
3. to destroy, let fall into disrepair
4. safety, protection
5. causes
6. to lose contact

4

5

4 WB p. 48/4

Complete the sentences with words from the text.

1. In a global economy, smaller companies often ___ in order to stand a better chance of survival and success.
2. However, it can be dangerous if one company becomes so powerful that it ___ the market.
3. Sometimes even state subsidies cannot guarantee the ___ of companies and the jobs they provide.
4. With the ___ of new technologies, traditional companies may face serious challenges to stay competitive.
5. Often this leads to a need to reduce costs by ___ plants to countries with cheaper labour.
6. If competitors are based abroad, there is sometimes a call for protecting the national market with ___.

6

5

Use the information and language from the text to explain which historical developments these images (7-9) refer to.

7

8

9

Webcode
You can download a word list for Part A here: DSW-73090-030

Step by step Viewing

Preview

In this Workshop, you will work on the feature film *Pride* (2014, director: Matthew Warchus). You will learn how to analyse a feature film, paying special attention to cinematic devices and their functions.

PRE-VIEWING

1 Group work (4)

As coal mines in the UK were heavily subsidized by the state, the British government under Prime Minister Margaret Thatcher wanted to close mines that were deemed unprofitable and inefficient. To do so, they had to break the trade unions' resistance to these closures. This conflict came to a head in 1984 and led to the miners' strike of 1984-85.

→ S15: How to describe pictures, p. 226

a) Look at the photos of the UK miners' strike of 1984-85. Choose one photo each and study it in detail. Describe your photos to each other. → SUPPORT D3, p. 178
b) Sum up what the photos tell you about what happened during the strike and what kind of atmosphere they convey. Read the info box on the next page for more background information. → SUPPORT D4, p. 178 → GRAMMAR G4, p. 193
c) Compare your results in class.

1 Orgreave coking plant near Sheffield, 4 June 1984

2 Newbridge, South Wales, 10 August 1984

3 Orgreave coking plant near Sheffield, 1984

4 London, 7 June 1984

Info

The 1984-85 miners' strike

In the early 1980s, Conservative Margaret Thatcher, who had become the UK's first female prime minister in 1979, aimed at turning the UK's ailing economy around. A key element of her strategy was to privatize state-owned companies, especially those that heavily relied on subsidies like coal mines and steel factories. At the same time, she wanted to weaken the power of the trade unions, which she considered too powerful, since the strikes of the National Union of Mineworkers had repeatedly brought the country to a halt in the 1970s. When a government plan which was expected to lead to the closure of about 20 pits and the loss of about 20,000 jobs was made public on 6 March 1984, a national strike was announced on the same day. With many miners joining the protest, a shutdown of many pits around the country followed. Police forces were dispatched to guard the mines and also to protect miners who still went to work. Those on strike, however, were involved in violent clashes with the police. The longer the strike lasted, the more difficult it became for the miners to feed their families with the financial support from the union. Over time, the number of strikebreakers rose until the strike officially ended on 3 March 1985.

2

a) Compare two stills from the 2014 feature film *Pride*, which is based on true events of the years 1984-85. Analyse what they convey about the plot and the atmosphere. Consider
- the banners and their messages,
- the setting (including the weather),
- the characters.

b) Speculate on how the stills and what you have found out about them in a) could be related to the title of the film.

Language support

... conveys the impression that ...
... draws attention to ...
... reminds one of ...
... reveals how ...
... focuses on ...
... puts ... at the centre

1

2

WHILE VIEWING

3 WB p. 49/1

Look at the categories field size, camera angle and point of view in the overview of cinematic devices on pages 108-109. Say which of the terms in the three categories apply to the two film stills. → SUPPORT D5, p. 179

Info

Editing

Every film is composed of **shots**. The beginning and end of a shot are marked by cuts, i.e. the change from one image to another one. Shots can be very short or – if the camera films without any interruption – long. In modern films, there are usually a lot of cuts so that shots that deal with the same part of the plot form a **sequence**.

The way shots are linked is referred to as **editing** or montage, which is usually done in a specific way to establish a meaningful relationship between the individual shots.

Typical examples of shots are:

Info

device	definition	function/effect
field size (distance between the camera and the object filmed)		
long shot	a view of characters or a setting from a distance	to provide an overview, often used as an introduction to a new scene or location 
full shot	a view of the entire figure of a person	to show a person in action or to give an impression of how the characters/ the characters and their environment are related to each other 
medium shot	a view of a person down to his/her waist	to give a better impression of a person's looks and behaviour, often used to present two people in conversation 
close-up	a full-screen shot of a person's face or other body part or object	to reveal a character's emotions by showing their facial expressions clearly; to draw attention to an object that is crucial to the plot or has symbolic value 
camera angle		
high-angle shot	the camera looks down on a person or object	to make a person/object seem smaller, less important, inferior 
low-angle shot	the camera looks up at the person or object	to make a person/object seem more powerful, more important, superior or even intimidating 
eye-level shot	the camera looks straight at a person or object	to provide a neutral view or to present two characters as equal and on the same level 
point of view/camera position		
point-of-view shot	a scene is filmed as if looking through a character's eyes	to experience a situation as if part of the scene, possibly to identify/ sympathize with the character
over-the-shoulder shot	the camera looks at a character from behind another character's back	to show two people in conversation and draw attention to a character's reaction to what is being said 
reverse-angle shot	a shot in a sequence of point of view shots in which the other character's perspective is shown	to allow the viewer to perceive how a conversation develops on both sides 

establishing shot	a shot that provides an overview of a scene/setting	to introduce the viewer to a new location or situation	
camera movement			
panning shot	the camera moves horizontally, e.g. from left to right	to follow an object or person, often used to speed up the action and make the viewer follow the plot development	
tilting shot	the camera moves vertically, i.e. upwards or downwards		
tracking shot	the camera follows a person or object	to follow an object or person, often used to speed up the action and make the viewer follow the plot development	
zooming in/out	the camera moves closer to or further away from a person or object	to draw attention to a detail or connect a detail to its environment	

4 Extract 1: 20:20-21:34

As a group of young gay and lesbian people in London see parallels between their struggle for acceptance and the miners' conflict with the government, they start LGSM (Lesbians and Gays Support the Miners) to collect money for miners who are on strike. Having had problems at first to find a mining community willing to accept money raised by a group of homosexuals, they are now sending their donations to the Dulais Valley in southern Wales. → SUPPORT D6, p. 179

→ **S16:** Checklist: Analysis of a film scene, p. 227

a) Before you watch the scene set in Onllwyn, a village in the Dulais Valley, copy the viewing grid below. Watch the scene several times and use the first three columns to take notes on
- what is happening,
- what different points of view on the donations by LGSM are voiced at the committee meeting.

setting	*characters*	*what is happening/ what they are discussing*	*what points of view are voiced*	*cinematic devices*	*function/effect*
in the village street	*Sian and her husband Martin, other miners*			• *tracking shot, then panning shot* • …	• *to convey an impression of how small the village is and that strike posters and other miners are never far away and dominate the place* • …
at the miners' welfare hall	*Sian and the members of the strike committee and*				

b) Sum up what the extract is about. Use your notes from a).

Webcode
You can download the grid here:
DSW-73090-031

→ S16: Checklist: Analysis of a film scene, p. 227

5 → SUPPORT D7, p. 180

a) Now work on the last two columns of the grid. While watching, note down the use of any of the following devices that you consider noteworthy in this extract:
- field size
- camera movement and camera angle
- point of view
- setting and costumes

After watching, fill in the last column.

b) **Pair work** Compare your notes with a partner's.

c) Present your findings in class. Add to or change the information in your grid where necessary.

d) Analyse how the people of Onllwyn are portrayed with the help of cinematic devices.

Tip
When you divide up an extract, a change in place and characters usually marks the beginning of a new part.

6 **Extract 2: 25:36–30:40**

Eventually, LGSM is invited to Onllwyn in spite of some resistance from the community. Copy the grid below before you watch the second extract from the film.

a) Decide which heading fits the extract as a whole best. Explain your choice.
1. Hostile miners
2. Nervousness on both sides
3. Overcoming prejudice

Webcode
You can download the grid here: DSW-73090-032

b) Fill in columns 2 and 3 of the grid. → SUPPORT D8, p. 180

setting	*characters*	*what is happening/what they are discussing*	*what points of view are voiced*	*cinematic devices*	*function/effect*
Welsh countryside, van					
outside the Onllwyn welfare hall and in its entrance hall				• *over-the-shoulder and reverse-angle shots of the LGSM group and the welfare hall* • *…*	• *to contrast the colourful young activists with the grey and traditional hall → clash of two worlds* • *…*
inside the kitchen	*strike committee (especially Dai (middle-aged) and Cliff (older)), women's support group (especially Sian, Hefina and Gwen)*				
inside the welfare hall	*Mark, …*			• *absolute silence when Mark is about to deliver his speech* • *…*	• *reservations and animosity among the locals* • *…*

7 → SUPPORT D9, p. 180

a) In order to analyse the extract, watch it again to take notes on the cinematic devices that are used in the grid you started in task 6 (columns 4 and 5). You need not note down every device, just concentrate on the ones that are meant to support the viewers' understanding of the extract. Apart from the different kinds of shots and their combination in the editing process, another important cinematic device is sound, especially music.

→ **S16:** Checklist: Analysis of a film scene, p. 227

Language support

Music	
Pace	**Mood**
fast | slow | frantic | monotonous	playful | cheerful | boisterous sad | solemn | sorrowful | mysterious | hesitant | yearning | sentimental scary | threatening | eerie | aggressive
The ... background music is used to create a ... atmosphere/evoke a ... feeling/support the action.	

b) Compare your grids in class. Add to or change the information in your grid where necessary.

8

Analyse how cinematic devices help to convey the atmosphere when the members of LGSM and some of the locals meet in the welfare hall in Onllwyn.

POST-VIEWING

9

Choose one of the characters from the film. Imagine you are at the welfare hall. Write down what goes through your mind when LGSM arrive and then enter the hall.

→ SUPPORT D10, pp. 180-181

Dai
- visited LGSM in London
- delivered an impressive speech in a gay club to thank them for their support
- is not sure how the other villagers will react to a group of gay and lesbian people

Mark
- has been the driving force behind LGSM
- does not always take other people's concerns seriously
- is usually very sure of himself

Sian
- stands up for what she believes in
- is not willing to accept local traditions
- is open-minded about new ideas

Practice Viewing

WHILE VIEWING

1 Extract 3: 33:27-36:22

The visitors from London are shown around the village and its surroundings while the miners are on strike or some, such as Lee and Carl, are even in prison for protesting.
Watch the third extract from *Pride* and outline LGSM's impact on the lives of the people of Onllwyn.

→ **S20:** How to listen/watch effectively, p. 234

2 WB pp. 50-52

Analyse how the relationship between LGSM and the miners changes and how this development is conveyed with the help of different cinematic devices.

→ **S16:** Checklist: Analysis of a film scene, p. 227

3

Assess to what extent this quotation captures the relationship between LGSM and the mining community.

"It is not our differences that divide us. It is our inability to recognize, accept, and celebrate those differences."
(Audre Lorde, 1934-1992, African American writer)

Industrialization and deindustrialization in the Midlands

1

Pair work Find the Midlands on the map. Then read the following text about industrial development in the Midlands and find headings for the paragraphs A-H.
→ SUPPORT D11, p. 181 → GRAMMAR G5, p. 194

2

Group work Create an infographic to illustrate the rise and fall of industry in the Midlands.
→ SUPPORT D12, p. 181-182

The Midlands played a crucial role in the process of English industrialization in the 18th and 19th centuries. This was primarily due to its geographical location and rich natural resources (coal, iron ore and clay), but also to the work of entrepreneurs, engineers and inventors based in the area.

A In 1771, Richard Arkwright invented the water-powered spinning wheel, making it possible to spin cotton and silk mechanically, which brought about the birth of the factory system. Built in Cromford in the East Midlands, his factory was the first ever to produce textiles.

Josiah Wedgwood was an entrepreneur and experienced producer of pottery. His pioneer work helped to establish the six towns of Stoke-on-Trent, known as "The Potteries", as the centre of the British ceramics industry, with over 300 factories producing tableware and industrial items such as tiles. 100,000 skilled workers were employed in this industry at the beginning of the 19th century.

B Transportation was of the utmost importance during the process of industrialization. In the 18th century canals were the most efficient and cheapest means of transporting raw materials and goods. Cutting through the English countryside, canals formed a close network in the Midlands. Having relocated his factory to land adjacent to the new Trent and Mersey Canal, Josiah Wedgwood proceeded to build a new village for his employees there, called Etruria. The expansion of the railways in the mid-19th century made the distribution of goods even easier.

C At the same time industrial expansion continued in the West Midlands: in Birmingham, the "city of a thousand trades", and the region west of the city, the so-called Black Country, which got its name from the coal in the area and the smoke and soot from the numerous factories. The production of iron and steel and metal processing were the most important industries in the area, facilitated by important inventions such as steam-powered furnaces. Industry and manufacturing were dependent on factory-based steam power, which in turn necessitated coal. In as many as 500 collieries in the area the coal was mined which was needed to run machines and to feed the furnaces in the foundries. The abundance of coal led to the West Midlands becoming the world's leading steel-producing region.

The Black Country in the 19th century

D This trend continued into the 20th century. Increasing steadily with the expansion of the railways, the demand for steel rose even more with the development of the automobile industry. Having begun the production of cars and other vehicles at the end of the 19th century, the town of Coventry in the West Midlands became the centre of the British motor industry. By 1950 there were 12 different car manufacturers in the area and the UK led the world in the export of cars in the early 1960s. Other associated industries such as rubber thrived, too.

A steel factory in Walsall

A strike at Jaguar in Coventry, 1980

E However, during the two post-war decades, government policy proved to be harmful to British manufacturing. The battle of ideologies between the different governments after the Second World War resulted in erratic government policy – the British steel industry was twice nationalized and twice privatized – which did not improve matters. Furthermore, globalization meant additional competition for British industry, both in the domestic as well as the former imperial markets. The textile industry in particular suffered greatly from the import of cheap clothing.

F In the 1970s, falling employment numbers in manufacturing resulting from a lack of demand led to unemployment and frequent strikes in mines and manufacturing. During the Conservative government of Margaret Thatcher (1979-1990), the government waged war against the powerful unions and the number of strikes increased. At the same time the interests of manufacturing were neglected, government policy focussed on financial services to the advantage of London. There was little incentive to invest in industry and – compared to countries like China – the costs for the manufacture of consumer goods were too high. UK industry experienced a long decline as economic recession and globalization took their toll.

G The national process of deindustrialization had a devastating effect on the industry of the Midlands. Today there are only very few traces left of the steel industry that once made the area great. The last colliery closed in 1993 and coalmines have been turned into museums and tourist attractions. The ceramics industry of The Potteries has also changed. Wanting to reduce labour costs, Wedgwood and other traditional companies outsourced production to Southeast Asia. In 1979 more than 50,000 people still worked in the ceramics factories. By 2008 this number was reduced to 10,000. Many textile mills in the East Midlands were also forced to close between 1992 and 2001. And the structure of the automotive industry has also changed significantly since the 1970s, with domestic firms such as British Leyland increasingly unable to compete in a world market.

H However, the 21st century has witnessed some hope of recovery in certain industries, for example ceramics. Due to an increased demand for premium ceramics "Made in England" rather than "Made in China", some firms have begun to bring their production back to the Stoke-on-Trent area. By upgrading their products and creating unique designs, they have been able to adapt to globalization. Having grown solidly over the past 15 years, the aerospace industry now employs more than 45,000 people. Moreover, a thriving start-up scene has attracted much investment. It remains to be seen what the real impact of Brexit and the Covid pandemic will be on Midlands businesses, but restructuring, innovation and government investment are necessary preconditions for a lasting economic revival.

Industrialization and deindustrialization in the Midlands: Working on novel extracts

→ S15: How to describe pictures, p. 226

1

a) Compare these images of Birmingham in the mid-19th century and Birmingham in the early 21st century. Describe what has changed. The following categories may help you: industry, transport, buildings, pollution.

b) The second illustration is from a website called *The Complete Guide to Living in Birmingham*. Say how Birmingham is depicted in the photograph and speculate on which groups of people it is aiming to attract. Explain your answer.

Language support

In comparison/contrast to ... | Likewise/similarly ... |
Whereas Birmingham in the 19th century ... | While the first image presents a picture of/depicts/portrays Birmingham as ..., the second one ... |
If one takes the aspect of ... into consideration ... it is obvious that ... |
Evidently, there have been drastic changes in ... |
On comparing the two images, it is possible to conclude that ...

2 **Jigsaw** → GRAMMAR G5, p. 194

→ S12: Checklist: Analysis – prose, p. 220

a) **Home groups** Work in groups of four. Each of you chooses one of the four novel extracts on pages 115-118 and works on these tasks:
   1 Outline the setting and the historical context.
   2 Summarize the developments in the process of industrialization depicted in the extract.
   3 Identify the narrator's attitude towards these developments and find examples in the text which underline this attitude.

b) **Expert groups** Form new groups. Work together with others who have worked on the same extract.
   1 Compare your results.
   2 Add any information you may have missed to your own notes.
   3 Prepare a short presentation of your results to give to your home groups.

c) **Home groups** Go back to your home groups.
   - Present your results to each other in chronological order.
   - Ask and answer any questions you may have about the presentations you have heard.

1 The Rainbow

by D.H. Lawrence (1915)

The Rainbow *is set in the East Midlands in the second half of the 19th century. It tells the story of three generations of the Brangwen family, traditionally farmers and craftsmen, against the background of increasing industrialization. The building of a canal through their land and the growing number of collieries changes the countryside radically. This extract describes the new industrial town of Wiggiston, where Tom Brangwen is now the pit manager.*

He lived in a large new house of red brick, standing outside a mass of homogeneous red-brick dwellings, called Wiggiston. Wiggiston was only seven years old. It had been a hamlet of eleven houses on the edge of heathy[1], half-agricultural country. Then the great seam of coal had been opened. In a year Wiggiston appeared, a great mass of pinkish rows of thin, unreal dwellings of five rooms each. The streets were like visions of pure ugliness; a grey-black macadamized[2] road, asphalt causeways, held in between a flat succession of wall, window, and door, a new-brick channel that began nowhere, and ended nowhere. Everything was amorphous[3], yet everything repeated itself endlessly. Only now and then, in one of the house-windows vegetables or small groceries were displayed for sale.

In the middle of the town was a large, open, shapeless space, or market-place, of black trodden earth, surrounded by the same flat material of dwellings, new red-brick becoming grimy, small oblong[4] windows, and oblong doors, repeated endlessly, with just, at one corner, a great and gaudy[5] public-house, and somewhere lost on one of the sides of the square, a large window opaque[6] and darkish green, which was the post-office.

The place had the strange desolation of a ruin. Colliers hanging about in gangs and groups, or passing along the asphalt pavements heavily to work, seemed not like living people, but like spectres. The rigidity of the blank streets, the homogeneous amorphous sterility of the whole suggested death rather than life. There was no meeting place, no centre, no artery, no organic formation. There it lay, like the new foundations of a red-brick confusion rapidly spreading, like a skin-disease.

Just outside of this, on a little hill, was Tom Brangwen's big, red-brick house. It looked from the front upon the edge of the place, a meaningless squalor[7] of ash-pits[8] and closets[9] and irregular rows of the backs of houses, each with its small activity made sordid by barren cohesion with the rest of the small activities. Farther off was the colliery that went night and day. And all around was the country, green with two winding streams, ragged with gorse[10], and heath, the darker woods in the distance.

The whole place was just unreal, just unreal. Even now, when he had been there for two years, Tom Brangwen did not believe in the actuality of the place. It was like some gruesome dream, some ugly, dead amorphous mood become concrete.

Annotations

[1] **heathy** = *Heide-*
[2] to **macadamize** = to build roads in a specific way invented by John McAdam ca. 1820
[3] **amorphous** = having no definite shape
[4] **oblong** = *rechteckig*
[5] **gaudy** = in an ugly way brightly coloured
[6] **opaque** = difficult or impossible to see through
[7] **squalor** = dirt and neglect
[8] **ash-pit** = the remains of a fire
[9] **closet** = outside toilet
[10] **gorse** = small bush with thorns

2 The Offing

by Benjamin Myers (2019)

The Offing *is set directly after the Second World War and tells the story of the friendship between a teenager from a mining family, Robert Appleby, and an eccentric older women, Dulcie, who introduces him to a different world of nature and culture. In this excerpt Robert has returned to his home and the mine after a summer in the countryside with Dulcie.*

In September I went to the pit. Yet instead of being handed a lamp and a hard hat, my father, perhaps recognizing that I wasn't suited to a life at the seam, and wanting me to have a position safer than the one he had held working the coalface for four decades, had somehow wrangled[1] an apprenticeship in the office above ground. [...]

I had lasted seven months as an apprenticed clerk at the colliery and confirmed member of a trade union. Even with many days off during the cold, cruel winter it was a gestation period[2] more than long enough to

Annotations

[1] to **wrangle** = to argue or fight (for sth)
[2] **gestation period** = time of development

Annotations
- [3] **drab** = uninteresting, dreary
- [4] **idleness** = laziness
- [5] to **pervade** = to be widespread
- [6] **shattered** = broken, shaken up
- [7] **Baltic** = *here:* very cold
- [8] **sinking** = digging of a vertical tunnel in a mine

birth in me a stifling sense of claustrophobia and a distrust of authority that endures to today.

I had quickly learned that if I didn't act otherwise I would be in that drab[3] office for life, and if witnessing a war, even from afar, like some sort of strange game played by adults that got out of hand, had taught me one thing it was life is short, and we each have only one shot at it, so as Easter approached – and against the pleas of my parents, who did little to disguise their disappointment, and despite the potential ostracism from those in the village who thought it a personal insult that I should walk away from a position of far greater privilege than those who risked their lives several hundred feet underground – I handed in my resignation. At the age of seventeen I retired from servitude.

My timing was good. Just two months earlier a notice had gone up at the gates announcing that the entire British coal industry was to be nationalized in order to address what the government called idleness[4] that pervaded[5] in those shattered[6] days of recuperation that followed the war. The harsh Baltic[7] winter

had scared the industry, too, and now the newly formed National Coal Board would oversee the management of the pits.

The long-held certainty that there would always be coal – and consequently there would always be work mining it – was the foundation of my village. But some of us saw that changing. Though money was still being invested in new sinkings[8] and mechanisation of the transportation of coal overground, the final chapter was already being written. The industry was contracting. It would be a long slow death. And I was glad to have got out.

3 Anita and Me

by Meera Syal (1997)

Annotations
- [1] **feted** = celebrated
- [2] **plucky** = brave
- [3] **thrusting** = energetic, determined
- [4] **Home Guard** = armed citizen militia during the Second World War
- [5] **dray** = wagon
- [6] **shire horse** = a certain race of horses
- [7] **able-bodied** = strong and healthy enough to work
- [8] **a gaggle of wheezy old geezers** = a collection of old men who are breathing heavily
- [9] **dour-faced** = gloomy-looking

Anita and Me *tells the story of Meena, growing up in the fictional village of Tollington in the 1960s and 70s. Tollington is a former mining town in the Midlands and Meena is the daughter of the only Punjabi family in the village. In this extract she finds out more about the history of Tollington and observes the changes that have taken place there.*

The Tollington mine had once employed the whole village; it had been feted[1] as a small but plucky[2] contributor to the Black Country's industrial growth, not as technically impressive as the nearby Cannock Pit, not as imposing and thrusting[3] as the one further afield in Wirley, but a respectable productive enterprise all the same.

Our adjoining neighbour, Mrs Worrall, had once shown me a newspaper cutting commemorating the day the Mayor of Wolverhampton had come to visit Tollington mine. It must have been during the war, for some of the grainy bystanders were decked out self-consciously in their Home Guard[4] uniforms and a coalman's dray[5] was parked in the left-hand corner of the photograph, where a shire horse[6] lurked with pricked ears. The mine and the village had been as intertwined as lovers, grateful lovers astonished by their mutual discovery; you could see it in the stiff backs of the men and the proud smiles of the women. [...]

Then the mine suddenly closed down in the late Fifties, no one seemed to know why. A few of the luckier miners were offered temporary jobs in the adjoining pits, but most of the able-bodied[7] men with families had moved on to look for work, leaving behind a gaggle of wheezy old geezers[8] and dozens of stout, dour-faced[9] miners' widows who had nowhere else to go. It had been a community of tough, broad-armed women and fragile old men until a few new families started moving in, drawn by the country air and dirt-cheap housing – families like us. [...]

All at once several cottage doors flew open like airholes on a concertina[10] and blew various women out of their houses [...] These women were commonly known as The Ballbearings[11] Committee as they all worked at a metal casings[12] factory in New Town, an industrial estate and shopping centre and our nearest contact with civilisation. The factory had opened, by way of compensation, soon after the mine closure, and everyone had assumed that the jobs would be given to the ex-colliers. But it was not the men they wanted; they wanted women, women who would do piecework and feel grateful, women whose nimble[13] fingers would negotiate their machines, women who, unlike their husbands, would not make demands or complain. So it was that in the space of a few months, the hormonal balance of Tollington was turned upside down. There must have been a time when women waved their men off on the doorsteps with lunch boxes and a resigned smile, but I could not remember it. It seemed to me that they had always run the village and they had always been as glamorous and shocking as they were now.

Annotations
[10] **concertina** = a musical instrument similar to an accordion
[11] **ballbearings** = *Kugellager*
[12] **casing** = *Gehäuse*
[13] **nimble** = quick and moving easily

4 Nice Work

by David Lodge (1988)

Extract 1

The novel takes place in 1986 in the fictional city of Rummidge (easily discernible as Birmingham) in the Dark Country (Black Country) and is set against the economic policies of the Thatcher era. As part of a shadow scheme, Robyn, a university lecturer specializing in the industrial novel, is given the task of shadowing Vic Wilcox, the manager of Pringle's, a factory producing iron casts and engineering parts for the automotive industry. In the first extract, Vic is driving to work.

Vic Wilcox has now, strictly speaking, left the city of Rummidge and passed into an area known as the Dark Country – so called because of the pall[1] of smoke that hung over it, and the film[2] of coal dust and soot that covered it, in the heyday of the Industrial Revolution. [...] The economy and outward appearance of the area have changed considerably since those days. As the seams of coal and iron were exhausted, or became unprofitable to work, mining and smelting diminished. But industries based on iron-casting, forging, engineering, all those kinds of manufacturing known generically as 'metal-bashing' – spread and multiplied, until their plants met and merged with the expanding industrial suburbs of Rummidge. [...] Nowadays the Dark Country is not noticeably darker than its neighbouring city, and of country there is precious little to be seen. Foreign visitors sometimes suppose that the region gets its name not from its environmental character but from the complexions of so many of its inhabitants, immigrant families from India, Pakistan and the Caribbean, drawn here in the boom years of the fifties and sixties, when jobs were plentiful, and now bearing the brunt of high unemployment.

All too soon it is time to slow down and leave the motorway, descending into smaller-scale streets, into the congestion of traffic lights, roundabouts, T-junctions. This is West Wallsbury, a district dominated by factories, large and small, old and new. Many are silent, some derelict, their windows starred[3] with smashed glass. Receiverships[4] and closures have ravaged the area in recent years, giving a desolate look to its streets. Since the election of the Tory Government of 1979 which allowed the pound to rise on the back of[5] North Sea oil in the early eighties and left British industry defenceless in the face of foreign competition, or (according to your point of view) exposed its inefficiency (Vic inclines to the first view, but in certain moods will admit the force of the second), one third of all the engineering companies in the West Midlands have closed down. [...] Well that won't happen at Pringle's, hopefully as they say. Hopefully.

Extract 2

In this extract Robyn is driving to Pringle's for the first time, thus entering a part of

Annotations
[1] **pall** = cloth covering a coffin
[2] **film** = thin layer
[3] **starred** = covered in star-shaped pieces
[4] **receivership** = *Konkursverwaltung*
[5] **on the back of** = because of

Rummidge she has never been to before. She is soon caught up in heavy traffic on the ring road and so able to observe the area she is driving through.

More shops, offices, garages, takeaways, Robyn passes a cinema converted into a bingo hall, a church converted into a community centre, a Co-op[6] converted into a freezer centre. [...] There are few trees and no parks to be seen. There are occasional strips of terraced houses, whose occupants seem to have given up the unequal struggle against the noise and pollution of the ring road, and retreated to their back rooms, for the frontages are peeling[7] and dilapidated and the curtains sag[8] at the windows with a permanently drawn look. Here and there an effort has been made at renovation but it is always in deplorable taste. [...] The shops

Birmingham in the 1980s

are either flashy or dingy. The windows of the former are piled with cheap mass-produced goods, banks of conjunctival[9] TVs twitching and blinking in unison, blinding white fridges and washing-machines, ugly shoes, ugly clothes and unbelievably ugly furniture, all plastic veneers[10] and synthetic fabrics.

Annotations
[6] **Co-op** = grocery store run as a cooperative (*Genossenschaft*)
[7] **peeling** = with the surface slowly coming off
[8] to **sag** = to become limp and thus hang down
[9] **conjunctival** = eye-like
[10] **veneer** /vəˈnɪə(r)/ = front, exterior

3

→ **S8:** How to improve your text, p. 209

In contrast to the information presented on the Facts pages (pp. 112-113), the literary extracts in this section offer a very personal view of industrial developments. Using your infographic from page 112, task 2 as a starting point, give examples from the extracts to illustrate how people were affected by the changes that took place as a result of industrial development.

4 WB pp. 53-54 → GRAMMAR G5, pp. 196-199

Tip
Look up any words you do not understand and also note down the adjectives associated with them. You can use them in b).

a) Work on the highlighted passages of the extracts on pages 115-118. Note down phrases or sentences that illustrate the expressions in the box below. → SUPPORT D13, p. 183

monotony | gloom | suffocation | apprehension | intimacy | upheaval | hopelessness

→ **S12:** Checklist: Analysis – prose, p. 220

b) CHALLENGE Choose a different extract from the one you worked on in task 2. Analyse how the author's choice of words and their use of rhetorical devices underline the atmosphere they wish to create. Use your examples from a).

Language support

The author creates/evokes/conjures up an atmosphere of ...
The ... atmosphere is evoked by the words ...
A sense of ... is suggested by the words/expression ...
The author uses the expression ... to underline the atmosphere of ...
An allusion to ... implies/indicates an atmosphere of ...
The repetition of the words/expressions ... emphasizes ...
The comparison of ... to ... accentuates ...

5 EXTRA

→ **S2:** Checklist: Creative writing, p. 199

a) Choose one of the extracts on pages 115-118 and create an identity for a person who lived in the setting described in the text. Consider the following aspects: employment, family, interests. → SUPPORT D14, p. 183
b) Think of questions your character would like to ask a person from another novel.
c) **Pair work** Talk to a partner and exchange information about your characters using your questions from b).
d) **Group work** Talk about the changes that have taken place in the Midlands during your characters' lives.

The remnants of industrialization: Working on poetry

1 Pair work → SUPPORT D15, p. 184 WB p. 55/1

In 2019, the *Places of Poetry Project* invited people around the UK to send in poems connected to different places in the country, particularly those with an industrial past.

a) Work on the following tasks, one of you working on the first, the other one on the second poem:
   1. Describe what the speaker says about the place the poem is about.
   2. Analyse how the speaker conveys their attitude towards the industrial past of their region.

b) Present your findings to each other and compare the views expressed in the poems.

→ **S10:** How to work on poetry, p. 215

Used to Be
by Rebecca Goodwin

Right there, she said,
There used to be a pub
Standing down beside the railway tracks
With soot-stained walls and frosted[1] windows
That held men's laughter on a Friday night
After the last fire was stoked[2]
And the engines had cooled
They stood at the bar or slumped on chairs
Supped[3] their pints and swapped their tales
Until just the dregs[4] were left, then they went
Out into the gas-lit gloom, returned
To the terraced rows they'd always called home.

That's where, she said,
My father – your great grandfather – heard
The news of your granda's[5] birth one winter's night
When the snow stuck to the window frames
And mixed with coal dust, turning black
On roofs and in the back yards of the houses
And your granda's dad spilled his pint
Overjoyed to have a lad[6] at last,
And I don't know what my dad said, but
Nine months later I was born,
So I reckon he must have known
That lad was meant for his little girl.

Well that's what he used to tell me, she said,
But all that was long ago,
Years before you were born, back when
There was still a pub down beside the railway
tracks.

Annotations
[1] **frosted** = when you cannot see through glass
[2] to **stoke** = *schüren*
[3] to **sup** = to make a sound while drinking
[4] **dregs** = what is left of a drink at the bottom of a glass
[5] **granda** = grandfather
[6] **lad** = boy

Magpie[1] Mine
by Naomi Crosby

A dark green information board charts in
vivid red the chequered[2] past of the mine
which closed for the last time in 1954.

Nothing to see here,
just the pit head[3] and chimney
and a few old workings[4].
No bodies, fires, floods or memorials
to men whose lives were cheap.

Nothing to hear;
No screams as men drowned,
nor wailing of their wives,
muttering incantations[5] as they
cursed the mine for ever.

Thick purple heather covers lead red soil,
Swallows[6] swoop[7] to pick up moths
and the hobby[8] dives;
a curlew[9] utters its desolate cry
as it circles the moor.

Annotations
[1] **magpie** = *Elster*
[2] **chequered** = *here:* with successful and unsuccessful periods
[3] **pit head** = the top of a coal mine
[4] **workings** = *here:* parts of machines
[5] **incantations** = words that are believed to have magic power when spoken
[6] **swallow** = *Schwalbe*
[7] to **swoop** = to dive
[8] **hobby** = *Baumfalke*
[9] **curlew** = *Brachvogel*

2 → **S2:** Checklist: Creative writing, p. 199

Choose one of the poems. Imagine you are the speaker of the poem. Use the information from the poem to write a diary entry about a visit to the place referred to in the poem.

Mediation: Deindustrialization in Germany

1 Across cultures WB p. 56/1 → **S19:** How to improve your mediation skills, p. 232

Your class is taking part in a project on deindustrialization in Britain and Germany with students from a school in the Midlands. Write an article for the project website in which you outline why the Ruhr area is a classic example of deindustrialization and how the region has been coping with this process. Write about 180 words. → SUPPORT D16, D17, p. 185

CHRISTIAN WERNICKE **Süddeutsche Zeitung, 15. Dezember 2018**

Mehr als nur Kohle

Bereits seit mehr als einem halben Jahrhundert schließen die Zechen im „Pott"[1]. Was die Menschen in der Region davor über Generationen zu Tage gefördert hatten, veränderte die Welt. Die Kohle von der Ruhr war das Fundament für Deutschlands Industrialisierung und seinen Aufstieg auch zur politischen Großmacht. Das schwarze Gold schuf Wohlstand – und befeuerte zwei Weltkriege und Katastrophen, die all dies zerstörten. Die Kohle war Treibstoff für Untergang und Neuanfang, auch für das Wirtschaftswunder der jungen Bundesrepublik. Die Republik dankte mit Milliarden, zeitweise verbrannte jeder Arbeitsplatz im Bergbau 80.000 Euro Staatszuschuss. Jedes Jahr. Niemand sollte abstürzen, also „ins Bergfreie fallen".

Und nun? Nun muss das Revier ohne den Rohstoff auskommen, auf dem es gegründet wurde. Die Kohle ist verbrannt, die Region muss lernen, „Asche zu machen" aus dem, was bleibt. Also umdenken und Geld verdienen in neuen Jobs, in anderen Betrieben und Branchen.

Strukturwandel nennt man diesen mühsamen, schmerzhaften Anpassungsprozess. Den durchleben und durchleiden die mehr als fünf Millionen Menschen im Ruhrgebiet seit nunmehr bald zwei Generationen. Vieles gelang, manches scheiterte, fertig ist nichts. Die Arbeitslosenquote dümpelt knapp unter zehn Prozent, in Duisburg und Essen, Gelsenkirchen oder Dortmund lebt jeder Fünfte von Hartz IV. [...]

In Wirklichkeit ist das Ruhrgebiet längst weiter. Vor gut 50 Jahren gab es hier 300.000 Kumpel[2] und keine Studenten – heute ist es umgekehrt. In einer Region, wo einst der Sohn im selben Stahlwerk oder auf demselben Pütt[3] wie Vater und Großvater anfing, weht Gründergeist. Vor allem im Umfeld der 22 Hochschulen gedeihen Start-ups. Bochum etwa erlebt bereits seinen dritten Strukturwandel: Auf jenem ehemaligen Zechengelände, wo Opel von den Sechzigerjahren bis 2015 Kadetts und Zafiras montieren ließ, siedeln sich nun Firmen und Institute für IT-Sicherheit an. In zwei Jahren wird der Standort doppelt so viele Jobs beherbergen, wie Opel kurz vor Toresschluss bot. Dortmund und Duisburg profilieren sich derweil als Logistikzentren, Gelsenkirchen wird gerade digitale Modellstadt.

Das ist die eine, die sonnige Seite. Im Schatten liegen Probleme, die das Ruhrgebiet seit Jahrzehnten plagen, die es nicht selbst lösen kann – und mit denen es bisher alleingelassen wird. Auch das mag an der falschen Bescheidenheit der Menschen liegen: Die Zeiten, da die Regierungen in Berlin oder Düsseldorf das Feuer einer „brennenden Ruhr" befürchteten, sind längst vorbei. Protestiert wird allenfalls „stickum", also heimlich, still und leise: per Votum für die AfD.

Der alte Westen wurde zum Opfer des neuen Ostens. Das spürt jeder, der in NRW über Autobahnen oder Bundesstraßen holpert. Nach dem Fall der Mauer 1989 strömte alle nationale Solidarität in die neuen Bundesländer. [...] Eine milliardenschwere Schuldenlast erdrückt die ärmsten Städte an Emscher und Ruhr, verhindert ihre Investitionen in die Zukunft, also in Kindergärten und Schulen. [...]

Dort, wo nach dem Zechentod die Malocher[4] wegzogen, fanden die Schwächsten ihre Bleibe mit bezahlbarer Miete: Arbeitslose, Hilfsarbeiter, Flüchtlinge. Halbe Stadtteile verkommen zu Zonen inländischer Abschiebung, zu Ghettos. Und diese Armut ist erblich: Kinder, die hier zur Schule gehen, haben kaum eine Chance aufs Abitur. (488 Wörter)

Annotations

[1] **Pott** = kurz für „Ruhrpott", ein Spitzname für das Ruhrgebiet
[2] **Kumpel** = Bergarbeiter
[3] **Pütt** = Bergwerk, Zeche
[4] **Malocher** = jemand, der schwer arbeitet

Globalization now and then

Webcode
You can download a word list for Part B here: DSW-73090-069

Webcode
You can find the video here: DSW-73090-033

→ **S20:** How to listen/watch effectively, p. 234

1 WB p. 57/1

a) Watch a video about the history of globalization. Before you watch, skim the questions. While watching, note down the correct answers. If you haven't got all of the answers, watch the video again.

1. About 2,000 years ago, the Silk Road was
   - a established by Asian and European traders.
   - b used to transport different metals and fabrics.
   - c covering a distance of more than 8,000 kilometres.
2. European colonization of the world
   - a started in the 18th century.
   - b partly depended on using slave labour.
   - c made Britain conquer about 25% of the world's territory.
3. The Industrial Revolution
   - a was accompanied by technological progress.
   - b marked the beginning of a free-market economy.
   - c started after the invention of new means of transport.
4. The global market was
   - a dominated by the US after World War II.
   - b threatened by changes in the tariff system.
   - c further developed by the invention of airplanes.
5. Global players
   - a intensified production of their goods.
   - b profited from better-educated workers abroad.
   - c forced many smaller companies to produce elsewhere.
6. Digital technology
   - a initially inhibited the progress of globalization.
   - b has not been equally available across the global market.
   - c allowed easier distribution of what companies had to offer.
7. It is seen critically that globalization has
   - a facilitated worldwide travel.
   - b been accompanied by increasing social differences.
   - c encouraged many people to leave their homes.
8. There is growing awareness of problems with globalization indicated by
   - a the lack of global medical standards.
   - b the increased focus on one's own country.
   - c the end of the protection of local markets.

b) Watch the video again and asses the impact digital technology has had on globalization. Think of examples from your daily lives.

2

In his 1999 book *The Lexus and the Olive Tree*, Thomas L. Friedman, an American journalist and expert on globalization, defined globalization as follows:

"[...] globalization involves the inexorable[1] integration of markets, nation-states, and technologies to a degree never witnessed before – in a way that is enabling individuals, corporations, and nation-states to reach around the world farther, faster, deeper, and cheaper than ever before, and in a way that is also producing a powerful backlash from those brutalized[2] or left behind by this new system."

a) Explain Friedman's definition in your own words.
b) Name examples that illustrate the developments included in Friedman's definition.

Annotations
[1] **inexorable** = unstoppable
[2] to **brutalize** sb = to hurt sb

3 → GRAMMAR G6, p. 197

In his 2016 book *Thank You for Being Late*, Friedman refers both to his old ideas of globalization and tries to come up with a new definition.

a) Read the following extract from the book and identify the three stages of globalization Friedman developed in *The World Is Flat*. → SUPPORT D18, p. 186

b) Explain which changes Friedman observes in globalization. → SUPPORT D19, p. 186

c) Compare your findings to Friedman's definition of globalization quoted in task 2. Discuss whether his 1999 definition is still valid or needs to be updated and, if so, how.

→ S9: How to structure a text, p. 212

Thank You for Being Late

by Thomas L. Friedman

When I wrote *The World Is Flat* in 2005, the argument was that globalization was once driven by countries – Spain discovering the "New World." Then it was driven by companies – think the Dutch East India Company two centuries ago or Apple today. And now, thanks to all of these digital flows, globalization is being driven by everyone and anyone – small groups, start-ups, individuals, and multinationals – and is fast connecting East and West, North and South, and South and South. So many people can now take advantage of digital globalization and the flows off the supernova, to go global on their own terms. No one has observed this transition more acutely than Jeff Immelt, the longtime CEO[1] of General Electric[2], who stepped down[3] in 2017.

"I think the world's gone from macro to micro," Immelt said to me in an interview at GE's Boston headquarters in March 2017. During the last forty or fifty years, he noted, globalization was shaped by big platforms created by big governments – like the World Trade Organization[4] or the World Bank[5]. But as he travels the world now, Immelt said he finds that the new globalizers have never heard of the WTO and have no clue who the U.S. ambassador is in their country.

"They don't even speak those languages," Immelt said. "They are just globalizing on their own. They use platforms like Alibaba and Tencent and Amazon." These new globalizers are really "good digitally"; the ones in China are all using WeChat and on their own they figure out how to connect "Chinese funding for a power plant in Pakistan with a Canadian export credit."

In this kind of a world, said Immelt, GE now sees itself as a "multilocal" not a multinational. It is pushing down power and opportunity to its local teams all over the world and encouraging them to link up with other teams and opportunities anywhere in the world. "None of them would even know how to bring a complaint to the WTO," added Immelt.

In 2000, 70 percent of GE's revenue was in the United States. In 2017, over 60 percent came from global markets. But this was not by outsourcing. "Outsourcing is yesterday's game," Immelt said in his 2017 annual report. "During the 1980s and 90s, business looked to the emerging markets as a cheap labor source. American jobs migrated to countries that welcomed U.S. companies with open arms. American workers lost in the game of wage arbitrage[6]. Chasing the lowest labor costs is yesterday's model."

In today's model there is no over here and over there. "We see substantial opportunity to grow around the world by investing, operating, and building relationships in the countries where we do business,"

Annotations

[1] **CEO** = chief executive officer, i.e. the most powerful manager in a company

[2] **General Electric** (GE) = a multinational US company operating in various fields

[3] to **step down** = to leave an official position or job

[4] **World Trade Organization** (WTO) = an organization of more than 160 member states that regulates international trade

[5] **World Bank** = an international organization of more than 170 countries that provides loans to countries

[6] **wage arbitrage** /ˈɑː(r)bɪˌtrɑːʒ/= making a profit by benefitting from low labour costs in one country and selling the product in another

Immelt said. "We partner with Chinese construction companies[7] and leverage[8] their funding to win contracts in Africa and Asia. Our investments have created jobs in China and the U.S., while making GE more competitive." The multinational companies that thrive in the age of accelerations will be those that digitally weave together the optimal production talents, design talents, logistics capabilities, financing, and market sales opportunities that look at every country as both a market and a source of skills. If they don't, their competitors will.

Annotations
[7] **construction company** /kən'strʌkʃ(ə)n ˌkʌmp(ə)ni/= *Bauunternehmen*
[8] to **leverage** /'liːvərɪdʒ/= to borrow the necessary capital for an investment, counting on future profits for covering the cost for interest rates and repayment

4

a) Look at the following infographic by the US international business consulting firm McKinsey & Company. Identify the main changes regarding globalization from the 20th to the 21st century. → SUPPORT D20, p. 186

b) Explain how the infographic relates to Friedman's and Immelt's statements in the extract from *Thank You for Being Late*.

California – the home of global players

1

a) In class, talk about
- what Silicon Valley is famous for,
- what companies are based there or in other parts of California.

b) **EXTRA** Do some research on major companies that are currently based in Silicon Valley. Name three examples and the products or services they are known for.

2

a) In 2017, Scott Galloway published his book *The Four* about the four most influential companies in the world. All of them are from the US, three of them with their headquarters in Silicon Valley. Guess which companies they are.

b) Scan the following extract from the first chapter of the book in order to find out which companies belong to "the Four". Referring to your own ideas in a), say whether any of them are a surprising choice for you.

c) Read the extract and find words with similar meanings to those listed below.

1. wealth
2. collection
3. never before
4. friendly and generous
5. private
6. to make known to sb
7. copied
8. opponents
9. to amount, combine
10. to be made less successful and powerful
11. to be placed in a very strong position that can hardly be challenged
12. collect, harvest
13. target of attack, victim
14. turn

→ **S9:** How to structure a text, p. 212

d) State what the author considers to be the positive and negative impact of the Four's achievements.

The Four

by Scott Galloway

Over the last twenty years, four technology giants have inspired more joy, connections, prosperity and discovery than any entity in history. Along the way, Apple, Amazon, Facebook, and Google have created hundreds of thousands of high-paying jobs. The Four are responsible for an array of products and services that are entwined into the daily lives of billions of people. They've put a supercomputer in your pocket, are bringing the internet into developing countries, and are mapping the Earth's land mass and oceans. The Four have generated unprecedented wealth [...] that, via stock ownership, has helped millions of families across the planet build economic security. In sum, they make the world a better place. [...] However, consider another view. [...] We know these companies aren't benevolent beings, yet we invite them into the most intimate areas of our lives. We willingly divulge personal updates, knowing they'll be used for profit. Our media elevate the executives running these companies to hero status – geniuses to be trusted and emulated. Our governments grant them special treatment regarding anti-trust regulation, taxes, even labor laws. And investors bid their stocks up, providing near-infinite capital and firepower to attract the most talented people on the planet or crush adversaries.

So, are these entities the Four Horsemen[1] of god, love, sex, and consumption? Or are they the Four Horsemen of the apocalypse? The answer is yes to both questions. I'll just call them the Four Horse-men.

Annotations

[1] **Four Horsemen** = reference to the Four Horsemen of the Apocalypse from the Book of Revelation in the Bible

How did these companies aggregate so much power? How can an inanimate, for-profit enterprise become so deeply ingrained in our psyche that it reshapes the rules of what a company can do and be? What does unprecedented scale and influence mean for the future of business and the global economy? Are they destined, like other titans[2] before them, to be eclipsed by younger, sexier rivals? Or have they become so entrenched that nobody – individual, enterprise, government, or otherwise – stands a chance? [...]

While billions of people derive significant value from these firms and their products, disturbingly few reap the economic benefits. General Motors created economic value of approximately $231,000 per employee (market cap[3]/workforce). This sounds impressive until you realize that Facebook has created an enterprise worth $20.5 *million* per employee ... or almost a hundred times the value per employee of the organizational icon of the last century. Imagine the economic output of a G-10[4] economy, generated by the population of Manhattan's Lower East Side. [...]

Governments, laws, and smaller firms appear helpless to stop the march, regardless of the Four's impact on business, society, or the planet. However, there's safety in hatred. Specifically, the Four hate each other. They are now competing directly, as their respective sectors are running out of easy prey.

Google signaled the end of the brand era as consumers, armed with search, no longer need to defer to[5] the brand, hurting Apple, who also finds itself competing with Amazon in music and film. Amazon

is Google's largest customer, but it's also threatening Google in search – 55 percent of people searching for a product start on Amazon (vs. 28 percent on search engines such as Google). Apple and Amazon are running, full speed, into each other in front of us, on our TV screens and phones, as Google fights Apple to be the operating system of the product that defines our age, the smartphone.

Meanwhile, both Siri (Apple) and Alexa (Amazon) have entered the thunderdome[6], where two voices enter, and only one will leave. Among online advertisers, Facebook is now taking share from Google as it completes the great pivot from desktop to mobile. And the technology likely creating more wealth over the next decade, the cloud – a delivery of hosted services over the internet – features the Ali vs. Frazier[7] battle of the tech age as Amazon and Google go head-to-head with their respective cloud offerings.

The Four are engaged in an epic race to become the operating system of our lives. The prize? A trillion-dollar-plus valuation, and power and influence greater than any entity in history.

Annotations

[2] **titan** = early god in Greek mythology, here referring to a very powerful person or entity

[3] **market cap** = market capitalization, the combined value of all the shares of a company

[4] **G-10** = group of ten, later eleven, economically strong countries that agreed to strengthen the Inter-national Monetary Fund in the 1960s

[5] to **defer to** = to accept sb's opinion or actions

[6] **thunderdome** = arena or stadium where a fight or sports event takes place; may be a reference to an arena in which fights to the death took place in the 1985 feature film *Mad Max Beyond Thunderdome*

[7] **Ali vs. Frazier** = famous 1971 boxing match between Muhammad Ali and Joe Frazier nicknamed The Fight of the Century

3 Language awareness

Analyse how the author's use of language conveys his view of the Four and their rivalry.

→ SUPPORT D21, pp. 186-187

→ **S13:** Checklist: Analysis – non-fictional texts, p. 222

4

Taking the information from the extract as well as your personal experiences as a starting point, discuss whether the Four have an overall more positive or negative influence on society.

→ **S6:** How to write an argumentative text, p. 206

5 EXTRA

Scott Galloway's book was published in 2017, which was some time ago considering how fast economic circumstances can change. Do some research to assess whether these four companies are still as powerful as Galloway presents them.

The global appeal of US entertainment

1

a) List your top three personal favourites for these categories and for each one the country they are from.
   1. feature films
   2. TV/streaming programmes
   3. singers/bands
   4. food/drinks
   5. kinds of clothes/clothing brands

b) Compare your results in class. Find possible reasons
   - why certain representatives rank so highly in their categories,
   - why certain countries are represented more than others.

2

a) Read the article by Steve Rose on pages 127-128. Outline how the influence of American pop culture has developed over the past 100 years.

b) Describe the challenges that the American entertainment industry is facing today.

3

Go through the article and find phrases that can be used to talk about the following issues related to pop culture.

Describing characteristics of successful cultural products	*Describing changes in the pop culture industry due to globalization*	*Describing the global influence of US pop culture*
"sophistication, glamour and influence" (l. 8)	*"wondering whether the era of US dominance is coming to an end" (ll. 16-17)*	*"usually paled in comparison to America's output" (ll. 6-7)*
"now queue up to collaborate with them" (l. 87)	*"provided another jolt to US supremacy" (ll. 27-28)*	*"became a global smash" (ll. 54-55)*
...	...	...

4

Analyse how the author's use of language is meant to convince his readers of his view of the current global role of US pop culture.

5

"It is a little early to be making predictions of America's demise." (ll. 147-148)
Assess to what extent you agree with the author's conclusion, considering also your and your peers' cultural habits.

STEVE ROSE

The Guardian, 12 September 2020

American horror story: how the US lost its grip on pop culture

[...] For the past century or so, in terms of pop culture, America *was* the party. If it wasn't happening in the US, it was barely happening at all. Whatever home-grown movies or TV programmes or music other countries produced, they usually paled in comparison[1] to America's output in terms of sophistication, glamour and influence. Other countries might occasionally muster[2] a world-beating movie or band, an *Amélie*[3] or an Abba[4] – and the UK has benefited from the common language like no other country – but these were always mere drops in an ocean of American pop culture that lapped[5] every shore.

Many are wondering whether the era of US dominance is coming to an end, with the coronavirus pandemic the final nail in the coffin. [...] Today's United States is a place of economic decline, rampant inequality and racial animosity. It is a place where culture is now discussed primarily in the context of warfare. [...]

Even before Covid, the tide was already turning. Sticking with the movies for the moment, the distant, carefree days of early 2020 provided another jolt[6] to US supremacy: for the first time, a non-English language movie won the Oscar for best picture: *Parasite*. Needless to say, [then President] Trump was not happy: "The winner is a movie from South Korea, what the hell was that all about?" he complained, "Can we get, like, *Gone With the Wind*[7] back please?" More prophetic was Bong Joon-ho[8]'s comment at the Golden Globes: "Once you overcome the one-inch-tall barrier of subtitles, you will be introduced to so many more amazing films." Those floodgates are open, and not just for films. Globalisation is a two-way street, and the US now finds itself receiving as well as transmitting.

On the small screen, the rise of streaming services has given global audiences more access to the non-American stuff they have been missing, and the language barriers are coming down. Take *Money Heist*, originally a hit on Spanish TV. In decades past, a US network might have bought the rights to it and remade it in New York with American actors. Instead, [streaming services] provided a platform for the original, and it became a global smash. There are still reams of quality US fare being made, but now it's in direct competition with German sci-fi (*Dark*), Israeli spy thrillers (*Fauda*), Indian crime sagas (*Sacred Games*), even British teen comedies (*Sex Education*). [...]

In the music industry, the streaming revolution has had a similar levelling effect. In decades past, the US was the gatekeeper: it owned most of the major record labels, it had MTV, and it was the market you had to crack before you could really say you'd made it (sorry, Oasis[9]). When it comes to the biggest acts in the world today, though, you could be talking about Puerto Rican rapper Bad Bunny, who was judged "the world's biggest pop star" by Bloomberg. Or Korean boyband BTS, who have had four No 1 albums in the US charts in the past two years and who pack out stadiums to adoring American and British fans, many of whom have started learning Korean to understand the lyrics. [...] Thanks to the internet, what were once regional genres, such as K-pop[10] or reggaeton[11], are now part of a global conversation.

Korean band **BTS**

Annotations

1 to **pale in comparison** = to be insignificant compared to
2 to **muster** = to gather strength to do sth
3 ***Amélie*** = 2001 French romantic comedy film
4 **Abba** = very successful Swedish 1970s pop group
5 to **lap** = waves that beat against a shore or coast
6 **jolt** = sudden strong feeling
7 ***Gone With the Wind*** = classic American feature film from 1939
8 **Bong Joon-ho** = South Korean film director who won the Oscars for Best director and Best picture for his film *Parasite* in 2020
9 **Oasis** = very successful British rock band who were never very successful in the US
10 **K-pop** = subgenre of pop music from South Korea
11 **reggaeton** = music style from Puerto Rico, influenced by reggae and hip hop

Annotations
[12] **J Balvin** = Colombian singer born in 1985, known as the Prince of Reggaeton
[13] **Rosalía** = Spanish singer and songwriter, born in 1992
[14] **Burna Boy** = Nigerian singer and songwriter, born in 1991
[15] **Christine and the Queens** = French singer and songwriter, born in 1988
[16] **primed** = ready
[17] **bit** = very small
[18] to **whet** sb**'s appetite** = to make sb want sth by giving them a small taste of it

And people who might have been local stars, such as Colombia's J Balvin[12], Spain's Rosalía[13], Nigeria's Burna Boy[14] or France's Christine and the Queens[15], are now international ones. US performers now queue up to collaborate with them.
It usually follows that centres of political and economic power also rule the cultural sphere. But the US was primed[16] to become the world's cultural exporter, says Lane Crothers, professor of politics at Illinois State University and author of Globalization and American Popular Culture. "If you think about when the movie and music industries developed, they were periods of enormous economic growth and enormous cultural diversity in the US, as vast immigrant populations were arriving," he says. "If you were going to produce something that was going to be popular in, say, New York in 1907 you were going to produce it for an audience that was already globally diverse, at least in the European, western hemisphere sense of that word, and so you had to figure out a way to make programming that was accessible to people across cultural and linguistic traditions. So when the opportunity emerged, post-second world war, to sell globally, US culture had already had plenty of practice."
After the second world war especially, the US was mindful of pop culture's soft-power applications. It had a pretty clear idea of the image it sought to project: leaders of the free world, the land of prosperity, opportunity, health and happiness. Even supposedly "anti-establishment" rock music was viewed as a strategic asset during the cold war – all the better to contrast with the boring Soviet alternative. Which would you prefer? Communist folk music or Prince and Guns N' Roses? Soviet propaganda films or *Beverly Hills Cop*? The American dream was both a national glue and an export commodity.
As economies have grown around the world, the US has had more consumers to export to, but this has entailed certain compromises. In terms of cinema, for example, international box office now makes up 60 to 70% of Hollywood's income. As China has grown into the world's second-largest cinema territory over the past decade, Hollywood has been watching with dollar signs in its eyes. But as well as casting Chinese actors in bit[17] parts to whet local appetites[18], Hollywood has been increasingly careful not to offend the country's ruling Communist party, which controls which foreign movies get released and for how long. That has meant cutting out all references to locally contentious matters [...].
It is a little early to be making predictions of America's demise. Let's not forget, the US still has a virtual monopoly over the means of production and distribution. As well as movie studios, that includes most streaming platforms and social media [...]. If the US can continue to pool the world's talents and use them to make great art – as it often does – that could still be a good thing.
But if insularity, nationalism and ruthless opportunism are America's future, the rest of the world might well decide it can live without it. If America has stopped believing in the American dream, why should the rest of us?

Writing an article on young people going global (Lernaufgabe)

1

a) Imagine your class is taking part in an Erasmus+ project on young people's futures in a globalized world. Collect examples of how young people can explore the world as part of their education, training or career.
b) Cluster your ideas on the board.

2

As part of your Erasmus+ project with students from other European countries, you are expected to write articles for the project website about how young people explore the world. You have chosen young German carpenter Johanna Röh as your case study to illustrate the German tradition of being a "journeyman/-woman". The article's headline is to be "Johanna Röh: Combining German traditions and crafts worldwide".
Listen to a German radio report about Johanna Röh. Take notes for your article, e.g. on

- where she went,
- what it meant to her to be a journeywoman or freemover,
- how she profited from her experiences,
- what one needs to bear in mind when going on such a journey.

Webcode
You can find the audio file here:
DSW-73090-035

→ **S20:** How to listen/watch effectively, p. 234

3

Using your notes, write your article about Johanna Röh for the project website.

→ **S8:** How to improve your text, p. 209

4

a) **Group work** Read your partners' articles and, as a group, choose the one that presents Johanna Röh's case best.
b) Present your group's article of choice in class and explain what makes it stand out from the rest.

5

Bearing in mind your ideas from task 1 and what you have found out about Johanna Röh, in class talk about

- whether or not travelling around as a journeyman/-woman would be an option for you,
- what other possible ways of going abroad as part of your education, training or career appeal to you and why,
- whether or not going abroad for some time as part of one's education or training is generally useful in the globalized world of today.

5 The digital age

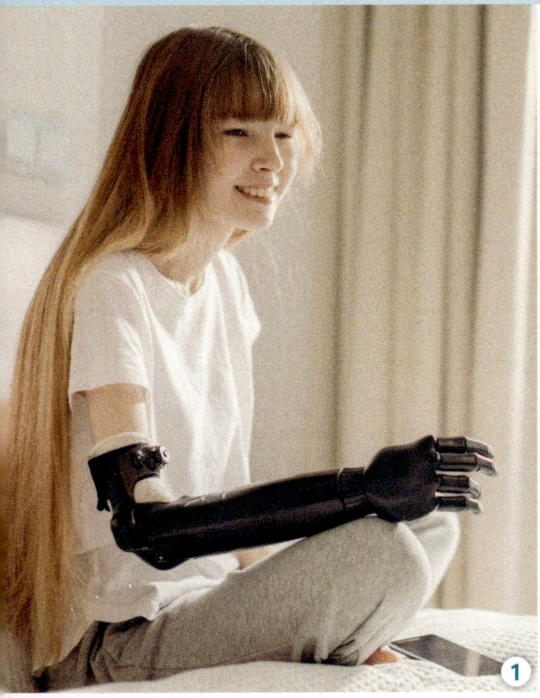
1

2

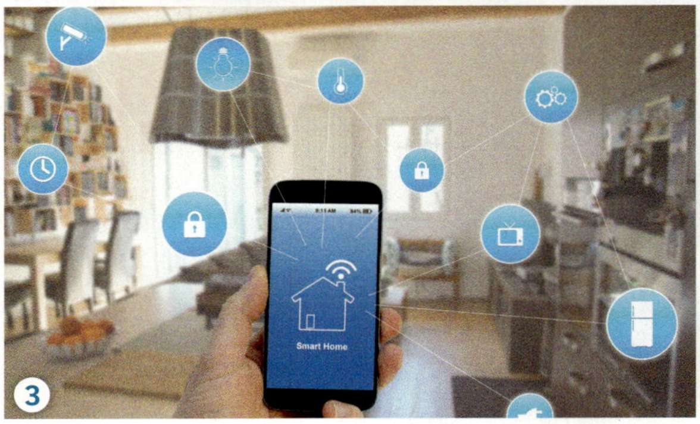

3

4

5

Webcode
You can download a word list for the Theme here: DSW-73090-036

1 Pair work

a) Describe the pictures on this double page and what they show about life in the 21st century.
b) Make a list of the situations displayed in the photos which are affected by digitalization and explain which of them you find most relevant to your life and to society as a whole.
c) The pictures present digitalization in a rather positive light. Discuss whether there are also possible downsides.
d) Using what you have talked about so far, create an acrostic poem with the letters of the term DIGITAL AGE.

2

a) Read the following quotations about the digital age and choose three that you can most relate to. Rank them according to their relevance to your life.
b) **Pair work** Present your top three to a partner and explain your choices and ranking.
c) Choose one of the quotations and write a personal statement on it in which you explain the quotation and give your opinion.

→ **S8:** How to improve your text, p. 209

1 Our movements and feelings are constantly monitored, because surveillance is the business model of the digital age.

Katharine Viner, editor-in-chief of the British newspaper The Guardian

2 I want to be part of the resurgence of things that are tangible, beautiful and soulful, rather than just give into the digital age. But when I talk to people about this they just say, 'Yeah, I know what you mean,' and stare at their mobiles.

Jack White, American musician

3 While the digital age has done so much to improve our world, it has dramatically changed our social structure, often further isolating us from each other.

Dean Ornish, American physician and researcher

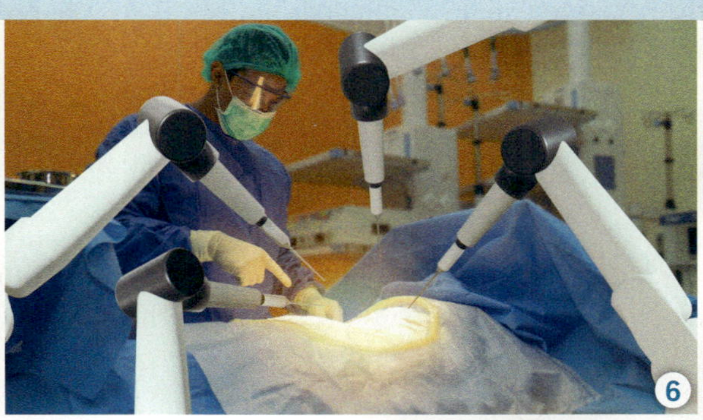

6

7

8

9

4 It's clear where the world is going. We're entering a world where every thermostat, every electrical heater, every air conditioner, every power plant, every medical device, every hospital, every traffic light, every automobile will be connected to the Internet. Think about what it will mean for the world when those devices are the subject of attack.

American journalist Andy Greenberg in his book Sandworm: A New Era of Cyberwar and the Hunt for the Kremlin's Most Dangerous Hackers

5 In the digital age, people spend countless hours throughout the day on social media and at the end of the day have absolutely nothing to show for it.

Germany Kent, American journalist

6 The digital world creates a situation where there are no secrets anymore.

Angela Merkel, former German chancellor

8 My own experience is use the tools that are out there. Use the digital world. But never lose sight of the need to reach out and talk to other people who don't share your view. Listen to them and see if you can find a way to compromise.

Colin Powell, American politician

9 Because of the internet, satellite TV, and the digital world, you can stay in touch, you can learn about other people from a young age.

Viggo Mortensen, Danish-American actor

Preview

In this Theme, you will learn about the impact of the internet and of technology on life in the current digital age.
In the **Workshop** you will practise writing argumentative texts on the advantages and disadvantages of being a digital nomad and of working from home.

7 Especially in the digital age, people want everything now, now, now.

Mark Waid, American author

The digital age has been a long time coming. Throughout the 19th and 20th centuries, we have moved from steam power and waterpower to electronics, we have introduced mass production and then further automated production using information technology. Eventually, the 21st century has brought us the fourth industrial revolution (Industry 4.0), the fusing of different kinds of advanced technologies and the infiltration of all aspects of people's lives – whether they like it or not.

EVERYDAY LIFE

Think about a typical day. Maybe you get up and listen to music on Spotify, a music streaming service. On your way to school, you probably scroll through social media platforms like Instagram or TikTok. Whereas your parents and grandparents may read the newspaper and watch TV to get the news of the day, you probably use the internet to stay informed about what you are interested in. Your smartwatch might even alert you to new relevant information. Even in your lessons at school, you probably use one of the many application programmes (also known as apps) available to stop time, create videos and audios or research topics. You use email to communicate with your teachers and messenger apps to stay in touch with your friends. Back home, you check your online calendar to remember what your plans are for the afternoon. Maybe there is time for some online shopping and even if you walk to the supermarket instead of having them deliver the products, you might pay using one of the many contactless payment services. Some of you already live in a smart home in which they monitor household appliances with their smartphones – one click and the blinds close, another one and the radiator powers up.

THE WORLD OF WORK

Not surprisingly, the world of work is just one more area which has been affected hugely by the developments of the digital age. Due to the many new forms of communication available to companies, it has become possible for teams to work together without being in the same office, city or even the same country. Employees more often have the choice to work from home or even from remote places that others go to on holiday.

Understandably, especially older people sometimes struggle with the rapid changes in what is expected from them, while on the other hand, young professionals are often confronted with the view that they lack a work ethic and are more focused on their social media presence than anything else. Overall, the newfound flexibility in several parts of the workplace offers both employers and employees a lot of chances but also poses challenges that need to be addressed.

CHANCES AND RISKS

This is also true for all other areas of our lives. While digital developments continue to make our lives easier and connect us with each other like never before, some people worry about possible downsides and there have been signs of certain dangers and risks. One example is that our dependence on technology may make us particularly vulnerable to certain kinds of attack, like hacker attacks on critical infrastructure. It is essential that people in the 21st century develop digital literacy, which means that they acquire the skills to successfully navigate a life more and more infused by digital technologies.

1

a) Find words highlighted in the text that are synonyms of these words:

1 distant
2 finally
3 vital
4 to collaborate
5 to tackle
6 normal
7 to impact
8 during
9 opportunity
10 disadvantage
11 to supervise

b) Find words highlighted in the text that are antonyms of these words:

1 irrelevant
2 to stop
3 evolution
4 analogue
5 basic
6 to destroy

2 WB p. 58/1

a) Read the definitions and find the corresponding words in the text.

1. to combine different things to form a new thing
2. to move a website up and down in order to be able to look at different parts
3. to make someone aware of something
4. machines like the coffee maker, the blender and the toaster
5. to start working (especially a machine)
6. far away from civilization
7. quick and sudden
8. the person or company who hires people to work for them
9. the ability to properly use digital devices and the internet

b) Find ten more words in the text that you can use to talk about the digital age and write a short definition for each one.

3 WB p. 58/2

You can easily extend your vocabulary by looking at the word families of words you already know. Use a dictionary to add at least one more word to every line.

noun	*verb*	*adjective*
production		
infiltration		
	to alert sb to sth	
		relevant
	to research	
employee		
	to develop	
	to acquire	

Webcode
You can download the grid here:
DSW-73090-037

4 Pair work WB p. 59/3

Discuss whether a typical day in your lives resembles the one described in the second paragraph of the text. Evaluate the impact digitalization has had on you and your everyday lives in comparison to the typical day depicted in the text.

Step by step Argumentative writing

PRE-WRITING

1 Pair work

→ **S15:** How to describe pictures, p. 226

a) Describe the photo and the feelings it evokes in you.
b) The person in the photo can be called a digital nomad. Talk about what you think digital nomads are and do.
c) Compare your results from b) to the following definition of the word "nomad":
"A member of a group of people without a permanent home who move from place to place to find pasture for their animals."
d) Talk about possible living circumstances and jobs that make it possible to live as a digital nomad.

Preview

In this Workshop, you will learn how to write a specific type of argumentative text which discusses a certain topic or statement. When asked to discuss a topic, you should use arguments for and against a certain viewpoint in a balanced way. At the end of your text, you should come to a logical conclusion in which you choose one side (for or against) and explain your choice.
To give you an introduction into the topic, you may be presented with a text first from which you can draw information and possible arguments. Similarly, in this Workshop, you will work on a newspaper article before practising step by step how to discuss a topic in written form. At the end, you will write an argumentative text in which you will discuss whether you would like to become a digital nomad.

COMPREHENSION

2

→ **S1:** Checklist: Summary, p. 198

Read the article on pages 134-136 and summarize the author's personal experience as a digital nomad.

3

a) In the article, several terms and phrases are used that have to do with (digital) work life. Make a list.
b) **Pair work** Compare your list with your partner's and expand your list if necessary.

4

→ **S9:** How to structure a text, p. 212

Outline the reasons mentioned in the article as to why the numbers of digital nomads have been increasing. Use terms and phrases from task 3.

GREG LEA — **The Guardian, 11 May 2019**

The world is my office: why I chose to become a digital nomad worker

1 I dismissed the idea at first. Over a picnic in south London's Brockwell Park last May my friend Tom asked whether I had ever considered leaving the UK behind and continuing my football journalism career abroad.

"Nice thought, mate," I replied. "But I can't see it happening. How would I make it work? Besides, I'd miss you too much." That last bit remains true, but the conversation got me thinking, and a few months later I became a digital nomad –

loosely defined as someone who uses the internet to work remotely without having a fixed home base. It's the best decision I have ever made.

2 The number of digital nomads in the world today is hard to ascertain: there is some overlap with groups such as remote workers, long-term travellers and expatriate online workers. How often do you have to be on the move to be considered a nomad? Do all your earnings have to be derived from the internet, or can you have other sources of income? […]

Helen Barlow is a freelance translator from Liverpool who has lived and worked in 15 countries since 2011. The freedom to travel and increased flexibility in working hours were the key factors behind her decision to take her job on the road.

"Every day is exciting, and there's always a new experience around the corner," she says of a lifestyle which has taken her to Europe, South America and Asia. "I feel like I'm constantly on holiday, and there's no such thing as the Monday morning blues, or the humdrum[1] of a daily commute. Life becomes simpler and more streamlined[2] as you realise you don't need many material possessions. And there's no keeping up with the Joneses[3]."

3 Pieter Levels, the founder of nomadlist.com – a website that ranks towns and cities by their nomad-friendliness based on factors such as cost of living, internet speed and entertainment options – estimates that there will be a billion digital nomads by 2035. That is a bold prediction, but in its support he cites the rise of freelance work, the increasing affordability of air travel, and the decline in home ownership and marriage. […]

4 I was reluctant to label myself a digital nomad before I arrived in Ho Chi Minh City, the largest city in Vietnam – still known as Saigon by almost everyone who lives here. I found the tag[4] a little pretentious, conjuring[5] Instagram influencers sipping[6] coconut water next to an unopened MacBook on a Bali beach. However, since arriving in January, I have met digital nomads from all walks of life. Jobs such as computer programming, copywriting[7], content marketing and web development are most conducive to the internet-itinerant[8] lifestyle, but I have also come across researchers, accountants and fellow journalists. They tend to be male, in their 20s or 30s and from western Europe, the US or Australia, but I have met a Taiwanese social media manager and a Brazilian graphic designer too. […]

"We live in a project-based economy, and more digital work is becoming available in more occupations, creating opportunities for people to go nomadic," says the Canadian-Pakistani, who is currently based in Greece. "Life goals are also different. Millennials[9] tend to favour experiences over possessions, which suits this kind of lifestyle."

The ability to travel and connect with people all over the world while still earning a living is my favourite thing about being a digital nomad. As Bill Nye, the US "science guy"[10], once said, "Everyone you will ever meet knows something you don't."

The constant sense of adventure that stems from being far from home is another plus. Many of my days here are not too dissimilar to my life in London – filing articles, editing copy for football websites The Set Pieces and FourFourTwo, consuming too much caffeine – but the unfamiliarity means there is excitement in the most mundane tasks, such as ordering lunch or taking a (motorbike) taxi. Using a popular co-working space also offers me the chance to regularly meet new people, and there is a thrill in not knowing who might walk through the door each day. Alas[11], no fellow Crystal Palace[12] fan has yet shown up. 5

Annotations

1 **humdrum** = monotony
2 to **streamline** = to optimize, to concentrate on what is important
3 to **keep up with the Joneses** = to envy what others have
4 **tag** = label
5 to **conjure** = to create an image in one's mind
6 to **sip** = to drink slowly
7 **copywriting** = writing the text for advertisements
8 **itinerant** = travelling around constantly
9 **Millennial** = member of the generation born between ca. 1980 and 2000
10 **Bill Nye the Science Guy** = American TV presenter known for science TV shows
11 **alas** = unfortunately
12 **Crystal Palace** = football club from London

6 It is not all fun and games, however, and the lifestyle would not suit everyone. The lack of permanence can be draining. Many digital nomads actively avoid becoming too attached to people or places, as they will soon be on the move. Barlow says: “I’ve had solitary times, especially when hopping from place to place in a short period, as I didn’t give myself the chance to commit to new friendships or activities. Maintaining a romantic relationship with someone who has more commitments at home and does not share the same freedom is another challenge. On the work side, battling dodgy wifi connections isn’t ideal when you’ve got deadlines.”

7 Pablo Genest, who quit his studies in France to begin building an online maths course from Vietnam, says: “You need to have a lot of discipline to live this way. My mum was a bit concerned that I was wasting my potential, which is understandable because a lot of older people don’t know what digital nomadism is. I get why she was apprehensive, but being able to work from anywhere is a real blessing.”

I could not agree more. I spent a few weeks in Japan in April, and plan to visit China, South Korea and Malaysia before the year is out. I am not sure how long I will stay in each place, and Saigon has already occupied a big enough place in my heart to make a return highly likely, but the opportunity to explore new places and continue to try and explain Brexit is too good to resist.

I owe my friend Tom a beer. 8

ANALYSIS

5

a) The article is divided into eight sections. Give each section a heading which summarizes its content.

b) Examine the purpose of each section and add it to your headings. Use the following terms: introduction, conclusion, argument, fact, example. Sometimes, more than just one term applies.

c) Take a look at the sections and analyse the line of argument the author applies. → SUPPORT D1, p. 187

→ **S13:** Checklist: Analysis – non-fictional texts, p. 222

WRITING: PLANNING THE INTRODUCTION

6

Now that you have become familiar with life as a digital nomad, you can start preparing your argumentative text, in which you will discuss whether you would like to become a digital nomad yourself. First, you will learn how to write a good introduction.

a) Read the info box and the example introduction and identify the different elements used here, which are marked in different colours.

Sitting at my desk studying for my final exams I often catch myself staring out the window imagining how nice it would be to do something else instead. Wouldn’t it be great if I could find a job where I would be able to sit in a hammock on a beach in Bali, working from there while sipping coconut water? Due to the increasing number of location-independent jobs, this fantasy of mine could become reality in the future if I decided to become a digital nomad. The question, however, is whether this lifestyle choice would really turn out to bring the absolute freedom that it seems to bring.

b) **Pair work** Collect further ideas on how to write an interesting introduction. You can also use the *Guardian* article for help.

Info

Introduction

You should start with an interesting introduction, which presents the issue of your text. To attract the reader’s attention, you can use facts or an anecdote related to the topic. Your introduction should also mention the fact that the topic will be discussed in a balanced way.

WRITING: PLANNING THE MAIN BODY

7

a) Read the following info box on how to write the main body of an argumentative text. Then make a list of arguments for and against becoming a digital nomad, using the arguments from the *Guardian* article. → SUPPORT D2, p. 187

b) Add your own arguments to both sides of the list.

c) Decide whether you are for or against becoming a digital nomad yourself.

d) Decide which arguments you are going to use and in which order. If you want to use the hourglass structure, number your arguments from most to least convincing for both sides. If you want to use the antithetical/ping pong structure, find the arguments for and against the topic that belong together and mark them using the same colour.

Info

Main body

In the main body, you present arguments for and against the issue at hand that you have prepared before writing the actual text. Before you start writing, make sure you know which side you support.

Each argument should have its own paragraph, starting with a **topic sentence**. A topic sentence is a thesis or statement which introduces the content of the whole paragraph, e.g.: *The most striking reason to live as a digital nomad is being able to see the world.*

This statement must now be explained in detail and supported with examples, facts, statistics or relevant quotations. After that you start a new paragraph with a new topic sentence introducing the next argument.

However, you should decide beforehand how you want to structure your arguments. When you discuss an issue, there are **two ways of structuring your main body**:

1 **Hourglass:** You first deal with the opposing viewpoint and then with your own. You start with the strongest argument of the opposing view, then the second strongest and so on until you reach the weakest counterargument. Then you introduce the weakest argument of your own line of argument and end with your strongest argument. That way, your strongest argument will stay in the reader's mind.

2 **Antithetical** ("ping pong"): You start with a counterargument and immediately refute it with an argument from your own side. This structure only makes sense if the arguments for and against the topic match each other. Again, you should end with your strongest argument.

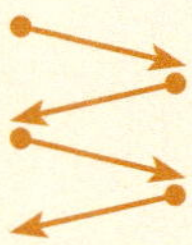

You are not expected to consider every argument there is. Instead it is a good idea to concentrate on about three arguments for each side, preferably the most important aspects, and to discuss these in detail.

WRITING: PLANNING THE CONCLUSION

8

a) Read this info box and the two conclusions (A and B) on page 138 and choose the one that you think is more suitable.

b) Pair work Explain your choice to a partner.

Info

Conclusion

Conclude your text with a paragraph that sums up the evidence and restates the topic. Here you state which side or perspective makes more sense or is more justified in your opinion. You may, at this point, also add personal feelings about the topic, say how you see the topic in the context of other related issues and/or give an outlook on how the issue in question might develop in the future. In any case, do not simply repeat arguments or add new ones! Instead, state your view in a concise way.

A Taking into account what has been said so far, I do not believe that becoming a digital nomad is the best lifestyle choice for me because it would not make me happy. The constant struggle of balancing the wish to explore the world and having to earn my living at the same time would be too stressful. I would rather keep my private and my work life separate and do a regular job to save up for travelling in my free time.

B Having considered the different arguments, I must admit that becoming a digital nomad initially sounds like the best lifestyle choice ever. However, this perfect image of working while sitting in a hammock in Bali omits the fact that life as a digital nomad is both stressful and lonely. So in conclusion, I would prefer a regular job in which I can earn money to sit in a hammock in Bali on vacation – without having to do any work.

WRITING THE TEXT

→ **S6:** How to write an argumentative text, p. 206

9
Now write your argumentative text: Discuss whether you would like to become a digital nomad yourself. Use your own introduction, main body and conclusion. Also use the language support for help.

Language support

Argumentative text

Introduction
The issue that is touched upon here is whether becoming a digital nomad is ...
The question raised here is whether ...

Line of argument: my point of view
Considering the fact that many jobs can be done location-independently ...
Another important argument/factor/point is ...
You also have to take into consideration that you still have to ...

Line of argument: balancing points of view
On the one hand becoming a digital nomad gives you the liberty to ..., on the other hand you cannot ... because ...
In contrast to this argument, one might argue that ...

Personal conclusion
Taking into account what has been said so far, I am of the opinion that becoming a digital nomad ...
To come to a final conclusion, I think the advantages of becoming a digital nomad ...
Looking at the two sides of life as a digital nomad, I have to say ...

Practice Argumentative writing

PRE-WRITING

1
The digitalization of work and of everyday life has opened up new opportunities for more flexible arrangements, for example in terms of an employee's workplace. While some work cannot be done remotely, there are a great number of jobs which allow employees to at least partly work from home.

a) In class, make three lists of jobs which can always, sometimes and never be done from home.
b) Considering your examples, talk about general job characteristics which support or complicate working from home and note them down below your lists.

2 WB p. 60/1

a) Pair work Take turns picking a photo and explaining the way it represents both advantages and disadvantages of working from home. Fill in the following grid. → SUPPORT D3, p. 187

potential advantages of working from home	*potential disadvantages of working from home*

b) Read the quotations and find out what CEOs and other executives from different companies have said about working from home. Add arguments in favour of and against working from home from an employer's perspective to your grid.

1 That unplanned kind of interaction that contributes so much to how we build relationships with people and how we build culture, those things are what are missing.
Andi Owen, chief executive of furniture producer Herman Miller Inc.

2 I am concerned that we would somehow believe that we can basically take kids from college, put them in front of Zoom, and think that three years from now, they'll be every bit as productive as they would have had they had the personal interaction [of work in an office].
Ronald J. Kruszewski, chief executive of Stifel Financial Corp.

3 I want to hire the best and the brightest even if they work from a different location [...]
Heyward Donigan, chief executive of American drugstore chain Rite Aid Corp.

4 Most of us are not hermits ... We need that social interaction, not only from a business standpoint but truly from a kind of personal-development standpoint.
Jim Fish , CEO of Waste Management Inc.

5 What I worry about the most is innovation. Innovation is hard to schedule – it's impossible to schedule.
Ellen Kullman, CEO of 3-D printing start-up Carbon Inc.

6 It [video conferencing technology] will make us more comfortable in providing more flexibility to employees, which, by the way, makes this a more attractive place for people to work.
David M. Solomon, CEO of investment bank Goldman Sachs

7 Maybe we don't need all the offices that we currently have around the world. So there is a major effort going, taking place as it relates to the costs in the business.
Dirk van de Put, CEO of multinational food and drink company Mondelez

c) Add at least two more arguments of your own to the grid.

WRITING

3 WB p. 62

In an argumentative text, discuss whether working from home is an arrangement you consider beneficial.

→ **S6:** How to write an argumentative text, p. 206

Has technology made us lazy and dependent?

Webcode

You can find the video here: **DSW-73090-038**

→ **S20:** How to listen/watch effectively, p. 234

1 WB p. 63/1-3

Several years ago, Pixar released a film called *Wall-E* set in the future, in which humans no longer occupy the earth. However, the robot Wall-E is left there to clean up after the humans. He then follows another robot to space, where he learns how humans live there and how they use digital devices.

a) Watch the clip from the film and note down how the humans live in space.

b) **Pair work** Discuss how much truth lies in the depiction of humans in the clip.

2 WB p. 65/1-2

a) Read the following article and list the examples given in the text which allegedly prove that we've become too dependent on technology.

b) **Pair work** Add your own examples to the list and compare your list with a partner's.

Are we too dependent on technology?

Terry Brown, 31 March 2020

When I was but a young, fresh-faced whipper-snapper[1] at school, I learned to do math in my head. I had my times tables up to 20 memorized and knew a slew[2] of mental math tricks I could call upon to add, subtract, divide, or multiply any two numbers you threw at me. Over the years, however, no doubt, as I became lazy and complacent[3] during my teens, I learned another trick – reach for my calculator. Today, if you were to give me a relatively simple sum like 74 + 113 – my hand would instinctively delve straight into my pocket for my smartphone. Why? Because, in all truth, it would probably be quicker – I've become so dependent on technology to perform calculations (calculators, smartphones, spreadsheet software) that I've lost all confidence in my ability to perform even simple sums in my head. In fact, sadly, now that I think about it, I've forgotten most of my multiplication tables, and those mental math tricks have all but vanished.

I can take some dubious solace[4] in the fact that I know I'm probably not alone here.

As a society, we have become dependent on technology to perform everything from mathematical calculations to communicating with friends, paying our bills and ordering a pizza. Hell, my cell even reminds me to go to sleep at night – and my smartwatch commands me to "Move!" when I've been sat on my butt too long.

But technology is, of course, the great enabler of the modern age. Cars, planes, Google, smartphones, computers, business software – it all makes us more efficient and less prone[5] to errors. But it begs

the question – what would happen if we had to go without our contraptions and gadgets? If computers and applications are our minds and our memories and machines, our hands and legs, could we cope without them? Could it be that we've become too dependent on technology? For all its power to increase our capabilities in both our private and professional lives, is our reliance on technology changing – even damaging – our brains?

Annotations

[1] **whipper-snapper** = a small fish; *here:* a young and unexperienced person

[2] **slew** = a large number

[3] **complacent** = self-satisfied, naive

[4] **solace** = relief, consolation

[5] to **be prone to** sth = to be very likely to happen

London taxi drivers are excellent navigators. To become licensed, they must pass the world-famous "Knowledge of London" test – usually abbreviated to "The Knowledge." To do so, they're required to memorize hundreds of routes and landmarks and demonstrate their knowledge of them in test situations. They commit to memory thousands of street names and can mentally visualize hundreds of journeys across the UK's biggest city. This impressive cognitive map is evident on an MRI[7] scan – in an enlarged part of the brain called the hippocampus.
However, as sat-navs and GPS technology have become commercially available and widespread, there have been calls in recent years for The Knowledge to be scrapped. Who needs to rely on their own memories in the digital age, right?
Well, a 2017 study by researchers at University College London (UCL) – published in *Nature Communications* – claims that when using automated systems to memorize directions and guide us where we need to go, the hippocampus and other areas of the brain used to think of different routes are "switched off." In other words, when we are dependent on technology for navigation, parts of our brain cease to be used – and when that happens, they stop growing. [...] While we're not all London cabbies[7], most of us these days now take turn-by-turn instructions from a GPS device to take the stress out of navigation. But scientists are finding that an underactive hippocampus could have broader implications for our health and well-being, particularly in terms of child development, mental health, and dementia[8]. By not regularly exercising the brain, just like a muscle, it becomes weak and unhealthy.

Annotations
[6] **MRI** = Magnetic resonance imaging, a technique that uses magnetic fields to form pictures of the body
[7] **cabby** = cab driver
[8] **dementia** = medical condition characterised by a growing loss of cognitive functions, i.e. remembering

3
Examine the strategies the author uses to convince his readers of his view. → SUPPORT D4, p. 188

→ **S13:** Checklist: Analysis – non-fictional texts, p. 222

4 WB p. 67/3
The article mainly uses arguments to support the view that technology has made us lazy and dependent. Collect arguments that refute this view, weigh up the pros and cons and write a letter to the editor in which you respond to his views.

→ **S4:** Writing a letter to the editor, p. 204

Advanced texts Mediation: Payment methods

1 Card survey
a) Ask your family members, friends and teachers about their preferred payment methods. Find out
- where they use cash and why,
- where they use other payment methods and why.

b) Cluster the cards on the board to identify which payment methods are used when and why.

Language support
to pay by credit card
to pay by debit card
to pay cash/in cash
to use contactless payment services

2
In class or in groups, discuss whether you think using cash will no longer exist in the future.

3 Across cultures → **S19:** How to improve your mediation skills, p. 232
During the summer holidays, your friend Harry from England visits you and he notices that, unlike people in his home country, Germans still use cash frequently. After Harry is back in England, you come across the article on the next page about the preferred payment methods in Europe, including Germany. Write Harry an email (about 200 words) in which you explain when and why Germans use cash and why this habit has been decreasing in recent years.

Bar oder unbar? EZB sieht Bedeutung von Schein und Münze schwinden

Von Jörn Bender, dpa, 02.12.2020

Die Corona-Krise verändert auch das Verhalten vieler Konsumenten: Einkäufe werden häufiger per Plastikkarte oder Smartphone beglichen. Doch noch hat die Mehrheit beim Bezahlen eine klare Präferenz.

Frankfurt/Main (dpa) – „Kontaktloses Bezahlen boomt", „Krisengewinner Girocard" – gemessen an mancher Überschrift des Corona-Jahres 2020 scheint die Bedeutung von Bargeld zu schrumpfen. Doch ändert die Krise das Bezahlverhalten der Menschen in Europa wirklich grundlegend – vor allem das der bargeldliebenden Deutschen?

Neueste Zahlen der Europäischen Zentralbank (EZB) bestätigen einen langjährigen Trend: Bereits im Jahr vor der Corona-Krise verlor Bargeld für Verbraucher weiter an Bedeutung. Zwar sind Scheine und Münzen demnach weiterhin das beliebteste Zahlungsmittel für kleinere Beträge an der Ladenkasse. Die Nutzung von Karten jedoch nimmt zu.

„In den letzten Jahren hat die digitale Revolution [...] dazu geführt, dass sich die Zahlungsgewohnheiten der Menschen stark verändert haben: Immer häufiger halten wir zum Bezahlen einfach eine Karte vor, wischen über unser Smartphone oder nutzen eine Smartwatch", fasst EZB-Direktoriumsmitglied Fabio Panetta zusammen.

Nach Angaben der Währungshüter griffen die Verbraucher im Euroraum im vergangenen Jahr bereits bei fast jedem vierten Bezahlvorgang (24 Prozent) zur Plastikkarte. Bei der Erhebung drei Jahre zuvor waren es noch 19 Prozent. Der Anteil der Bargeldzahlungen sank im gleichen Zeitraum von 79 auf 73 Prozent.

Besonders häufig kommt Bargeld der EZB-Auswertung zufolge in Malta (88 Prozent der Transaktionen) sowie Zypern und Spanien (je 83 Prozent) zum Einsatz. Deutschland liegt mit 77 Prozent in der oberen Hälfte der 19 Euroländer. Am seltensten greifen die Niederländer zu Schein und Münze (34 Prozent). Deutschland liegt gemessen an den täglichen Kartenzahlungen pro Kopf unter dem Schnitt der Euroländer.

Sicher ist: Die Pandemie hat dem bargeldlosen Bezahlen auch hierzulande einen Schub gegeben. In Zeiten des grassierenden Virus gilt etwa das kontaktlose Bezahlen an der Ladenkasse als sehr hygienisch. [...]

Das Handelsforschungsinstitut EHI geht davon aus, dass im laufenden Jahr rund eine Milliarde Einkäufe weniger im deutschen Einzelhandel mit Bargeld beglichen werden als 2019. [...]

In einer EZB-Erhebung in den Euroländern im Juli 2020 gaben vier von zehn Befragten an, seit Beginn der Pandemie seltener Bargeld verwendet zu haben. Die Werbung für kontaktloses Bezahlen in der aktuellen Krise zeigt Wirkung. [...] Fast 90 Prozent derjenigen, die in der aktuellen Krise häufiger auf Bargeld verzichten, wollen dies nach der Pandemie beibehalten (46 Prozent sicher, 41 Prozent wahrscheinlich).

Allerdings: Auf Cash ganz verzichten will die Mehrheit der Verbraucher bislang nicht. Betrachtet man beispielsweise die Gesamtzahl der Einkäufe im deutschen Einzelhandel, kommt Bargeld immer noch bei zwei Drittel aller Zahlungen zum Einsatz.

Und auch in der am Mittwoch vorgelegten EZB-Bezahlstudie betonen 55 Prozent der Befragten, wie wichtig es ihnen ist, auch in Zukunft die Möglichkeit zu haben, auf Scheine und Münzen zurückgreifen zu können. [...]

Währungshüter Panetta zeigt [...] Verständnis: „Selbst wenn digitale Zahlungen möglichst robust gestaltet werden, so bleiben sie doch anfällig für Störungen wie Stromausfälle, Cyberbedrohungen oder technische Störungen." Bargeld stelle dann „eine wichtige Absicherung und einen zuverlässigen Wertspeicher" dar. Zudem gebe es auch Menschen ohne Bankkonto oder diejenigen, die mangels digitaler Kenntnisse lieber auf Bargeld zurückgreifen.

„Wir sind daher weiterhin fest entschlossen, dafür zu sorgen, dass Bargeld auch künftig im gesamten Euroraum weithin verfügbar ist und akzeptiert wird", bekräftigte Panetta. Zugleich jedoch treibt die EZB ihre Arbeiten an einer digitalen Version des Euro voran – als Ergänzung zur gedruckten und geprägten Gemeinschaftswährung. „Die Digitalisierung hat das Potenzial, den Zahlungsverkehr zu revolutionieren", resümierte Panetta. „Dennoch ist es wichtig, dass die privaten Haushalte und die Unternehmen in Europa weiterhin eine Wahl haben."

(579 Wörter)

Planning and hosting a chat show (Lernaufgabe)

You are going to plan and host a chat show with different guests on the following topic:
The impact of digitalization on our daily lives

1
Divide the class up into groups. Decide which group will prepare which role for the chat show. Two students should focus on being the hosts of the show while the other groups can be bigger.

2
In your group, write down arguments for your respective role. Also take into consideration which arguments the other groups might use. Use your results from the tasks in this Theme.

3
Study your role card below, which serves as a starting point. In your group, you may give your role a biography and personality to be more convincing during the chat show.

4
Stage the chat show.

Webcode
You can download the role cards here:
DSW-73090-065

role card
host
As an impartial host, you consider all perspectives in a balanced way. You should anticipate possible arguments and prepare challenging questions to ask your guests.

role card
tech start up CEO
As the CEO of a tech company, you need to be able to compete with other international tech companies. The digitalization of work is important to you because it makes work processes more efficient.

role card
former social media influencer
As a fitness blogger and influencer, you have made your fair share of money. However, the ongoing pressure to perform and display a perfect body has resulted in serious health issues so now you are sceptical of the influence of social media.

role card
remote worker
As a journalist and copywriter, you are able to work remotely as long as you have a good wifi connection. You believe this freedom to live and work anywhere you want is crucial to your happiness.

role card
unemployed worker
After 25 years in the same company, you have been laid off because your job can now be done by a robot. Being middle-aged with a family to support, you desperately need a new job, but have trouble finding one.

role card
labour union employee
In your opinion, digitalization is inevitable, however, you are worried about the negative effects on society. This is why you think both politics and the economy must cooperate to ensure a steady and well-planned transformation.

role card
therapist
You have been noticing that the constant use of digital devices has made your patients lazy and isolated because they spend their time at home instead of going outside to meet and interact with other people. You believe this often affects your patients' psychological health.

role card
online activist
Thanks to the internet, it has become so simple to find like-minded people from all over the world. This is why you support digitalization, as this has enabled you to participate in international protest movements.

6 English as a lingua franca

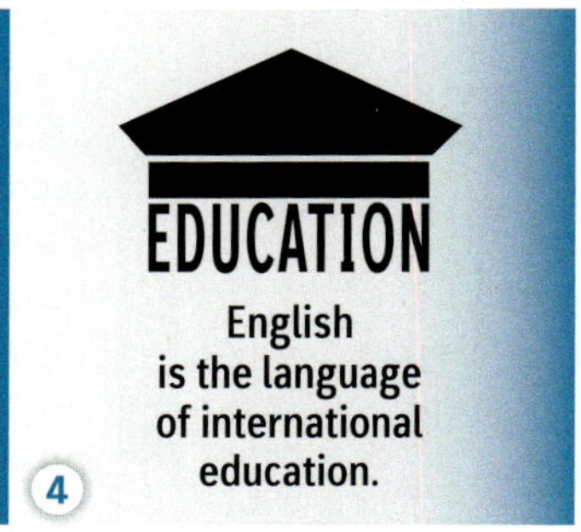

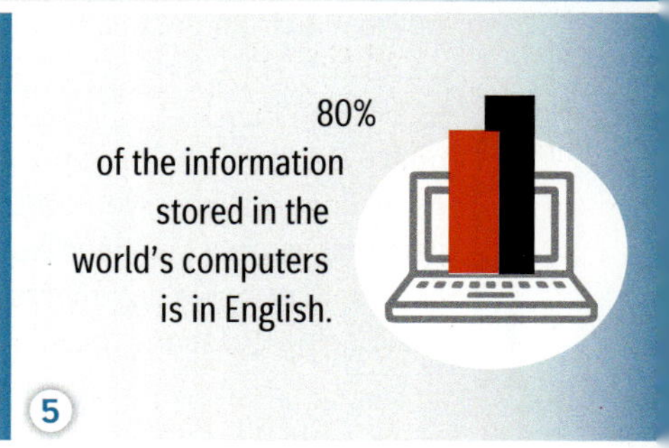

1 → **S18:** How to analyse statistics, p. 230

English is spoken by more than 1.5 billion people all over the world and is the official language in many countries. It is taught in schools in countless other countries and speaking English is considered an important skill. Study the infographics above and explain the importance of English in your own words.

2

a) Look at the advertising posters for different English language courses. Describe what they highlight about English.

b) Using your knowledge about English, design your own poster advertising the benefits of learning the language.

Webcode

You can download a word list for the Theme here: DSW-73090-039

English is the third largest language by number of native speakers, after Mandarin Chinese and Spanish. Combining native and non-native speakers it is considered to be the most commonly spoken language worldwide.
About 400 million people speak English as their first language.

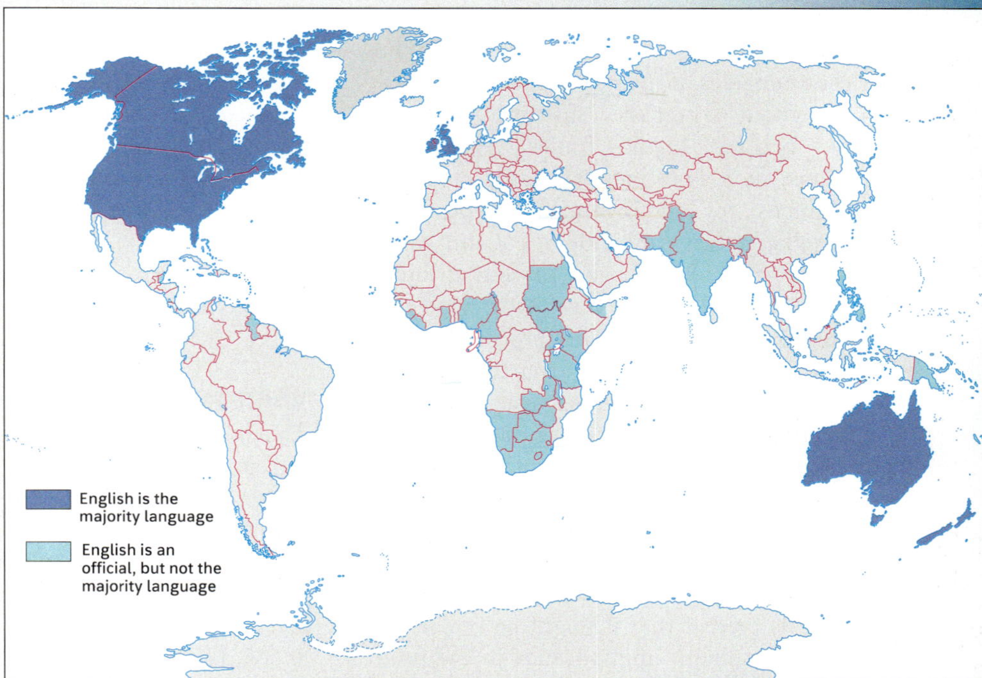

6

Preview

This Theme deals with English as a global lingua franca and the varieties of it that exist.
In the **Workshop** of this Theme, you will improve your mediation skills:

- ✓ considering the addressee
- ✓ identifying the situational context of your text
- ✓ considering the type of text that should be produced
- ✓ knowing what aspects of the text to focus on

3 EXTRA

Because so many people all over the world speak English, many varieties of the language can be found. Read the text on p. 146 and list the varieties that are mentioned there. Do some research on a particular form of English and present your findings to the class. If possible, include a speech sample (video or audio).

→ **S26:** How to design a poster, p. 244
→ **S27:** Evaluating online sources, p. 245

WHAT IS A LINGUA FRANCA?

Lingua francas, sometimes also known as bridge languages, are languages that are used to enable communication between groups of people who do not speak the same native language. When communicating in a lingua franca, members of such groups can show various degrees of fluency in that language.

Throughout human history, languages have become lingua francas for various reasons, such as to facilitate trade or cultural exchanges, for administrative purposes and to exchange scientific findings. Latin, Greek, Farsi, Swahili, French and of course English all evolved into lingua francas at some point in the past or present. This process has been subject to constant change over the millennia; new lingua francas emerge, reach their peak, their importance is diminished again and the number of speakers declines, until a new lingua franca displaces the old language. While lingua francas have been used for centuries, English as a lingua franca is a special case because of the extent to which it is used, although some scientists predict that it might be replaced by another dominant lingua franca in the future, such as Chinese.

THE PREDOMINANCE OF ENGLISH

Currently, the world's predominant language in areas such as international trade, seafaring and airfaring, science, mass media, news, international telecommunications as well as diplomacy and international relations is English. English is one of six official languages of the United Nations. Many other worldwide international organizations use English in official statements or even as their working language. Many international scientific endeavours are conducted entirely in English. Therefore, having fluency in English as a second language is considered an asset today and proves useful in a multitude of contexts. To facilitate international communication, several attempts have been made to develop a simplified standard English, sometimes called Globish.

THE DISTRIBUTION OF ENGLISH

Though few countries have English as their primary language, it is currently the language most often taught as a foreign language. It is the most widely spoken foreign language in most EU countries. Because of its usefulness, being able to speak English carries a certain prestige, but most non-native speakers today acquire it for practical rather than ideological reasons. When decolonization began, many countries did not reject the language of their former colonizers in the process, but rather chose English as their own language or continued to use it interchangeably with native languages.

Throughout this process, English itself has undergone many changes and transformations, so that many varieties of the language exist today.

VARIETIES OF ENGLISH

The oldest variety of English is British English, but it is only spoken by about 60 million native speakers. All the other English native speakers speak some variant of English such as American English, Australian English, South African English or Indian English, to name just a few. Collectively, these variants are known as World Englishes. American English is the variety of English with the largest number of native speakers: 225 million. Its sound and vocabulary have been shaped by many influences, most notably the great waves of forced and voluntary migration of people from Africa, Europe, Asia and the Americas to the United States. It might not be surprising then that American and Irish speakers of English sometimes sound quite similar given the large number of Irish immigrants to the USA in the 19th century.

Some varieties of English, often having evolved out of colonial contact between English-speaking rulers and a non-English-speaking (slave) population, are so unique that they classify as languages in their own right. An example of this is Patwa or Jamaican Creole, spoken in Jamaica. It features elements of English, West African languages and new creations. Jamaicans are proud of their distinctive language and strive to preserve it.

1

Replace the underlined words or phrases with words from the text. Note: you may have to change the form, e.g. singular/plural, different tense.

1. The use of Swahili made it possible for Arab and African traders to do business with each other.
2. The importance of Farsi as a lingua franca in Asia declined with the rise of Russia and Britain as global powers.
3. It is hard to tell which language will become the next world language.
4. At a number of universities in continental Europe, English has become the main language of instruction.
5. Over the course of time, the English language has developed into many "Englishes".
6. It can be hard to understand people with noticable accents.

2 WB p. 68/1

a) Complete the grid with the corresponding words. Use a dictionary, if necessary.

b) Find words from the grid to match these definitions.

1. when something is very respected
2. to make something easier to understand or learn
3. to make sure that something survives
4. to say that something will happen in the future
5. someone who is able to talk to people well is ...
6. slow change over time
7. the ability to speak a language very well

noun	adjective	verb
communication	...	...
...	*1) variant* *2) various*	...
...		*to evolve*
...	*fluent*	
acquisition	...	...
prestige	...	
...		*to preserve*
...	*simple*	...
...	...	*to influence*
...	*similar*	
prediction	...	...

Webcode
You can download the grid here:
DSW-73090-040

3 WB p. 68/2, p. 69/3

a) Match the words from A with the words from B to form collocations.

A to carry | to use | to preserve | to reach | to embark | to facilitate | to go into

B a peak | prestige | on an endeavour | communication | decline | the status quo | interchangeably

b) Complete the sentences with the collocations from a).

1. Latin as an elite lingua franca ___ with the rise of French in the 18th century.
2. Being fluent in English greatly ___ in education and business.
3. Languages are evolving constantly. It's pointless to try ___.
4. The use of English has ___. Will it be replaced by another lingua franca soon?
5. Having a good education ___ in many societies.
6. People who are bilingual are able ___ two languages ___.
7. ___, like moving abroad, can be quite hard at first.

Step by step Mediation

Preview

In this Workshop, you are going to work on a mediation task. When working on such a task, do not translate the German text literally. Instead, write an English text of your own in which you include relevant information from the German text. Before you start writing your text, it is important to fully understand the task in order to identify the following four points:

- who is the addressee?
- what is the situational context?
- what type of text are you asked to produce?
- what information from the German text should you include?

1 Across cultures

This is the task you are going to work on. Read the instructions below. Match the colours to the four points in the Preview above.

You are taking part in an international youth conference on the role of media in society. On the last day, there will be a panel discussion with young people from different countries on the influence of the media on the way we communicate and how TV and other mass media influence the way we use language. Your task will be to speak about the benefits of the availability of English-language media for young Germans.
As preparation, you have done some research and found the article by Klaus Ungerer.
Write an introductory speech to the panel discussion focusing on

- the way Germans have consumed English-language media up to now and the consequences,
- changes the author is seeing at the moment.

2

→ **S19:** How to improve your mediation skills, p. 232

Prepare a short checklist for the introductory speech you need to produce. Include points on all relevant aspects of a mediation task. Your checklist may look like this:

checklist		
addressee	*young people …*	✓
situational context	…	

3

a) Read the following article and take notes on points that are relevant to your task.
b) Across cultures Identify relevant aspects or examples that might not be understandable without knowledge of German culture and take notes on how you want to explain these to your audience.

4

→ **S5:** Checklist: Writing a speech, p. 205

Write your introductory speech (50 words). Include your explanations of culture-specific concepts if necessary.

KLAUS UNGERER

Frankfurter Allgemeine Zeitung, 4. März 2017

Lustig? Nicht auf Deutsch!

Deutsche Zuschauer erleben die Stars der Film- und Serienwelt nur als bewegte Abziehbilder. Die Synchronisation raubt ihnen den eigenen Ton und die Sprache. Ein Selbstversuch zeigt, was uns dabei alles entgeht.

Mein Opa hat sein Abitur noch mit knoff und kneff bestritten. Sie hatten Englisch als mündliche Prüfung, so erzählte er manchmal, aber mündliches Englisch hatte im Unterricht nie stattgefunden, damals. Sie hatten die Sprache ungefähr so kennengelernt, wie man einem lateinischen Text gegenübersitzt. Sie hatten sich braverweise die Formen eingepaukt, und mit den Formen gingen sie dann in die mündliche

Prüfung: weiß, wusste, gewusst – knoff, kneff, knoffn. Und so weiter. Es muss eine quälende Sache gewesen sein, die einen zwischen Scham und Lachen zerrissen hätte, und vielleicht wussten es nicht einmal ihre Lehrer viel besser, damals, irgendwo in Südniedersachsen kurz nach dem Ersten Weltkrieg. […]

Abiturklasse 1920

Müheloses Switchen zwischen den Sprachen

Und auch selbst denkt man nur ungern zurück an die Zeit in Schweden als Austauschstudent: Sie mochten nicht ganz so hochtrabend gebildet sein, die schwedischen Kommilitonen, wie man selbst, ihre Uni mochte verschulter sein – aber mit ihrem jederzeit fließenden Englisch machten sie aus dem deutschen Austauschstudenten binnen Sekunden einen stammelnden Globalisierungsverlierer.

Mühelos switchten sie von ihrer Heimatsprache ins Englische hinüber und zurück, und es mochte ihnen an Rechtschreibung und Grammatikkenntnissen fehlen, doch sie beherrschten das Wunder der Sprache: sich jederzeit auszudrücken, geschmeidig mit jedem kommunizieren zu können. Woran aber liegt es, dass sie im entlegenen, menschenleeren Norden eine solche selbstverständliche Weltläufigkeit entwickeln konnten, derweil der Durchschnittsdeutsche im Herzen Europas als Provinzdepp herangewachsen ist?

Viele Elemente gehen verloren

Ausnahmsweise ist hier eine einfache Antwort möglich. Sie sind da oben so sprachstark und wir so verblödet, weil die Leute in Hollywood dunnemals den Tonfilm erfunden haben, und weil der Tonfilm kurz darauf eine geistige Verfinsterung über uns brachte, von der skandinavische Länder oder auch die Niederlande verschont blieben. In Deutschland wurde immer alles synchronisiert, und synchronisiert heißt: Man nimmt ein Filmkunstwerk voller Schauspieler und Sprache, voller Körperlichkeit, Timing und Sprachwitz. Zieht das alles ab. Behält die Bildspur bei. Und klatscht eine neue, teutsche Tonspur druff. Was da alles verloren geht! Erste Opfer sind seit Urzeiten Dialekt und Soziolekt, unrettbar. Denn wie will man einen Dialekt übersetzen, ohne dass es peinlich wird? Wie soll überleben, was da mitschwingt, wenn in einem amerikanischen Film plötzlich jemand mit britischem Akzent auftaucht? Wie soll man den Graben eindeutschen, der schon sprachlich zwischen einem Afroamerikaner und dem Redneck-Polizisten klafft? Rein ins Hannoversche Bühnendeutsch alles. Perdü, vorbei.

Ein Experiment mit den eigenen Lieblingsserien

[…] Einen Nachmittag lang wage ich das Experiment. Und schaue mir ein paar Lieblingsserien an. Im Original habe ich sie staffelweise gefressen. Jetzt mal auf Deutsch. Schauen wir mal. Hören wir mal. Praktisch unvermeidlich: dass oft der Sprachwitz auf der Strecke bleibt. Viele englische Ausdrücke lassen sich nicht übertragen, mancherlei Anspielungen würden im Deutschen sinnlos verpuffen. […]

Etwas hat sich geändert

[…] Hoffnung aber ist immer. In meinem Fall ist sie 13 Jahre alt und flitzt nach der Schule am liebsten in ihr Zimmer. Sie guckt Netflix. „Big Bang Theory", „Dr. Who", „Pretty Little Liars". Hat sie alle schon durch. Manchmal taucht sie aus ihrem Zimmer wieder auf, manchmal sprechen wir Englisch. Achte Klasse, wie soll ich sagen? Mühsam holperten wir uns damals durch das englische Gestrüpp, nie werden wir fit sein für die globalisierte Welt. Die Tochter aber spricht fließend, und sie spricht mit bewundernswertem amerikanischem Akzent. Sich das Zeug auf Deutsch reinzuziehen käme ihr nie in den Sinn. Der Uropa hätte seine Freude an ihr. Er würde lächeln – über sich selbst, über kneff und knoff und all das Verpasste. (601 Wörter)

Practice Mediation

1 Across cultures → SUPPORT D1, p. 188 WB pp. 70-73

→ **S19:** How to improve your mediation skills, p. 232

You are on a high school exchange in America. Your English teacher asks you to give a short presentation about English as the "global language" from a German perspective. After some research, you find the blog post below. Use it to write the script for your short presentation for the class (150 words). Focus on reasons that speak against English as the global language from the author's point of view.

Warum Englisch nicht als Weltsprache taugt

Wer die Welt beherrscht, beherrscht auch die Sprache. [...] Jetzt kommen mir aber auch immer wieder Versuche unter, das Vorherrschen des Englischen mit einer allgemeinen sprachlichen Überlegenheit gegenüber dem Deutschen zu begründen. Einige dieser Argumente greife ich hier auf. [...]

Kürzer = schwieriger zu lernen.

Ganz objektiv lässt sich dagegen sagen, dass englische Formulierungen kürzer sind als deutsche. Und das wird der Sprache auch ständig hoch angerechnet. Zu Unrecht – wie ich meine. Wenn Kürze so erstrebenswert ist, stellt sich nämlich die Frage, warum wir dann nicht gleich Kanji, die chinesischen Schriftzeichen, statt einer Lautschrift verwenden. [...] Wenn Du von Kanji schon gehört hast, wirst Du jetzt vielleicht gleich aufschreien: »Ja, aber von denen gibt es doch Tausende. Wie soll man sich die denn alle merken?« Und ja, da gebe ich Dir recht. Der springende Punkt ist nur: Die Verkürzung im Englischen gegenüber dem Deutschen bekommt man ebenso wenig für lau. Das Deutsche wird gerne für Wortungetüme wie Kraftfahrzeughaftpflichtversicherung [...] kritisiert. [...] Der Vorteil solcher zusammengesetzten Wörter ist aber, dass sie sich einfach herleiten lassen. Man könnte die Kraftfahrzeughaftpflichtversicherung auch einfach Krafag nennen. Aber kein Mensch, der dieses Vokabel nicht stur auswendig gelernt hat, wird dann noch wissen, wovon die Rede ist. Im Englischen ist das der Normalfall, wie ich an folgender »Schweinerei« demonstriere: [...]

pig	**wild boar**	**warthog**	**swine**	**pork**
Schwein	Wild-schwein	Warzen-schwein	Haus-schwein	Schweine-fleisch

Kürzer = schwieriger zu verstehen.

Kurze Ausdrücke haben noch ein zweites Problem: Sie sind störungsanfällig. [...] Akzente, Radios, lärmende Nachbarn, eine Schießerei vor dem Haus, Pfropfen aus Ohrschmalz im Gehörgang, ... irgendetwas trägt immer dazu bei, dass beim Hörenden nicht alles ankommt, was der Sprechende von sich geben wollte. [...] Am Weihnachtstisch kann man »pork« (»Schweinefleisch«) schon mal leicht mit »fork« (»Gabel«) oder »dork« (»Depp«) verwechseln. Um »Schweinefleisch« falsch zu verstehen, muss dagegen schon sehr viel schief gehen. Vielleicht ist ja auch das der Grund, warum es Leute gibt, die Deutsch für witzlos halten – weil man den Cousin beim Weihnachtsessen nicht ungestraft als Depp bezeichnen kann. [...]

Fazit: Englisch kocht auch nur mit Wasser.

Ist Englisch also gut als gemeinsame Sprache aller Länder geeignet? Nein, definitiv nicht. In der Kürze liegt nicht nur Würze, sondern auch ordentlich Pfeffer und zum Sprechen ist die Sprache schlechter geeignet als zum Schreiben. [...] Damit will ich umgekehrt nicht sagen, dass eine andere Sprache besser wäre. [...] Mir fehlt ein ausreichender Überblick, um eine einzelne Fremdsprache wirklich in Relation setzen zu können. Deutsch hat als meine Muttersprache natürlich einen klaren Sympathiebonus, aber ich glaube trotzdem jedem, dass zumindest die deutsche Grammatik schwieriger als in Englisch zu erlernen ist. Als dritte Sprache könnte ich bestenfalls noch auf ein paar Jahre Lateinunterricht verweisen. Aber davon ist außer ein paar pseudointellektuellen Sprüchen nicht mehr viel übrig. Sic transit gloria mundi. [...]

(469 Wörter)

The global language of the future

PRE-LISTENING

1

a) Look at the infographic below and describe what it shows.
b) Now discuss the implications in class. Consider:
- what you have learned
- what you found surprising

c) Use the diagram to speculate on future global languages.

→ **S18:** How to analyse statistics, p. 230

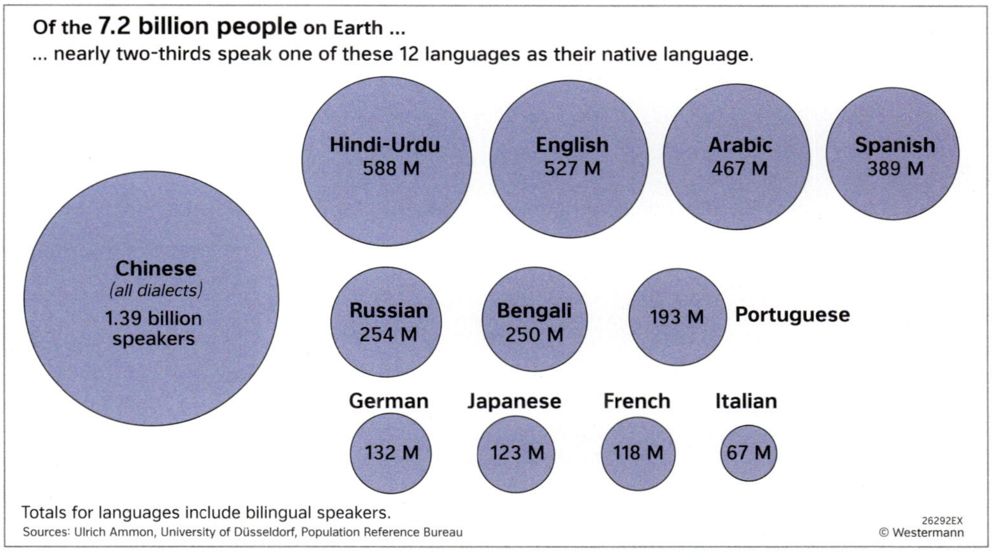

2

In a talk for the British Council, renowned linguist David Crystal uses these terms:

futurologists | predominantly | "money talks" | air traffic control | to retain | it is not "rocket science" | to diminish | diminution

If necessary, use a dictionary to look up their meanings. Then speculate about what aspect(s) of the topic "English as a global language" the talk might be about.

→ **S25:** How to work with a dictionary, p. 242

LISTENING

3 WB p. 74/1-2

Listen to part of the talk by David Crystal. Then take notes on the following questions:
1. Why, according to Crystal, did English become the global language in the past?
2. What are reasons it still has this status today?
3. Under what circumstances might English remain the global language in the future?
4. What other three likely scenarios does Crystal describe?

Webcode
You can find the audio file here: **DSW-73090-041**

→ **S20:** How to listen/watch effectively, p. 234

WRITING

4

CHALLENGE Should Mandarin, the predominant Chinese dialect, be made a compulsory subject in European schools? Discuss this question in no more than 200 words.

→ **S6:** How to write an argumentative text, p. 206

Varieties of English: Analysing modern poetry

Webcode
You can find the video here: DSW-73090-042

1
Watch part of a poetry recital with the sound turned off. Talk about your first impressions in class, considering the following questions: What might the presenter be talking about? What might his attitude be? What do his gestures and facial expressions hint at?

Webcode
You can find the video here: DSW-73090-043

2
Watch and listen to the whole recital with sound. Write down in one sentence what the poem is about.

→ **S27:** Evaluating online sources, p. 245

3
This poem by Guyanese-British poet John Agard is titled *Listen Mr Oxford Don*. Do some research and write down what is commonly associated with someone who is an "Oxford don".

4 → **S10:** How to work on poetry, p. 217
Write an analysis of the poem, considering the structure and stylistic devices used.

Info

Caribbean English

From the 1700s, thousands of people from Africa were transported as slaves to the British island colonies in the Caribbean. As a result a new form of English developed: Caribbean English. In its most extreme form, it can be very difficult to understand for outsiders. There are a number of elements that characterize Caribbean English. The lack of the verb "to be" in statements such as *she dreaming*, where Standard English requires *she's dreaming*, is typical of the type of structure that occurs in a creole language. Similarly, verbs might not always carry a tense marker as in the statement *Him tell me dat yesterday* for *He told me that yesterday*.

Annotations
1 **Me not no** = double negatives to express negative meaning ➡ I am not
2 **de** = the
3 **I ent** = I don't
4 **yu** = your
5 **dem** = they
6 to **serve time** = to go to prison
7 **I rekking** = I think/believe it to be
8 **wit mih** = with my
9 **mek dem** = make them
10 **I ent serving** = I am not going to serve

Listen Mr Oxford Don

Me not no[1] Oxford don
me a simple immigrant
from Clapham Common
I didn't graduate
I immigrate

But listen Mr Oxford don
I'm a man on de[2] run
and a man on de run
is a dangerous one

I ent[3] have no gun
I ent have no knife
but mugging de Queen's English
is the story of my life

I don't need no axe
to split up yu[4] syntax
I don't need no hammer
to mash up yu grammar

I warning you Mr Oxford don
I'm a wanted man
and a wanted man
is a dangerous one

Dem[5] accuse me of assault
on de Oxford dictionary
imagine a concise peaceful man like me
dem want me serve time[6]
for inciting rhyme to riot
but I rekking[7] it quiet
down here in Clapham Common

I'm not a violent man Mr Oxford don
I only armed wit mih[8] human breath
but human breath
is a dangerous weapon

So mek dem[9] send one big word after me
I ent serving[10] no jail sentence
I slashing suffix in self defence
I bashing future wit present tense
and if necessary
I making de Queen's English accessory to
my offence

John Agard

5 Language awareness WB p. 75/1, p. 76/2
In the poem, Agard challenges the view that Standard English is the correct form of English and that other forms of English are of a lesser status. Comment on this view.

→ **S6:** How to write an argumentative text, p. 206

The future of English

1 WB pp. 73-75

Read the article by Nicholas Ostler and use it to create an illustrated and annotated timeline of English as a global language. Include Ostler's predictions for the future, too.

NICHOLAS OSTLER **The Guardian, 27 February 2018**

Have we reached peak English in the world?

One of Britain's greatest strengths is set to diminish as China asserts itself on the world stage

[...] Beyond doubt, the use of English is greater than ever, and far more widespread than any other language in the world. All non-English-speaking powers of our globalised world recognise it as the first foreign language to learn; it is also, uniquely, in practical use worldwide. The British Council reckons that English is spoken at a useful level by some 1.75 billion people, a quarter of the world's population. It is taught from primary level up in all China's schools; it is the working language of the whole European Union.

[...] This global acceptance of English [...] has effectively grown up in just a century – neatly, and a little paradoxically, since the 1919 treaty of Versailles. In deference[1] to the US, this was the first international treaty written in English; but it also turned out to mark the incipient decline of the world's greatest English-speaking institution, the British empire. From a language point of view, however, British power had the good fortune to be succeeded by its cousin in North America, so that the usual historic lag[2], as political command leads on to linguistic imitation, was disguised.

[...] But all this while, especially from the 1920s to the 1990s, the focus of US expansion was changing, moving from North America to the world, leading to influence on trade, engineering, telecommunications, mining, media, science and finance, as the dollar moved to replace sterling[3] as the world's reserve currency. This was followed by the digital information revolution, creating new fortunes based in Silicon Valley at the turn of the 21st century. These were all positive for the world role of English (a role founded by Great Britain), but should have been expected to peak later, in the growth of soft power and the increased popularity of American culture.

It is this lagged growth of English, reflecting US influence hitherto[4], that we are now experiencing. Yet it is happening in a 21st century when other nations, particularly in Asia but also in South America and Africa, are far outpacing the US (let alone Britain and the European Union) in economic growth rates. This is an amazing juncture[5] in world history. And two questions arise. Is the position of English a real asset to the states that speak it natively? And is the language likely to hold this position in the pecking order[6] indefinitely? [...]

But special knowledge of a language is an asset that wastes all too soon when it becomes global property. World English will have just a historic connection to Britain or the US, and knowing it well is no longer exclusive to native speakers. [...] Transnational lingua francas, once established, always give off an aura of permanence. Yet when circumstances change, they fall. And the change is clearly coming.

And so the natural expectation will be that after the new powers, such as China, India or Brazil, establish themselves economically, politically (and probably militarily), their linguistic and cultural influence too will come to be felt, among those who want to do business with them, and then with one another. But as with all newly dominant languages, there will be a lag. [...]

Evolving translation technologies may make languages largely interchangeable, pushing national cultures into the background. Whatever, there will be no special deference to the current English-speaking tradition. [...]

For English, therefore, its current peak is likely to be as good as it will ever get, its glory as a world language lasting just a couple of centuries [...] And on present form, its fall is likely to coincide with the latest rise of China, whose documented history has run for three millennia.

Annotations

1 **deference** /ˈdefərəns/= behaviour that shows great respect towards sb

2 **lag** /læg/= a period of time between one event and another

3 **sterling** = pound sterling (British currency)

4 **hitherto** /ˌhɪðə(r)ˈtuː/= until now

5 **juncture** = *here:* critical point in time

6 **pecking order** = the order of power in a group

2 → **S1:** Checklist: Summary, p. 198

a) Read the article below and summarize the changes in the English language in no more than 120 words.

b) Language awareness Look at the different highlighted parts in the article. What kinds of English are they examples of? Sort the words and phrases into categories.

c) EXTRA Find more examples for your categories.

category	*examples*
US English	• *"get a cookie",* • *"I'm good" …*
US pronunciation	*…*
…	*…*

What will the English language be like in 100 years?

Simon Horobin, 10 November 2015

One way of predicting the future is to look back at the past. The global role English plays today as a lingua franca – used as a means of communication by speakers of different languages – has parallels in the Latin of pre-modern Europe.

Having been spread by the success of the Roman Empire, Classical Latin was kept alive as a standard written medium throughout Europe long after the fall of Rome. But the Vulgar Latin used in speech continued to change, forming new dialects, which in time gave rise to the modern Romance languages: French, Spanish, Portuguese, Romanian and Italian.

Similar developments may be traced today in the use of English around the globe, especially in countries where it functions as a second language. New "interlanguages" are emerging, in which features of English are mingled[1] with those of other native tongues and their pronunciations. […]

Looking back to the early 20th century, it was the Standard English used in England, spoken with the accent known as "Received Pronunciation", that carried prestige.

But today the largest concentration of native speakers is in the US, and the influence of US English can be heard throughout the world: *can I get a cookie, I'm good, did you eat, the movies,* "skedule" rather than *"shedule"*. In the future, to speak English will be to speak US English.

US spellings such as *disk* and *program* are already preferred to British equivalents *disc* and *programme* in computing. The dominance of US usage in the digital world will lead to the wider acceptance of further American preferences, such as *favorite, donut, dialog, center*.

What is being lost?

In the 20th century, it was feared that English dialects were dying out with their speakers. Projects such as the Survey of English Dialects (1950-61) were launched at the time to collect and preserve endangered words before they were lost forever.

A similar study undertaken by the BBC's Voices Project in 2004 turned up a rich range of local accents and regional terms […] But […] the word *chav*[2] was found throughout England, demonstrating how features of the Estuary English spoken in the Greater London area are displacing local dialects, especially among younger generations. […]

In the online world, attitudes to consistency and correctness are considerably more relaxed: variant spellings are accepted and punctuation marks omitted, or repurposed to convey a range of attitudes. Research has shown that in electronic discourse exclamation marks can carry a range of exclamatory functions, including apologising, challenging, thanking, agreeing, and showing solidarity.

Capital letters are used to show anger, misspellings convey humour and establish group identity, and smiley-faces or emoticons express a range of reactions.

Getting shorter

Some have questioned whether the increasing development and adoption of emoji pictograms, which allow speakers to communicate without the need for language, mean that we will cease to communicate in English at all? ;-) The fast-changing world of social media is also responsible for the coining and spreading of neologisms, or "new words". Recent updates to Oxford Dictionaries give a flavour: *mansplaining*[3], *awesomesauce*[4], *rly*[5], *bants*[6], *TL;DR* (too long; didn't read). Clipped forms, acronyms, blends and abbreviations have long been productive methods of word formation in English (think of *bus, smog* and *scuba*) but the huge increase in such coinages[7] means that they will be far more prominent in the English of 2115.

Annotations

[1] to **mingle** = to mix; [2] **chav** a usually young British person, stereotypically known for aggressive behaviour and wearing flashy jewelry and casual clothing (such as tracksuits); [3] to **mansplain** = to explain sth to a woman in a condescending way; [4] **awesomesauce** (*infml.*) = extremely good; [5] **rly** = really; [6] **bants** = *Geblödel, dummes Geschwätz*; [7] **coinage** /ˈkɔɪnɪdʒ/ = *here:* a recently created word or phrase

Lingua francas through the ages (Lernaufgabe)

Nowadays, English is considered THE lingua franca of the world. But through the ages as well as around the world, other languages have held and still hold this position. Here is a list of languages commonly acknowledged as lingua francas (past and present).

- Akkadian
- Arabic
- Farsi
- French
- Hausa
- Hindi-Urdu
- Koine Greek
- Latin
- Mandarin Chinese
- Mediterranean Lingua Franca
- Old Aramaic
- Old Church Slavonic
- Plains Sign Language
- Portuguese
- Russian
- Sogdian
- Spanish
- Swahili

To counterbalance what is often seen as a problematic dominance of Western culture and languages, your school has decided to hold a "bazaar of languages", where other important languages apart from English will be presented to expand the students' (and teachers') horizons.

1

Decide whether you want to work
- in a small group.
- in a pair.
- alone.

2

From the list above, choose a language you would like to work on.

Fragment from the Epic of Gilgamesh: Akkadian (18th century BC)

3

Do some research on your chosen language. These prompts can help you:

✓ **Where** was/is your language spoken?
✓ **When** was it spoken?/Since when has it been spoken?
✓ **Who** were/are the speakers of your language?
✓ **Why** was/is it important?
✓ **What** characteristics of your language made/make it suitable as a lingua franca?
✓ If it is no longer spoken: Why?
✓ If it is still spoken: Why is it not THE lingua franca of today's world?

→ **S27:** Evaluating online sources, p. 245

4

Plan a poster for the bazaar. Ask yourself how you can present your language in an informative as well as appealing way.

→ **S26:** How to design a poster, p. 244

5

Find visuals to make your poster more attractive, such as maps, timelines, script examples, photos, ancient texts, ...

6

Create your poster and display it in the school building. You can also organize an opening event and invite other classes, etc.

→ **S26:** How to design a poster, p. 244

Indian street sign in Hindi and English

1 Visions of the future

Workshop: Step by step

D1 SUPPORT FOR TASK 3A (P. 16)

Explaining the effect of a device or narrative perspective on the reader is often the most difficult part of an analysis. In the part highlighted in orange, the reader gets to know Winston's thought process. He asks himself questions, and the feelings he has when having certain thoughts are described. Before writing your analysis, think about what effect this has on the reader. These questions may help you:

- Do you, as reader, know more than Winston, e.g. whether his activities are being observed by Big Brother, or are you dependent on his view?
- Does the narrative perspective make you identify with Winston?
- Do you get a balanced view of Winston's situation?

Webcode
You can download the grid here: DSW-73090-044

D2 SUPPORT FOR TASK 6 (P. 20)

aspect	quotation	direct/ indirect?	interpretation
1. Outward appearance physical features/clothes/ body language	Syme has "large, protuberant eyes, at once mournful and derisive". (ll. 13-14)	direct and indirect	The way Syme's eyes are described directly, makes him seem physically rather unattractive. At the same time, they are also described as being reflective of his character: his eyes are both "mournful" (l. 14), showing sadness and perhaps regret, as well as "derisive" (l. 14). This second adjective suggests that Syme is full of contempt and scorn for others. It contradicts Winston's first introduction of Syme as his "friend" and we learn that Winston might not feel very positively towards Syme after all.
2. Character traits e.g. modesty, courage, uncertainty			
3. Behaviour how a character acts (or does not act) gives an impression of their motives, abilities or moral standing.	"'It was a good hanging,' said Syme reminiscently. 'I think it spoils it when they tie their feet together. I like to see them kicking. And above all, at the end, the tongue sticking right out, and blue – a quite bright blue. That's the detail that appeals to me'." (ll. 26-32)	indirect	Syme talks about the hanging in a way that 'normal' people would not; he seems to derive a perverse joy from seeing others suffer that marks him out as a sadist. The use of the adverb "reminiscently" (l. 27), which would normally be used in a context were somebody remembers a pleasant experience, underlines his distorted view of the executions. The same is true for the use of "that appeals to me" (ll. 31f.) a bit later. However, it is not entirely clear whether he really means what he is saying. In that case, he might want to be provocative and shock Winston with his words.

aspect	quotation	direct/ indirect?	interpretation
4. Mood the emotional state of a character			
5. Language e.g. correct or incorrect use of grammar, simple or academic vocabulary, colloquial language; reflects a character's social background, education, attitudes, etc.	Syme "continued speaking, with a sort of pedant's passion." (ll. 72f.)	direct	Syme's way of speaking reveals that he is very pedantic, meaning that he is excessively concerned with formalism, accuracy and precision. At the same time, he is very passionate about this. He is presented as somebody who takes his work, namely the destruction of the old and implementation of a new, greatly reduced language, very seriously.
	"'You haven't a real appreciation of Newspeak, Winston,' he said almost sadly." (ll. 106f.)	indirect	Syme uses the negative form of "have" incorrectly by just saying "haven't" instead of "haven't got" or "don't have". It shows that he shortens the language and therefore lives by what he believes.
6. Family/social background			
7. Relationships with others how a character interacts with others and is perceived by them	"'You haven't a real appreciation of Newspeak, Winston,' he said almost sadly." (ll. 106f.)	indirect	Here, Syme is shown as seeing through Winston's façade of the eager Big Brother-supporter. Syme seems to like Winston, because it makes him "almost sad" (l. 106) that Winston obviously does not support the society's goals.

D3 SUPPORT FOR TASK 8 (P. 22)

When writing a characterization, it is useful to broaden your vocabulary in order to describe a character's traits.

a) Match the adjectives (1-13) with the correct definitions or synonyms (A-M).

1 ambitious	A not truthful
2 assertive	B trying to control other people's behaviour
3 courageous	C provoking disgust
4 deceptive	D doing or saying sth (negative) to cause a certain reaction
5 defiant	E showing very unpleasant behaviour
6 faithful	F not giving in, willing to resist
7 generous	G enthusiastic
8 humorous	H bold, confident
9 manipulative	I loyal
10 obnoxious	J having a sense of humour, being funny
11 passionate	K willing to give a lot to others
12 provocative	L wanting to be successful in what you're doing
13 repulsive	M brave

b) Find a noun for each of these adjectives. Use a dictionary if necessary.

ambitious – ambition
assertive – …
…

D4 SUPPORT FOR TASK 8 (P. 22)

For your characterization of Syme, you are asked to start with a central claim. It serves as a guideline which you can use to structure your text. Your central claim could look like this:

In this extract, it becomes evident that Syme is a cunning, cruel man and devout follower of Big Brother, who takes pleasure in destruction and strives to find people guilty of "Thoughtcrime". As such, he might become very dangerous for Winston.

Workshop: Practice

Webcode
You can download the graphic organizer here: DSW-73090-045

D5 SUPPORT FOR TASK 2 (P. 23)

a) Arrange the information about the world in Lanchester's *The Wall* in a graphic organizer like the one below.
b) Present your graphic organizers in class.

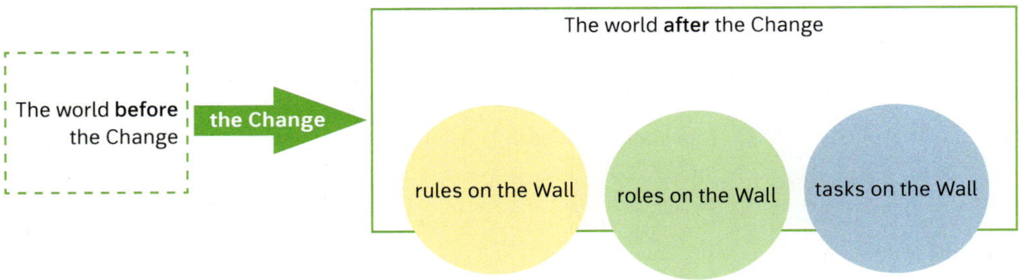

Theme task

D6 SUPPORT FOR TASK 1 (P. 33)

Here are some ideas:

1. *surveillance, climate change/global warming, data mining, …*
2. …
3. …
4. *abandoned, grim, clean, overgrown with plants, dried up, frozen, polluted, …*
5. *a big corporation, artificial intelligence, a person like a queen or a dictator, …*
6. *elegant, mean, inconspicuous, destructive, cunning, hypocritical, arrogant, …*
7. *a drought, a storm or tsunami, a meteor, an uprising of a certain group of people, a rather unremarkable incident, …*
8. *activities, certain emotions, books, …*
9. *the amount of money people are allowed to earn, the job you pick, what kind of family you live in, what you look like, who you love, …*
10. …

D7 SUPPORT FOR TASK 2 (P. 33)

Plan your story in even more detail. Mark the aspects you want to mention directly in one colour and information you only want to allude to in another. Also write down how you are planning on introducing certain details – consider rhetorical devices like metaphors, a specific choice of words, etc.

2 Postcolonial experiences

Intro

D1 SUPPORT FOR TASK 4A (P. 35)

There are many words and expressions that are derived from the word "colony". Look at the words (1-6) and match them with the correct definitions (A-F).

1	colonialism	A	the act of sending people to live in and govern another country
2	postcolonialism	B	the process in which a colony becomes independent
3	colonisation	C	the imperialist expansion of Europe to the rest of the world
4	decolonisation	D	a study of the effects of colonialism on cultures and societies
5	colonists	E	people who have lived in a colony for a long time
6	colonials	F	the people who start a colony or are among the first to live there

D2 SUPPORT FOR TASK 4B (P. 35)

Language support

Colonialism has contributed to ...
Britain's contemporary society reflects ...
Certain aspects of Britain's contemporary culture can be attributed to ...
One important effect of Britain's colonial past is ...
Politically and economically, Britain ...
Britain's former colonies have profited/suffered as a result of ...
Whereas British rule was responsible for ... it was also ...
Former British colonies have been burdened with ...

In 1948, the *Windrush* carried immigrants from the Caribbean to Britain.

Part A: India

Texts

India – a country of contrasts

D3 SUPPORT FOR TASK 4A (P. 40)

a) Here are some suggestions of how to start your text:

b) The adjectives in the box below might help you to describe the place or situation. Make sure you understand all the words and choose some for your texts.

Language support

This is it – the place of my dreams: ...
We got here after a long train ride, but it's definitely worth it: ...
So glad we came here: ...
I would never have expected it like this: ...
You know I've always enjoyed ..., so it's no surprise that ...
To be honest I was a bit worried about ..., but ...
You wouldn't believe ...

amazing | awe-inspiring | bizarre | breathtaking | challenging | colourful | crowded | difficult to cope with | exotic | fascinating | frantic | full of live | intimidating | laid-back | out of this world | peaceful | relaxing | strange | stressful | stunning | unbelievable | unexpected

c) This is how you can express expectations:

Language support

I had hoped to ... /for ... | I was expecting to be .../find ... | I had prepared myself to ... | What I had been looking for was ... | I had imagined myself in ... /to ...

Workshop: Step by step

D4 SUPPORT FOR TASK 3B (P. 44)

When you work on a new text and are not allowed to write in the book, these tips might help you:

- Identify the paragraphs in which the required information can be found.
- Make notes on the information that is related to the task you are dealing with. It may be helpful to work with different colours and graphic elements, e.g. → ↕ =
- You can use the different colours to highlight important words or phrases such as relevant facts, definitions, examples, criticism, etc.
- Use the dictionary for help where necessary.

a) Read the notes and match them to the paragraphs of the text.

b) Work in the same way on the remaining paragraphs of the text on pp. 44-45.

c) Use your notes to sum up the text in your own words.

→ reason for Seema's discrimination: her caste → a Dalit
→ caste system abolished in 1950
↕
→ caste discrimination continues → no access to programs for poor
→ violence and aggression → Seema forced to give up samosa stall in market

A Seema and her husband did quite well when they first opened a samosa stall in the local market of a town in Bihar state, northeastern India. But then other vendors found out who Seema was. They yelled at her customers for buying her samosas. They threatened her husband for "polluting" the market by selling food prepared by her. She put up with it for months before giving up.

B What had Seema done wrong? She had been born a Dalit, a member of the "untouchables", the lowest group in India's ancient and now officially obsolete caste system. [...]

C India officially outlawed caste-based discrimination in 1950. But it continues to be a fact of life for the estimated 200 million of India's 1.4 billion population who are Dalits.

D They are even discriminated against when applying for programs established to help them.

D5 SUPPORT FOR TASK 4 (P. 45)

a) Read the following notes on the author's line of argumentation and put them in the right order. Copy the table on the right and write them down under the correct headings:

- generalizes Seema's fate of discrimination and rejection as typical for treatment of Dalit women
- illustrates discrepancy between official situation of abolished caste system andreality
- unmasks bureaucracy as weapon to maintain the status quo / to prevent social mobility
- exemplifies Seema's vocational training as strife for a better life
- criticises India's reluctance to establish a caste-free society and gives a resigned outlook
- explains concept of microloans as tool to reduce poverty and examines why implementation fails when applied to Dalit women
- describes humiliating discrimination on basis of caste-certificate
- presents the problem of Dalits in a slice-of-life story

Introduction
1. ...
2. ...

Main part
3. ...
4. ...
5. ...
6. ...
7. ...

Conclusion
8. ...

b) Use the notes to describe the author's line of argumentation.

EXAMPLE:
The author introduces her article by referring to the 70th anniversary of independence from Britain, praising the historic achievement of the non-violent fight for freedom. But she reminds the reader that the pride felt by many Indians is not fully justified.

In the main part, she questions the definition of freedom and ...

Workshop: Practice

D6 SUPPORT FOR TASK 2 (P. 48)

1. Analysing the structure
Read the description of different parts of the article "Full steam ahead" and identify the respective paragraphs/lines in the text.

- presentation of Ghandi Nagar project and plans for the future
- situation in Rajasthan
- identifying Kala as one of 40 women working in the same place
- slice-of-life story depicting Chandra Kala at work at the station
- outlook: inspiration for young women
- background information on situation of female workforce in India
- specification of topic: low rate of women in jobs
- presentation of project as success story

EXAMPLE:
– slice-of-life story depicting Chandra Kala at work at the station → ll. 1-10
– identifying Kala as one of 40 women working in the same place → ...

2. Analysing language
a) Read the quotes and put them in the right category (choice of words, stylistic devices, rhetorical strategies).

"male bastion" (l. 90) | "financial windfall" (ll. 50-51) | "improvements" (l. 78) | "20 million women ..." (l. 36) | "trailblazers" (l. 28) | "appreciate" (l. 82) | "faster service" (l. 79) | "7,000 commuters" (l. 62) | "inspire" (l. 118) | "smaller queues, better information and cleanliness" (ll. 79-80) | "I used to feel very shy" (l. 15) | "record earnings" (l. 52) | "providing hope" (l. 29) | "trigger a change" (l. 120) | "equipped the station with CCTV cameras, deployed an all-women police force, [...] and created temporary daycare" (ll. 114-117)

device/strategy	*quote (evidence)*	*function/effect*
choice of words/word fields		
words with positive connotations		
word field "success", "progress"		
stylistic devices		
imagery/methaphor	*"male bastion"*	
enumeration		
parallelism		
rhetorical strategies		
quotation		
facts and figures		

b) Consider the context of the quotes and explain their function/effect.

Webcode
You can download the grid here:
DSW-73090-046

Texts

Working on a short story

D7 SUPPORT FOR TASK 2A (P. 49)

In preparation of the task, it can be helpful to read the first extract and collect information on the different characters.

Webcode
You can download the grid here: DSW-73090-047

Anamika	*Vikram*	*Adinah*
	- doctor at hospital *- does cancer research* *- wants to marry Anamika* *- dark-skinned* *- Dalit?*	

D8 SUPPORT FOR TASK 4 (P. 50)

a) When writing an interior monologue, it is important to understand a person's character. The following questions may help you to get an insight into Adinah's character and the role he sees himself in.

Tip
Work together with a partner to understand Adinah better. One of you plays the role of Adinah and the other one asks him these questions. When all the questions are answered, switch roles. You can also come up with additional questions of your own.

- What is his relationship with his sister? What was it like in their childhood days?
- How did he feel when Anamika was allowed to go to Mumbai to study medicine? What did he think about his parents' reaction to her plans?
- How did he feel when he spotted Anamika with a strange man on Facebook?
- Why did he show the photo to his parents? Was he sent by them or did he go to Mumbai on his own accord?
- What went through his mind while travelling to Mumbai?
- What makes him so aggressive? Consider his sister's profession and behaviour.
- How does he look upon Vikram and his career?
- What does he not understand, or not want to understand, about Anamika's life?
- How does he define his own role? How does he justify his actions? Will they affect his position in the family?

b) Since an interior monologue represents the thoughts that go through a person's mind, the language you use is that of spoken English. Consequently you can use
- elliptical sentences (incomplete sentences),
- questions that can also be incomplete,
- admonition addressed to oneself (what one should or shouldn't have done),
- accusations against others,
- exclamations,
- harsh language to reveal despair, aggression, frustration, etc.

Note down one or two examples for each category that fit the context and could be part of the interior monologue you are going to write.

D9 SUPPORT FOR TASK 7 (P. 51)

a) Read the quotes from the short story and explain what they reveal about Anamika's mother.

quote	interpretation
"Her brother threw her luggage in her room and her mother locked her in."	
"The only person who looked after her was her mother – who always locked the door after tending to her."	
"Her mother began to worry. The girl was too thin, she looked like a scarecrow. Who would ever accept to take her as a wife?"	
"She took her daughter by the shoulders and swung her around, like a rag doll."	
"... she screamed ..."	
"'... you are as dirty as a Dalit!'"	
"She wailed, wringing her hands."	
"She looked up at him [the Vishnu god] and he frowned down at her, fierce and ready to combat sin."	
"Your soul is saved", she murmured in her [Anamika's] ear.	

Webcode
You can download the grid here: DSW-73090-048

b) Study the adjectives in the box and make sure you understand them all. Use a dictionary for help if necessary.

abusive | aggressive | annoyed | appalled | apprehensive | ashamed | cheated | compassionate | considerate | deceived | desperate | determined | devastated | disgraced | disgusted | disrespected | empathic | enraged | frustrated | full of foreboding | furious | harsh | honourable | humiliated | justified | mournful | obliged | proud | self-righteous | relieved | reproachful | ruthless | violent

c) Choose adjectives from the box to describe the mother's feelings and her behaviour.

Part C: South Africa

Texts

Living under apartheid

D10 SUPPORT FOR TASK 2B (P. 57)

If you need help with this task, copy the grid below and use it for your notes.

Webcode

You can download the grid here: DSW-73090-049

laws and rules of apartheid	effect on non-white South Africans
criminalization of "race-mixing"	
classification of people into racial groups	
white-collar jobs and skilled-labour jobs reserved for whites; menial jobs reserved for blacks	
minimal reforms in the early 1980s in reaction to international protests	
black people were only allowed in cities for work; they had to live either in the "homelands" or in "townships"	

D11 SUPPORT FOR TASK 2C (P. 57)

The adjectives in the box can be used to describe the way Trevor Noah characterizes his mother. Look up any words you do not know and then find examples from the text to support five of the adjectives.

ambitious | bold | defiant | independent | proud | resourceful | respectable | strong-willed

D12 SUPPORT FOR TASK 3 (P. 58)

Trevor Noah employs a number of techniques to create humour despite the seriousness of his theme:

- irony – describing things in the opposite way to what you expect
- self-deprecating humour – showing that he can laugh about himself
- satire – use of humour or exaggeration to show how foolish other people's ideas are

Identify the kind of humour used in the following quotations:

1. "I grew up in South Africa during apartheid, which was awkward because I was raised in a mixed family, with me being the mixed one in the family."
2. "There were whole police squads whose only job it was to go round peeking through windows – clearly an assignment for the finest law enforcement officers."
3. "At the time, a black woman learning how to type was like a blind person learning to drive."

Find other examples of these types of humour in the extract.

Advanced texts

South Africa today

D13 SUPPORT FOR TASK 1B (P. 61)

a) While watching the film, answer the questions about it in a few words. Use the column in the middle for your answers.

questions	answers	issues
1. What does the boy 'Johnson' beg for in the first scene?	*money for beer and food*	*poverty, drugs*
2. What class does the young Zach watching TV represent?		
3. What kind of job does the supermarket worker have?		
4. Why do Zach's aunt and uncle want him to come to Australia?		
5. What does Zach's girlfriend, Tash, accuse him of doing?		
6. What did Zach's parents do to Eunice after she became pregnant?		
7. What happened to the car that Eunice was driving?		
8. Why does Johnson stab and rob Zach in the end?		

Webcode
You can download the grid here:
DSW-73090-050

b) In the right-hand column, note down the issues which are illustrated in each scene, e.g. poverty, inequality, racism, etc.

D14 SUPPORT FOR TASK 2 (P. 61)

a) When asked to examine Zach's attitude towards South Africa, you need to look more closely at the content of the film. Who does Zach find in his backyard, what do they represent and how does he react to them?
Use the grid in D13 as a guideline and note down
- what group of people they represent
- Zach's reaction to them.

The first four scenes have been done for you:

Scene 1: Young Johnson represents the poor black youth, uneducated and unemployed and having to beg for money. Zach is both annoyed and surprised by the intrusion, but gives Johnson money although he suspects him of buying drink or drugs.
Scene 2: Young Zach's life is contrasted with Johnson's. He represents the privileged white youth. He switches off Mandela's inauguration and watches a commercial, illustrating a disinterest in the end of apartheid rule and politics.
Scene 3: The man pushing the supermarket trolleys represents those uneducated black workers who can only do menial work. Zach's attitude towards him is neutral although he almost gets run over.
Scene 4: The family members who moved to Australia stand for the greed and the racist attitude of those South Africans who have abandoned the country. Zach doesn't share this attitude and wants to stay.
Scene 5: ...

b) Choose words from the box that describe Zach's attitude towards South Africa in your opinion. Look up any words you do not understand.

ambivalent | bitter | condescending | contemptuous | critical | cynical | enthusiastic | matter-of-fact | negative | objective | optimistic | patronizing | pessimistic | positive | reflective

Language support

Zach's attitude towards South Africa seems to be rather ambivalent. On the one hand he ... but on the other hand he ...
By confronting many of the problems facing South Africa, Zach underlines his ... attitude towards his country.
Zach appears to be very ... towards ...
While his attitude towards his country is not completely ... he nevertheless criticizes/condemns ...
Whereas his attitude towards ... is reflected in his behaviour towards/treatment of ..., he still maintains an open mind on the topic of ...

D15 SUPPORT FOR TASK 7 (P. 63)

In order to persuade a reader of their opinion, authors have a number of devices and strategies at their fingertips, which they can employ when writing an article.

- Attract the reader's attention with a catchy headline and a first paragraph that clearly states the author's point of view.
- Use photographs which support this view.
- Quote experts and/or facts and figures to convince the reader of the authenticity of their arguments.
- Present balanced arguments to underline the author's objectivity and appeal to the reader's sense of logic.
- Use "you" and "your" or "we" and "our" to directly address the reader and get them on their side.
- Use emotive language and devices such as rhetorical questions and imagery to appeal to the reader's imagination.

When asked to analyse the means an author uses to support his or her view, you should look for examples of these strategies.

Part D: Nigeria

Texts

Working on novel extracts

D16 SUPPORT FOR TASK 1A (P. 66)

Reading between the lines: for each character, match the quotes (numbers) with the interpretations (letters).

quotes: Obinze

1 skimmed Ifemelu's email "wishing it were longer"
2 "He had hated it ... the photo of the black American ... made him send her a cold reply"
3 "Obinze laughed, a little too heartily"
4 "He wanted to tell Gabriel that his girlfriend from university had just e-mailed him"
5 "for a confused moment he thought it was Ifemelu ringing from America"

interpretation: what is revealed

A he can't bear the idea of Ifemelu and another man, even though he is married; reacts in a humiliated way
B the fact that he wants to share his feelings shows how much this means to him
C there is nothing but Ifemelu on his mind
D he has been longing to hear from Ifemelu
E he is overexcited about the prospect of seeing Ifemelu again

quotes: Ifemelu

1 "... had called him Ceiling"
2 "kedu?"
3 "... wished him happiness ... and mentioned the black American she was living with"
4 "when he e-mailed her again... she did not reply"

interpretation: what is revealed

A retaliates when she learns about his marriage
B hurt, not interested in keeping in touch superficially
C sounds very intimate using the nickname she gave him
D uses Igbo in her email to allude to common background

D17 SUPPORT FOR TASK 2 (P. 67)

To describe Obinze's life, consider what you learn about

- his family,
- his lifestyle (house, choice of furniture, food, space, staff),
- his wife,
- his work and his projects.

D18 SUPPORT FOR TASK 3 (P. 67)

Read the following statements about Obinze's feelings and find the corresponding passage in the text.

1. The passage illustrates Obinze's feeling in a metaphorical way: he has the impression that all he has achieved is weighing him down. Instead of feeling satisfied about his luxurious lifestyle and his economic success, he wishes he could get rid of all the assets he has acquired to feel free again.
2. Obinze is depicted as a person in a serious crisis when he wonders if he really enjoys his life or just pretends to do so because that is what everyone expects of him.
3. It becomes obvious that Obinze has reservations about the way his wife behaves. He appreciates her beauty, but it irritates him that she would rather not be considered a black person while he seems to be proud of his roots.

➡

4. The fact that Obinze would prefer to wear more casual clothes instead of the outrageously expensive and extravagant caftan his wife has chosen for him reveals that he considers aspects of his life as exaggerated and pretentious.
5. Obinze seems disappointed that his wife does not really take an interest in what he is doing, she is merely interested in the wealth his work generates.

EXAMPLE:
– Statement number 1 corresponds to ll. 21-27.
– Number 2 corresponds to …

Advanced texts

Nollywood – Nigeria's dream factory

D19 SUPPORT FOR TASK 1B (P. 71)

Here are some ideas for functions a film may fulfil:

educate the viewer by offering role models | entertain | manipulate people to adopt a certain attitude or behaviour | convey an authentic impression of historic events | open up new worlds to the audience beyond their personal experience | portray social problems | confront the audience with the harsh realities of life | create empathy and enable the viewer to understand conflicts at an emotional level | promote consumerism

Part E: Europe and the colonial past

Texts

Statues, monuments and other remnants of colonialism

D20 SUPPORT FOR TASK 2 (P. 74)

Language support

Expressing your opinion in a differentiated way

For me, In my view, As far as I'm concerned, I would say that I would agree that I can't believe that I doubt that I would favour	it would (not) be a/the best solution … an obvious solution would be … the difficulties lie in …	
	it is hardly/absolutely/definitely	feasible … convincing to … (un)necessary to … essential that … evident … unbearable … an absolute must … inconceivable … comprehensible … useless … meaningless …

Advanced texts

Decolonizing the curriculum

D21 SUPPORT FOR TASK 2 (P. 76)

Match the highlighted parts (1-7) with their function in the introduction of the article (A-E). There are two more highlighted parts than necessary.

The medley of (1) jubilant black, brown and white faces cheering the destruction of Edward Colston's statue has had many rethinking. (2) Discussing even. (3) Britain, a nation not keen on making much of a fuss, is having to talk about slavery. (4) For too long we would rather have dunked our digestives into mugs of tea and not bothered with dredging up our past. But (5) what if we had all learned at school that the history of our great British brew is inseparable from our history of empire? While Brits have been embracing lockdown baking, how many will know our (6) national sweet tooth is the direct (7) result of slave labour on Caribbean sugar cane fields?

A elliptic phrase intensifies impression that this is an unexpected but necessary reaction of the public
B criticism that the necessary discussion about the past has been avoided for years
C rhetorical question as reference to school education as a means to raise awareness
D refers to people of all ethnic backgrounds who rejoice in the new awareness of historic wrong
E description of British national character pretending to be oblivious of unpleasant facts

3 New York – a global city

Workshop: Step by step

D1 SUPPORT FOR TASK 2A (P. 83)

When you work on task 2a), you will notice that there is some information on all three options, as you will hear about the population of "Kleindeutschland", the way other immigrants like the Irish saw the Germans and the German way of life in New York City. The task, however, asks you to focus on the gist. So consider what the reporter's main point is in this extract.

D2 SUPPORT FOR TASK 2B (P. 83)

In the extract, the reporter mentions various examples of German life in New York City at the time. You need to note down only **two** examples, so concentrate on the ones you understand clearly. Make sure that you actually list distinct points. Imagine the reporter mentions "traditional German suits and dresses", then you should not write down "traditional German suits" as your first example and "traditional German dresses" as your second example because both could be summarized as "traditional German clothes" and therefore do not count as two separate examples.

D3 SUPPORT FOR TASK 3 (P. 84)

In a multiple-choice task, the answers you can choose from are often based on paraphrases or synonyms of expressions used in the audio clip. The sentences below include some of the words from the podcast about "Kleindeutschland". Rewrite these sentences by replacing the words highlighted in green by synonyms or paraphrases.

1. Before Germany became a unified nation-state, it was a federation of distinctive regions and cultures.

➡

2. People of German descent bound for a new life in the US in the mid-1800s were characterized by different culinary traditions and religious persuasions, for example.
3. Residents of Little Germany identified rather as Bavarians or Prussians than as Germans although they were often seen as a monolithic community.
4. It was still highly improbable for people from different homelands to build a life together as there were still tensions between them.
5. However, the facets of their new lives in the US brought them more closely together than in Germany, as their immigrant experience took an emotional toll and put them under pressure of assimilation.
6. Eventually, the Germans of Little Germany were on the move again and spread out to other parts of the US.
7. People who are well-versed on the topic warn of collapsing different migrant communities and rather consider it imperative to distinguish between migrants with very specific backgrounds.

D4 SUPPORT FOR TASK 4B (P. 84)

When you are asked to infer meaning, you need to find out the underlying message of what is said. The tips below may help you find the right answer.

Why does Mark Turin, the reporter, refer to the expanse of New York City?

a to raise doubts about the term "most linguistically diverse city" → Does the reporter disagree with the term that is mentioned in the clip or report about critical voices that call into question that NYC is linguistically diverse?

b to emphasize the exceptional nature of the language situation there → Does the reporter focus on what makes the language situation in NYC special but not add any personal judgment?

c to express his surprise about the number of languages spoken there → Is the reporter surprised about the language situation in NYC or does he think of it as something that is to be expected of this city?

D5 SUPPORT FOR TASK 5 (P. 85)

The following information may help you follow the report better.

The interview partner:
Hoong Yee Lee Krakauer is the executive director of the Queens Council on the Arts. She was born and raised in the New York borough of Queens as a child of Chinese immigrants. She still lives in Queens with her Jewish husband and their three children.

The subway line:
The "7" trains are part of the New York City Subway Service and operate between Flushing, Queens and Manhattan and pass various neighbourhoods along their way.

Texts

New York is not America

D6 SUPPORT FOR TASK 1A (P. 88)

Alicia Keys' song title refers to various terms familiar to Americans:

- The state of New York is also known by its nickname "Empire State". The origin of this term is not quite clear, but explanations often refer to the size, the geographical advantages of New York's location, its resources and economic power.
- As a consequence, buildings such as the Empire State Building have picked up this nickname.
- The phrase "state of mind" can be defined as follows: a person's mood and the effect that mood has on the person's thoughts and behaviour.

D7 SUPPORT FOR TASK 1C (P. 88)

a) Go through the text and find examples of expressions that show that New York is
- a city that never sleeps. Why is it such a busy place?
- a place that is bigger and more impressive than other cities. How does the atmosphere of the city influence people?

b) Go through the text and find examples of expressions that show that New Yorkers
- hope to achieve their dreams in that city.
- work hard to get by.

D8 SUPPORT FOR TASK 3 (P. 90)

The author uses language in various ways to express how she feels about New York City. Look at the examples below and identify the effect her use of language is supposed to have on the readers.

	use of language	examples from the article
choice of words	colloquial/informal/ slang expressions	"weirdos" (l. 3); "kerfuffle" (l. 8); "roll with that" (l. 24)
	more formal expressions	"transcend societal expectations" (ll. 63f.); "Cisgendered men" (l. 67)
stylistic devices	alliteration	"intoxicating and infectious" (ll. 43f.)
	figurative language	"rat race" (l. 78)
	repetition/parallelism	"crying in public, fighting in public, making out in public, ..." (ll. 32f.); "Even when I'm not in a hurry, here I'm in a hurry. Generally, however, I'm in a hurry." (ll. 44-46)
	enumeration	"in dresses, mini-skirts, and mink stoles with a dashing lapel pin" (ll. 67-69)
rhetorical strategies	use of personal pronouns	use of "we", e.g. "We're not unfriendly" (l. 39); use of "I", e.g. "I can make a living" (ll. 85f.)
	use of imperatives	"Just don't get in our way." (ll. 36f.)
	ellipsis (leaving out words)	"Remember the kerfuffle ...?" (l. 8); "nice of them not to bother ..." (ll. 82f.)
	use of humour/irony	"Instagram masterpiece" (l. 36)
	comments in brackets	"(it happens)" (l. 51)

Texts

9/11 and New York

D9 SUPPORT FOR TASK 3 (P. 91)

When you read the prologue of *Hope and Other Punch Lines* to find out how Abbi Hope Goldstein sees the 9/11 attacks, you may follow the steps below to examine her view.

1. Read up to "A before." (l. 2) and analyse what Abbi associates with Tuesday as the day of the week on which the attacks happened. Pay special attention to expressions such as "least descriptive" and "nothing day" as well as the sentence structures.
2. Read the second part of the short extract up to "... you look up." (l. 3) and analyse how Abbi describes the morning before the attacks. Pay special attention to expressions such as "a blue sky" and "clean breath" as well as the sentence structures.
3. The extract ends with the sentence "And the world splits itself in two." (ll. 3f.). Explain what she refers to and what these words try to express about it. Compare this sentence to the lines before and examine whether anything she says before already hints at the message of the last sentence.

Language support

to contrast ... and ... /be contrary to ...
to depart from ...
to coincide
to foreshadow the disaster that is about to happen
impression/thought/what is going through one's mind
ominous/foreboding
unimaginable/inconceivable vs. mundane/ordinary/everyday
terrible/atrocious/barbaric vs. peaceful/innocent/calm

D10 SUPPORT FOR TASK 4C (P. 91)

Find examples of sentences or expressions that illustrate the following thoughts and feelings Abbi has.

1. comparing her life to a fairy tale
2. having doubts about whether she really deserves to be alive
3. being unable to control and escape her past
4. being constantly confronted with death in spite of her survival of 9/11
5. feeling haunted by her unwanted fame
6. desperate to find happiness on her own terms
7. afraid of being caught up by events of the past

D11 SUPPORT FOR TASK 5A (P. 92)

Copy the grids and complete them with information from the extracts.

Webcode
You can download the grids here: DSW-73090-051

extract 2 – Noah: 9/11 Memorial and Museum	
Why did he visit the museum?	
What is on display?	
How are victims and their families involved?	
How does he feel about the museum?	
Why?	

extract 3 – Abbi: Oakdale 9/11 memorial garden	
When does she visit the memorial garden?	
What is on display/done there?	
How are victims and their families involved?	
How does she feel about the monument?	
Why?	

Texts

New York – social disparities

D12 SUPPORT FOR TASK 3A (P. 95)

a) Read the highlighted words or phrases and select the ones that have a negative connotation. Explain these connotations for each of them.

The ultimate real-life test of "trickle down" – the notion that we all prosper when the rich get richer – may well be New York. The Big Apple, after all, certainly abounds in rich getting richer. No city in the world now hosts more of humanity's super rich.

Researchers at Wealth-X last month put the New York billionaire total at 103, ten more than Hong Kong. Top 1 percenters in New York overall are now taking in over 40 percent of the city's income, about double the top 1 percent's income share nationally in the United States.

Numbers like these don't happen by accident. Local and state officials in New York have worked diligently for decades to make their city as attractive as possible to the ten-digit set.

"If we could get every billionaire around the world to move here," as then mayor of New York Michael Bloomberg, himself a billionaire, noted in 2013, "it would be a godsend."

At that mission, Bloomberg and his pals would prove remarkably successful. The fantastically rich physically dominate New York as never before. Luxury residential towers over 75 stories tall now look down upon midtown Manhattan, casting shadows that darken ever wider swathes of Central Park.

Fancy restaurants abound throughout Manhattan and beyond. Broadway is booming. Millions of tourists are trampling on streets free from grit and grime. New York, the city's most ardent cheerleaders proclaim, has never been a better place.

[...]

EXAMPLE:

The word "dominate" is considered negative because it is associated with exerting power over a weaker individual.

b) Now look at the words and phrases that normally have a positive connotation and examine them in the current context.

EXAMPLE:

Normally, the phrase "work diligently" is a positive statement as it suggests that a person is focused and hard-working. In the context of working hard only to make the rich richer it is used ironically as it is meant as a criticism.

c) The phrase "trickle down" is a technical term meaning that if the rich get richer everyone will become wealthier. It uses the image of water trickling down through the soil. Seen in the context of the article, it still has a negative aspect as it describes a very slow movement. Explain.

D13 SUPPORT FOR TASK 3B (P. 95)

Copy the grid and complete it.

		proof from the article/quote	*effect/function*
rhetorical strategies	*facts and figures/ statistics*		*to reveal the imbalance between the numbers of super rich and of poor or struggling New Yorkers*
			to prove that the horrendous sums at which apartments are sold are entirely unaffordable for the average person
	quotes		*quoting the mayor to unmask his prioritization and focus of interest*
		"'just one paycheck away,' writes Baker, 'from disaster'" (ll. 49f.)	
	examples/ exemplifications	*"the story of a proprietor of one of New York's vanished small businesses ... paying $7,000 a month ... The landlord upped that to $21,000." (ll. 80-84)*	
			to show that places for the general public to enjoy are being reduced
		"What happens when arithmetic like this happens?" (ll. 98f.)	
stylistic devices			*to emphasize the contrast between the rich and the less wealthy*
	metaphor	*"cornucopia of consumption options" (ll. 72f.)*	
	alliteration		*to draw attention to the extremely negative effect of rising rents in NYC*

Webcode
You can download the grid here: DSW-73090-052

D14 SUPPORT FOR TASK 4 (P. 95)

Language support

For me/in my view/in my opinion, the photo represents ...
The photo depicts .../reveals .../shows .../illustrates .../reflects .../unmasks ...
The photo is related to/refers to the description/example/statement/to the fact that ...

D15 SUPPORT FOR TASK 5C (P. 95)

a) Use a T-chart to sort the words from the box into positive and negative adjectives.

alarming | considerate | depressing | detrimental | discouraging | discriminating | effective | efficient | encouraging | favourable | harmful | helpful | hopeless | inconsiderate | irreversible | outrageous | preferable | reassuring

b) Depending on the role you have chosen, select two or three adjectives that you can use in your comment to describe your view of the situation.

c) Read the sentences that could be used as an opening and complete them. Try to present different perspectives/views and decide which of the roles they might fit.

- It is easy to criticize ... but ...
- For a long time, people complained about the run-down character of some parts of New York City ...
- We all want to live in a world that offers equal chances ...
- I'm very proud to say that ...
- This city is everything for me but ...
- In a globalized world, New York City has to compete with other cities around the world, so ...
- For me, it is obvious that things have gone from bad to worse: ...
- It is no surprise that ...

Advanced texts

The High Line

D16 SUPPORT FOR TASK 2C (P. 96)

a) These photos can help you analyse some of the imagery used in the highlighted paragraph:

bird sitting on a perch

nest

sprouting plant

b) Consider the phrase "choked with out-of-town visitors" and explain the metaphorical language.

D17 SUPPORT FOR TASK 4 (P. 98)

There are many ways to weigh different aspects. Use the phrases on the right to talk about the pros and cons of the High Line.

Language support

on the one hand ... , on the other hand ...
in contrast to .../on the contrary
as a consequence/consequently
this has caused .../triggered .../led to ...

Advanced texts

The arts and New York City

D18 SUPPORT FOR TASK 1B (P. 100)

a) Match the highlighted phrases from the mission statement (1-8) to the expressions below (A-H).

As the leader in its field, Public Art Fund brings dynamic (1) contemporary art to a (2) broad audience in New York City and beyond by mounting ambitious (3) free exhibitions of international scope and impact that offer (4) the public powerful (5) experiences with art and the urban environment. [...]
Since its (6) inception, Public Art Fund has presented more than five hundred artists' exhibitions and projects at sites throughout New York City's five boroughs, making it possible for artists (7) to engage diverse audiences and, along the way, (8) redefine public art in relation to the changing nature of contemporary art.

A art of our day and age
B involving many people
C exhibitions open to everybody without paying for a ticket
D all citizens
E a new way of seeing their city through art
F beginning
G to communicate with people from all ethnic groups or social classes
H make people look at art in a new way

b) Use some of the phrases to describe the aims of the Public Art Fund in your own words.

Theme task

D19 SUPPORT FOR TASK 3 (P. 101)

Here is a planner template for a typical podcast episode:

Parts (duration)	Description/Example
1. Intro tag (a few seconds)	Name the creator, sponsors, etc.: *This podcast is brought to you by ...* *Thanks to ... who keep our podcast running.*
2. Intro monologue (15 to 45 seconds)	Introduce yourselves and the topic you are going to talk about. Try to create interest in you and your topic. *Welcome to ... with ....* *We believe it is important/our mission is ...* *Today's episode brings you the latest on...* *In today's episode, we talk about .../explore the topic of ...*
3. Intro jingle/music (25 to 45 seconds)	Play a short piece of music or a recognizable melody to introduce your programme.
4. Show content/topic (2 to 5 minutes)	Make a script; determine the different roles; make sure you answer all *wh*-questions. Roles: HOST CO-HOST GUEST(S), EXPERTS, PEOPLE ON THE STREETS, etc.

Parts (duration)	Description/Example
5. Closing remarks (1 to 2 minutes)	Thank your audience, your guests and give a teaser for your next show. *Thank you so much, ..., for coming to NYC tonight and ... Thank you all for listening. If you liked this episode, give me a ... on ... Next week on "Empire State of Mind": ...*
6. Closing music/jingle (a few seconds)	Play a short piece of music or a recognizable melody as an outro.

4 Industrialization and globalization

Intro

Webcode
You can download the grid here:
DSW-73090-053

D1 SUPPORT FOR TASK 3B (P. 102)

The grid has been partly filled in for you. Complete it while watching the video.

	"fourth industrial revolution"	*first industrial revolution*	*second industrial revolution*	*third industrial revolution*
when it takes/took place	*now, according to Klaus Schwab*			*second half of ...*
key inventions and technologies		*steam ...*		
major changes and developments			*mass ..., new industries like ...*	

D2 SUPPORT FOR TASK 5 (P. 103)

alliteration | assonance | ellipsis | exclamation | metaphor | pun | repetition | rhetorical question

a) Which rhetorical device(s) are used in the headlines? Match the rhetorical devices in the box with the highlighted parts of the headlines.

1. New research highlights impact of the digital divide
2. The die was cast for Midland Steel industry
3. The Silicon Valley economy is here. And it's a nightmare!
4. How England's broken ceramics industry put itself back together again
5. A dozen dead whales washed ashore in the bay area
6. No dirt? No farm? No problem. The potential for soil-less agriculture is huge
7. UK factory output rebounds after increase in demand
8. Did Derby build the world? How the Museum of Making bounced back

b) The aim of a newspaper headline is to grab the readers' attention and make them want to read the news article. There are different ways of doing this, e.g.
- repetition of the same sounds or words to focus attention,
- use of wordplay to create a humorous effect,
- omission of unnecessary words to emphasize a point more succinctly,
- punctuation to create shock or surprise.

Choose two of the headlines in a) and write a short analysis of them. Describe the rhetorical devices used and their effect on the reader.

Part A: Industrialization and deindustrialization in Britain

Workshop: Step by step

D3 SUPPORT FOR TASK 1A (P. 106)

When describing and analysing a photo, you may follow this structure:

general introduction	This photo shows a scene at/in/... and seems to deal with ... It might have been taken in/at ... / when ... The general impression it conveys is that the situation seems ... because ...
detailed description	In the middle/foreground/background/top-left corner, one can see ... On the right/left, ... At the top/bottom, ... The colours/the lack of colour ... make ... appear ... There is a contrast between ... and ...
analysis/interpretation/putting the photo into a wider context	The facial expressions of ... /the gestures of ... /the body posture of ... suggest(s) that ... /convey(s) the impression that ... The look on their faces makes one think of ... /expresses that ... The situation depicted in the photo is related to the wider context of ... The atmosphere conveyed in the photo makes the viewer take sides with ... /get an idea of what it means to ...
conclusion	All in all, the aim of the photographer seems to be to ...

D4 SUPPORT FOR TASK 1B (P. 106)

Look at the photos and decide which atmosphere they convey. Choose adjectives that fit and explain why you think so.

alarming | busy | cheerful | cooperative | desolate | dignified | ecstatic | friendly | gloomy | harmonious | hostile | light-hearted | peaceful | scary | sombre | tense | terrifying | threatening | vivacious | warm | welcoming

1

2

3

4

D5 SUPPORT FOR TASK 3 (P. 107)

Look at the photos and the terms for cinematic devices next to them. For each photo, choose the ones that fit.

1
- close-up
- full shot
- high-angle shot
- low-angle shot
- over-the-shoulder shot

2
- close-up
- establishing shot
- medium shot
- low-angle shot
- over-the-shoulder shot

3
- establishing shot
- eye-level shot
- long shot
- low-angle shot
- medium shot

4
- close-up
- eye-level shot
- full shot
- over-the-shoulder shot
- reverse-angle shot

D6 SUPPORT FOR TASK 4 (P. 109)

These phrases may help you to describe what is going on in the first extract from *Pride*:

- to speak up for the gay support group
- to be criticized for voicing one's opinion
- to unpack boxes of tinned food
- to say goodbye to her husband
- to walk over to the welfare hall
- to express concerns about inviting the gay support group
- to join other miners to drive to the picket line[1]
- to interfere in the strike committee's discussion
- to express support for each other
- to discuss what to do about the gay support group

[1] **picket line** = a group of protesters outside a place of work

D7 SUPPORT FOR TASK 5 (P. 110)

These phrases may help you to describe the function/effect of the cinematic devices used in that scene:

- to present the discussion from the characters' point of view
- to show the distance between the welfare committee and the other people present
- to draw attention to the character's facial expression
- to reveal the tension between those participating in the discussion
- to underline the gloomy atmosphere of a poor mining village
- to help the viewers understand the importance of the strike for the community

D8 SUPPORT FOR TASK 6B (P. 110)

Decide which pieces of information do **not** match the film.

1	*Welsh countryside, van*	A the LGSM members have lost their way	B some are unpleasantly surprised by the sight of the village	C their arrival is met with disbelief by the local youth
2	*outside the Onllwyn welfare hall and in its entrance hall*	A Mark and his friends hesitate nervously before entering the hall	B some of them appear confident once inside	C they are noticed by one of the locals
3	*inside the kitchen*	A Dai introduces his wife and other members of the mining community	B LGSM have to sign in so that they can be officially introduced to the mining community	C all the locals are welcoming and curious to find out more about gays and lesbians
4	*inside the welfare hall*	A Dai introduces LGSM to the audience	B Mark manages to establish a relationship with the audience	C some locals leave following Mark's speech

D9 SUPPORT FOR TASK 7 (P. 111)

When analysing the way this scene is filmed, consider some of the points below.

1. Consider the costumes/clothes, e.g. colourful, modern, formal, informal, traditional, etc., and what they say about the people wearing them.
2. Pay attention to facial expressions and body language, e.g. welcoming smiles, stern faces, signs of nervousness, etc.
3. Consider the atmosphere, e.g. lively chatter, awkward silence, friendly small talk, reserved conversation.
4. Watch out for the use of reverse-angle shots, point-of-view shots, full shots and close-ups, as they help to reveal people's relationships, state of mind, feelings, etc.

D10 SUPPORT FOR TASK 9 (P. 111)

a) Before you start writing, consider the following points about your character:
   - What situation is he/she in? What does it mean to him/her?
   - What is his/her character like?
   - What are his/her thoughts, feelings, associations, etc.?

b) Make sure that your style of writing imitates what may go through one's mind.
   - Ask yourself questions.

- Address problems, hopes, fears, etc.
- Refer to your expectations and the actual course of events.
- Express your feelings and how they change over time.
- You may switch from one thought to another.
- Sentences can be incomplete.
- There may be pauses or you stop a sentence in the middle and continue with another thought.
- You use exclamation marks to show your emotions.

c) You may use the following sentences as a beginning.

I don't really know any more why LGSM is/we are here now. Last-minute nerves maybe. Has it really been such a good idea? Is Onllwyn ready for a group of gays and lesbians? But why shouldn't they/we be here? They/we were the ones who collected and sent all that money here. A true sign of solidarity! ...

Facts

D11 SUPPORT FOR TASK 1 (P. 112)

Match the headings (1-9) to the paragraphs (A-H) on pp. 112f. There is one more heading than you need.

1 Coal, iron and steel in the Black Country
2 Thatcher versus the unions
3 Pioneers in engineering and business
4 A beam of hope
5 The heart of the British car industry
6 A system of waterways
7 The importance of trade
8 Post-war policy
9 Death of traditional industry

D12 SUPPORT FOR TASK 2 (P. 112)

An infographic aims to illustrate a process or problem clearly and succinctly. When creating an infographic, it is helpful to follow these steps.

1. Identify the topic.
Which of the following themes best fits task 2?

A Explain the growth of industry in the Midlands during the industrial revolution.
B Show industrialization and deindustrialization in the Midlands from the 18th to the 21st century.
C Outline the progress of the car industry in the Midlands in the 20th century.

2. Collect the necessary data.
- Use the facts page as a source for your data.
- Divide the text between the group members and note down relevant information.
- Decide as a group which information to include. It is important not to overload your infographic with text.

➡

3. Decide how to visualize the data.
There are various types of visualization to choose from. Decide which of the templates below best fits your topic.

Timeline:
Suitable to show change over time

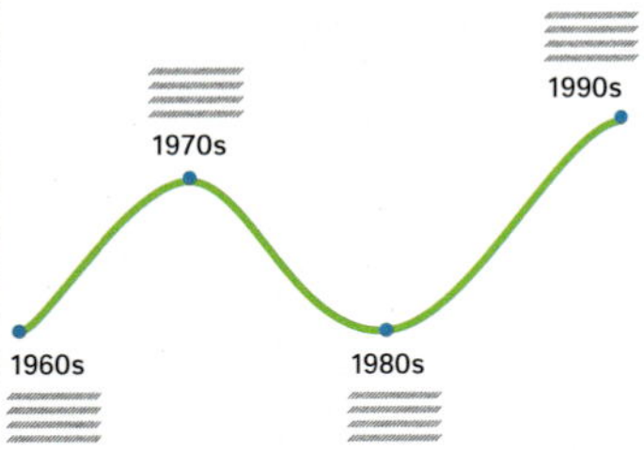

Flowchart:
Can be used to visualize organisational questions or questions with different possible outcomes

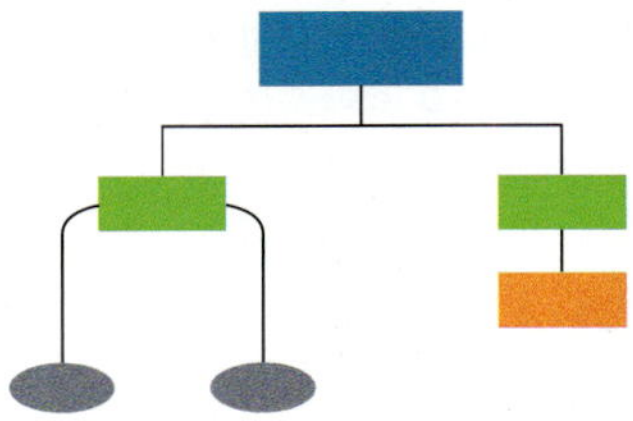

Informational:
Similar to a poster, it can be used to highlight different aspects in lists or specific sections

Hierarchical:
Suitable to imagine hierarchical structures and ideas; example: food pyramid

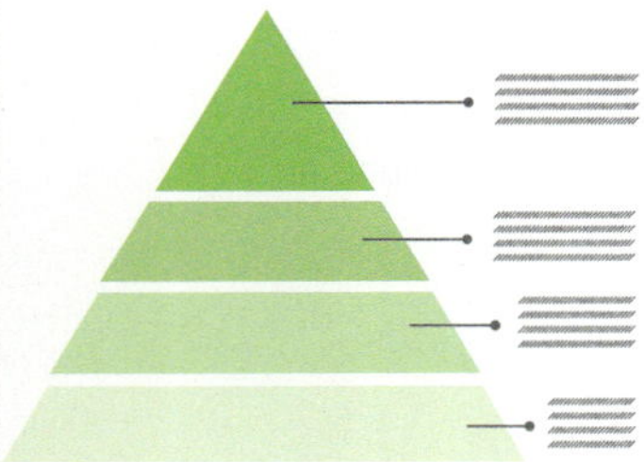

Process:
Helps to visualize steps that have been or need to be taken

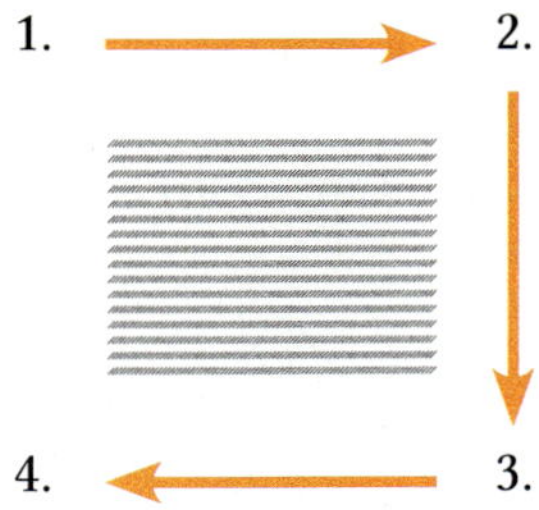

Comparison:
Organizes data that compares two or more ideas, places, people or things

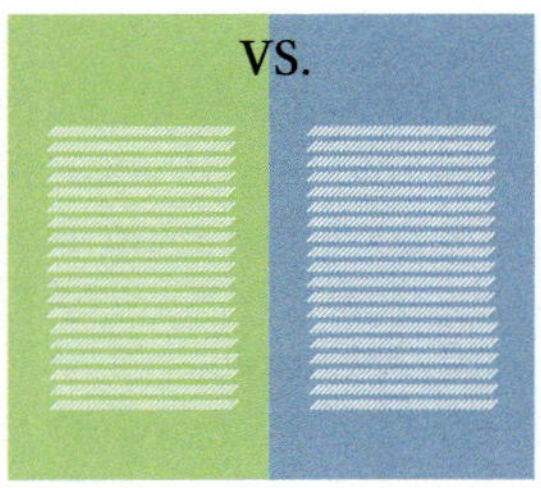

4. Write a short headline.
Keep the headline short and snappy. Here are some options:
- The process of industrialization in the Midlands
- Industrialization and deindustrialization – the Midlands
- The rise and fall of industry in the Midlands
- The history of industrialization – the Midlands

5. Make your infographic attractive.
Choose illustrations, icons, and decide which colours and fonts you are going to use.

Texts

Industrialization and deindustrialization in the Midlands: Working on novel extracts

D13 SUPPORT FOR TASK 4A (P. 118)

Match the quotations from the literary extracts (1-10) with the descriptions of atmosphere (A-G). There are various possibilities.

1 ... a stifling sense of claustrophobia ...
2 ... the frontages are peeling and dilapidated ...
3 ... piled with cheap mass-produced goods ... ugly shoes, ugly clothes and unbelievably ugly furniture ...
4 The mine and the village had been as intertwined as lovers ...
5 ... the whole suggested death rather than life.
6 ... closures have ravaged the area in recent years, giving a desolate look to its streets.
7 ... yet everything repeated itself endlessly. ... small oblong windows, and oblong doors, repeated endlessly ...
8 ... the hormonal balance of Tollington was turned upside down.
9 ... rapidly spreading, like a skin-disease.
10 It would be a long slow death.

A monotony
B gloom
C suffocation
D apprehension
E intimacy
F upheaval
G hopelessness

D14 SUPPORT FOR TASK 5A (P. 118)

Here are some ideas:

- Tom Brangwen
- A collier living in Wiggiston
- Robert Appleby
- A woman working in the factory in New Town
- An unemployed metal worker of Caribbean origin
- A factory worker at Pringle's

Advanced texts

The remnants of industrialization: Working on poetry

D15 SUPPORT FOR TASK 1 (P. 119)

When analysing a poem, there are various aspects you can consider. Use the grid to examine what feelings and impressions are conveyed through choice of words, stylistic devices and the structure of the poems.

Webcode
You can download the grid here: **DSW-73090-054**

poem 1: Used to Be		*poem 2: Magpie Mine*	
1. Choice of words			
soot-stained (l. 4)	*conveys the impression of an old and run-down place that is heavily affected by the dust and dirt of the mine where the men work hard; the signs of their working life are everywhere*	*cheap (l. 8)*	*suggests that the men's lives did not matter to the owners of the mine; the men's well-being was not important, as workers could be replaced and the needs of the coal industry came before minimizing the dangers of working there*
gloom (l. 11)		*drowned (l. 10)*	
slumped (l. 8)		*wailing (l. 11)*	
laughter (l. 5)		*cursed (l. 13)*	
overjoyed (l. 20)		*desolate (l. 17)*	
2. Stylistic devices			
alliteration: soot-stained (l. 4); gas-lit gloom (l. 11)		*alliteration: wailing/wives (l. 11)*	*highlights that the dangers of working in the coal mine affected not only the men working there but also their wives who worried for their husbands or even had to mourn their deceased partners*
enumeration: stood at the bar or slumped on chairs/Supped their pints and swapped their tales (ll. 8f.)		*enumeration: Swallows swoop to pick up moths and the hobby dives; a curlew utters its desolate cry (ll. 15-17)*	
repetition: pub … beside the railway tracks (ll. 2f. + 28f.)	*emphasizes that the place is the focal point of the speaker's memories, but it is gone, just like the industry*	*metaphor: lives were cheap (l. 8)*	
3. Structure			
2 stanzas of 12 lines each, 1 stanza of 4 lines		*3 stanzas of 5 lines each*	
stanza 1: Right there …	*focus on the memories of a place that formed the positive hub of the mining community*	*stanza 1: Nothing to see here …*	*focus on the memories of what people used to be able to see around the mine*
stanza 2: That's where …		*stanza 2: Nothing to hear …*	
stanza 3:		*stanza 3:*	

Advanced texts

Deindustrialization in Germany

D16 SUPPORT FOR TASK 1 (P. 120)

a) Read the task and decide which of the following tips apply.

Your class is taking part in a project on deindustrialization in Britain and Germany with students from a school in the Midlands. Write an article for the project website in which you outline why the Ruhr area is a classic example of deindustrialization and how the region has been coping with this process.

1. Your language should be relatively formal because you write an article for a project website.
2. Your language can be quite colloquial because you write for a young audience.
3. Your text should include – among other things – a headline and a conclusion.
4. You can follow the structure of the article from *Süddeutsche Zeitung* for your article.
5. You need to rearrange relevant information for your article.
6. You may include your own assessment of how well the Ruhr has coped with change.

b) Before you start writing your article, note down ideas from the article that need to be included.

why the Ruhr area is an example of deindustrialisation	how it has been coping with that change
• *coal industry in the Ruhr area as the basis of the rise of German industrialization* • *but days of coal industry over* • ...	• *new businesses need to be developed* • ...

Webcode
You can download the grid here:
DSW-73090-055

D17 SUPPORT FOR TASK 1 (P. 120)

In a mediation task, there are different ways to express ideas from a German-language article:
- using an English equivalent for a German expression
- paraphrasing a German expression, i.e. explaining a concept in your own words

For each expression below, find both an English equivalent and a paraphrase, where possible.

EXAMPLE:

Gründergeist

English equivalent:
founders' spirit,
spirit of the founders,
start-up spirit

paraphrase:
optimistic attitude of those founding companies

1. Wohlstand
2. Wirtschaftswunder
3. Anpassungsprozess
4. Feuer einer „brennenden Ruhr“
5. Schuldenlast
6. Zechentod
7. Malocher

Part B: Globalization

Texts

Globalization now and then

D18 SUPPORT FOR TASK 3A (P. 122)

Copy the grid and complete it with the help of the information from the first part of the extract.

Webcode
You can download the grid here:
DSW-73090-056

The three stages of globalization:			
stage of globalization	1	2	3
main driving force/agent	...	...	...
typical developments/effects	...	...	...
size of the world	*L ("macro")*	*M*	*S ("micro")*

D19 SUPPORT FOR TASK 3B (P. 122)

Explain the old and new forms of globalization. Consider the following notions related to each form of globalization.

- "Old globalization":
  WTO, World Bank, outsourcing, multinational
- "New globalization":
  globalizing on their own, no over here and over there, multilocal, age of accelerations

D20 SUPPORT FOR TASK 4A (P. 123)

Match the following descriptions with elements in the infographic.

1. Developing countries are involved in the global economy.
2. New inventions and developments spread only slowly from one country to the next.
3. Technological progress is achieved in the developed world and then exported elsewhere.
4. The internet makes it possible for everyone worldwide to use knowledge online.
5. The global economy depends mainly on financial investment and the workforce.
6. It is more important that digital information and services are exchanged.
7. In an economy that increasingly relies on IT, digital services can be provided with the help of a computer with internet access anywhere in the world.
8. Open-source software, for example, and other data are made available free of charge online.

Texts

California – the home of global players

D21 SUPPORT FOR TASK 3 (P. 125)

Go through the extract from Scott Galloway's book *The Four* to find examples of the author's use of language that are meant to have the following effects:

- to make readers develop a critical attitude towards the rise of those companies
- to emphasize in how many ways these companies have changed our everyday lives
- to convey a clear sense of the rivalry that exists between those companies
- to evoke images of a fight without inhibitions
- to contrast the pros and cons of the products and services these companies have developed
- to underline that the power of these companies exceeds that of states
- to allude to the biblical vision of the end of the world
- to present the Four as if they were human beings

5 The digital age

Workshop: Step by step

D1 SUPPORT FOR TASK 5C (P. 136)

When you analyse the line of argument, you must focus on **how** the author structures his or her text and **what effect** this structure has on you, the reader. Also, you should ask yourself which intention the author pursues with his/her text. Is it simply to inform you about a certain topic or to convince you of a certain point? Or both?

Pay attention to ...
... the headline,
... the introduction (e.g. is there an example or a quotation?),
... the use of examples, anecdotes or personal experiences,
... the use of quotations from experts,
... the use of facts and figures,
... the ending (e.g. is there an appeal to the reader? Is there a reference to the introduction?),
... the structure in general (chronological, contrastive/antithetical).

Possible effects can be ...
... to catch the reader's attention,
... so the reader can identify with the author/the experiences mentioned,
... to explain, compare, contrast, to underline, to support, to criticize, to illustrate, ... something.

EXAMPLE: *Section 1: In the beginning of his article, the author uses an anecdote from his personal life to catch the readers' attention and to make the readers imagine themselves in the same situation as the author before moving to the actual topic of the article.*

D2 SUPPORT FOR TASK 7A (P. 137)

A grid can be useful for collecting pro and contra arguments. The table below has been partly filled in for you.

Webcode
You can download the grid here:
DSW-73090-058

arguments for becoming a digital nomad	*arguments against becoming a digital nomad*
– *according to Helen Barlow, every day is exciting because there are always new experiences* – *to have the possibility to live a lifestyle valuing experiences over possessions* ...	– *some digital nomads avoid deep connections with others abroad to not become attached to them when they move* ... ...

Workshop: Practice

D3 SUPPORT FOR TASK 2A (P. 138)

Here are some aspects related to potential advantages and disadvantages of working from home:

comfortable clothes | creating your perfect work space | distractions like pets, children, spouses, ... | feeling tired/isolated | flexibility to do other things in between | no communication with colleagues | no motivation to get dressed | no proper separation between job and home | no room for a proper desk | opportunity to look after children when they are at home | staying in touch with colleagues/clients (globally) using video conference tools | working too many hours (into the night)

Texts

Has technology made us lazy and dependent?

D4 SUPPORT FOR TASK 3 (P. 141)

Strategies for persuasive writing can be related to the content of a text but also to the way language is used to convince the reader of a certain view.
For **content-related strategies** (e.g. use of examples), take a look at **D1** on p. 187.
For **language-related strategies**, pay special attention to the following aspects when reading the article again:

- use of a personal anecdote: "When I was but a young ... and those mental math tricks have all but vanished." (ll. 1-23)
- use of humour: "Hell, my cell even reminds to go to sleep at night – and my smartwatch commands me to 'Move!' when I've been sat on my butt too long" (ll. 30-33)
- metaphorical language: "When I was but a young, fresh-faced whipper-snapper" (ll. 1f.), "the hippocampus [...] used to think of different routes are 'switched off'" (ll. 74-76)
- (rhetorical) questions to activate the reader: "could we cope without them?" (ll. 43f.), "Could it be that we've become too dependent on technology?" (ll. 44f.), "Who needs to rely on their own memories in the digital age, right?"
- use of personal pronouns to involve the reader
- informal language, use of short forms: "Hell, my cell even reminds me ... too long" (ll. 30-33), "While we're not all London cabbies" (l. 80)

6 English as a lingua franca

Workshop: Practice

D1 SUPPORT FOR TASK 1 (P. 150)

This checklist can help you:

Checklist

Mediation

✓ Identify
- addressee,
- situational context,
- topic,
- type of text/register.

✓ Note down the information from the German text which you need for your presentation.

✓ Note down the words and expressions which have no direct English equivalent.
- Decide whether you need them for your presentation.
- If so, find a way to explain them in English so you can include the information.

Language support

The text/article/comment consists of ... /can be divided into ... sections/parts/paragraphs.
In the beginning the author starts by pointing out that/presenting the thesis that/using an example ...
In the next paragraph, the author contrasts the view/idea/point by ...
In the following paragraph ... is emphasized/is listed/in order to/to achieve the effect that ...
By quoting several experts, the author supports/explains/criticizes/illustrates that ...
The article closes with an appeal to the reader in which ...

G1 Emphasis

If you want to emphasize certain elements of what you are saying, these elements are often – but not always – moved to the beginning of the sentence. There are different ways an element in a sentence can be emphasized: emphatic *do*, inversion and cleft sentences.

→ Theme 1, pp. 31-32

Emphatic *do*

If you want to emphasize a verb, simply put a form of *do* in front of it. The use of emphatic *do* is more common in oral than in (formal) written communication:

I ***do*** *hope you are happy now.*
He ***did*** *help him in the end.*
She ***does*** *know what she is doing.*

1

Use the emphatic *do* to rewrite these sentences about *Brave New World*.

1 *Brave New World* became Aldous Huxley's most important work.
2 Bernard seems to think too much about his life.
3 Lenina enjoys listening to the radio.
4 She takes soma to feel happy.

Webcode

You can find the solutions to all grammar tasks here: **DSW-73090-066**

Inversion

Inversion occurs when the normal word order in a sentence (subject – verb – object) is changed so that the verb is placed in front of the subject.

Inversion with *here/there*

You can use inversion with *here/there* in combination with verbs of motion to achieve a slight dramatic effect and emphasis:
Here comes the sun.
There goes the last one.
There remains the question of financing.

Inversion after certain adverbs

Inversion can occur when certain adverbs are moved to the beginning of the sentence for emphasis. These adverbs usually have a somewhat negative meaning, such as *never (before/again), seldom, only once, only then, barely, under no circumstances*. You need an auxiliary verb to form an inverted sentence. If the verb of the sentence you want to invert is in a progressive or perfect form or other combined form like the *will* future, simply use the form of *be* or *have* or *will*. If it is in a simple form, use a form of *do*. This type of emphasis is more formal.

Barely had *she touched her food when he started to speak.*
Seldom have *I seen such a blue sky.*
Under no circumstances will *I go back.*
Only once did *I sleep in a tent.*
Only then did *she understand what was happening.*

2

a) Use inversion with the help of *here/there* to write sentences about these situations.

1 In a meeting, you and a few others have discussed a number of questions and now you want to use a certain dramatic effect to emphasize that only one last question is left to discuss.
2 You and a few others are waiting for your friend Emma. Then you suddenly see her and you want to announce her arrival to the others.
3 You and your team had one last chance of winning the game and now it is gone.

b) Use inversion to rewrite these sentences about Lenina and Bernard from *Brave New World*.

1 Lenina had never before talked to someone like Bernard.
2 Bernard couldn't accept her answer under no circumstances.
3 Lenina didn't want to have such a conversation ever again.
4 Bernard understood only then that he couldn't really talk to Lenina about anything important.

Cleft sentences, part 1: cleft sentences with *It is/was*

You can use this kind of cleft sentence to emphasize the subject of a sentence, an object or an adverbial of time, place or reason by moving it to the beginning of the sentence.

***It was** in Hamburg **that** we wanted to meet.* (We wanted to meet in Hamburg.)
***It is** Patrick **who** I wanted to meet there.* (I wanted to meet Patrick there.)
***It is** because she didn't like the band **that** she left the concert early.* (She left the concert early because she didn't like the band)

3

Use cleft sentences with *It is/was* to reformulate these sentences from the extract from *Brave New World* on pp. 31-32.

1 On their way back across the Channel, Bernard insisted on stopping his propeller.
2 Bernard had switched off the current.
3 But Lenina was crying.
4 You're saying the most awful things.

Cleft sentences, part 2: cleft sentences with *What ... is/was*

Another way of forming cleft sentences is by using the construction *What ... is/are*.
Here, what you want to emphasize comes at the end of the sentence, after the *is/was*.

***What** she really wants to buy **is** a new coat.* (She really wants to buy a new coat.)
***What** he likes more than anything else **is** spaghetti.* (He likes spaghetti more than anything else.)
***What** they believe in **is** magic.* (They believe in magic.)
***What** was published in August **was** her new book.* (Her new book was published in August.)

If you want to emphasize the verb of a sentence, you can also use this kind of cleft sentence, but you need to insert a form of *do* in front of the *is/was*. The form of *do* takes the tense of the original sentence, whereas the verb after the *is/was* is always an infinitive.

***What** she **doesn't do is speak** Italian.* (She **doesn't speak** Italian.)
***What** they really **want to do is help** their mother.* (They really **want to help** their mother.)
***What** she **is going to do** next month **is write** a novel* (She **is going to write** a novel next month.)
***What** he never **did was wear** a suit.* (He never **wore** a suit.)

4

Use cleft sentences with *What ... is/was* to rewrite these sentences from the extract from *Brave New World* on pp. 31-32.

1 She reached for the dialling knob on the dashboard.
2 I want to look at the sea in peace.
3 Lenina was shocked by his blasphemy.
4 He looked at her in silence.

5

Use cleft sentences, inversion or the emphatic *do* to emphasize the highlighted parts of the following sentences.

1 People in *Brave New World* usually follow the rules.
2 The notion that you cannot make your own decisions seems dreadful to me.
3 Bernard tries to connect with Lenina on a higher level.
4 Lenina has never been interested in exchanging ideas and emotions.
5 She is very much a product of the state she lives in.
6 I think that especially Betas, Gammas, Deltas and Epsilons enjoy lives without worries.
7 *Brave New World* citizens think that they are happy, although they really aren't.
8 Lenina was not only bewildered, but also upset.
9 He realized the importance of the topic only after Lenina had left.
10 After dinner that day, Lenina felt a sharp pain in her stomach.

G2 Conditional clauses

→ Theme 3, pp. 88-90

1

In your text for task 4 on page 90, it makes sense to use some conditional clauses, also known as *if* clauses. For practice, complete these conditional clauses. Be careful about the tenses.

Webcode

You can download the sentences here: DSW-73090-060

1 If I had the chance to spend a gap year in the US, 1
2 If I got a place to stay in New York City, 2
3 I would have visited the US years ago if 3
4 I will travel around in the US if 4
5 If one of my friends goes to the US as an au-pair after school, 5
6 If my parents had been offered jobs in the US, 6
7 I would try to make some friends in NYC online if 7
8 If my school had an exchange programme with a school in the US, 8
9 I will definitely go to NYC if 9
10 If offered the chance to live anywhere in New York City 10
11 Even if I had enough money 11
12 If my parents allow it 12

G3 Aspect

→ Theme 4, pp. 102-103

When you look at the headlines and news snippets on pp. 102-103, you will notice that they contain many different verb forms. You will find active and passive forms as well as different tenses, indicating when something happens. But there is something else called aspect. The aspect of a verb gives you additional information about the action.

The **continuous aspect** tells you that the action is, was or will be ongoing or happening over a longer period of time. The continuous aspect is formed by using a form of *be* together with the *-ing* form of the verb (present participle).
The **perfect aspect** tells you that the action is finished. The result of the action may be what is important. The perfect aspect is formed by using a form of *have* together with the *-ed* form of the verb (past participle).
Here are two examples from the news snippets on pages 102-103:

The electrification of the auto industry ***is speeding up****.*
➡ **continuous aspect:** the action is going on at the moment.

British industry ***has declined*** *over the past 100 years.*
➡ **perfect aspect:** industry is no longer declining, the process is at its end. And the result is important, i.e. there is hardly any industry left.

Simple forms like the simple present and the simple past do not have an aspect.

Here are some more examples:
Many researchers ***are working*** *on ways of using hydrogen as an alternative to petrol.*
➡ This is happening at this moment and it is an ongoing process.

Workers ***were hoping*** *for new job opportunities when their mines closed down.*
➡ They had been hoping for new job opportunities for some time. If the simple past (*hoped*) was used instead, this would mean that the workers only started hoping at the moment their mines closed.

Ordinary mobile phones ***had become*** *household items when smartphones revolutionized user habits.* ➡ The process was already finished when smartphones entered the market.

Experts say that many coal-fuelled power plants ***will have closed down*** *by 2040.*
➡ The process (the closing of many coal-fuelled power plants) will already have come to an end by 2040, i.e. over a longer period of time leading up to 2040, many power plants will close down.

1

Complete these sentences with the verbs in brackets using the right tense and aspect.

Webcode
You can download the sentences here: **DSW-73090-061**

1 Most people 1 (work) as farmers when the Industrial Revolution 2 (start) in the 18th century.
2 Studies suggest that electric cars 3 (replace) petrol cars by the middle of this century.
3 Car manufacturers 4 (invest) billions of euros over the past few years to switch their production to electric cars.
4 Customers 5 (become) so used to doing all kinds of things with their mobiles that they 6 (be) willing to pay a lot of money for a new smartphone.
5 Some companies like Google or Facebook 7 (gain) so much power and influence that smaller companies in the field 8 (struggle) to survive.
6 In the 1970s, more and more coal mines in Germany and the UK 9 (become) unprofitable, so it 10 (not come) as a surprise that many 11 (be forced) to close in the 1980s.
7 These days, we 12 (use) the Internet with many electronic devices without noticing it.
8 Social media 13 (make) it much easier to stay in touch with people abroad than it 14 (be) in the past.

G4 Defining and non-defining relative clauses

The info box about the miner's strike on page 107 contains many relative clauses. Two kinds of relative clause can be distinguished: defining and non-defining relative clauses.

→ Theme 4, pp. 106ff

type of relative clause	examples from the info box on p. 107
defining relative clause: the relative clause further specifies the noun it refers to – no comma	*When a government plan* ***which was expected to lead to the closure of about 20 pits and the loss of about 20,000 jobs*** *was made public on 6 March 1984, ...* ➡ "a government plan" does not give the reader an idea of what plan it is, the relative clause defines which government plan is actually meant, namely the one about the mines. *... to protect miners* ***who still went to work.*** ➡ In this sentence not all miners are meant, but only those who were still working in spite of the miners' strike. The relative clause helps to identify the group among the miners that the author has in mind.
type of relative clause	**examples from the info box on p. 107**
non-defining relative clause: the noun already tells you which people/things/... the author wants to refer to, it does not need to be further specified. So the relative clause gives only extra information – comma necessary	*... weaken the power of the trade unions****, which she considered too powerful,*** *...* ➡ Thatcher thought of all trade unions, so the relative clause does not further specify a certain group of powerful trade unions. It just gives extra information about the trade unions, namely that Thatcher thought of them as having too much influence. *Conservative Margaret Thatcher****, who had become the UK's first female prime minister in 1979,*** *...* ➡ By giving the name, it is clear which person the author refers to, so the relative clause only gives extra information about Thatcher.

1

Look at the sentences below and rewrite them using relative clauses. Add commas when necessary.

1 After her speech in 1976, Thatcher was given the nickname *the Iron Lady* by a Soviet journal. The speech criticized the Soviet Union.
2 In 2011, Hollywood actress Meryl Streep portrayed Thatcher in the feature film *The Iron Lady*. The film also deals with her battle with dementia in the last years of her life.
3 In 1982, the Falklands War was a 10-week conflict between the UK and Argentina. Argentina had invaded the UK-owned Falkland Islands off the Argentinian coast.
4 After her death in 2013, a social media campaign helped the 1939 song "Ding-Dong! The Witch Is Dead" to reach No. 2 in the charts. The campaign had been started by anti-Conservative activists.
5 BBC Radio 1 did not play the complete song in its chart programme, but instead played a news report. It put the song and Thatcher's life and death into a wider context.
6 Thatcher is also a main character in the fourth season of the TV series *The Crown*. The series deals with the history of the Royal family after World War II.

Webcode
You can download the sentences here: DSW-73090-062

2

→ Theme 4, pp. 112-113, 115-118

Having read the Facts page and the novel extracts dealing with industrialization and deindustrialization in the Midlands, work on the sentences below.

a) Note down the correct relative pronoun (*who, which* or *whose*) to fill the gaps in the sentences below.

b) Decide which relative clauses are defining and which are non-defining and therefore need to be separated by commas.

Webcode
You can download the sentences here: DSW-73090-059

1 In 1771, Richard Arkwright invented the water-powered spinning wheel [1] brought about the birth of the factory system.
2 Industry and manufacturing were dependent on factory-based steam power [2] in turn necessitated coal.
3 In as many as 500 collieries in the area the coal was mined [3] was needed to run machines and to feed the furnaces in the foundries.
4 Against the pleas of my parents [4] did little to disguise their disappointment, and despite the potential ostracism from those in the village [5] thought it a personal insult that I should walk away from a position of far greater privilege than those [6] risked their lives several hundred feet underground – I handed in my resignation.
5 Most of the able-bodied men with families had moved on to look for work, leaving behind a gaggle of wheezy old geezers and dozens of stout, dour-faced miners' widows [7] had nowhere else to go.
6 They wanted women, women [8] would do piecework and feel grateful, women [9] nimble fingers would negotiate their machines, women [10] would not make demands or complain.
7 There are occasional strips of terraced houses [11] occupants seem to have given up the unequal struggle against the noise and pollution of the ring road.

3

Write down six sentences about films or TV series you like. Include a relative clause in each sentence – all in all three defining and three non-defining ones. You can use this language support.

Language support

My favourite film genre are films ...
... is my favourite film of all time because ...
I really like the actor/actress ... is best known for ...
If there are a lot of special effects ... it makes watching a film ...
Watching TV series ... at home is much better/worse than going to the cinema.
Whenever I want to take a break from reality, I watch films ...

G5 Participles

→ Theme 4, pp. 112-113, 115-118

Participles are derived from verbs. They can function as adjectives or be part of participle clauses. Participle clauses are particularly useful to write and say things in English in a shorter way.

There are three types of participles:
present participles: going, seeing, laughing, etc.
past participles: gone, seen, laughed, etc.
perfect participles: having gone, having seen, having laughed, etc.

function of the participles	examples from the text on pages 112-113 and 115-118
Present and **past** participles can be used as adjectives to modify nouns.	*Josiah Wedgwood was an entrepreneur and* ***experienced*** *producer of pottery.* *In the 1970s,* ***falling*** *employment numbers ... led to unemployment ...*
Participle clauses can be used to join two sentences. The **perfect participle** can be used to emphasise that one thing happened before another. It can also describe reasons or causes.	***Built*** *in Cromford in the East Midlands, his factory was the first ever to produce textiles.* (His factory was built in Cromford in the East Midlands. It was the first ever to produce textiles.) ***Cutting*** *through the English countryside, canals formed a close network in the Midlands.* (Canals cut through the English countryside. They formed a close network in the Midlands.) ***Having relocated*** *his factory to ..., Josiah Wedgwood proceeded to build a new village ...* (Josiah Wedgwood relocated his factory to ... He proceeded to build a new village ...)
Participle clauses can be used to shorten sentences, e.g. by omitting constructions with relative pronouns (*who, which*) or the conjunctions *since, because, as, so.* Note that *since* and *as* can have temporal as well as causal meaning.	*In 1771, Richard Arkwright invented the water-powered spinning wheel,* ***making*** *it possible to spin cotton and silk mechanically ...* (In 1771, Richard Arkwright invented ..., **which made** it possible to ...) *His pioneer work helped to establish the six towns of Stoke-on-Trent,* ***known*** *as "The Potteries", ...* (His pioneer work helped to establish the six towns of Stoke-on-Trent, **which were known** as "The Potteries", ...) ***Having begun*** *the production of cars and other vehicles at the end of the 19th century, the town of Coventry in the West Midlands became the centre of the British motor industry.* (**Since/As it had begun** the production of cars and other vehicles at the end of the 19th century, the town of Coventry in the West Midlands became the centre of the British motor industry.) ***Having*** *many members* ***willing*** *to go on strike, the unions became very powerful.* (**Since** they **had** many members who **were willing** to go on strike, the unions became very powerful.)
If, in the construction you intend to shorten, the main clause and the subordinate clause each have their own subject, the **subject of the subordinate clause** becomes the subject of the participle clause (*eigenes Sinnsubjekt*).	***Money*** *still being invested in new sinkings and mechanisation of the transportation of coal overground, the final chapter was already being written.* (Though **money** was still being invested in new sinkings and mechanisation of the transportation of coal overground, the final chapter was already being written.)

1

Find at least three other examples of participles in the text on pages 112-113 and identify their functions.

Tip:
The past participle is often used to describe feelings, whereas the present participle describes the thing or situation which has caused the feeling.

Webcode

You can download the sentences here: DSW-73090-063

2

Use either the present or past participles of the verbs in brackets to complete the sentences below. Be careful! Some participles change their meaning when used as adjectives.

1 Men, women and children worked 1 (to exhaust) shifts of twelve or more hours a day in the textile factories.
The 2 (to exhaust) child fell asleep during his shift and had a terrible accident.
2 There are some 3 (to fascinate) examples of 19th-century industrial architecture in the Midlands.
The 4 (to fascinate) guests were able to watch the production of ceramics at the visitor centre.
3 The men working in the coal mine felt 5 (to alarm) when the lights went out.
There are some rather 6 (to alarm) statistics which reveal how the politics of the Thatcher era caused the economic decline of the Midlands.
4 Globalization has had a 7 (to devastate) effect on the British car industry.
There are many 8 (to devastate) areas in the region.
5 The 9 (to shock) employees left the factory in tears after being made redundant.
At the turn of the century, many factory workers still lived in 10 (to shock) conditions.

3

Join the following sentences using a participle clause. Use each type of participle (present, past, perfect participle) twice.

EXAMPLE:

The steelworkers had been on strike for six months. Then they were forced to capitulate.
Having been on strike for six months, the steelworkers were forced to capitulate.

1 The UK manufacturing industry experienced a decline at the end of the 20th century. It was further hit by the global financial crisis in 2008.
2 The powerful unions protested against government policy. They organized industrial action and strikes.
3 Japanese clients were impressed by the quality of Wedgwood china. They wanted products made in England.
4 Many mines closed down. They later became museums and tourist attractions.
5 The railway was invented in the early 19th century. It transformed the countryside and made transport of goods easier.
6 The metal industry grew up around Birmingham. It became the most important industry in the area.

4

Shorten these sentences using a participle clause.

EXAMPLE:

Since the people in the Black Country are very proud of their past, they often live there for generations.
Being very proud of their past, the people in the Black Country often live there for generations.

1 The six towns of Stoke-on-Trent, which are situated in the heart of the Midlands, are known as "The Potteries".
2 Since the factory was conveniently located near the canal system, it could transport manufactured goods easily.
3 The steam engine, which was invented by James Watt in 1765, revolutionized the factories.

4 After the government had restructured the industry in the area, it was able to reduce unemployment.
5 By 1984, the government waged a war against the unions. More strikes were the result.
6 The production of cars proved too expensive, so it was moved to Asia.
7 Margaret Thatcher left office in 1990, fellow party member John Major took up her position.
8 David Cameron, who was elected prime minister in May 2010, was responsible for the Brexit referendum.

G6 Gerunds

→ **Theme 4, pp. 122-123, 124-125**

A gerund is formed by adding *-ing* to a verb and is used as a noun. Here are some examples from the texts on pages 122-123 and 124-125:

***Outsourcing** is yesterday's game.*	➡ gerund as subject
*We see opportunity to grow by **investing**, **operating**, and **building** relationships in the countries where we do business.*	➡ gerund after a preposition (*after, before, by, in spite of, on, without*)
*We partner with Chinese construction companies [...] to win contracts in Asia. Apple [...] finds itself **competing** with Amazon.*	➡ gerund as object, especially after certain verbs (*admit, consider, don't mind, find, keep on, recommend, risk, suggest, ...*)

1

Use these notes to write sentences about globalization. Make sure you include a gerund.

1 people today / be / more mobile / because of / fly
2 speak / Chinese / be / an asset for / jobs in multinational companies
3 governments / see / reduce taxes / as / way to / increase business
4 customers / find hard / resist / buy / cheap goods
5 customers / avoid / think about / production methods
6 companies / hope / make profit from / reduce / safety standards
7 by / use / solar power / countries / want / fight / climate change
8 have / access to the internet / be / crucial to / economic success

2

→ **S25:** How to work with a dictionary, p. 242

Write seven sentences about your own experiences with globalization. Use some of the verbs and ideas below. You may use your own ideas as well. Be careful: some verbs combine with the gerund, others with the *to* infinitive. Check in a dictionary if you are not sure.

to forget to begin to enjoy to avoid to consider to recommend to suggest to decide to expect to hope to manage to need to volunteer	find out where my clothes were produced think about the effects of my actions on the environment be connected with people worldwide via the internet work in a soup kitchen understand how similar shops and restaurants are around the world use English as a language to communicate with almost anyone enjoy the variety of products from around the world in the local supermarket travel to faraway places

S1 Checklist: Summary

A summary is for someone who has not read a text and needs to know the essence of what it is about. The readers of your summary do not expect details; instead they want a short version of the text. Therefore, a written summary only gives a general idea of what a text is about and the most important information. Usually, tasks requiring you to write a summary of a text begin with "Summarize" or "Sum up". But bear in mind: many tasks starting with these words ask you to focus on a certain aspect of a text (e.g. *Summarize the developments in the process of industrialization depicted in the extract.*). and not to summarize the whole text. Always read the task carefully.

<table>
<tr><td>Dos</td><td>Before writing:
✓ Read the text carefully and highlight key words and/or key sentences.
✓ Divide the text up into parts or subsections.
✓ Find an appropriate sentence or keywords to summarize each subsection.

Writing an introduction:
✓ The introductory sentence of your summary should include the author, title, type of text, the place and date of publication, and the main idea.
In other words, you need to answer these wh-questions:
→ Who is the author?
→ When was the text published?
→ Where was it published?
→ What type of text is it?
→ What topic does the text deal with? State the underlying problem or conflict, and not simply its content.

Writing the main part:
✓ Focus on the essentials/on basic facts.
✓ Use the simple present.
✓ Use your own words.
✓ Use formal language.
✓ Use connectives to link your sentences.</td></tr>
<tr><td>Don'ts</td><td>✗ Don't include irrelevant details.
✗ Don't use the present progressive.
✗ Don't use quotations or direct speech.
✗ Don't give your personal opinion.
✗ Don't start analysing the text.
✗ Don't try to create suspense.</td></tr>
</table>

Language support

Introduction:
- *The short story/novel/article/poem/... "[title]" ...*
- *The extract from the short story/novel/... "[title]" by [author] ...*
- *... written by [author] in [year] ...*
- *... written by [author] and published in [source] in [year] ...*
- *... deals with/is about/shows/illustrates ...*

Stating the topic/purpose of a text:
- *The text/story ... is about/shows/presents/depicts/alludes to/refers to/criticizes/targets/comments on/exposes the fact that/the problem of ...*

Main part:
- *According to the author, ...*
- *The author believes/claims/emphasizes/states/points out ...*
- *From the author's point of view, ...*
- *The author is of the opinion that ...*

S2 Checklist: Creative writing

A. Continuation of a prose text

When you are asked to continue a prose text you have read, it is important that you write in a similar way as the author. Pay attention to the author's style and the developments in the story. Decide if your continuation is plausible and fits in with what has happened before.

Dos	**Content:** ✓ Stay in line with the plot and atmosphere. → You are not entirely free as you are expected to show in your text production that you have digested the original text. You have to use the information from that text as a basis for a plausible sequel. → Mention certain features (places, details of landscape or weather) that have been introduced. → Make sure you present the characters in a way that does not contradict their previous behaviour unless this change in character is part of your story. → If possible refer back to events in the text you have dealt with. **Point of view (narrative perspective):** ✓ Adopt the same narrative perspective: → First-person narrator → Third-person narrator • Omniscient (knowing and commenting on all the characters' thoughts and feelings, foreshadowing future events etc.) • Limited (having insight into one of the characters' thoughts and feelings only) **Language:** ✓ Stay in line with the author's style and try to imitate it. → Consider the amount of descriptive as opposed to dramatic passages that mainly consist of dialogue. → Use either long, elaborate sentences or short simple ones like the author. → Employ imagery (symbolic or metaphorical language) if it occurs in the original text; you need not always think of new images but pick up the ones used and extend them. → Adopt the author's use of language to place a character in a particular social class or reveal his/her emotions.

B. Change of perspective

You may be asked to consider the fictional situation from the point of view of a different character, writing

- a dialogue
- a diary entry/an interior monologue
- a letter to a friend

Dos	**Content:** ✓ Consider the relationship between the characters involved, their age, their social standing, the way they might be personally affected by what has happened. ✓ For your character, imagine how he/she feels in the circumstances. ✓ Decide how he/she would comment → on the situation or conflict, → on other characters and their behaviour. **Language:** ✓ Age, relationships to other characters, social class and profession determine the way a person speaks. ✓ Make sure you use an appropriate register (formal, informal, colloquial, scientific, educated etc.). ✓ Emotions may alter a person's behaviour and speech. ✓ Use typical elements of spoken language like exclamations, incomplete sentences (ellipses), questions, etc.
Don'ts	✗ Don't stray from the original text you were given. ✗ Don't create an entirely new universe. ✗ Don't quote when you refer back to instances in the original text, but make the references part of your own narrative.

C. Change of narrative perspective

You may be asked to rewrite an extract from a novel or short story using a different narrative perspective. In this case your text will be mainly based on the same content but you will have to modify it according to the narrative perspective you have to work with. All the information above about changing perspective is relevant here as well, but there are also other things you have to bear in mind.

a) First-person narrator

When you are asked to retell a story as a first-person narrator, first determine what the character from the extract who has now become the narrator is like. In the original text, identify how he/she experiences the situation and how he/she would talk about it. Even though you have to keep the main elements of the plot, you can rearrange them to include the narrator's thoughts and feelings or comments he/she might make. Depending on the character, his/her age and social background, the style you have to use will differ, e.g. with snappy and clipped colloquial wording for a teenager or a more elaborate choice of words and sentence structure for a parent, teacher, judge etc.

b) Third-person narrator: omniscient or limited

As an omniscient narrator you can look inside all the characters in the extract: you know their thoughts and feelings. You might even know how the story will end and provide some foreshadowing. However, the elements that you include should be in keeping with the original text.

As a limited narrator, you retell the story from the perspective of one of the characters, but you use the third person. Remember to limit your focus to the things your character knows about.

Dos	**Content:** ✓ Use the tense of the original text. ✓ As a first-person/third-person limited narrator → determine the narrator's character, → include his/her views, feelings, thoughts about the incident or conflict dealt with in the extract or the people involved, → limit your text to what he/she actually knows or experiences, → include speculations or hopes and worries where he/she has no obvious knowledge, → stay within the framework of the original text. ✓ As an omniscient narrator → refer to thoughts and feelings of all characters, → add comments and judgements on what is happening or on the characters' behaviour and the possible outcome of the narrative. **Language:** ✓ As a first-person narrator → adapt your style to the narrator's character, consider age, social background, emotional state, etc. → use elements of spoken language. ✓ As a third-person narrator (limited or omniscient), you are quite free in what kind of language you use.
Don'ts	✗ Don't invent things that are not linked to the original text. ✗ Don't simply imitate the style of the original text.

Language support

When a **first-person narrator** is telling the story, features of spoken language like questions, incomplete sentences or exclamations are often included:

- *Why on earth haven't I ...?*
- *How could X do this?*
- *Seriously?/The nerve!/Brilliant!*

When a **third-person narrator** is telling the story, the feelings and thoughts of the narrator/different characters can be presented. Phrases to describe feelings may be helpful:

- *X felt/was lonely/misunderstood/relieved/ overwhelmed/...*
- *X often thought that .../wondered why .../ doubted if .../underestimated ...*
- *X had lost all self-respect/hope/ inhibitions.*
- *To his/her relief/surprise/annoyance ...*

An **omniscient narrator** might comment or hint at a future outcome or include judgements:

- *It was obvious/to be expected/proved inevitable that ...*
- *It was only much later that he/she found out/understood ...*
- *This would prove to be a problem when ...*

S3 Checklist: Formal letter / formal email

There are many different types of formal letters or formal emails that you could be expected to write, e.g. a letter of request, a letter of inquiry, a letter of complaint, a letter of application (often called a covering letter). Whatever kind of letter or mail it is, the response you get will greatly depend on the way they are written. Formal letters are generally precise and to the point, without unnecessary detail. It is also important that you adopt the right tone, i.e. it should sound business-like rather than emotional. Finally you must also think about the layout of your letter and the type of language you use. The language used in this type of letter should not be chatty and personal but rather formal and reserved. Before you start writing you should first ask yourself:

- Who am I writing to?
- Why am I writing?
- What do I need to tell them?
- What do I want them to do?

Dos	**Before writing:** ✓ Observe the rules for the layout of a formal letter (see next page). ✓ Use formal language. ✓ Choose a more formal font for your letter or email if you use a computer, e.g. *Times New Roman* or *Arial*. ✓ Draft and edit your letter or email before you send it. Poor grammar and punctuation or spelling mistakes do not make a good impression. ✓ Plan the structure of your letter to include the following parts: **Salutation and introduction:** ✓ Address the person you are writing to correctly: → If you know the person's name write: *Dear Ms* (for a woman whose marital status is not known) *Mrs, Mr, Dr Smith*, etc. → If you do not know the person's name: *Dear Sir or Madam*, ✓ Start the first sentence with a capital letter. ✓ State the purpose of your letter in the first paragraph. ✓ Refer to any correspondence that may already have taken place. **Main part:** ✓ Organize your ideas into paragraphs. ✓ Include important and/or relevant details such as exact names, dates and addresses, e.g. where you saw the job advertised, when and where you bought the defective goods etc. ✓ Keep to the point and avoid unnecessary details. ✓ Be polite and tactful. **Conclusion and ending:** ✓ Outline how you expect the recipient to react, e.g. send you information, give you a refund, reply to your application etc. ✓ End the letter in the appropriate way: → *Yours sincerely* if you address them by name in the salutation → *Yours faithfully* if you use *Sir or Madam* in the salutation ✓ Type your full name and sign the letter by hand.
Don'ts	✗ Don't write your name above the address. ✗ Don't use inappropriate or informal language, e.g. slang, short forms, abbreviations, ...

Language support

Say why you are writing:

to reply:
- *In response to your letter of September 23rd ...*

to complain:
- *I am writing to express my dissatisfaction with ...*
- *Unfortunately, I am forced to write this letter in order to complain about ...*

to inquire:
- *I am writing to inquire about the possibility of ...*
- *I would be very grateful if you would send me further information about ...*
- *Would you kindly tell me how ...?*

to apply:
- *I wish to apply for the post of ...*
- *I am writing to apply for ...*
- *With reference to your advertisement in the Daily News of March 3rd, I should like to apply for the position of ...*

Say how you expect the recipient to reply to ...

your complaint:
- *Under the circumstances, I feel an apology should be offered.*
- *I would be grateful if you could deal with the problem as soon as possible.*
- *I must insist that you refund me my money immediately.*

your inquiry:
- *I would like to thank you in advance for your assistance.*
- *Please accept my thanks for your help.*

your application:
- *I look forward to hearing from you.*
- *I will be glad to supply you with any further information you may require.*
- *I have attached/enclosed the following documents.*

The example formal letter below details the general layout that your letter should conform to.

Write your address and email in the top right-hand corner or on the left above the recipient's address.

The address of the person you are writing to should be on the left.

Leave a line and write the date below your address.

Say why you are writing the letter in the first paragraph.

The main part of the letter should include any other necessary information.

In the last part of the letter, say how you expect the recipient to reply.

End the letter in an appropriate way.

68, Wood Lane
Romford RM12 8JY
sgoodenough@internet.com

November 1, 2022

Ms Diane Poole
Personnel Department
Debenhams Ltd.
Romford RM10 6NX

Dear Ms Poole,

With reference to your advertisement in the Romford Recorder of October 24th, I would like to apply for a summer job in your Department Store. My final examinations finish on June 23rd and I will be available to start work any time after that date.

I am just completing my final year at Hornchurch Grammar School and have applied to do Business Studies and French at Bristol University in October. Meanwhile, I would like to gain some experience in a large organization such as yours, and of course earn some extra money to help finance my university course.

Having worked in a local supermarket on Saturdays for the past two years, I have gained a lot of experience in dealing with customers. I also greatly enjoy working in a team and was always a popular member of any group presentation at school because I always do my share of the work. In my last year at school I was a prefect and also captain of the hockey team, which shows I have a sense of responsibility towards others. My teachers have always considered me to be a reliable and conscientious student.

I have attached my CV and will be glad to supply you with any other information you require, for example, the names of referees. Thank you for considering my application.
I look forward to hearing from you soon.

Yours sincerely,

S. Goodenough

S4 Checklist: Letter to the editor

Readers of newspapers often write a letter to the editor to comment on something they have read, usually in the hope that the letter will be published in the newspaper. When writing a letter to the editor, take the aspects for writing a formal letter into account. Use formal language, but include strong statements. Before you start writing the letter, you will need to note down important facts and points from the text you are reacting to. Note down any other ideas you have and arrange all of them in a logical order.

Dos	**Introduction:** ✓ Start with *Sir,* or *Madam,* ✓ Leave out any introductory or closing remarks with which you show your politeness or personal interest. Concentrate on the point you are trying to make. ✓ Name the article you refer to at the beginning of your letter. ✓ Give the reason why you are writing the letter, i.e. what you support/criticize/would like to comment on about the article. **Main part:** ✓ Follow a clear line of argument and stick to the most important point(s). ✓ Explain why you share or oppose the author's point of view. ✓ Support your arguments with evidence and examples. **Conclusion:** ✓ End with a strong statement that sums up your position and/or says what you expect from future articles on the issue. ✓ Just sign your name and state your place of residence at the end.
Don'ts	✗ Don't use *Yours sincerely/faithfully* at the end. ✗ Don't quote from the original article unless it is absolutely necessary. ✗ Don't retell the article and explain it to the editor, but explain your view.

Language support

Starting the letter:
- *I am writing to you in response to the article ...*
- *Having read your article ..., I would like to point out ...*
- *In the article ..., the author ... claims that ...*
- *The article ... by ... raises the question of whether ...*

Expressing your opinion in the main part of the text:
- *I would like to congratulate you on ...*
- *I personally believe that ...*
- *I could not have put it better myself.*
- *It is beyond doubt that ...*
- *You are absolutely right when you say .../I utterly agree with you that ...*
- *I wholeheartedly endorse ...*
- *As a firm believer in .../As a supporter of ..., I totally agree/I see no reason why ...*
- *Although I understand why ..., I cannot accept the overall conclusion that ...*
- *I see the author's point, but I still feel that ...*
- *I think ... is mistaken if he/she believes ...*
- *What you need to keep in mind is ...*
- *I would question the argument that ...*
- *Your author overlooks the fact that ...*

Ending with a strong statement:
- *The question can no longer be whether ..., but ...*
- *However, doesn't the evidence I have cited prove that ...?*
- *All in all, there can be no doubt that ...*
- *Ultimately, what matters is (that) ...*

S5 Checklist: Writing a speech

When you give a speech, you are aiming to get people to agree with your views. As your speech will only be heard and not read by your audience, you have to be careful how you present what you have to say. Speeches are meant to be spoken, so your language should not be too formal. You may use short forms and contractions like *don't, we're, haven't, I'm*, etc.
It may help you to read out loud to yourself what you have written to check whether your style creates the desired effect.

Dos	**Plan the structure of your speech to include the following parts:** **Introduction:** ✓ Directly address the audience at the beginning. ✓ Begin your introduction with an "attention-getter" to capture your audience's attention, e.g. a story, a rhetorical question, a quotation. ✓ Clearly state the topic of your speech and your personal stance on it. **Main part:** ✓ Explain the topic/problem. ✓ Quote facts and people to persuade your audience. ✓ Show your emotional involvement and appeal to the emotions of the audience. **Conclusion:** ✓ Briefly highlight your main points and end with something strong, e.g. an appeal for support. ✓ Show that the speech has ended, e.g. by thanking your audience for listening.
Don'ts	✗ Don't put too many ideas in your speech, but give the listeners two or three important things to remember. ✗ Don't just read the speech out loud to your audience. ✗ Don't use expressions that are too complex. ✗ Don't write very long sentences – listeners must be able to follow your point. ✗ Don't use modifiers, e.g. *might be, possibly, probably, more or less* – you must be very direct and specific to be convincing.

Language support

Introduction:
- Address the audience: *Ladies and gentlemen, Fellow students, My friends, Members of* ..., etc.

Main part:
- Relate your speech to your listeners. Use receiver-including pronouns and words like *we, us, our, my friends*, etc.
- Use connectives to structure your speech: *firstly, finally*, etc.
  Link the different points by using phrases such as: *Having discussed ... it is now appropriate to mention ...*
- Use adverbial phrases to underline your own convictions and win over the audience: *undoubtedly, certainly, undeniably, definitely, indeed, paradoxically, surprisingly, strangely enough, primarily, first and foremost, above all*, etc.
- Include rhetorical questions like: *Don't we all agree/want to ...?*
- Include stylistic devices like repetition, exaggeration/hyperbole, alliteration, etc.

Conclusion:
- *Finally, fellow friends of the environment, ...*
- Clearly indicate the end of your speech: *Thank you for your attention, ladies and gentlemen.*

Webcode
You can read excerpts from some famous speeches here: DSW-73090-067

S6 How to write an argumentative text

Many tasks require you to write an argumentative text. Often, you are asked to discuss or comment on a question, problem or statement. For both kinds of tasks you will have to state your opinion. When discussing a question, you need to weigh up arguments in favour of both sides of a debate in order to come to a well-founded conclusion, whereas commenting allows you to focus more on your opinion. But if it helps your case, you can also include arguments for the other side.

<table>
<tr><th></th><th>discussing</th><th>commenting</th></tr>
<tr><td>preparation</td><td colspan="2">1 Know what your line of argument is before you start writing. To accomplish this, **prewrite or brainstorm** your ideas on paper until you have developed a working thesis.
2 Write a **rough outline** to structure your essay: It begins with a **thesis statement**. A thesis statement is an argument that you want to prove. Then add three to five **facts or examples** that support your thesis. End your outline with a short **conclusion** that essentially restates the thesis.</td></tr>
<tr><td>introduction</td><td colspan="2">3 The first sentences should be an interesting **introduction that presents the problem** your argumentative essay will discuss. The last sentence of the paragraph should **clearly state the thesis or the basic question, argument or problem**.</td></tr>
<tr><td>main part</td><td>4 First line of argument
Look at the problem from one side (e.g. the side of those in favour, the arguments for a particular question). Write a handful of **paragraphs – at least three – that support your thesis**. If you are making an argument about a literary text like a novel or poem, you can select **quotes** from the text that support your argument. If you are discussing a political controversy, choose **reasons** that bolster your claim, and find **relevant quotes and statistics** to cite.
5 Second line of argument
Then consider the problem from a different side (e.g. the side of those against, the arguments against a particular question). Address any **counterclaims** in the main body of your argument as well. For example, if your argument is in favour of capital punishment, refute commonly held beliefs about why capital punishment is either morally wrong or ineffective. Counterclaims might not apply in a literary argumentative essay, but usually do in one about politics.</td><td>4 Your line of argument
Look at the problem **from your point of view**. Refer to **at least three aspects** of the topic and say what your position is on these. Do not forget to give **plausible reasons** for what you think. **Support your view** by means of examples, statistics, relevant quotes etc.
[5 Other lines of argument (optional)]
Although not strictly necessary for a comment, it might be useful to also refer to **views of an issue that are in opposition to your position**. It might help to prove your point when you show that you are able to think of counter-arguments and how you deal with them. But again: **plausible reasons supported by evidence** are essential.</td></tr>
</table>

	note: • Instead of discussing first arguments in favour and then arguments against, you may also contrast each argument for with an argument against the issue right away. • The examiner does *not* expect you to consider *every* argument there is. So, instead of listing, say, twelve different points, it is a good idea to concentrate on about three, preferably the most important aspects and discuss these in detail.
conclusion	6 Conclude your argumentative text with a **paragraph that sums up the evidence presented and restates the thesis**. Here you say which side or perspective makes more sense or is more justified to you. You may, at this point, also **add personal feelings** about the topic, say how you see the topic **in the context of other related issues** and/or **give an outlook** on how the issue in question might develop in the future. In any case, mere repetition of arguments must be avoided!

Language support

Introduction
- *The text/book raises the question of .../ introduces the problem of ...*
- *The problem/issue that is touched upon here is ...*
- *The statement/text illuminates the basic problem/dilemma of ...*

Lines of argument: my point of view
- *Considering the fact that ...*
- *Another important point/factor/argument is ...*
- *You also have to take into consideration that ...*
- *I am convinced (that) ...*
- *Above all, it is important to note .../it must be said .../one cannot ignore (that) ...*
- *to be in favour of sth*
- *to (strongly) support/oppose sth*
- *to argue for/against sth*

Lines of argument: balancing points of view
- *On the one hand ..., on the other hand ...*
- *Whereas A ..., B ...*
- *In contrast to A, B ...*
- *From B's point of view, however, ...*
- *Looking at the problem from A's side, you have to admit that ...*
- *Supporters/Opponents of .... argue/might argue that ...*
- *Another argument/point/reason that is often put forward is ...*
- *Others maintain/claim/assert that ...*

Personal conclusion
- *I rather agree/disagree with ...*
- *As opposed to ..., I definitely believe that ...*
- *In my opinion, .../As I see it, .../ Personally, ...*
- *As far as I am concerned, ...*
- *Finally, I would like to point out that ...*
- *Taking into account what has been said so far, I ...*
- *Having considered the different arguments, I ...*
- *Looking at the two sides, I have to say ...*
- *To sum up, I am of the opinion that ...*
- *To come to a final conclusion, I think ...*

S7 Checklist: Writing a blog post

In an exam, you may be asked to write a blog post. A blog is a regularly updated website run by an individual or a group. Blog posts are usually written in a personal, informal or conversational style to engage with readers. It is important to keep in mind who you are writing for. Your target group determines what you write about and how you do it.

Dos	**The structure:** ✓ Give the blog post an eye-catching title that will grab the readers' attention. This is the first thing they see. It will help them decide if it is of interest to them. ✓ Outline the main point in the first paragraph. This will help readers decide whether they want to read on. ✓ Put the details in the following paragraphs. ✓ Add background information if necessary. ✓ End with a conclusion that invites comments or reactions from your readers and other bloggers. ✓ Add your name if you wish to. **Your style:** ✓ Write in a friendly and informal style. ✓ Use first person *I*. ✓ Try to include references to your own experience. ✓ Describe rather than tell. For instance, instead of saying you thought a book was great, try to explain why you enjoyed it. ✓ Use vivid words, conjunctions and modifiers to make the reading more interesting and to improve the flow. ✓ Keep your sentences short and simple. ✓ Always be polite, informative and respectful of other cultures and opinions. ✓ Ask your readers to respond to what you have written. ✓ On the next page, you will find some useful phrases, but make sure your blog post has a personal touch.
Don'ts	✗ Don't be overly negative. ✗ Don't use the passive voice. ✗ Don't try to impose your beliefs on others. ✗ Don't be rude or impolite. ✗ Don't write overly long paragraphs. ✗ Don't write overly long and mindless texts. ✗ Don't include links to commercial sites or inappropriate materials. ✗ Don't give specific names, places, addresses or contact details.

Language support

Introducing a topic
- *Today, I want to address ...*
- *It seems that everybody is talking about ... at the moment.*
- *Today's topic is ...*

Introducing an opinion
- *I think/believe/reckon/find ...*
- *As far as I'm concerned, ...*
- *I've been thinking about this over the last few days and ...*
- *I've got to be honest, I think ... is fantastic.*
- *I'm not a massive fan of ...*

Adding further detail
- *But that's not all.*
- *But what's more, ...*
- *That's all well and good, however, ...*
- *Nonetheless, there's a whole other side to this.*
- *Let's not forget ...*

Concluding
- *Whichever side of the debate you're on, I'm sure you'll agree this is a really interesting subject.*
- *That's where we are at the moment, but we'll have to watch how this develops in the future.*
- *Just to sum up this week's post, ...*

S8 How to improve your text

Once you have written your text, read it carefully again and check whether you have considered the criteria listed below. Revise your text accordingly.

a) **Content:**
- Has your text taken all aspects of the assignment into consideration?
- Have you given evidence to support your arguments?
- Have you referred adequately to the text that has to be analysed (lines, quotations)?
- Have you avoided repetitions?

b) **Structure and logical order:**
- Are the following parts included?
  - introduction, introductory sentence
  - main part, divided up into several paragraphs
  - conclusion
- Is the text clearly structured and therefore easy to follow with the help of visible paragraphs and a clear order of arguments or examples?

c) **Language and style:**
- Have you used the correct tense, e.g. the simple present tense in a summary?
- Have you used the correct language, e.g. formal language in a letter to the editor?
- Are your sentences complete and not too long or complicated?
- Have you avoided waffling, i.e. excluded all unnecessary words?
- Have you varied your vocabulary by using synonyms? Look at the language support on the next page for some ideas.
- Do you use connectives effectively to make your text coherent? Again, the language support will help you.

➡

Language support

Synonyms: certain adjectives and nouns
You should ban the following words from your range of vocabulary – at least when writing a formal text like an analysis or characterization:

SAD HAPPY NICE BAD
INTERESTING SITUATION

Use some of these synonyms instead:
- For "sad" people you could use: *downcast, depressed, downhearted, dejected, dispirited, frustrated, discouraged, sorrowful*
- For a "sad" atmosphere you could use: *dark, gloomy, dismal, dreary, depressing, desolate, melancholy, hopeless, cheerless, bleak*
- For "happy" people you could use: *cheerful, contented, relaxed, pleased, delighted, light-hearted, merry, lively, vivacious, animated, buoyant, spirited*
- For "nice" people you could use: *amiable, kind-hearted, good-natured, gentle, congenial, easy-going, pleasant, sympathetic*
- For a "nice" atmosphere you could use: *cheerful, relaxed, pleasant, harmonious, idyllic, picturesque, familiar, friendly, warm*
- For "bad" people you could use: *despicable, contemptible, loathsome, hateful, detestable, reprehensible, awful, vile, mean, repulsive, horrible, dreadful, terrible*
- For "interesting" you could use: *appealing, exciting, fascinating, remarkable, significant, captivating, intriguing, attractive*
- For "situation" you could use: *circumstance, case, state of affairs, condition, predicament, position, dilemma*
- For "normal" you could use: *average, ordinary, standard, usual, regular, typical*

Language support

Synonyms: "author"
Depending on the type of text you are writing about, use one of these synonyms instead of repeating the word "author" too often:
- literary texts: *novelist, playwright, poet, writer*
- newspaper articles: *journalist, reporter, columnist, writer, essayist*

Varying your vocabulary
Similarly, you should avoid writing "the author says", but use more precise alternatives instead. Here are several examples of verbs you could use:

"the author says"
- *refers to ...*
- *alludes to ...*
- *talks about/mentions ...*
- *addresses the issue of ...*
- *examines ...*
- *raises the question of whether ...*
- *claims/maintains/argues that ...*
- *assumes/supposes/presumes that ...*
- *asserts ...*
- *believes ...*
- *states ...*
- *insists ...*
- *emphasizes ...*

"the author argues"
- *weighs up the arguments ...*
- *is in two minds about ...*
- *blames sth/sb ...*
- *criticizes ...*
- *reproaches sb for ...-ing ...*
- *rejects (the idea of) ...*
- *abandons the idea of ...-ing ...*
- *opposes the idea of ...-ing ...*
- *refutes the argument ...*
- *sides with ...*
- *backs up his argument with ...*
- *is in favour of ...-ing ...*
- *puts forward another argument ...*
- *doubts ...*
- *attacks/accuses sb of ...-ing ...*

"the author doesn't say"
- *leaves ... unanswered ...*
- *avoids this issue ...*
- *does not consider ...*

Language support

Connectives
Use some of these connectives to ensure that your text continues to flow for the reader:

- **Connectives to show sequence:**
  firstly, secondly, thirdly
  next
  consequently
  previously
  simultaneously
  afterwards
  subsequently
  finally
  later
  before
  Firstly, ... In addition, ...
  Equally important, ...

- **Connectives to compare different aspects:**
  in comparison
  furthermore
  likewise
  similarly
  moreover
  in addition
  additionally
  otherwise
  On the one hand, ... On the other hand, ...

- **Connectives to show time:**
  soon
  then
  by this time
  as soon as
  meanwhile
  presently

- **Connectives to give specific examples:**
  for example
  for instance
  in this case
  specifically
  with regard to
  that is to say that
  For example, ... Also ... In addition, ...

- **Connectives to contrast:**
  in contrast
  whereas
  nonetheless
  however
  on the contrary
  nevertheless
  although
  conversely
  despite this
  in spite of the fact that
  regardless
  even though

- **Connectives to signal conclusion:**
  in conclusion
  therefore
  as a result (of this)
  in short
  generally
  all in all
  because of this
  evidently

Language support

Adverbs
Using adverbs is an essential way to help you strengthen your writing.

Adverbs to add clarity
thoroughly
extremly
urgently
significantly

Adverbs for emphasis or contrast
actually
certainly
undoubtedly
contrarily
contrastingly

Be careful: Only use adverbs when the information that follows is connected to it, e.g. don't use the adverb "obviously", if the information that follows isn't obvious.

S9 How to structure a text

When analysing a text or commenting on an issue, for example, you should not only pay attention to the content and the correct use of language (grammar, choice of words, etc.), but also to the structure of your text.

In order to write a well-structured text, you should follow the structure of introduction – main part – conclusion. Make sure that you plan how to present your ideas effectively in a sequence of paragraphs before you start writing.

Moreover, you should make the relationships between your points clear by using connectives, e.g. to express cause and effect or to point out contrasts and contradictions.

Apart from creative writing tasks, which require you to follow the specific criteria for the kind of text you need to produce (e.g. a newspaper article or a lètter), there are basically three types of texts you may be asked to write, especially in an exam context:

1. comprehension (e.g. Describe/State/Outline/Summarize/...)
2. analysis (e.g. Analyse/Examine/Compare/Explain/...)
3. argumentative writing (e.g. Comment on/Assess/Discuss/...)

Below are some tips to help you structure your texts for all three general text types.

INTRODUCTION			
general tips	**comprehension**	**analysis**	**argumentative writing**
Refer back to the task, if necessary.	• Give the general information on the text at hand (e.g. author, title, etc.). • State the issue the text deals with.	• Make a general statement that sums up what you are expected to find out.	• Make it clear what makes the issue you discuss topical or controversial. • Explain its relevance with regard to the text at hand, if possible or necessary. • Express your general view on the issue.
(The examples for **comprehension** and **analysis** are from Nick McDonell's novel *Twelve*.)	Example: Summarize White Mike's encounter with Lionel and Jessica.	Example: Analyse White Mike's character in the passage at hand.	Example: Discuss whether a gap year is worth taking after school.
	The extract from chapter 23 of Nick McDonell's novel *Twelve*, first published in 2002, deals with how White Mike becomes aware of the destructive nature of the drug Twelve and its consequences.	Although White Mike is an experienced drug dealer, his acute observation and ability to empathize make him start to realize that he cannot cope with the effects Twelve has on his job as a dealer.	Thousands of students decide to take a year off from education once they have graduated from school and do not want to start studying straight away. As the article "Why Malia Obama is right to take a gap year" has suggested, a gap year may provide valuable experiences. However, I do not believe that travelling the world for a year, which is what most people seem to do, is of much benefit for your personal development or your career.

MAIN PART			
general tips	**comprehension**	**analysis**	**argumentative writing**
Divide the text up into paragraphs that each deal with one aspect. Link ideas and paragraphs, e.g. with connectives and participle constructions.	• Present the relevant content in your own words.	Follow this structure in your paragraph writing: • P - Point: an introductory sentence that outlines the point you are trying to make in this paragraph so that the reader immediately knows what you are referring to • E - Evidence: examples from the text (including quotations) – in an argumentative text also arguments and examples that you know from other contexts – that can be used to prove your point (P) • A - Analysis: explanation of your examples/quotations/arguments to make it clear which function your evidence (E) has in proving your point (P). Express your general view on the issue.	
(The examples for **comprehension** and **analysis** are from Nick McDonell's novel *Twelve*.)	Example: Summarize White Mike's encounter with Lionel and Jessica.	Example: Analyse White Mike's character in the passage at hand.	Example: Discuss whether a gap year is worth taking after school.
	Having been called by Jessica, White Mike is joined by another more professional dealer, Lionel, to meet her. Feeling uneasy in Lionel's company, White Mike walks to the meeting point at 91st Street where he already notices Jessica from a distance.	White Mike empathizes with Jessica and tries to establish some kind of relationship with her. At one point he "tries to look her right in the eye but can't catch her gaze". As White Mike is aware of Jessica's inexperience in dealing with that kind of situation and her strong urge to buy Twelve, he hopes to make her focus on the deal and not come across as an easy victim for Lionel. By trying to make eye contact, he hopes to keep her focused and possibly guide her through the situation without losing respect and dignity.	What kind of activity you do in your time abroad needs to be chosen wisely if it is to be relevant beyond your gap year. If you intend to become a doctor, it might be a good idea to volunteer in a hospital or nursing home. Similarly, those interested in a career in social work or education are more likely to profit from spending some time in a nursing home or school. As a consequence, the choice of a subject for your university studies or your apprenticeship is bound to be a more informed one and you may already gain practical experience in a field that will come in handy when approaching relevant topics at university.

➡

CONCLUSION			
general tips	**comprehension**	**analysis**	**argumentative writing**
Refer back to the opening paragraph, if possible, at least implicitly.	• Usually, no conclusion is necessary unless you need to lead over to the analysis.	• Summarize the most important findings concisely without repeating all the details and using the same words again.	• Draw a conclusion by weighing up the pros and cons and stating your opinion clearly.
(The examples for **comprehension** and **analysis** are from Nick McDonell's novel *Twelve*.)	Example: Summarize White Mike's encounter with Lionel and Jessica.	Example: Analyse White Mike's character in the passage at hand.	Example: Discuss whether a gap year is worth taking after school.
	As it has become clear above, White Mike is the character that connects Jessica as a high-school student who is roughly his age and Lionel, who represents the drug dealing part of White Mike's life. In order to see how White Mike's character deals with this particular situation, his behaviour deserves a closer analysis.	All in all, White Mike displays a more sensitive side as he realizes how much a person like Jessica is changing as a consequence of taking and demanding more Twelve. Furthermore, he is aware of his own role as someone linking two very different worlds he is not part of – Jessica's circle of wealthy teenagers and Lionel's world of violence and crime.	All in all, I strongly believe that a gap year needs to be filled with meaningful activities to justify taking a one-year break. Partying for a year in the sun is definitely not worth postponing your studies for, whereas internships or social work can be justified both with regard to career opportunities and personal development.

S10 How to work on poetry

Many students feel insecure when asked to analyse a poem. However, working on poetry can be very rewarding. The following tips will help you to read, enjoy and work successfully with poetry.

Step 1: First reading

The aim of the first reading is to get a general sense of what the poem is about. At this stage you should not worry if you do not understand all the lines but concentrate on your first impressions. Try to identify the topic/subject of the poem. If possible, listen to someone read the poem out loud in order to get a feeling for the rhythm of the poem. If there is no recording, read it out loud to yourself or to a partner.

Listen to this reading of the poem *Fire and Ice* by Robert Frost and read two first impressions.

The poem appears to be about the end of the world and whether this will be caused by fire or by ice.

The poem is concerned with the destruction of the world either by fire or by ice.

Step 2: Studying the poem

a) Annotations

While studying the poem you should keep **a set of notes**. Preferably these notes should be **annotations** on and around the poem itself. If you are not allowed to write in the book, make a large copy of the poem, on which you

- underline or highlight key passages or words.
- write down short explanations of your thoughts and interpretations.
- use question marks **?** or wavy lines ~~~ to mark passages that you find difficult to understand.
- use exclamation marks **!** to show that you agree with or are impressed by an idea in the poem.
- use different colours to highlight recurring ideas or emotions.

Annotations

Theme of the poem, end of the world/destruction of mankind?

The contrast between fire and ice.

What does the narrator mean by "tasting desire"? Reference to Frost's own romantic experiences?

The poet thinks the end of the world will most likely come as a result of fire. I agree that it is more likely than an ice age.

Poem

Fire and Ice

Some say the world will end in fire,
Some say in ice.
From what I've tasted of desire
I hold with those who favor fire. **!**
But if it had to perish twice,
I think I know enough of hate
To say that for destruction ice
Is also great
And would suffice.

Robert Frost

Form

Three different rhymes.

Lines of four or eight syllables.

End-stopped lines (lines 1,2,4,5,9)

enjambment (line 7)

Webcode

You can listen to the poem here:
DSW-73090-068

b) Form and rhythm

What makes a poem a poem and not a piece of prose? Look what happens if Robert Frost's lines are written as prose.

Some say the world will end in fire. Some say in ice. From what I've tasted of desire I hold with those who favor fire. But if it had to perish twice, I think I know enough of hate to say that, for destruction, ice is also great and would suffice.

➡

The language remains but the poetic effect is lost. **Form** and **rhythm** are necessary to transform the lines into a poem.

- **Form** refers to the type of poem, e.g. sonnet, and the way it is organized. Poems are usually organized in groups of lines called **stanzas**. Many poems are organized into stanzas of equal length (3 or 4 lines). Contemporary poems, however, often contain stanzas of varying lengths, without a formal pattern.
- The **rhythm** of a poem refers to the way its sound pattern is organized. It is determined by its stressed and unstressed syllables and by punctuation.

The poem *Fire and Ice* is not organized into stanzas of equal length but consists of nine lines of either four or eight syllables. The form is what makes this poem so special.

If you listen to the poem again, you should be able to detect a rhythm. The stressed syllables are marked with ´.

Sóme sáy the wórld will énd in fíre
Sóme sáy in íce
From whát I've tásted óf desíre
I hóld with thóse who fávor fíre.

Many of the lines can be read as **iambic**. That means that an unstressed syllable is followed by a stressed syllable. But this rhythm is not consistent. In the first two lines the poet makes a point of stressing the two different views on the destruction of the earth. By using and stressing the word "some", he underlines that this is not a personal view but rather a universal truth.

The poet also employs the following poetic techniques, which affect the rhythm:

- **End-stopped lines** in lines 1,2,4,5 and 9. The lines end in a comma or a full stop creating a natural pause and slowing down the speed.
- The **enjambment** in line 7 has the opposite effect. By continuing the idea into a new line, the pace of the poem is increased. The reader cannot comfortably pause at the end of the line.

c) Language

Having identified the theme of the poem and studied its form and rhythm, you should then look more closely at the language.

1. Choice of words

The poet's choice of words determines his/her style and adds to the meaning of a poem. The choice of vocabulary in a poem will depend to a certain extent on its theme. The style may be **formal** or **informal**, **simple** or **complex**, **straightforward** or **ambiguous**.

The poem *Fire and Ice*, written in 1923, employs formal language to pursue the theme of the destruction of the world, a topic of scientific debate at the time. Some scientists believed that the world would end as a result of explosions of fire from its core. Some scientists believed that an ice age would destroy all living things. Frost states this clearly in the first two lines. The language is straightforward and concise, underlining the scientific nature of the subject matter.

However, the poem also employs **connotations** and **imagery**, introducing a more emotional side to the topic.

- The **connotations** of a word are the **associations** it evokes.
- **Imagery** refers to any aspect of a piece of writing that appeals to the reader's senses. It also refers to the use of comparisons, specifically **similes**, **metaphors** and **personifications**.

In this poem, Frost associates passionate desire with fire and hatred with ice. He thus creates the image of the world as a relationship, which may be destroyed by too much passion or fire or alternatively by icy indifference and hatred. The metaphorical view of the two elements begins in the first two lines and is developed over the whole poem.

2. Grammar and syntax

When analysing the language of a poem, it is also important to look at grammar and syntax (the way the words are arranged).

- Are there any **questions**, **commands** or **exclamations**? To what effect?
- Is the normal **word order** changed in order to emphasize certain words? To what effect?
- Are certain structures repeated (**parallelism**)? To what effect?
- Is the poem written in the **first person** (I, me)? What feelings and attitudes does the narrator convey?

The use of parallelism in the first two lines "Some say ..." underlines that only two options are open as far as the final cause of the destruction of the world is concerned. The narrator, introduced in line 3, initially refers to his own experience of desire and maintains that fire is more likely to be the cause of destruction. However, he finally admits that the world could just as easily end in ice, revealing his own experience of hate.

3. Sound

The sound of a poem is not just determined by its rhythm but also by the vocabulary used. The following techniques can create a musical effect, making the poem easier to read but there are often other important effects. It is not enough just to identify the techniques, you must also explain their effect.

- **Rhyme:** It is not difficult to identify rhymes but more difficult to talk about their effects. Rhyme can give a poem momentum as well as an evenness of tone. Poems without a regular rhyme scheme are called **free verse**.
- **Alliteration:** This is when two or more words begin with the same sound, e.g. favor fire.
- **Assonance:** This is the rhyming of vowel sounds within two or more words, e.g. hold with those.

The poem *Fire and Ice* incorporates three sets of interwoven rhymes. Each line ends with an -ire, -ice, or -ate rhyme. The rhymes bring particular words together that are important for the meaning/message of the poem. "Desire" not only connotes "fire", it also rhymes with it. "Hate" is "great" in the sense of excessive or huge and thus the final message that hatred can also cause destruction is drummed home and further emphasized by the rhyme of "ice" and "suffice". The use of alliteration in line 4, "favor fire" and assonance in line 5, "hold with those" both accentuates the narrator's initial preference for destruction by fire and contrasts strongly with the final message of the last four lines, which come as quite a shock.

S11 How to work on a play

Together with poetry and prose, drama is one of the three main literary genres. Drama is a representation of people in conflict with each other and the world around them, which is intended to be performed on stage. It relies on dialogue, interaction and set design.

Types of plays

Tragedies like the famous plays *Romeo and Juliet* or *Hamlet* by William Shakespeare explore human nature and end in a **catastrophe** due to the tragic hero's misjudgement or hubris, causing his/her own death and that of others.

History plays like *Henry V* use historical events to analyse the machinations of politics and warfare, revealing their impact on people's lives. Thus, history plays comment indirectly on the political situation of the time.

Comedies entertain audiences by making them laugh at the quirks and follies of everyday life. But in spite of all the confusion in a comedy, which might also expose and criticize the shortcomings of society, there is no catastrophe but rather a **happy ending**.
Comedy, especially as **social satire**, is a device used to expose corruption and the foolishness of the individual or to unmask current problems and dangerous trends in society.

A special variety of postwar drama is the **theatre of the absurd**, which illustrates the problem of dysfunctional communication, i.e. the inability to communicate in a meaningful way. Its aim is to shock us out of our complacency and to suggest that our world cannot be rationally comprehended.

Structure

A play is divided into **acts** and **scenes**. In ancient Greece, the action had to take place in one day and one place (**unity of time, place and action**) – an idea based on the writings of philosopher Aristotle. In the late 16th century, these conventions started to be challenged by the inventive playwright William Shakespeare who used subplots and switched between different locations on his stage. Normally, the development of the plot follows the following structure:

The **climax** is the point of highest tension and can consequently also be referred to as the **crisis**.

During the **rising action** suspense builds up due to unexpected obstacles, complications or a clash of conflicting interests and controversial attitudes.

The **falling action** shows how the conflict is resolved …

In the **exposition** the main characters, the setting and the topic/conflict are introduced.

… and leads to the final part, the **resolution** or **denouement**.

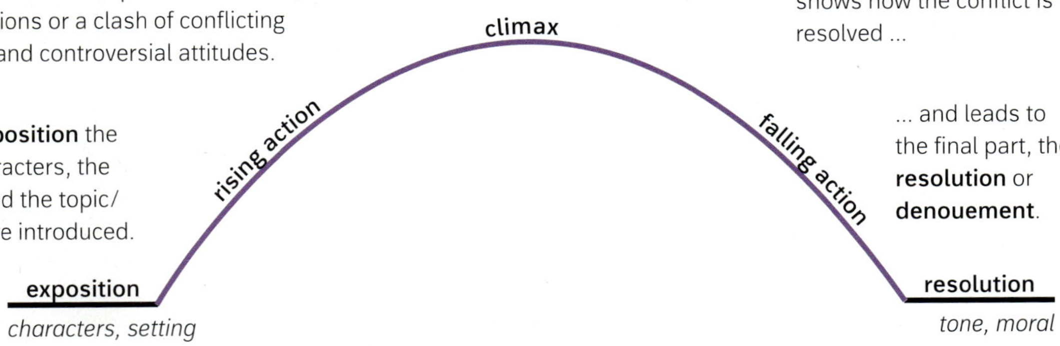

Dramatic devices

The script of a play – or a film – is meant to come alive on stage – or on set. The text consists of dialogue and monologue and the stage directions, which help the actors to interpret and perform the play.

The characters are defined by what they say and do. Their ideolect, the language typical of an individual speaker, reveals a lot about their class and education (e.g. by grammatical incorrectness, lower class slang, sophisticated vocabulary), their personality, their mood (e.g. by an aggressive/ polite/reserved/enthusiastic choice of words) and their role (e.g. domineering/hesitant/intimidated/ uncertain, indicated by pauses, incomplete sentences or repetition).

Dramatic devices	
Dialogue	The verbal exchange between two or more characters
Monologue	A long speech or statement by a single character without any interruption
Soliloquy	Alone on stage, the character voices his innermost thoughts and feelings. Just think of Hamlet's famous words "To be or not to be".
Aside	With several characters present, one of them makes a comment or hints at a plan in a way that makes it obvious that the others cannot hear what is said. This is often used to create suspense by giving the audience some idea of further complications in the plot.
Dramatic irony	Relies on the audience knowing more about the course of action than a character on stage and consequently leads them to anticipate what traps he or she might fall into or what relevance his or her seemingly unimportant words have. For example, the audience knows that the protagonist in a tragedy will be murdered but other characters are unaware of that, so that his or her words and actions suggest a different meaning to the audience.
Reported action	The theatre is a limited space and sometimes details about what happened years ago or in a different place are necessary to explain a character's behaviour or motives or their relationship to others. This can be achieved by characters telling the story and providing the relevant background information.
Comic relief	A favourite device of Shakespeare's, this is a means of breaking the tension and giving temporary relief in a serious or tragic situation by introducing an amusing scene, a comic remark or incident.

Analysis

Plot

- What is the main problem/ conflict?
- How is the conflict introduced? How does it develop? How is it resolved?
- What creates suspense?
- Are there any subplots? How are they linked to the main plot?

Character

- How is a character presented in the stage directions?
- What does his/her ideolect reveal?
- How does the character interact with others?
- What does the dialogue reveal about the role he/ she is assuming?

Devices

- What type of register/what choice of words is used by the individual characters?
- How are pauses/volume/ interruptions used?
- Does the audience know more than a character on stage?
- Is there additional information about past events/experiences and what is its relevance?

S12 Checklist: Analysis – prose

When analysing a prose text, i.e. an extract from a novel or a short story, you will be likely to work through the text chronologically, but when writing your analysis, it is often more advisable to **use a topical order**. The task usually requires a focus on particular aspects. These include:

- stylistic devices,
- choice of words,
- characterization and/or
- narrative perspective,

Structure your ideas along these aspects – this allows you to combine passages that are taken from different parts of the text but are closely related, and to rearrange them in a way that suits your analysis best.

Consequently, you should **plan your text carefully** before you start writing your analysis. You should decide which passages are most relevant to the task and what they illustrate so that you can group similar points together. Put them in a logical order that makes your analysis flow naturally. For a characterization, for example, it would be advisable to start with general information on a character like age and family background before you move on to other aspects such as attitudes and feelings. Once you have decided on an outline for your analysis, make sure your answer follows the structure of **introduction** – **main part** – **conclusion** (see pp. 214-216).

Do not just consider the content, but always **examine the language** used by the author and explain **what it reveals about the narrator or a character** or **what effect** it is supposed to have on the reader. Pay attention to features such as **narrative techniques**, **choice of words** and **stylistic devices**.

Dos	✓ Begin with a central claim that forms a first conclusion on the task, e.g. in the case of a characterization, what a character's central character trait appears to be. ✓ Structure your text logically and divide it into paragraphs. ✓ Organize your analysis around the specific aspects you are asked to focus on (unless the task specifically asks you to work on the development and chronology of the text). ✓ Always combine findings on language/structure and content/message. ✓ Quote from the text to support your findings or refer to the text in your own words. ✓ Use the present tense. ✓ Use connectives to link your ideas. ✓ Use formal and neutral language. ✓ End with a conclusion that does not only sum up your findings, but also refers back to the task and states your results on a more abstract level.
Don'ts	✗ Don't use the past tense. ✗ Don't just paraphrase the text you are analysing. ✗ Don't speculate – your findings must be based on evidence from the text. ✗ Don't write about every detail.

Language support

Writing about characters:
- *The frequent use of* ***direct characterization*** *creates a convincing/ clear/positive/negative picture of .../helps the reader to ...*
- *X is directly characterized by ...*
- *The direct characterization by family and friends*
  - → *seems/appears to be controversial/ contradictory/...*
  - → *shows/reveals different sides of X as each of them perceives X in his/her own way/in an individual way.*
- *X is mainly* ***characterized indirectly*** *by/ through his/her ...*
- *From the way he/she addresses .../reacts to .../behaves when ... we can infer/ conclude that ...*
- *The protagonist seems/appears to be ...*
- *X's behaviour/the way he/she speaks/ dresses/... suggests that ...*
- *As X is presented/described as ..., it becomes clear/it is emphasized/it is highlighted that ...*
- *X's reaction/comment/... reveals/makes the reader feel/believe/understand that ...*

Writing about narrative perspective:
- *By granting the reader access to the character's/characters' mind(s), the narrator draws attention to/makes the reader see/feel ...*
- *The narrator tells the story from a first-/ third person* ***point of view****.*
- *Due to the* ***first-/third-person narration*** *(with a* ***limited/omniscient point of view****), it is (not so) easy for the reader to identify with ...*
- *As the story is told by ..., the reader knows more/does not know more than the character(s) in the story ...*
- *The reader needs to be careful not to take all he/she reads for granted as he/she experiences the development through the main character's eyes ...*

Writing about atmosphere/choice of words/stylistic devices:
- *The author makes use of/uses ... to create a/an ... atmosphere.*
- *The use of short forms and colloquial language in direct speech suggests that ...*
- *The simple short sentences in this passage quicken the pace of the action in order to ...*
- *By incorporating a lot of direct speech in this part of the chapter, the narrator manages to ...*
- *The author uses metaphorical language to ... /employs stylistic devices to ...*
- *The author's use of stylistic devices underlines/enhances the arguments/ message of the text.*
- *The stylistic device/metaphor/... brings out/emphasizes/underlines/supports/ affirms the message ...*
- *to examine/explain/analyse the stylistic devices*
- *The description of the sounds / colours / smells creates a feeling of ...*
- *The tension is created by ...*

Writing about structre:
- *The story has a simple/complex plot ...*
- *The action arises/falls when ...*
- *The narrator uses flashbacks to ...*
- *Suspense is created through the use of ...*
- *The main conflict arises between ... and ...*
- *The events are presented in chronological order ...*
- *The problem is solved by/when ...*
- *The plot has a surprise ending ...*

S13 Checklist: Analysis – non-fictional texts

When analysing non-fictional texts, i.e. a newspaper article or a speech, you need to look at the analysis task very carefully in order to decide whether you should analyse the text in the order in which it is written or by focusing on a certain aspect.

- If you are asked to work on the line of argument, it is advisable to follow the structure of the text and see how the author/speaker moves from one point to the next. If, however, the task requires you to analyse the use of stylistic devices, for instance, it makes more sense to structure your findings according to the different types of devices that are used – no matter in which order they appear.
- Take your time to **plan your text carefully** before you start writing. Decide how to divide your findings up into paragraphs. Your answer should have a coherent structure, consisting of an **introduction**, **main part** and **conclusion** (see pp. 214-216).
- Apart from the overall structure, consider the different **strategies and devices** the author/ speaker may use to inform/influence/convince or entertain the reader or – in the case of a speech – the audience.
- Similarly, **the author's point of view** and **the type of text** can have a significant impact on the way a text is written. So watch out for the way facts and opinions are combined, to what extent the text is biased and what the ultimate **goal of the article or speech** is.
- However, it is not sufficient just to identify these devices. Analysing a text means that you have to **explain why these devices are used** and what **the desired effect** on the reader is.

Dos	✓ Begin with a central claim. In order to do this, keep the central message or problem of the text in mind, but also the task you are working on. Your central claim should set out what you expect to find in your analysis, e.g. what a speaker's overall aim and strategy is in a speech. ✓ Structure your text logically and write in paragraphs. ✓ Analyse the text either in the order in which it is written or according to each of its various aspects in turn – depending on what fits the task best. ✓ Give examples of important stylistic devices, rhetorical strategies, choice of words and structure (included in your analysis as direct or indirect quotations), explain them/their meaning and analyse their effect on the reader. ✓ Always combine findings on language/structure and content/message. ✓ Use the present tense. ✓ Use connectives to link your ideas. ✓ Use formal and neutral language. ✓ End with a conclusion that not only sums up your findings, but also refers back to the task and states your results on a more abstract level.
Don'ts	✗ Don't use the past tense. ✗ Don't only paraphrase the text you are analysing. ✗ Don't just state that a certain stylistic device is used, but explain its function. Refer only to those devices that you can use as evidence for what you claim. ✗ Don't speculate – you must use evidence from the text to support your findings. ✗ Don't write about every detail. Choose evidence carefully and concentrate on the examples that reveal the most about the author's intention; you can mention similar examples without going into too much detail.

Language support

Writing about language/style:

- *formal/informal/colloquial/vulgar/academic/clear/objective/vivid/... language*
- *complex/simple sentences*
- *a serious/friendly/humorous/ironic/polite/rude/critical/optimistic/... tone*
- *The style of the text is plain/condensed/vivid/pompous/artificial/...*

Writing about choice of words:

- *to use emotive adjectives/adverbs that ... to appeal to the readers' emotions*
- *to express ideas in a more informal or colloquial way in order to ...*
- *to associate ... with positive/negative words such as ... in order to ...*
- *the ... connotations of words like ... are meant to make the reader ...*

Writing about stylistic devices:

- *The author uses metaphorical language to ...*
- *The author employs stylistic devices to ...*
- *The author uses figures of speech to ...*
- *The stylistic devices underline/enhance the arguments/message of the text.*
- *The stylistic device supports/affirms the author's/the text's message.*
- *The stylistic device/metaphor/... brings out the message ...*
- *to examine/explain/analyse the stylistic devices*
- *to make a comparison ...*
- *The author makes use of/uses ...*
  ... formal/informal language ...
  ... imagery/metaphors/symbols ...
  ... a unique/clear/sophisticated style ...
  ... irony/satire to ...

S14 How to analyse a speech

There are many types of speeches that are delivered on numerous different occasions to different types of audiences. The type of speech a speaker makes depends on the occasion and the objective. Speeches can aim to inform, to persuade or to entertain. Often speeches are a mixture of all three, e.g. the intention of a political speech may be primarily to convince the audience of a particular policy, but it will probably also include important information and might well be entertaining at times, in order to maintain the audience's attention. There is no point in speaking to an audience that does not listen. In your English classes you are more likely to be confronted with political speeches, e.g. a president making a particular statement.

Step 1: Identifying the speaker's objective

The first thing you should do before planning your speech analysis is to decide what the speaker wants to achieve with his/her speech. Read the speech and try to identify the purpose of the speech. The following questions will help you:

- **When and where** is the speech delivered?
  → on a social occasion? in honour of someone/something? in a political context? in public? in private?
- **Who is the speaker?** What can you find out about him/her?
  → a politician? a public figure? a private individual? an entertainer?
- **What kind of audience** is it?
  → small or large? members of the media? politicians? people who share a common goal? representatives of a particular group?
- **What general theme** is covered by the speech?
  → Is it political, cultural, scientific, economic? Is it concerned with biographical information and/or personal achievements?

➡

- **What kind of language** does the speaker use?
  → Is it emotional, powerful, graphic? Can you detect humour, irony, or satire? Does the speaker employ stylistic devices? (see the glossary at the end of your textbook for more definitions of different stylistic devices)

Stylistic devices often used in speeches	
alliteration	"They are part of the finest fighting force that the world has ever known." (Barack Obama, US president, 10 November 2009, Washington D.C.)
antithesis	"That's one small step for man, one giant leap for mankind." (Neil Armstrong, American astronaut, 21 July 1969, on the moon)
parallelism	"I speak not for myself, but for all girls and boys. Those who have fought for their rights: Their right to live in peace. Their right to be treated with dignity. Their right to equality of opportunity. Their right to be educated." (Malala Yousafzai, Pakistani Nobel prize laureate, 12 July 2013, New York City)
repetition	"How dare you? [...] How dare you?" (Greta Thunberg, climate activist, 23 September 2019, New York City)
simile	"We will not be satisfied until justice rolls down like waters, and righteousness like a mighty stream." (Martin Luther King Jr., 28 August 1963, Washington D.C.)

Tip: If you have the opportunity to **listen to the speech or even watch the speech being delivered** you should do so. The tone of voice of the speaker, the emphasis of certain words, lowering and raising of the voice, will give you good insight into his/her objective.
If a video of the speech is available, you can also take facial expressions and gestures into account.

One of the most famous speeches ever made was by Martin Luther King Jr. on 28 August 1963 in Washington D.C. Read the first lines of the speech and try to answer the questions about it. You may have to do some research concerning the period of time and the speaker.

I Have A Dream

I am happy to join with you today in what will go down in history as the greatest demonstration for freedom in the history of our nation. Five score years ago, a great American, in whose symbolic shadow we stand today, signed the Emancipation Proclamation. This momentous decree came as a great beacon light of hope to millions of Negro slaves who had been seared in the flames of withering injustice. It came as a joyous daybreak to end the long night of their captivity.
But one hundred years later, the Negro still is not free. One hundred years later, the life of the Negro is still sadly crippled by the manacles of segregation and the chains of discrimination. One hundred years later, the Negro lives on a lonely island of poverty in the midst of a vast ocean of material prosperity. One hundred years later, the Negro is still languished in the corners of American society and finds himself an exile in his own land. And so we've come here today to dramatize a shameful condition. [...]

Step 2: Planning and writing your analysis

A speech analysis should adhere to the structure you are familiar with and consist of an **introduction**, a **main body** and a **conclusion**.
The following checklist outlines the information you should include in each part.

Checklist

Introduction
- ✓ Name the speaker and his/her position.
- ✓ Say when, on what occasion and to whom the speech was delivered.
- ✓ Identify the theme/topic.
- ✓ Specify the purpose of the speech (briefly).

Main body
- ✓ Outline the structure of the speech.
- ✓ Summarize the speaker's main arguments.
- ✓ Quote examples of stylistic devices and strategies employed by the speaker and explain their function.

Conclusion
- ✓ Sum up your conclusions.
- ✓ If necessary put the speech into its historical context.
- ✓ Depending on the task, give your personal opinion on whether the speech succeeds in fulfilling the speaker's objectives.

Language support

Introduction
- *The speaker, ... , a civil rights leader, makes/gives/delivers the speech during a demonstration in .../in an election campaign in the year ...*
- *The speech is made/delivered to an audience of .../The speaker faces an audience of ...*
- *The speaker addresses the topic/theme of ...*
- *His/Her purpose/aim/objective is to persuade/convince the audience/to explain the necessity for ...*

Main body
- *In the first few lines the speaker informs the audience/argues that/puts forward the idea of ...*
- *He/She continues by expanding his/her arguments on/offering further proof of ...*
- *About halfway through the speech he/she appeals to the audience by ...*
- *The scientific evidence cited in lines ... offers a powerful argument on behalf of ...*
- *Throughout his/her speech ... employs a number of stylistic devices to underline/illustrate/emphasize his/her point of view.*
- *In lines ... the repeated use of 'we' is a strong appeal to the audience to ...*
- *A recurring/much-used/frequently employed stylistic device is the use of ... in order to emphasize ...*

Conclusion
- *In general I have come to the conclusion that ....*
- *All in all the speaker convincingly argues his/her case on behalf of ...*
- *Martin Luther King's speech on ... was a landmark in the struggle for ...*
- *The speaker has not achieved his/her objective as far as I am concerned.*
- *His/Her arguments fail to convince me/overcome my doubts about ...*
- *Despite the extensive use of rhetorical strategies, the speaker does not succeed in ...*

Step 3: Proofreading

Very few pieces of writing are printed exactly the way they were first written. A first draft needs to be revised and improved. That may mean changing the order of paragraphs or arguments or including more quotations or references to the text.
In an exam situation you won't have time to redraft a whole piece of writing but you can proofread it. The final read should concentrate on spelling, punctuation and grammar.
You should try to identify your own weaknesses and look for mistakes in these areas, e.g. the wrong use of commas and other punctuation or word order.

S15 How to describe pictures

Pictures often say more than words and may be used in many different ways to illustrate a topic. There are many different types of pictures and it is important that you follow these steps when working with them:

- Identify and name the kind of picture you are asked to describe in your introductory sentence.
- Describe the different elements in the picture in detail.

Finally, you may be asked to speculate on a particular aspect of the picture or give your own interpretation.

1. **Opening sentence.**
   e.g. The picture shows the 1872 painting *American Progress* by John Gast.

2. **On the left-hand side** there is a group of native Americans and a herd of buffalo, apparently fleeing.

3. **In the background** you can see dark clouds on the left-hand side that become lighter towards the right-hand side of the painting. On the very right, you can see the sun and the clouds have scattered.

4. **On the right-hand side** you can see three steam trains, a line of telegraph wire and some ships in a bay.

5. **In the centre** you can see a young blonde woman in a long white gown with a yellow star on her forehead. She carries a book in her right hand and lays out telegraph wire with her left. Moreover you can see a stagecoach, a covered wagon and a rider all going from right to left.

6. **In the bottom right-hand corner** there are some peasants with two oxen and a plow.

7. **In the foreground** of the painting there are four men, one of them on horseback.

8. **Speculation or interpretation.**
   Possible questions you could ask yourself are:
   - What is the difference between light and dark, clouds and sun meant to convey?
   - What is the role of the female figure?
   - Why is everyone and everything in the painting moving from right to left?
   - What does it mean that the native Americans are fleeing?
   - What is the overall message of the painting?

Language support

Different types of pictures and artists
- *advertisement, caricature, collage, drawing, film still, illustration, (oil) painting, photograph portrait, poster, sketch, watercolour*
- *graphic designer, artist, portrait painter, photographer*

Describing where to find different elements
- *in the top right-hand/left-hand corner*
- *in the foreground/background*
- *at the top/bottom*
- *in the middle/centre*
- *on the left/right*

Speculating
- *It seems likely/probable that ...*
- *One might assume that ...*
- *The choice of ... might mean that ...*
- *It seems to be the intention of the artist to ...*
- *The body language of the central figure suggests ...*

Interpreting
e.g. atmosphere, tone, etc.
- *The atmosphere created by the colours is ...*
- *There is a certain humorous/mocking/critical/light-hearted/grave/optimistic tone about the ...*
- *The choice of ... underlines the intention of the artist/graphic designer/photographer to ...*
- *The painting captures the feeling of ...*
- *The serious/loving/hateful expression on the face of the figure on the right/left/in the centre corresponds with/contrasts strongly with ...*

S16 Checklist: Analysis of a film scene

In order to analyse a film scene, it is necessary to watch the scene multiple times. What and how much you are expected to analyse depends on the task you are given. Sometimes you will have to analyse a film scene as a whole, often in the context of the complete film. In other cases, your task may only be to analyse how stylistic devices are used in a scene. During the viewing process, you should keep a **viewing log**. Having a viewing log makes it easier for you to remember and refer back to important points during the writing process.
A viewing log may look like this:

scene	action	cinematic devices	function/effect
...	...	...	...

You can find an overview of cinematic devices and their primary functions on pages 108-109. When you write your analysis, you can use the checklist on the next page.

➡

Dos	**Introduction** ✓ Refer back to the task. ✓ Name the film, its director and the year it was released. ✓ In the introduction, it often makes sense to make a central claim that sums up what you are going to prove in your essay. **Main part** ✓ Present your points in a well-structured and logical way. Guide your reader through your text and express connections between points in the text explicitly. ✓ Divide your main part up into meaningful paragraphs. Decide whether those paragraphs will reflect a chronological analysis of the excerpt or represent certain aspects or focal points. ✓ Within those paragraphs, it usually makes sense to follow the structure Point – Evidence – Analysis: a point you want to make, evidence to support the point and an analysis of the evidence (see S9: How to structure a text, pp. 214-216) ✓ For an analysis of a film scene as a whole, you should include and combine • an analysis of the dialogue, • an analysis of the action, • an analysis of images (like objects, landscapes that have metaphorical meaning etc.) • an analysis of the camera operations and • an analysis of other important cinematic devices (like music, lighting, etc.). ✓ For an analysis of a film scene as a whole, you might want to consider • how the scene moves the action forward and creates suspense, • if/how it represents a turning point, • whether it shows a new/important character trait of a protagonist or • introduces something new (character, conflict, etc.) or • defines the relationship between characters. ✓ For an analysis of a scene as a whole, put your findings into a broader context if necessary, i.e. explain them in the context of the complete film: use your knowledge about the plot, the characters etc. **Conclusion** ✓ Refer back to your introduction. ✓ Summarize your most important findings concisely.
Don'ts	✗ In the conclusion, do not repeat every single detail of your findings. ✗ In the conclusion, do not introduce new details.

Language support

The scene conveys/suggests/indicates/reveals/highlights …
The character's position/stance/facial expression suggests/indicates/reveals/seems to reveal …
The music intensifies/emphasizes/has the effect of …/evokes a feeling of …/creates a(n) … atmosphere.
The sound effects intensify/emphasize/have the effect of …/evoke a feeling of …/create a(n) … atmosphere.
The setting suggests/indicates/has the effect of …/evokes a feeling of …
The use of colour underlines/has the effect of …/creates a(n) … atmosphere.

S17 How to work on cartoons

Cartoons are often used to make a critical comment on a serious issue in a humorous way. They are often published in newspapers or magazines. In order to understand the cartoon it is important to look at the details, and you should consider the connection between the picture, the punch line and any speech bubbles.

Issue
Before you study the cartoon in detail, decide what the issue is.

Presentation of characters
Are the characters in the cartoon caricatures of real people like politicians or other persons of public interest, or do they stand for a particular group?

Scene/Setting
What is the situation depicted in the cartoon? Where is it set? Who are the characters involved? What are they doing?

Source
The cartoon may be published in a newspaper or a magazine. What is the general attitude represented by the paper? Is it more conservative or more liberal? When was the cartoon first published?

Punch line, caption or written comment
Is the punch line presented as direct speech or as a general statement? Does the caption contain a play on words or a double meaning? Does it suggest a parallel with past or present situations or events?

Language support

Describing cartoons

- *At the top/bottom of the cartoon …*
- *In the foreground/background …*
- *On the right/left …*
- *In the centre …*
- *In the top/bottom right-hand/left-hand corner …*
- *The cartoonist shows …*
- *There are … in the picture.*
- *The situation reminds one/me/you of …*
- *The cartoon describes …*

Interpreting cartoons

- *The topic/issue addressed by the cartoon is …*
- *The figures represent/symbolize …*
- *The caption suggests/implies/underlines …*
- *The cartoonist ridicules/draws attention to/caricatures/is making fun of …*
- *The … is a caricature of …*
- *The message is accentuated by …*
- *The message in the speech bubble conveys the idea that …*
- *I agree/don't agree with the cartoonist …*

S18 How to analyse statistics

Statistics can appear in different forms. Usually, they take one of the forms below:

bar chart

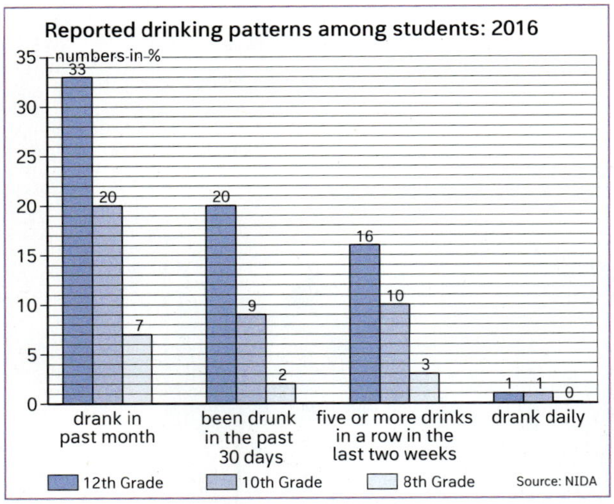

pie chart

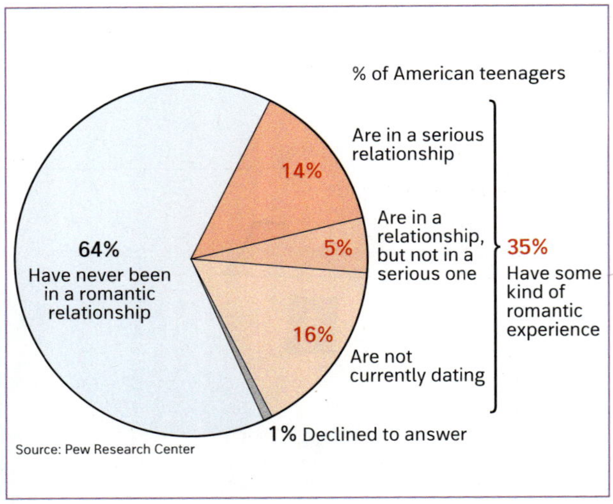

line graph

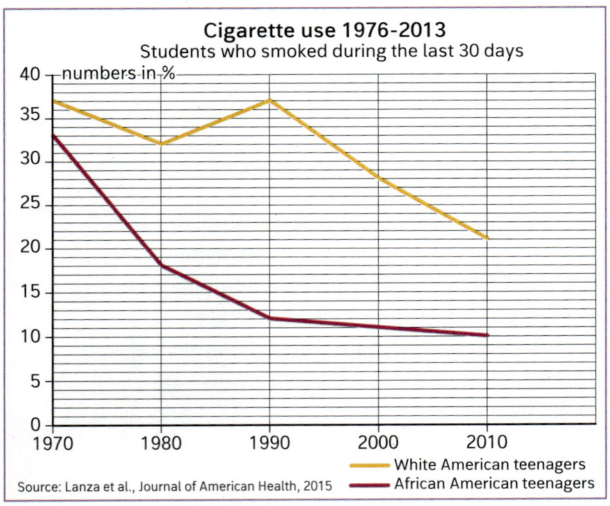

table

Among adult American smartphone owners, % who use...

	Messaging apps	Auto-delete apps	Anonymous apps
Men	31	24	4
Women	27	23	7
18-29	42	56	10
30-49	29	13	6
50+	19	9	<1
Highschool or less	28	24	5
Some college	25	27	8
College+	33	21	4
Less than $ 50 K/year	28	27	5
$ 50.000+	29	22	6
Total	**29%**	**24%**	**5%**

Survey conducted March/April 2016 Source: Social Media Update 2016, Pew Resaerch Center

Studying the figures

1. In order to analyse statistics, make sure you study the graph/chart/table carefully. Find out what the statistics are about.

2. Study the legend and the figures and check if they are absolute numbers or percentages. Pay special attention to the way the figures are presented visually to make sure that proportions are represented accurately, for example.

3. Look for general trends or noteworthy figures or correlations. What you can find out depends largely on the type of visualization. Pie charts and bar charts usually deal with the relative size/importance of data, line graphs and tables often emphasize certain developments including changes in trends.

Language support

Describing and interpreting the figures

Introduction: • How are the figures presented? • What is the graph/chart/table about? • What is the source (author/date of publication) of the figures?	• *The graph/chart/table shows/presents/provides information on/deals with ..., covering a period of ...* • *The topic/subject/theme of the graph/chart/table is ...* • *It is taken from/The source of the data is ...* • *The graph/chart/table was published by ... on ...*
Description: • How do the figures develop? • What is the highest/lowest point? • What are the most striking points? • Are there any irregular figures? • If there are figures to compare, are there any similarities/differences?	• *The horizontal/vertical axis shows ...* • *There is a considerable/steady/sharp/slight/marked increase/decrease in the number of ...* • *The number/amount/proportion of ... has changed slightly/clearly since ...* • *After 1980 ... rose dramatically/soared.* • *The numbers drop/fall/decrease ...* • *The figures remain constant/steady ...* • *The figures reach a peak/a trough in ...* • *In ..., X reached its lowest point at 21%/peaked at 37%.* • *The downturn began in ...* • *The average figure for ... is ...* • *The pie is subdivided into segments that represent ...* • *The chart/graph/table reveals/shows that ...* • *The numbers for ... are about twice as high as those ...* • *The ... with the highest frequency/number of ... is ...* • *Compared to ...* • *Nearly half of ...*
Conclusion and evaluation: • What general conclusion can be drawn from the figures? • What could be reasons for the figures? • How can the figures be related to each other? • What can be predicted on the basis of these figures? • How do the figures relate to what you know about the topic? Are they objective or biased?	• *All in all/By and large, the statistics for ... reveal/show/... that ...* • *This development clearly shows/indicates that ...* • *It seems likely/unlikely that the figures for ... will (not) continue to ...* • *Against the background of ..., the figures/ results are (not) very surprising/revealing/enlightening ...* • *The data confirms/contradicts/is (not) consistent with ...* • *The graph/chart/table conveys a false/one-sided impression because ...*

S19 How to improve your mediation skills

You are very likely to be confronted with situations where people who do not speak German need your help because some information they need is only available in German.
Such situations are very similar to those that you find in mediation tasks.

Step 1: Understanding the task

Before you start working on a mediation task, make sure that you fully understand what is required from you. Mediation does not mean translating the German original word for word.

a) What is the type of text you need to produce?

In the example below, you can see that the German original is an article, but the text you should produce is an email. This means that you must change the way the information is presented to you in German. In order to do this, you need to remember what is typical of that particular kind of text. In the case of an email, you should first address your partner, introduce your email stating the reason for it, (e.g. by referring to the given situation), write a main part which includes the relevant information from the text and finish your email appropriately.

> Together with an English and a Polish partner school, your school is working on a Comenius project about immigration to Europe. You are a member of your school's Comenius group and you have found the following article in the German magazine Der Spiegel. Use the information given here to write an email in English informing the other partners about immigration laws and the conclusions drawn by the magazine.

Other common types of text that you may come across in this context are:

- poster
- brochure
- email to a friend or other young person
- formal letter or email to an institution/ authority
- article for a website or online magazine
- article for the school newspaper or website
- newspaper article
- (info)graphics and statistics
- blog post

b) What information is needed?

Read the task carefully to find out what information is needed. Certain passages or elements of the German text are likely to be irrelevant to the task. You should leave this information out in your text.

c) Who is the addressee?

In a mediation task, another factor that should influence the way you deal with the text is the addressee that is mentioned in the task. Select the aspects that are relevant for the addressee. Explain relevant terms that your addressee would otherwise not understand. If you write a text for teenagers, your text should be less formal and technical than if you were writing about a difficult topic for experts in a particular field, for example.

d) What style and register should you use?

Choose the style and register that fits the text type you have to produce (e.g. an email, letter, speech).

Step 2: Working on the task

a) Reading

- Highlight all the information relevant to the task (see Step 1b).
- Make notes in English.
- Remember that you are not supposed to write a word-by-word translation of passages from the text. If you decide that the translation of a certain expression is necessary to do the task properly, do not get stuck looking for a literal translation of a German expression. Sometimes it doesn't exist and you can paraphrase the idea you want to express. For example, there may be a German idiomatic expression like "das Zeitliche segnen" which you cannot translate directly. So you need to find either an English idiom that has a similar meaning or go for a more neutral expression, for example "to die".

b) Writing the English text

- Arrange the information you highlighted and noted down in a logical order that fits the type of text you are expected to write. Structure it in such a way that it is easy to understand for the people who are supposed to read your text.
- As stated above, you shouldn't translate the German text word for word. It is important that all the relevant information is presented clearly. Leave out anything that is not related to the task, also leave out any personal comments unless the task invites you to include them.
- Be careful with expressions and concepts that are very specific to German and Germany. You may have to include an explanation to someone from abroad. For example, a text may include references to people or institutions that most Germans know, but people from abroad do not know. So you need to add a short explanation: *Many Germans watch the news programme "Tagesschau" at 8 o'clock at night on ARD, which is a public TV channel.*

c) Editing the text

- Make sure that you have included all the relevant information required by the task and not used anything that goes beyond it.
- Check that your text fits the criteria of the type of text that the task has asked you to produce.
- Don't forget that the style and register of the text must suit the addressees that the text is intended for. If necessary, make some changes to style and register.
- Check your text for grammatical correctness and the right choice of words.
- Do a spell-check and make sure the punctuation is correct (check your use of commas, quotation marks, apostrophes, etc.).

S20 How to listen/watch effectively

Learning a foreign language properly is impossible without learning to listen and sometimes also watch effectively. Listening and viewing comprehension tasks, however, can take very different forms as you may have to listen to a dialogue, a speech, a song or watch an interview, a news report, an episode from a TV series, etc. The situations – whether it's in parliament or a family context – vary as much as the accents or pace of the speakers.

a) Before listening/viewing

- Make sure you read the task carefully.
- Think about the topic you have been discussing in class. If there are photos, headings, additional texts, study them so that you already have some ideas of what the listening text or the video may be about.
- Consider the context of the situation. Where are the people? What do people typically do or talk about in such a situation?
- Think about your expectations and assumptions concerning the video or audio clip. What do you think will happen? What will you see or hear?

b) While listening/viewing

- When you listen to an audio or video clip for the first time, listen for gist, i.e. the main ideas. Key words that are repeated several times may help you work out what the clip is about.
- While listening/watching, keep the task in mind and try to remember where in the clip there are relevant passages you should concentrate on when you listen to or watch it for a second time.
- Aim to understand the general message; don't worry if you can't make out every word. If you listen to a clip a second time, you will notice that you understand a lot more. You will then be able to work out the meaning of words from the context or from similarities they have with other words you know in English (e.g. high – height, clean – cleanliness), German or another language (e.g. to deny so. sth. – French: dénier).
- In video clips, gestures and body language can help you to understand the content. The body language of the people speaking, for example, tells you a lot about their feelings and thoughts and thereby can help you to figure out the meaning of unknown words.
- Try to think ahead. What might happen next? What might the speakers say? How are the people possibly going to act? Make predictions.

c) After listening/viewing

- Answer the key questions: **Who? Where? When? What? Why?**
- Note down important facts, key words and words you didn't understand.
- Were your guesses right? Did the people do or say what you expected them to? Correct your assumptions based on what you have heard or seen.
- If you are not quite sure whether you understood everything, try to guess what the people could have said by using all the information you got with the help of visual and/or acoustic hints.
- Look up key words that you think are essential for the understanding of the clip. Try to guess other words you don't know by using all other available information.
- If you hear or watch the clip again, set yourself an aim: What do you want to focus on?

d) Working on the task

- Use a pencil to take notes or, if it is a multiple-choice test, mark the correct answers.
- Add to your notes when you listen again.
- If it is not a test, check with your partner to see if you understood the same things.

S21 How to succeed in oral exams

Oral exams can be rather intimidating. In order to overcome your fears and to be able to prepare, it is important that you know what to expect in the exam and what the examiner expects of you.

In all oral examinations marks will be given both for the **content** of your answers and your **language competence**.

Content

The exam may be based on topics you have studied in class. In this case you can prepare by noting down useful information and learning it.
You will in many cases get one or more spontaneous "prompts" to start you talking about a particular topic. These are likely to be visuals such as pictures, cartoons etc., in some cases short texts. You will be expected to use these "prompts" together with your own knowledge to give a short talk or presentation (**monologue**) or as the basis for a discussion with a partner or small group (**dialogue**). In an **interview** you may have to react spontaneously to questions without preparation or prompts.

Language competence

A good way to make sure that your discourse runs fluently is to use **discourse markers**. These words and phrases help the listener to follow what the speaker is saying by signalling certain aspects of speech. The following discourse markers are common in everyday speech.

so – marks the beginning of a new part of conversation
well – marks a change in focus
right/OK/if you like – mark a response/an agreement
I mean/you know/as I say – mark explanations or re-phrasings
actually – marks a different point of view or the introduction of a new aspect
anyway – marks a shift in topic

Look at the following short discussion:

A: So, I think the first picture is concerned with the consequences of cyber-bullying.
B: Well, that could be the case but it could also just show the importance of social networking.
A: Right. That's what I think, too. But it can still be misused.
B: Actually, I think misuse is not as widespread as many people believe. I mean, most of us don't send threatening texts to our classmates, do they?
A: OK, I suppose you have a point. Anyway, I think we should change the subject and move on to the next topic.

You can also use discourse markers to sequence what you say.

Language support

Beginnings are often introduced by:
- *First (of all), ...*
- *For a start, ...*
- *Firstly* (more formal)

Further points may be introduced by:
- *On top of that, ...*
- *What's more, ...*
- *Next/Second(ly)/Third(ly)*

Endings may be signalled by:
- *Last of all, ... To sum up, ...*
- *Finally, ... In the end, ...*

Reacting to what others said:
- *I agree/disagree with what you said ...*
- *I see your point, but I think that ...*
- *As far as I'm concerned/If you ask me ...*
- *I'd like to add that ...*

➡

Apart from ensuring that you speak fluently, it is also important not to make too many mistakes. Although no one expects you to be flawless, bear in mind these two points:

- Try to avoid basic grammar mistakes. Know your own weaknesses and practice structures that you have difficulty with, or avoid these structures if they cause you too many problems.
- Concentrate on communicating your ideas successfully. Do not express yourself in a too complicated way. Learn some useful phrases to structure your answers.

Parts of the exam

Usually, an oral exam consists of two or all of the following parts:

1. Interview

This is the most spontaneous type of oral exam and it is not always possible to prepare for it. The examiner is interested in how you can respond spontaneously to his or her questions on a particular topic that will usually be revealed shortly before the interview begins.
The important thing is to keep calm and to listen carefully to the examiner's questions before you answer. Here are some tips:

Checklist

✓ If you do not quite understand, ask the examiner to repeat or rephrase the question:
I'm not quite sure whether I have understood you/the question. Would you mind repeating it, please?

✓ If you are not immediately sure about your answer, try to win some time by using phrases such as:
Let me just think about that for a moment. • *As I was saying ...*
or by rephrasing or repeating the question:
You asked me whether .... Personally, I ...

✓ If it is a partner exam and the other student has to answer the same questions as you, you can refer to what the other candidate has said and agree or disagree with it:
Actually there isn't very much I can add to what the other candidate has just said.
I completely agree with him/her that ...
But generally, you should always try to add aspects of your own.

2. Monologue

In this kind of exam, you will be expected to demonstrate that you can speak coherently for some time on a particular topic. This usually takes the form of a short presentation based on some visual prompts such as photographs and a leading question.

Here is an example:
Talk about these pictures. What do they reveal about the importance of social media in the communication between young adults?

In many cases, you will have little or no time to prepare so that you will have to be able to present your topic quite spontaneously. Here are some tips:

Checklist

✓ If you are given time to prepare, use it well. Read the task and look at the pictures carefully (noting down useful information and your own ideas).

✓ Structure your talk e.g. by using phrases from the language support on the next page.

✓ Begin your talk by referring in detail to the pictures/material you have been given but then move on to include other relevant information or opinions while answering the leading question.

✓ Remember the examiner is interested in hearing what you have to say in the relatively short time given. Make sure you use that time effectively, avoiding long periods of silence, but do not "waffle", i.e. spend a lot of time talking about irrelevant aspects. Keep to the point.

3. Dialogue

In this kind of examination, you will have a conversation or a discussion with one or two other candidates based on prompts such as short texts or pictures and a leading question.
Here is an example:
Talk about which of the media in the following pictures have had the greatest impact on society.

Often you will be asked to come to some kind of agreement with the other examinee(s).
The examiner expects you to show the following oral skills:

Checklist

- ✓ listening actively to what the other person says
- ✓ keeping a conversation going
- ✓ reacting to what the other person says by taking turns, agreeing and/or disagreeing
- ✓ stating your own view clearly
- ✓ clarifying and asking for clarification if something you or the other person says is not immediately clear
- ✓ making suggestions and compromises in order to reach an agreement

Language support

Active listening You can use certain discourse markers to show that you are listening and are interested in what is being said.	• *Absolutely.* • *Really?* • *You don't say.* • *I see.* • *Exactly.* • *Sure.*
Keeping a conversation going Sometimes it is necessary to actively involve the person you are talking to, or bring him/her back into the conversation.	• *So what do you think?* • *What makes you so sure?* • *Wouldn't you say so?*
Agreeing and disagreeing It is more idiomatic in speaking to use phrases which are not too direct, especially when disagreeing	• *That's just what I think/how I see it.* • *Well, I'm not sure about that.* • *You could be right, but ...* • *I see your point but ...*
Stating your own view clearly It is possible to say "in my opinion/view", but in spoken English this sounds rather formal.	• *I'd say ...* • *If you ask me, ...* • *From my point of view ...* • *I'm sure/convinced that ...* • *As I see it ...*
Clarifying if someone doesn't understand your point	• *What I really mean is ...* • *In other words ...* • *What I'm trying to say is ...*
Asking for clarification if you do not understand another person	• *I'm sorry, I didn't quite understand what you mean.* • *When you talk about ..., do you mean ...?*
Making suggestions/compromises	• *What about ...?/How about ...?* • *What do you think about ...?* • *Well, I suppose that's a possibility.* • *Why not?*

S22 How to stage a debate

A debate is a good way of discussing varied opinions which argue for or against an idea. Through the format of a debate, different opinions and evidence can be shared and considered. The goal of the debate may be to convince the other side of your point of view, or to reach a common consensus through compromises.
Here is some help:

Step 1: Choosing a motion

Identify a clear topic or motion where there is a division of opinion. In these circumstances, the different groups can argue either for or against it. An example of such a motion would be:

> "Driverless cars should save their driver and passengers at all costs."

Step 2: Splitting into two groups

Usually, two groups are formed based on common arguments both for and against the motion. However, the people in a single group do not necessarily have to share the exact same motivations or reasoning for their choice of argument. Bringing in different ideas is part of the debating process.

Step 3: Preparing your arguments

Each side of the argument has time to prepare their arguments. Part of a debate is finding weaknesses or flaws in the opposition's argument. Therefore, it is important that you research beforehand and identify evidence which will support your claims. In the same way, you can anticipate what the other side's arguments will be and prepare arguments against their ideas.

Step 4: Having the debate

The group supporting (or putting forward) the motion begins the debate by making an opening statement. This should summarize the key reasons why they are arguing for the topic. Afterwards, the spokesperson for the other side makes a similar opening statement. At this point, the debate really begins. Each group takes it in turns expressing their ideas, as well as exposing weaknesses in their opponent's thoughts.

Step 5: The results of the debate

To conclude the debate, a final vote is held in which everyone involved votes for or against the original motion. At this stage, group members are allowed to vote independently. That is to say that they might have been convinced by the opposition's side of the argument and vote with them on the issue.

Language support

We strongly believe that ...
We are firm believers that/in ...
We support the motion proposed here today because ...
It is our view that ...

On the contrary, ...
I agree to a certain extent but ...
He/she claims that ... but ...
It is unjustifiable to say that ...

In my opinion, ...
If you ask me, ...
In my experience, ...
I'd like to point out that ...
Personally, I feel/think/believe/suggest ...
As far as I'm concerned, ...
Just to be clear, I believe ...

To recap the main points, ...
In summary, ...
To conclude our side of the debate, ...

S23 How to quote

When referring to/working on a text, you need quotations from that text to support your statements and findings with evidence. You can quote directly or indirectly, and you can integrate quotations into your own sentences or quote passages to back up what you have said in your own words. As opposed to German, in the English language, quotation marks always appear at the top of the word.

Language support

You may ...	Examples
1) ... quote indirectly from a text, i.e. say something that can be found in the text in your own words. This is often used when stating facts that need no in-depth interpretation. To show that you haven't quoted directly from the text, use "cf."[1].	• *Ed works as a taxi driver and plays cards with his friends Audrey and Marvin on a regular basis (cf. p. 40).*
2) ... integrate direct quotes into your own sentence. But be careful: Don't change the meaning of the quotation, and make sure the resulting sentence is grammatically correct. To show that you are quoting directly from the text, use inverted commas.	• *Ed comes from one of the parts of the town where the poorer, less educated people live, which he himself describes as a "dirty secret" (p. 41).*
3) ... quote a short passage or sentence directly to back up what you have already said in your own words. Again, use inverted commas to show that it is a direct quotation.	• *Ed states clearly that he is not content with his life: "No real career. No respect in the community. Nothing." (p. 40).*

Annotations
[1] **Cf.** = is short for the Latin word *confer*, which means *compare*

Checklist

When you quote from a text, ...

✓ don't quote very long passages. Quotes should underline or support what you have to say, not say it for you.
✓ don't use quotes simply to fill paper space – they must refer to your findings.
✓ quote the exact wording and punctuation from the text. If you leave something out or change something to make it fit into your sentence, you have to indicate that clearly by using [...]. You may only make minor changes and mustn't alter the meaning of your quote.
✓ don't use quotations to retell a text or story.
✓ make sure the quotes are meaningful.
✓ always refer to lines or pages (l. 1/ll. 5-7/p. 8/pp. 8-9, etc.). Use "l." for one line, "ll." for more than one line, "p." for one page and "pp." for more than one page.
✓ you should set off the quoted passage further away from the left-hand margin if the quoted text is more than two or three sentences long.

S24 How to give feedback/peer edit

Giving constructive feedback is a helpful way to improve the quality of your own and of your classmates' work.

A. Feedback on a presentation

Make sure that the feedback you give ...

- is worded in such a way that your classmates can accept it without being embarrassed.
- is objective and not personal.
- focuses more on the corrected form and does not dwell on the mistake.
- highlights the use of good language.

Language support

Here are some phrases you can use to give positive feedback on a presentation by your classmates:

- *What I really liked was that you ...*
- *What really impressed me was ...*
- *I particularly liked ...*
- *I think it was a good idea to ...*
- *You managed to ...*

If you need to be more critical, these expressions can help you:

- *The explanations/facts given were not (quite) correct.*
- *What could be improved is ...*
- *I would have liked to learn more about ...*
- *I missed information about ...*
- *You did not manage to ...*

B. Peer editing

A good method of improving your writing is peer editing. It means working with someone from your class to help you to improve, revise and edit each other's writing.

When editing a text check the following aspects:

- **Topic:** Check whether the writer stays on topic. Information that is not relevant should be left out.
- **Choice of words:** Make sure the writer uses interesting words and not too many "overused" words (e.g. *really, very, nice, interesting*). A writer should also use language which is appropriate for the relevant text type (e.g. register, thematic vocabulary, etc.).
- **Sentences:** Check for sentences that are either too long or too short. A good writer also uses linking words to join his/her sentences.
- **Text structure:** A good text should be well organized and easy to understand. An introduction should immediately grab the reader's attention.

When peer editing a text, you should keep three aspects in mind:

- **Compliments:** The most important rule of peer editing is to BE POSITIVE! Always start with compliments. Remember, you are helping to improve someone else's work. First tell the writer what you think he/she did well. Here are some phrases you can use to give positive feedback:

  This was fun to read because ...
  I liked the way you ...
  My favourite part was ... because ...
  I think you used a lot of good details.

- **Suggestions:** Make suggestions by giving some specific ideas about how to improve the piece of writing. Remember to try and stay positive and always try to provide constructive criticism.

  For example, don't say to your partner:
  This paragraph doesn't make any sense.
  Tell him/her: *If you add more details after this sentence, it will be clearer.*

  Rather than saying: *Your choice of words was boring*, say:
  Instead of using the word 'good', maybe you can use the word 'exceptional'.

- **Corrections:** Only after you and your partner have agreed on how to change your pieces of writing can you actually start with the final step in the peer-editing process: making corrections.

  Swap your texts and check your partner's work for:
  - spelling mistakes
  - grammar mistakes
  - missing or wrong punctuation

Checklist

Here is some advice on how to spot mistakes:

✓ Read the text more than once and concentrate on one aspect at a time, e.g. spelling mistakes.
✓ If you have typed your text on the computer, use the spellchecker in Word.
✓ After you have finished writing your text, take a break before you check it for mistakes.
✓ Reading "backwards", i.e. from end to beginning, might do the trick to spot mistakes.

S25 How to work with a dictionary

Many tasks, especially reading and writing tasks, involve the use of a dictionary. There are **monolingual dictionaries**, which provide definitions in English and **bilingual dictionaries**, which give you the German equivalents. Most of the time you will be using a bilingual dictionary.

A. English – German

When working on texts you may not always understand all the words, so you will need to refer to a dictionary. The use of the dictionary, however, may be determined by the situation you are in.

- Don't look up every single word you don't know but apply the **strategies** you have learnt to **understand words from the context** first.
- **Limit the number of words to look up** as using the dictionary is quite time-consuming.
- Depending on the task you are given it may be necessary to **check all the words you don't understand**. If you read a novel or a longer text of course you will need to use your strategies of understanding words from the context, from cognates, etc. But sometimes you need to get a detailed understanding of the text.
- Having gone to the trouble of finding the word, try and use it to build and **extend your active vocabulary**.
  - → Decide if the word may be useful for later use.
  - → Collect the words you have selected in word fields.
  - → Add collocations or idioms to avoid possible mistakes in the future.
  - → Use the newly acquired words and phrases in your homework/written texts. This is the best way to remember them.

How to look the word up properly

- Make sure you look the word up in its **correct spelling** or you may end up with an incorrect translation. Examples of this are: *board-bored, fair-fare, sail-sale*.
- Determine whether the word you are looking up is a noun, a verb, an adjective, etc. and read the corresponding part of the entry. With verbs, make sure you look for the infinitive.
- There may still be different meanings. Read the complete entry and decide which translation fits the context of your text best.
- Avoid mistakes by checking what grammatical construction is needed with the word you want to use, for example *used to* ***do*** as opposed to *get used to* ***doing***.

The phonetic transcription shows you how to pronounce a word correctly. It not only reflects the sound but also gives you the intonation of a word, which may be different depending on the function of the word (e.g. pre'sent v – 'present n).

n, vi, vt, adj tell you what type of word it is (noun, verb, etc.). If there are abbreviations you don't understand, check the explanations in the dictionary.

The headword helps you to find the word more easily.

chest [tʃest] n 1. *(torso)* Brust f, Brustkorb m; **to fold one's arm across one's ~** die Arme vor der Brust verschränken – 2. *(trunk)* Truhe; *(box)* Kiste – 3. *(treasury)* Schatzkästchen

The different meanings of a word are listed under numbers. Make sure that you read the whole entry to find the meaning that fits the context.

Expressions in bold letters give you examples of how to use the word correctly in typical phrases or idioms (e.g. "heavy: ~ accent, with a ~ heart").

B. German – English

When writing texts you will, with time, want to make your phrasing more precise, varied and differentiated.

Typical needs

- **Spelling:** You are not sure how the English word you want to use is written.
  → Check for changes in spelling in different grammatical contexts.

- **Vocabulary:** You want to use a particular word.
  → Make sure you have the correct German spelling. For example: The word *Widerspruch* will be hard to find if you think it is spelt with *ie*.
  → Read through **all** the possible meanings and consider the specific lexical area in which you want to use the word. For example: The German word *Bank* can mean either *bank* or *bench* in English.
  → If collocations are given, try to use the whole phrase or a parallel construction in your own text.

- **Style variation (synonyms/antonyms):** When writing a text and editing it you will find that you have repeated certain words.
  → Use the definitions of the German word you have looked up to find other ways in English of expressing it.

Internet dictionaries

It may seem the quickest route to use an internet dictionary, but this often is the quickest way to making lots of mistakes: internet dictionaries often offer a one-to-one translation which may not always fit. So don't go for the first option but check carefully in which context the respective word can be used: Look for synonyms, example sentences, and other elements you know from a print dictionary.

Tip: Since you will have to work with a non-digital dictionary in your exams, you should practise working with one in class and at home.
- You will start to get quicker at finding words.
- You will start to get more confident in choosing the right meaning.
- You will get used to benefitting from the additional information the dictionary offers you.

S26 How to design a poster

A good poster captures the viewer's attention and communicates the right message and information without being overloaded. Remember that a poster is a visual form of presenting something, so make sure to find the right balance between visuals and text elements.

When creating a poster, you need to decide on these key aspects:
- the **addressee** you wish to reach with the poster
- the **composition** of the different elements on the poster
- the use of **text** elements (and the **font(s)**[1] you want to use)
- any **images** or **photos** you want to include
- the **colour scheme** you are going to employ
- how you are going to use **white space** throughout your poster

1 **font** = a set of printable text characters in a specific style and size

Composition

Aim for a poster that is neither empty nor overloaded and think about how you want to guide your viewer through the information. For that, decide on one focal point and then on the order you want to arrange the other elements in, making it easy for the audience to follow your thoughts behind the composition. Also make sure everything is aligned.

Poster design tips

Use bold and contrasting colours to draw attention.

Never use more than three different fonts. Choose easy-to-read fonts.

Ag

Emphasize or highlight the main information.

Keep your written content very brief.

Use images to enhance the visual impact of your poster.

Think about where your poster will be presented or shared.

Colour scheme

- You want your poster – and your message – to stand out, so go for bold, strong colours.
- Do not use too many different colours and decide whether you want complementing (e.g. all shades of one colour, all warm colours) or contrasting colours.
- Try to use no more than four different hues.

Images

- Posters should have appealing visual elements. Images and photos are a great way to add those.
- Make sure the images are of high quality and fit your target audience, message, and overall style of the poster.

Text and fonts

- Do not use too many words – this is a poster, not a handout or essay.
- Keep it short and simple and use a font or different fonts that are easy to read and fairly big – try reading your poster from across the classroom to decide whether a font is big enough.
- If you use different fonts, do not use too many and choose them in accordance with your composition; so different fonts for different parts, etc.

White space

You do not only have to consider where on your poster to put which elements, but also which areas of the poster to leave empty. White space makes your design stand out more and helps your audience "read" your poster.

Addressee

- Keep all parts of your poster (colours, text, images, composition, overall style) relevant for your audience.
- Ask yourself whether it needs to look professional, business-like, casual, playful, modern, etc. for your target group, and whether you are aiming for a more complex depiction or something that is easy to understand and quick to take in.

S27 Evaluating online sources

When looking for material to include in a presentation or for a written assignment, you should ideally use a variety of sources, including books, newspaper articles, and websites, i.e. the internet should not be your only source. Especially with internet sources, you cannot always be sure that the information you find is correct, so it is important to determine its quality. Here are some strategies to keep in mind when evaluating online sources:

Checklist

Accuracy	✓ How was the information presented gathered? ✓ Does the website give sources for their information or are they just presented as matters of fact?
Authority	✓ Who is the author? Does he/she have experience in a specific field? ✓ Where was the information published? Is it a well-known news website, a personal blog or an organizational website?
Objectivity	✓ Is the way the information is presented factual or does it contain opinions? ✓ Is the author biased in his/her opinion or does he/she promote certain political views?
Timeliness	✓ When was the article published?

Especially the rise of social media has seen an increase of misleading or false information presented as news, usually termed "fake news". Fake news usually aim to manipulate people's opinions and can have damaging effects on the credibility of serious or "real" media coverage, because they often cannot be identified as fabricated at first glance. The following checklist can help you identifiying false information online:

Checklist

- ✓ When you are unsure if a website is reliable, check the source. Major websites usually have an imprint or "About Us" page that informs about the organization.
- ✓ Check the URL domain. Websites ending in ".org" or ".edu" are maintained by non-profit organizations or educational institutions – so their information can usually be trusted.
- ✓ In case of a news story, check if other sources also report about the issue and what they say about it.
- ✓ Credible sources will usually include facts, quotes from experts or present data and statistics. If these are missing, the story might be false.
- ✓ Check the photos. Do they look altered or cropped? Use a reverse image search to check if the photos have been used in other contexts.
- ✓ Sometimes, people will claim that truthful stories are fake news, because they don't agree with them. In this case, be extra careful and examine the source critically.

Literary terms

	literary term	definition	example
A	**act**	One of the parts that a play is divided into. Each act is divided into two or more scenes.	
	action	everything that happens in a fictional text; events that form part of a play or film	
	addressee	the person to whom something is addressed	
	alliteration	emphasis that occurs through the repetition of initial consonant letters of two or more neighbouring words	"bigger box", "red rose"
	allusion	a reference to a familiar or famous historical or literary figure or event	
	antithesis/ contrast	a contrast between two things; denotes the opposing of ideas by means of grammatically parallel arrangements of words, clauses or sentences so as to produce an effective contrast	"It used to be hot, it becomes cool. It used to be strong, it becomes weak." (Malcolm X)
	antonym	a word that means the opposite of another word	night – day, wet – dry, hot – cold
	atmosphere	the feeling or mood created by the author, through the description of events, setting, etc.	"For a moment, a cloud drifted past the moon and the sky turned greenish gray."
B	**bias**	A prejudice in favour of or against one thing, person or group. It is a tendency to hold a certain point of view at the expense of other alternatives. An article is biased if information is presented in a one-sided way and based on personal opinion rather than facts.	
	body language	the movements or positions of your body that show other people what you are thinking or feeling	
C	**caption**	words printed near or on a picture that explain sth about the picture; a joke that is printed underneath a humorous drawing or photograph	
	caricature	a presentation in which sb's/sth's features are exaggerated to produce a comic or grotesque effect	
	character	a person who takes part in the action of a fictional text	
	characteri-zation	The way in which a writer creates characters in a book, play, film etc. The author may present his characters in two ways: directly by describing them (explicit/direct), or indirectly through their actions, thoughts or feelings and words (implicit/indirect).	"I was too lazy at school." "Audrey always sits opposite me, no matter where we play." ➡ She seems to be interested in the narrator.
	close-up	a full-screen shot of a person's face or other body part or object; to reveal a character's emotions by showing their facial expressions; to draw attention to an object	
	comparison/ contrast	analysing two ore more things and examining them for their similarities (comparison) or differences (contrast)	

	literary term	definition	example
	conclusion	the final part of a speech, an article or a piece of writing	
	conflict	the disagreement between opposing forces which is the basis of the plot of a story or a play	
	connotation	an additional idea or emotion that a word suggests to you that is not part of its usual meaning	
	content	the information a text contains	
D	**dialogue**	the words that characters speak in a fictional text, play or film	
	direct address	when the audience is spoken to in the second person	"Ask not what your country can do for you – ask what you can do for your country." (John F. Kennedy)
E	**ellipsis**	leaving out words from a sentence that can be understood from the context in order to avoid repetition and to give a statement more emphasis	"Anyone's guess."
	empathy	the ability to understand how someone feels because you can imagine what it is like to be them	
	end-stopped line	when a phrase or sentence is the same length as the line containing it	"To be, or not to be, that is the question." (William Shakespeare)
	enjambment/ run-on line	a structure/construction in which a thought or statement in one line runs into the next	"To the Mind's gaining that prophetic sense / Of future change, that point of vision, whence / May be discovered what in soul ye are."
	enumeration	a listing of words or phrases	
	establishing shot	a shot that provides an overview of a scene/setting, to introduce the viewer to a new location or situation	
	euphemism	word used for sth unpleasant to make it sound less unpleasant	"to pass away" instead of "to die"
	exclamation	something that you say suddenly and loudly because you are surprised, impressed, angry etc.	
	eye-level shot	the camera looks straight at a person or object, to provide a neutral view	
F	**facial expression**	how a person uses his/her face to show what he/she is feeling	
	fiction	A piece of writing that comes from a writer's imagination. Fiction is not factual but may be sometimes based on facts, real experiences or people the writer has known.	

	literary term	definition	example
	fictional text	a text that isn't based on facts but on the imagination of an author.	
	flashback	a scene that shows what happened in the past and thus interrupts the chronological order of the plot	
	flat character	a character who doesn't undergo much change and who often lacks a multi-faceted personality.	
	fore-shadowing	the technique of hinting at future events in such a way that the reader/viewer is prepared for them or can even anticipate them	
	free verse	a poem with no regular metre or rhyme	"What you recall are impressions; we have the facts. We called the tune." (Carol Ann Duffy)
	full shot	a view of the entire figure of a person, to show a person in action or to give an impression of how the characters are related to each other	
G	**genre**	a particular style used in cinema or writing which can be recognized by certain features, such as subject matter, theme, type of characters, etc.	comedy, thriller, horror, romance
	gesture	how a person uses his/her body to communicate messages	
H	**headline**	the title of a cartoon, a newspaper article, etc.	
	high-angle shot	the camera looks down on a person or object, to make a person/object seem smaller, less important, inferior	
	hyperbole/ exaggera-tion	representing (something) as being larger, greater, better, or worse than it really is	"We've heard this complaint a thousand times."
I	**imagery**	use of vivid or descriptive language to represent objects, actions or ideas	
	inclusive language	including the audience to create a sense of unity or identity	"we", "my friends", "fellow countrymen"
	interior monologue	an expression of the thoughts and feelings passing through a character's mind	
	introduction	the part at the beginning of any text	
L	**line**	a unit of verse ending in a visual or typographic break	
	line of argument	the views that an author takes on a certain issue and how he/she goes about supporting them	
	long shot	a view of characters or a setting from a distance, to provide an overview	
	low-angle shot	the camera looks up at the person or object, to make a person/object seem more powerful/important, superior or even intimidating	

	literary term	definition	example
M	**main part/ body**	the body/main part of a book or document, not including the introduction, conclusion or the notes	
	medium shot	a view of a person down to his/her waist, to give an impression of a person's looks and behaviour, often used to present two people in conversation	
	message	the main idea that you want people to remember from a speech, advertisement, article, poem, etc.	
	metaphor	Two ideas that are not normally linked are compared in a metaphor without using "as" or "like". This creates an image in the reader's mind and makes the description more powerful.	"They blazed a trail toward freedom through the darkest of nights." (Barack Obama)
	metre	the pattern of stressed and unstressed syllables	
	monologue	part of a literary work in which only one character speaks (as opposed to a dialogue)	
	mood	the feeling that the writer tries to evoke	excitement, anger, sadness, happiness, pity, ...
N	**narrative**	any writing that tells a story	
	narrator	A usually fictitious person who tells the story in a novel or film. The story can be told by a **first-person** or a **third-person narrator**. The narrator can be a character in or outside the story. The third-person narrator can be **omniscient** (knowing everything about the characters), **selective** (perceiving and knowing the same things as one character), or an **observer narrator** who merely reports the events without having access to the thoughts and feelings of the characters. A **reliable narrator** is one that readers can trust because he or she seems well-informed. An **unreliable narrator** seems untrustworthy and dishonest, so that readers might not trust what he or she is telling them.	
	non-fiction	texts that provide facts about real events, things or people	newspaper article, university lecture, political speech, etc.
	novel	A fairly long fictional prose narrative. Normally it has a plot which develops through the actions, speech, and thoughts of its characters.	
O	**outward appearance**	of or relating to the outside of the body	"I have dark hair, half-tanned skin, coffee brown eyes."
	over-the-shoulder shot	the camera looks at a character from behind another character's back, to show two people in conversation and draw attention to a character's reaction to what is being said	
P	**pace**	the speed at which sth happens or is done	

	literary term	definition	example
	panning shot	the camera moves horizontally, e.g. from left to right, to follow an object or person	
	paragraph	a section of a piece of writing that begins on a new line and contains a group of several interrelated sentences	
	parallelism	the repetition of a sentence pattern	"... look at you. Look at us ..."
	personifi-cation	A thing, an idea or an animal is given human attributes. Non-human objects are portrayed in such a way that we feel they have the ability to act like human beings.	"When well-appareled April on the heel / Of limping winter treads." (William Shakespeare)
	plot	a series of related events that make up the main story in a book, film, etc.	
	poetry	A literary piece of writing characterized by musical (such as rhythm and rhyme) and literary elements (such as metaphor or simile). Poems are divided into lines and often grouped into stanzas.	
	point of view	the relation in which the narrator stands to the story, a mental viewpoint or attitude • **limited point of view:** The story is told by and shaped through one character's thoughts and experiences. The narration is limited to what he or she knows. • **unlimited point of view:** The narrator knows all the thoughts and feelings of every character, i.e. he or she is omniscient (→ narrator)	
	point-of-view shot	a scene is filmed as if looking through a character's eyes; to experience a situation as if part of the scene	
	protagonist	the main character in a fictional text	
Q	**quote/quo-tation**	words from a book, play, film etc. that you use in a piece of writing	"To be, or not to be" is a famous quote from Shakespeare's tragedy *Hamlet*.
R	**register**	the degree of formality in language use: formal, neutral, informal, colloquial, familiar, intimate	formal: "I must say I'm not particularly fond of his films."; neutral: "I've never liked his films."; familiar: "God, I can't stand his films."
	repetition	words or phrases that are used more than once in a text, catching the reader's attention	"I have fought against white domination and I have fought against black domination."
	reverse-angle shot	a shot in a sequence of point-of-view shots in which the other character's perspective is shown, to allow the viewer to perceive how a conversation develops on both sides	
	review	a report in a newspaper, magazine or online in which a critic gives his views on a new film, novel, etc.	

	literary term	definition	example
	round character	A round character is usually complex, has a multi-facetted personality and/or undergoes a development as the story progresses (≠ flat character)	
	rhetorical question	an assertion in the form of a question which strongly suggests a particular response	"The tribe's code of behavior was broken. The new faith could not keep the tribe together. How could it?"
	rhyme	the repetition of sounds usually at the end of two or more lines	"You've lost your head. / If that's how easily you're led"
	rhyme scheme	the pattern created by the repetition of sounds at the end of lines	abab, abba, aabb, etc.
	rhythm	The pace or "movement" of a poem. The rhythm is determined by the metre and by the length of lines.	
S	**scene**	a part of an act in a play or film in which events happen in the same place or period of time	
	setting	the place and time at which the action of a fictional text takes place	
	short story	A work of fiction which usually deals with one or two major characters and one major conflict. The elements of a short story are character, plot, setting and theme.	
	simile	a comparison of two ideas, usually linked by "as" or "like"	"Like a magic kingdom that belonged only to Grace and her mother."
	social back-ground	The social background describes various facts about a person, including how he/she was raised and what ethnic group he/she belongs to.	
	sonnet	A poem consisting of 14 lines. Various forms have been created. A Shakespearean sonnet consists of three four-line verses (or quatrains) followed by a two-line verse (or couplet).	
	speaker	the voice that speaks in a poem, from whose perspective the poem is written	
	special effects	an unusual piece of action in a film for which particular technical equipment is used	
	stage directions	Notes in a play telling the actors how to speak and act. They also say what the characters and the stage should look like and where and when the action takes place.	ARCHIE *(proud).* [...] BETH *(disappointed).* [...] *Everyone hesitates, suddenly embarrassed.*
	stanza	a section of a poem consisting of a group of lines	
	stereotype	A stereotype is a simplified and generalized understanding, usually of a person or a group of people, based on what you expect from them or have experienced with them. It is a kind of image that immediately arises in your imagination as soon as you hear a name, for example.	Germans wear leather trousers.

	literary term	definition	example
	still	a photograph taken from one of the scenes in a film	
	stress	a stressed syllable is one which has the most emphasis when it is spoken	In "emphasis" the first syllable ("em") is stressed.
	structure	the organization of the elements of a text	
	style	the special, often personal and individual way in which a writer expresses ideas depending on personal factors and the type of text he/she is writing	
	stylistic device	technique used to convince the reader/listener of the author's idea	repetition, enumeration, irony, exaggeration, metaphor
	subheading	the title of one section of a longer piece of writing	
	suspense	a feeling of excitement or worry that makes a reader curious about the outcome of a fictional text	
	symbol	sth concrete that also carries an abstract meaning	the colour white symbolizes innocence, a dove symbolizes peace
T	**tension**	the feeling evoked by the conflicts of a fictional text	
	tilting shot	the camera moves vertically, i.e. upwards or downwards, to follow an object or person	
	theme	the main idea the writer wants to present	
	tone	the tone the author uses to convey his/her attitude towards the subject	ironic, sarcastic, serious, sentimental, humorous
	tracking shot	the camera follows a person or object	
	trailer	a short filmed advertisement for a film	
	trait	a particular quality in someone's character	
	turning point	the point at which the action takes a different, often unexpected direction	
V	**verse**	a section of a poem consisting of a group of lines	
Z	**zooming in/ zooming out**	the camera moves closer to or further away from a person or object, to draw attention to a detail or connect a detail to its environment	

Standardized language for tasks *(Operatoren)*

In *Camden Town Oberstufe*, the same standardized language for tasks *(Operatoren)* is used as in the *Abitur* and in tests. Always make sure you understand what is expected of you before you start working on a task.

Operator	What you have to do	Example
analyse, examine	describe and explain in detail	Analyse the way(s) in which atmosphere is created. Examine the opposing views on social class held by the two protagonists.
assess, evaluate	express a well-founded opinion on the nature or quality of sb/sth	Assess the importance of learning languages for somebody's future. Evaluate the success of the steps taken so far to reduce pollution.
give/write a characterization of	provide a thorough analysis of a character	Give a characterization of the protagonist in the excerpt.
comment (on)	state one's opinion clearly and support one's view with evidence or reasons	Comment on the writer's view on gender roles.
compare	show similarities and differences	Compare the opinions on education held by the experts presented in the text.
describe	give a detailed account of what sb/sth is like	Describe the soldier's outward appearance.
discuss	give arguments or reasons for and against, especially to come to a well-founded conclusion	Discuss whether social status determines somebody's future options.
explain	make sth clear	Explain the protagonist's obsession with money.
illustrate	use examples to explain or make clear	Illustrate the way in which school life in Britain differs from that in Germany.
interpret	explain the meaning or purpose of sth	Interpret the message of the cartoon.
outline	give the main features, structure or general principles of sth	Outline the writer's views on love, marriage and divorce.
point out, state	present the main aspects of sth briefly and clearly	Point out the author's ideas on… State your reasons for applying for a high school year.
summarize, sum up	give a concise account of the main points or ideas of a text, issue or topic	Summarize the text. Sum up the information given about green energy.
write (+ *text type*)	produce a text with specific features	Write the ending of the story / a letter to the editor / a dialogue, etc.

BILDQUELLEN

|akg-images GmbH, Berlin: 76.1; Quagga Media UG 114.1. |Alamy Stock Photo, Abingdon/Oxfordshire: Apollo, Mark 95.3; Armyagov, Andrey 40.3; Black Country Images 118.1; Blossey, Hans 120.1; Cowell, Margaret 119.1; Dagnall, Ian 86.2; Eye Ubiquitous 78.2; Fox, Andrew 113.1; Gorodenkov, Aleksei 103.2; Graham, Jeremy 95.1; Heritage Image Partnership Ltd 56.3; imageBROKER 10.1; Jeff Morgan 01 106.2; Korzeniewski, Daniel 40.7; Levine, Richard 95.2, 99.1, 99.3, 99.4; Michele and Tom Grimm 56.4; PA Images 73.1, 106.4; Pobirchiy, Andriy 52.5; Purepix 40.1; Radharc Images 170.1; Retro AdArchives 31.1; Roberts, Frances 78.5; Rosenstock, Stacy Walsh 99.2; shoults 40.6; Slusarczyk, Marek 102.2; Smith, Trevor 106.3; Trinity Mirror/Mirrorpix 106.1, 113.2; Tuul and Bruno Morandi 40.5; Universal Images Group North America LLC 90.1; UPI 87.1; Vespasian 78.3; Wake, Elizabeth 84.1; World History Archive 112.1. |Alamy Stock Photo (RMB), Abingdon/Oxfordshire: Boethling, Joerg 64.3; Byhre, Rey T. 64.4; Chung, Stephen 39.1; Cole, David 129.1; Contraband Collection 159.1; Johnny Greig Int 66.1; Pictorial Press Ltd 14.1; Robert Estall photo agency 52.4; Roll, Liz 96.3; Singh, Raj 44.1; TaniaL 132.1; The Granger Collection 34.1; ZUMA Press, Inc. 32.1. |Art Explosion, Calabasas, CA: 144.1. |Bridgeman Images, Berlin: Underwood Archives/UIG 96.1. |CartoonStock.com, Bath: 87.2, 87.3; Allan Plenderleith 229.1. |Das Bundesarchiv, Koblenz: Bild 146-2001-011-31 / Ballin und Rabe 149.1. |Domke, Franz-Josef, Wunstorf: 41.1, 65.1, 137.1. |fotolia.com, New York: bernardbodo 178.1; bonciutoma 178.2; Kneschke, Robert 141.1; Pekchar 144.3; S. Engels 98.3; wildworx 33.1. |Fuchs, Oliver, Berlin: 108.1, 108.2, 108.3, 108.4, 108.5, 108.6, 108.7, 108.8, 108.9, 109.1, 109.2, 109.3, 109.4, 249.1, 250.1, 251.1, 252.1, 254.1, 254.2. |Getty Images, München: AFP/Ojisua, Philip 65.3; CORBIS/Turnley, David 56.1. |Imago, Berlin: Lucas, Hans 135.1. |IMO Charity, Blackburn: 144.5. |Interfoto, München: Granger, NYC 226.1; Mary Evans/Library of Congress 35.1. |iStockphoto.com, Calgary: 3000ad 13.2; Alan_P 105.9; AleksandarNakic 139.5; aluxum 86.3; AnaBGD 139.2; bonetta 140.2; Bylo, Petro 105.5; Chiosea, Feodora 105.2, 105.3; Clivia 142.1; DaniloAndjus 139.6; deberarr Titel; Dronandy 30.1; Ekkasit919 131.2; elenab 105.1; filrom 98.2; Flory Titel; focusstock 86.1; Fudio 53.1; GaudiLab 134.1, 139.1; Global_Pics 146.1; Golden Sikorka 105.4; HomoCosmicos 64.5; HRAUN 130.2; joezc 105.6; Jun 139.4; Kanawa_Studio 140.1; Keating, Courtney 186.1; lcepparo 79.2; len-pri 218.1; MauMyHaT 105.7; Media Raw Stock 130.3; MGSmith 105.8; narvikk 103.3; Nikada 40.2; peeterv 79.1; photographer 130.1; sarawuth702 102.3; shalamov 129.3; svetikd 139.3; THEGIFT777 58.2; tommy 245.1; traveler1116 34.2; twinsterphoto 131.4; Veronica Bogaerts 52.2; Viisimaa, Peeter 64.2; VioletaStoimenova 131.1; wwing 92.1; YakobchukOlena 131.6; zimmytws 124.1. |Küstner, Moritz, Hannover: 74.1. |mauritius images GmbH, Mittenwald: Alamy Stock Photos / ZUMA Press 96.4. |McKinsey & Company Inc., Düsseldorf: 123.1. |Penguin Random House LLC, New York: 57.1; THE CIRCLE by Dave Eggers, copyright © 2013 by Dave Eggers. Used by permission of Alfred A. Knopf, an imprint of the Knopf Doubleday Publishing Group, a division of Random House LLC. All rights reserved. 27.1. |Picture-Alliance GmbH, Frankfurt a.M.: AP Photo / Weitz, Udo 60.1; dpa/Barry, Daniel 121.1; dpa/Berg, Oliver 129.2; dpa/EPA/esiri 68.1; dpa/Horsten, Christina 100.1; empics/Denette, Nathan 54.1; epa afp/Booher, Andrea 90.2; epd/Schulze, Jens 59.1; Everett Collection/Library of Congress 96.2; Globe-ZUMA/Cotler, Bruce 127.1; Mary Evans Picture Library/Worsley, Roger 116.1; Marzullo, Joseph/MediaPunch 79.3; NurPhoto/Creative Touch Imaging Ltd 52.3; PA_Archive 42.1; Reuters/Akinleye, Akintunde 71.2; REUTERS/Sotunde, Afolabi 71.1; SZ Photo/Schellnegger, Alessandra 155.1; United Archiv/World History Archiv 56.2. |plainpicture, Hamburg: DEEPOL/Maskot 26.1; Pietsch, H. 178.4. |Shutterstock.com, New York: Ajay PTP 155.2; Bachlakov, Sergei 52.1; Bell, Gonzalo 40.4; Bellers, Lance 179.3; Bruining, Nik 179.4; Cara-Foto 179.1; Crockett, David 145.1; Cumming, Jim 175.1; Doerr, Miriam/Frommherz, Martin 10.5; Grochev, Igor 64.1; Hywit Dimyadi 144.2; iurii 10.3; JackEmpireCTRL 79.6; Jackson, Brian A 13.1; Karandashich, Barandash 10.4; koya979 10.2; kram-9 175.3; Kraulis, Juris 175.2; Lesniewski, Rainer 38.1, 81.1; Marco Rubino/ Reuterswärd, Carl Fredrik: Non violence (c) VG Bild-Kunst, Bonn 2021 78.1; melitas 147.1, 147.2; mentatdgt 179.2; nortongo 144.4; Ogbebor, Orighomisan 69.1; Oksana, Belikova 79.5; Pit Stock 172.1; PR Image Factory 122.1; Reinch. Nataly 67.1; Stock, Pit 93.1; T photography 81.2; Talukdar, David 47.1; Who is Danny 132.3. |Shutterstock.com (RM), New York: Lionsgate/Kobal/ Jennifer Lawrence, The Hunger Games - 2012 11.1; Nicola Dove/Pathe/Bbc/Proud/Bfi/Canal+/Kobal 107.1, 107.2; Per Arnesen/Netflix/Kobal The Rain (2019) 11.4; Red Wagon Entertainment/Kobal Shailene Woodley, Theo James, Divergent - 2014 11.2; Sophie Giraud/MGM/Hulu/Kobal Ann Dowd as Aunt Lydia Clements, ‚The Handmaid's Tale' TV Show Season 3 - 2019 11.3. |stock.adobe.com, Dublin: black_kira 18.1; Boehmer, Oliver 102.1; Crockett, Ian 103.1; Daxiao Productions 131.5; Dierks, Janina 25.1; Feodora 133.1; Goldengel 178.3; Helfman, Yuval 125.1; Kateryna 131.3; kinwun 132.2; Kneschke, Robert 141.2; mangpor2004 132.4; Marco 88.1, 101.1; Margarita 22.1; Mariakray 78.6; Peter 98.1; Roux, Francois 97.1; USII BELL 114.2; vvoe 78.4. |The Dusty Rebel LLC, Tillson, NY: Albanese, Daniel 79.4. |ullstein bild, Berlin: AP 65.2; Archiv Gerstenberg 37.1; Ex-Press 58.1.

TEXTQUELLEN

14-19 *Nineteen-Eighty-Four* by George Orwell, Secker & Warburg, London 1949.

23-25 *The Wall* by John Lanchester, Norton, New York 2019.

26-27 „Überwachungs-Apps werden missbraucht" by Andrea Fischer Schulthess and Sharmila Egger Stone, *Tagesanzeiger*, 23 October 2018.

27-29 *The Circle* by Dave Eggers, Knopf, New York 2014. Lizenzgeber: Knopf/Penguin Books, London

30 "Dave Eggers' 'The Circle' uncomfortably close to Internet reality" by Silke Wünsch, *Deutsche Welle*, 14 August 2014.

31-32 *Brave New World* by Aldous Huxley, Chatto & Windus, London 1932.

32 Quotation by Margaret Atwood, *Penguin* Website, 08 February 2017. London

34 Quotation from *Winston Churchill: An Intimate Portrait* by Violet Bonham Carter, Harcourt, Brace & World 1965.

44-45 "India's 'untouchable' women face discrimination even in schemes meant to help them" by Kanika Meshram, *The Conversation*, 28 December 2022. © The Conversation Media Group Ltd, Paris

47-48 "Full steam ahead: India's first women-run train station blazes a trail" by Annie Banerji, reuters.com, 15 October 2018, Thomson Reuters Foundation.

49-51 "Death on Facebook" by Claude Forthomme, in *Death on Facebook. Short stories for the digital age*, Amazon Digital Services LLC 2012. Seattle

53-54 "What does it mean to be Canadian?" by Quincy De Vries, varsity.com, 22 December 2021. "Population breakdown by race"

57-58 *Born a Crime. Stories from a South African Childhood* by Trevor Noah, Spiegel and Grau, New York, 2016.

59-60 Speech by Archbishop Desmond Tutu given at the University of Toronto, 24 February 2000. © Anglican Consultative Council, London.

62-63 "South Africa's apartheid regime ended 25 years ago" by Evan Lieberman, *The Washington Post*, 27 April 2019. From The Washington Post. © 2019 The Washington Post. All rights reserved. Used under license.

66-67 *Americanah* by Chimamanda Ngozi Adichie, Harper Collins: London 2013.

68-69 *Oil on Water* by Helon Habila, Penguin: London 2011.

70-71 "Shell in Nigeria: Polluted communities 'can sue in English courts'" by Ishaq Khalid, bbc.com, 12 February 2021.

72 *Nollywood – The Making of a Film Empire* by Emily Witt, Columbia Global Reports- The Trustees of Columbia University in the City of New York. New York 2017.

73-74 "Toppling of UK statue fuels debate on monuments to slave traders" by Sonia Elks, reuters.com, 08. June 2020.

74-75 „Die Schatten des deutschen Kolonialismus" by Christoph Hasselbach, *Deutsche Welle*, 18 June 2020.

76 "'White guilt on its own won't fix racism': decolonising Britain's schools" by Lola Okolosie, *The Guardian*, 10 June 2020. Copyright Guardian News & Media Ltd 2021.

77 "Decolonisation", Museum of British Colonialism.

78 Quotation from *Decoded* by Jay-Z, Penguin Random House, New York 2010.

79 Quotation from *Is Everyone Hanging Out Without Me? (and other concerns)* by Mindy Kaling, Crown Archetype, New York 2011.

79 Quotation from "Making of a New Yorker" by John Steinbeck, *The New York Times*, 01.02.1953.

79 Quotation from "All hail Awkwafina, the Queen of Queens", *TimeOut*, 12 June 2019.

79 Quotation from *Open City* by Teju Cole, Random House,

2011.
79 Quotation from "Greenwich Village As It Is" by Djuna Barnes, *Pearson's Magazine*, Oktober 2016.
85 "Dazzling Map Shows NYC's Incredible Linguistic Diversity" by Christopher Robbins, *Gothamist*, New York Public Radio, 03 December 2019.
88 Empire State of Mind (Part II). Text (OT): Carter, Shawn/Hunter, Angela/Keyes, Bert/Keys, Alicia/Robinson, Sylvia/Sewell, Janet/Shuckburgh, Alexander; Copyright: KMR II GT Publishing Ltd./Kobalt Music Publishing Ltd., London/Printrechte Hal Leonard Europe GmbH
89-90 "How New York City is not an American City" by Remington Write, *The Ascent*, 18 March 2019. Hrs. A Medium Corporation, San Francisco
91-93 *Hope and Other Punch Lines* by Julie Buxbaum, Delacorte Press, 2019. Toronto.
94-95 "New York, New York, What a Less than Wonderful Town" by Sam Pizzigati, inequality.org, Institute for Policy Studies, Washington, DC, 20 June 2018.
97 "New York's High Line park marks 10 years of transformation" by Karen Matthews, Associated Press, 09 June 2019, © dpa.
98-99 „Zeche Zollverein: Vom Ort der Maloche zum UNESCO-Welterbe", nrw-tourismus.de, Tourismus NRW e.V.
100 "Mission & History", Public Art Fund, New York.
102 "What Is Globalization?" by Melina Kolb, Peterson Institute for International Economics, Washington, DC, 29 October 2018 (Update: 24 August 2021).
102 "Gone to pot" by Mian Ridge, *The Guardian*, 29 May 2002.
102 Midlands Engine, Crown Copyright 2023, Nottingham 23.09.2020.
102 "New high-tech food manufacturing campus to create up to 4,500 jobs in Derby, UK", *Food and Drink Technology*, Bell Publishing, Gravesend, UK, 04 August 2020.
103 "With Oil Industry in Slump, California Offers a Break on Some Well Regulations" by Ted Goldberg, KQED Inc., San Francisco, 14 May 2020.
103 "The electrification of the auto industry is speeding up—and shaking up the energy economy" by Jeffrey Ball, *Fortune*, 16 February 2021. New York.
103 "Massive biotech hub planned for San Diego's waterfront" by Jonathan Horn, abc 10 News, San Diego, Scripps Local Media, 29 September 2020.
111 Quotation by Audre Lourde.
115 *The Rainbow* by D.H. Lawrence, Methuen & Co, London 1915.
115-116 *The Offing* by Benjamin Myers, Bloomsbury Circus, London 2019.
116-117 *Anita and Me* by Meera Syal, New Press, New York 1997.
117-118 *Nice Work* by David Lodge, Secker & Warburg, London 1988.
119 *Used to Be* by Rebecca Goodwin, Places of Poetry.
119 *Magpie Mine* by Naomi Crosby, Places of Poetry.
120 „Mehr als nur Kohle" by Christian Wernicke, *Süddeutsche Zeitung*, 15 December 2018.
121 *The lexus and the olive tree* by Thomas L. Friedman, Macmillan, London 2012.
122-123 *Thank you for being late* by Thomas L. Friedman, Farrar Straus & Giroux, New York 2016.
124-125 *The Four* by Scott Galloway, Penguin Random House, London 2017.
127-128 "American horror story: how the US lost its grip on pop culture" by Steve Rose, *The Guardian*, 12 September 2020.
130 Quotation from "Katharine Viner: in turbulent times, we need good journalism more than ever" by Graham Ruddick, *The Guardian*, London. 16 November 2017.
130 Quotation from "'I don't want to give in to the digital age'" by Will Hodgkinson, *The Guardian*, London. 03 July 2009.
130 Quotation from "Can Online Communities Be Healing?" by Dean Ornish, *Huffington Post*, 19 November 2013.
131 Quotation from *Sandworm: A New Era of Cyberwar and the Hunt for the Kremlin's Most Dangerous Hackers* by Andy Greenberg, Doubleday, New York 2019.
131 Quotation by Germany Kent., San Francisco.; Angela Merkel.; Mark Waid; Colin Powell, "Viggo Mortensen, Man of the World" by Emma Brown, *Interview Magazine*, New York. 05 May 2015.
134-136 "The world is my office: why I chose to become a digital nomad worker" by Greg Lea, *The Guardian*, 11 May 2019, Copyright Guardian News & Media Ltd 2021.
139 Quotations from "What CEOs Really Think About Remote Work" by Chip Cutter, www.brandknewmag.com.
139 Quotation from "Fortune 500 CEOs and Executives on Remote Work: Then and Now" by Collette Parker, staffing.com, Toptal, LLC, 24 March 2021.
139 Quotation from "More big employers are talking about permanent work-from-home positions" by Adedayo Akala, CNBC LLC, NBCUniversal, 01 May 2020.
140-141 "Are We Too Dependent on Technology?" by Terry Brown, IT Chronicles, Toronto, 31 March 2020.
142 „Nur Bares ist Wahres?" by Monika Skolimowska, 02 December 2020, © dpa.
148-149 „Lustig? Nicht auf Deutsch!" by Klaus Ungerer, *Frankfurter Allgemeine Zeitung*, 04 March 2017.
150 „Warum Englisch nicht als Weltsprache taugt" by Michael Treml, wiesoso.com, Wien, 19 January 2018.
152 *Listen Mr Oxford don* by John Agard, *Alternative Anthem: Selected Poems* by J. Agard, Bloodaxe Books, Hexham 2009.
153 "Have we reached peak English in the world?" by Nicholas Ostler, *The Guardian*, 27 February 2018, Copyright Guardian News & Media Ltd 2021.
154 "What will the English language be like in 100 years?" by Simon Horobin, theconversation.com, Lizenzgeber: The Conversation Media Group Ltd, Paris 10 November 2015.
217 *Fire and Ice* by Robert Frost, *The poetry of Robert Frost*, edited by Edward Connery Lathem, Henry Holt and Company, New York1951.
226 "I Have a Dream" speech by Martin Luther King, Jr., Washington, 28 August 1963.

AUDIOS

83, 84 How to be American. The history of migration and immigration, Why can't I be both? The Tenement Museum, New York City, © Tenement Museum Collection.
84, 85 Our language in our hands: New York, Mark Turin, BBC, December 2012.
86 ©2015 National Public Radio, Inc. NPR report titled "Museum Asks Visitors To Listen To New York's Buildings" was originally broadcast on NPR's All Things Considered on March 10, 2015, and is used with the permission of NPR. Any unauthorized duplication is strictly prohibited.
87 ©2021 National Public Radio, Inc. Excerpts from NPR report titled "The Statue Of Liberty's (Very) Little Sister Is Coming To Town" were originally broadcast on NPR's All Things Considered on July 2, 2021, and are used with the permission of NPR. Any unauthorized duplication is strictly prohibited.
126 ©2020 National Public Radio, Inc. Excerpt from NPR report titled "The Rise of Netflix" was originally broadcast on NPR's It's Been a Minute with Sam Sanders on August 11, 2020, and is used with the permission of NPR. Any unauthorized duplication is strictly prohibited.
129 Fachkräfte auf der Wanderschaft Als Frau auf der Walz, Susanne Lettenbauer, Deutschlandfunk/Campus & Karriere.
151 Will English always be the global language?, David Crystal, British Council, 9 November 2013.

VIDEOS

23 The Human Impact of Climate Change: Personal Stories from Somalia, Ghana, and Kenya, The Climate Reality Project, Washington, DC, 23 October 2013.
53 Prime Minister Trudeau delivers a speech at Canada House in London, 02 March 2016.
55 South Africa - Swearing-In, AP News, 10 May 1994, © BoClips.
61 My Backyard, Ari Kruger, Sketchbook Studios, 2011.
81 Here grows New York, Myles Zhang
86 NYC On a Budget, © Westermann Gruppe.
90 9/11: A Modern History, Step Back History, 9 June 2018, © BoClips.
102 What is the Fourth Industrial Revolution? CNBC LLC, NBCUniversal, 22 January 2019.
121 Put simply – how did globalization come about? Deutsche Welle, 01 July 2020.
140 Wall.E, Walt Disney Pictures, Pixar Animation Studios, 2008.
152 Listen Mr Oxford don, John Agard, Alternative Anthem: Selected poems, Bloodaxe Books, 2009.